SIBERIA

Westview Series on the Post-Soviet Republics

Alexander J. Motyl, Series Editor

Siberia: Worlds Apart, Victor L. Mote

The Central Asian States: Discovering Independence, Gregory Gleason

Lithuania: The Rebel Nation, V. Stanley Vardys and Judith B. Sedaitis

Belarus: At a Crossroads in History, Jan Zaprudnik

Estonia: Return to Independence, Rein Taagepera

◾ SIBERIA ◾
Worlds Apart

VICTOR L. MOTE
University of Houston, University Park

Westview Press
A Member of Perseus Books, L.L.C.

Westview Series on the Post-Soviet Republics

Cartography by Vadim Myachin

Copyright © 1998 by Westview Press, A Member of Perseus Books, L.L.C.

Published in 1998 in the United States of America by Westview Press, 5500 Central Avenue, Boulder, Colorado 80301-2877, and in the United Kingdom by Westview Press, 12 Hid's Copse Road, Cumnor Hill, Oxford OX2 9JJ

A CIP catalog record for this book is available from the Library of Congress
ISBN 0-8133-1298-1 (hardcover); 0-8133-1837-8 (pbk.)

The paper used in this publication meets the requirements of the American National Standard for Permanence of Paper for Printed Library Materials Z39.48-1984.

10   9   8   7   6   5   4   3   2   1

· Contents ·

Tables and Illustrations   ix
Preface   xi
Acknowledgments   xiii
Author's Note on Transliteration   xvi

1   Greater Siberia: A Resource Frontier   1
Introduction, 1
Greater Siberia: Russia's "Foreign Territory," 2
The Periphery as a Resource Frontier, 5
Conclusion, 10
Notes, 10

2   Greater Siberia: The Land and Its People   13
Introduction, 13
Western Siberia, 13
Eastern Siberia, 19
The Russian Far East, 25
Conclusion, 29
Notes, 29

3   The Little Siberians: On the Planet's Periphery   31
Introduction, 31
The Peopling of Siberia, 31
Ethnography Before the Russians, 32
Russians in Siberia, 39
Conclusion, 51
Notes, 52

**4   Regionalism, Separatism, and
     Russification Before the Revolution**   57
The Birth of a Region, 57
Russification and the Siberians Before 1917, 66

Changes in the Indigenous People
  on the Eve of the Soviet Period, 72
Conclusion, 74
Notes, 74

5 **Revolution, Civil War, and Stalinism in Greater Siberia**   79
Regionalists and Revolutionaries, 79
Siberia in the Civil War, 81
The NEP and Greater Siberia, 85
Greater Siberia Under Stalin, 90
Stalinism and the Native Question, 99
Conclusion, 100
Notes, 101

6 **Salad Days: The East-West Debate and Greater Siberia**   105
Introduction, 105
Labor, Research, and Development After Stalin, 106
The Siberian Economy, 1950–1985, 109
Siberian Politicians After the Stigma, 114
Greater Siberian Indigenes, 1953–1985, 123
Conclusion, 124
Notes, 125

7 **Dog Days and the Rise of the Little Siberians, 1985–1993**   131
Introduction, 131
Kuzbas Goes on Strike, 132
Nationalities Policies, 137
Regionalism and Federalism, 142
Conclusion, 149
Notes, 149

8 **Greater Siberia Today: Roaring Mice and Wage Arrears**   155
October's Aftermath: National Supremacy
  vs. Ethnoregional Rights? 155
Organized Interest Groups, 157
The Mice That Roar, 178
Conclusion, 192
Notes, 195

Appendixes   203
Selected Bibliography   210
Index   228

▪ Tables and Illustrations ▪

Tables

A.1 Greater Siberian Governorships in 1917
    and Ethnoregions in 1997   204

B.1 Socioeconomic Characteristics of Ethnoregions
    in Greater Siberia in 1997   206

Maps

1.1 Greater Siberia and the Little Siberias, 1998   3

2.1 Greater Siberia: Physical Geography   14
2.2 Greater Siberia: Ethnic Groups   20

3.1 Conquest of Siberia, 1584–1860   42

5.1 Infamous Siberian Railway Projects and the Gulag   98

6.1 Ob' Basin Oil and Gas Fields   113
6.2 The Baykal-Amur Main Line (BAM)   120

8.1 Results of the 1996 Russian Presidential
    Runoff Election in Greater Siberia   173

Photos

The *Rossiya* (Russia) rolls from Moscow to
    Vladivostok in eight days   xii

3.1 Bust of Andronovian woman ca. 2000 B.C.   35

3.2 Man of mixed race, Baraba Steppe, near the time of Christ 36

5.1 Novosibirsk Railway Station, on the Trans-Siberian Railroad 92

6.1 Yegor Kuz'mich Ligachev 106

7.1 Miner on strike in the Kuzbas 134
7.2 Severe air pollution at the West Siberian Steel Mill,
   near Novokuznetsk 135
7.3 Shor hunter with dog 138
7.4 Khant man with reindeer 140
7.5 Ninety-two-year-old Nanay woman with pipe 142
7.6 Aman Tuleyev, Boris Yeltsin, and miners'
   strike leader Gennadiy Golikov in Kemerovo 148

8.1 Russian Prime Minister Viktor Chernomyrdin
   and Vitaliy Mukha, governor of Novosibirsk
   and chairperson of the Siberian Agreement 161
8.2 Yevgeniy Nazdratenko, governor of Primorskiy kray 168
8.3 Yevdokiya Gayer, former member of the Federation
   Council 175
8.4 East Surgut oil field, Khantia-Mansia 180
8.5 Mikhail Nikolayev, President of Sakha (Yakutia) 183
8.6 Lenin as antihero at Kemerovo Meeting Hall, 1991 188
8.7 Aman Tuleyev, the "Kazakh from Kemerovo" 189

· Preface ·

My research for this book spanned a period of 30 years and seven extensive visits to the Soviet Union, Russia, and Siberia. My romance with Siberia began vicariously in 1967. It was not until 1973, however, that I actually set foot in the region. I recall how tired I was when I descended onto the apron of the Novosibirsk Airport from the plane that had flown me from Tashkent. The importunate Intourist guides insisted that I "must" have my whirlwind excursion about the Siberian capital, even though I could barely keep my eyes open. When the *Rossiya* (Russia) (Photo 0.1) embarked for Irkutsk that afternoon, I had been awake for 48 hours. I slept through Krasnoyarsk, barely noticed Tayshet and Cheremkhovo, and trundled into Irkutsk quite inebriated and lubricated from a late repast of vodka and suet, which had magically appeared from the briefcase of my compartment mate, a robust Buryat colonel of the Soviet Army. In the environs of Irkutsk for two days, I toured Baykal by hydrofoil and ate *omul* with a Frenchman in a poky restaurant on the shores of the big lake. The train for Khabarovsk left at night, so I missed—as all tourists did in those days—the most interesting part of the Trans-Siberian journey, a harrowing twist around the south end of Lake Baykal. It took three days to reach Khabarovsk, and another to alight in Nakhodka. I remember the rusty-brown water of my bath in Khabarovsk, but a wrapper around my toilet seat assured me that everything was okay: A note on the wrapper indicated it had been *dezinfitsirovanno* (disinfected). Twelve years would pass before I would return to the land of my research, this time as a so-called Siberia expert and a specialist on the Baykal-Amur Main Line (BAM) railway. For one month, together with my KGB guide, I saw much of the western BAM, Yakutsk, and the Vilyuy Basin. In several of these places, I was the first American, if not the first foreigner, my hosts had ever seen. It was exciting to be the first *inostranets* (alien) to do some things, such as to milk a cow in Berkakit!

Two years later, as a month-long guest of the Heilongjiang Academy of Social Sciences in Harbin, China, I obtained a backdoor view of Siberia by

The Rossiya *(Russia) rolls from Moscow to Vladivostok in eight days.* SOURCE: *ITAR-TASS.*

twice traveling the length of the Chinese Eastern Railway between Suifenhe and Manzhouli near their respective Soviet border crossings at Grodekovo and Zabaykal'sk. This romantic visit to the land of Genghis Khan bound me to Asiatic Russia more than ever before.

The significance of these journeys and the associated scholarship is that they enabled me to secure a visiting research fellowship at Hokkaido University's Slavic Research Center in Sapporo, Japan, in 1988–1989. The experience in Japan thoroughly enriched my life by exposing me to international scholars who were themselves specialists on "Greater Siberia" (see Chapter 1). Upon the completion of my research at Hokkadai, I returned to Siberia once more, this time by way of Vladivostok (which was still a closed city then), where I became the first geographer from the United States to visit that city in half a century or more.

This book is the sum of my observations and experiences during those travels as well as my research of the scholarly literature. My approach is holistic and multidisciplinary, stressing not only my own field of geography but also relevant aspects of anthropology, history, regional economics, and politics. Ultimately, my goal is to reveal, for better or for worse, the post-Soviet transformation of Siberia and its implications for Russia and the global economy.

Victor L. Mote
Houston, Texas

▪ Acknowledgments ▪

I wish first to thank my former student Ed Lewis, currently the president and CEO of Industrial Information Resources, Inc. (IIR) in Houston, Texas, for granting me the time and use of the equipment to complete the latest version of this manuscript. Without his understanding, the book might have suffered several more delays. I am also indebted to George Williams and Andrea Chadwell, who in their off hours at IIR, proofread the manuscript for any "land mines" that I may have missed in my own reading. I am grateful to a host of anonymous librarians at the branch libraries of the University of Washington, the University of Houston, the Library of Congress, Hokkaido University (Hokkadai), and the Khabarovsk Regional Library. I am particularly indebted to Akizuki Takako and her husband, Akizuki Toshiyuki, senior librarians at the Hokkadai campus. My thanks also go to Patricia Polansky of the University of Hawaii Library, who volunteered thoughtful long-distance advice and assistance during the past two decades. Generous kudos should go as well to Vadim Myachin, who waited four years for my draft maps, from which he derived the handsome computerized versions in this book. He also deserves credit for the index.

I am certainly grateful to Alexander Motyl, the steadfast editor of Westview's series on the post-Soviet republics. Dr. Motyl first contacted me about participating in this project in late 1990, and he never panicked when my manuscript subsequently fell hopelessly behind schedule. Moreover, without the inspiration of, encouragement by, and occasional consultation with the following people, this volume might not have come to fruition: Abel Aganbegyan, Georgiy Arbatov, Aleksey Arbatov, Tony Allison, Sergey Averin, Pyotr Baklanov, Marjorie Mandelstam Balzer, Brent Barr, Mark Bassin, Umit Bayulken, Larry Black, Andy Bond, Kathy Braden, Michael Bradshaw, Capt. Lawson Brigham, Peter Buckley, Tanya Buckley, Boris Chichlo, Curt Clemenson, David Collins, Frances Cooley, Violet Connoly, George Demko, Leslie Dienes, Genna Demoura, Stepan Demoura, Peter DeSouza, Andy Durkin, Herb Ellison, Murray Feshbach, Gennadiy Fil'shin, Volodya Fogel, Gail Fondahl, Tony French, James R.

Gibson, Paul Goble, Bob Gohstand, Marshall Goldman, Leonid Gor-yushkin, Alexander Granberg, Paul Gregory, Vladimir Gukov, Nikolay Gushchin, Walton Hall, Chung Han-ku, Chauncy Harris, Gary Haus-laden, Milan Hauner, Art Hill, Kimura Hiroshi, Jade Hlavinka, David Hooson, Doris Hughes, Holland Hunter, Chris Iles, Birgitta Ingemanson, Bob Jensen, Doug Jackson, Xu Jinxue, Walter Joyce, Mochizuki Kiichi, Stuart Kirby, Dan Kitt, Carol Kitt, Dima Korobeynikov, Boris Korovin, Yevgeniy Kovrigin, John Kratovil, Kostya Kroujilov, Cindy Kroujilova, Richard Levine, Bob Lewis, Valeriy Lifshits, Richard Lonsdale, Paul Ly-dolph, Viktor Lysenko, Peter Maffitt, Pat Micklin, Elisa B. Miller, Dick Moore, Mikhail Morozov, Nikolay Nekhayenko, Jim Nichols, Joe Nogee, Bob North, Aleksey Novikov, Sergey Ostroumov, Dmitriy Pines, Lyuda Pines, Nataliya Pisarenko, Phil Pryde, Peg Purser, Brian Redman, Larissa Redman, Oleg Renzin, Allan Rodgers, Matt Sagers, John Sallnow, Sergey Savoskul, Ota Seizo, Ted Shabad, Denis Shaw, Alexander Sheyngauz, Tabata Shinichiro, Sunita Singh, Valera Slyusarev, Mike Speckhard, Derek Spring, John Stephan, John Massey Stewart, Michael Strauss, Sophya Tabarovsky, Ito Takayuki, Hara Teryuki, Stuart Tonks, Margaret Tonks, Donald Treadgold, Hasegawa Tsuyoshi, Nataliya Usenko, Sveta Vas-siliyeva, Piers Vitebsky, William Wallace, Harry Walsh, John Albert White, Allen Whiting, David Wilson, Ronald Wixman, Kim Won-Suk, Alan Wood, Feng Xiaobing, Kim Yu-Nam, Craig ZumBrunnen, and Yevgeniy Zykov.

John Stephan, the nonpareil historian of the Far East at the University of Hawaii at Manao, deserves special mention for his consistent, unselfish support for twenty years, even though we have never met personally. It was he who directed me to the venerable historian of Siberia, John Albert White, who now lives in retirement in the old Quaker settlement of Friendswood, on the outskirts of Houston.

For their special assistance, I am especially thankful for the contributions of my former students Art Hill, Walton Hall, and Grant Robinson. Art Hill worked in Moscow between 1992 and 1997 and faithfully sent me key materials on Russian politics. Despite poor health, Walton Hall spent hours helping me to organize and assemble my home computer station. Grant Robinson produced an excellent term paper on Siberian autonomy movements.

I am deeply grateful to Dr. Aleksey Novikov of Moscow State University for providing me with helpful information and a number of photographs for Chapter 8 (Photos 8.1, 8.2, 8.3, 8.5, and 8.7). I am again grateful to my friend, colleague, and fellow geographer, Dr. Vadim Myachin, for putting me in contact with Dr. Novikov.

I am indebted in too many ways to the patient people at Westview Press. Since I signed the contract to produce this book, I have had the pleasure of working with Susan McEachern, Alison Auch, Rebecca Ritke, Rob Williams, and Kristin Milavec. Without their forbearance in the face of my long delays, my task would have been a great deal more painful.

This book has been funded in part by support from Industrial Information Resources, Inc.; Vinson & Elkins; World Wise, Inc.; and Prudential Relocation Services, all of Houston, Texas. In the early going, research was facilitated by stipends from Hokkaido University in Sapporo, Japan, and from Booz Allen & Hamilton in Bethesda, Maryland.

V.L.M.

· Author's Note ·
on Transliteration

In most instances, I have chosen to use the transliteration system of the U.S. Board of Geographic Names. Hard and soft signs are thus indicated as " and ', respectively; *i, ii, ia, iu,* and *e* are written *y, iy, ya, yu,* and *ye* except when *e* follows a hard consonant, as in *reka* (river). Thus, the more familiar "Baikal" is rendered "Baykal" in this work. I also decided to use the Russian "tsar" without the soft sign (tsar') in lieu of "czar"; however, I chose "taiga" (the spelling used in the current edition of *Merriam-Webster's Collegiate Dictionary*) instead of "tayga." I also opted for "Alexander" rather than "Aleksandr," but retained "Viktor," "Nikolay," "Georgiy," and other Russian spellings for names of Russians, except when the persons are very well known in English as in "Peter" the Great, "Catherine" the Great, Boris "Yeltsin" (not Yel'tsin) and so on.

I bear complete responsibility for any shortcomings or inaccuracies that may appear in the book.

ONE

Greater Siberia:
A Resource Frontier

Sibir' tozhe russkaya zemlya *(Siberia is also Russian land).*
—**Old Russian song**

INTRODUCTION

There is a place so enormous that were it truly independent, it would be the world's largest country; yet, it is treated as a mere appendage of the world's largest country. The old day ends and the new day begins near its eastern margin—the gateway to eight other time zones, the last of which crumpled, along its western margin, against another continent 250 million years ago. It is Asia sutured to Europe. To most mortals, it is a great white void, an arcane, gelid world unto itself. On closer inspection, however, it appears to be many worlds, unified only by the common experience of living on the edge of the earth; or more exactly, many netherworlds—worlds apart from the security and comfort of geographies blessed by moderation and civility.

As geographer Gail Fondahl has observed, Siberia is "people poor," as it is home to a mere 22 percent of Russia's population; but it is simultaneously "peoples rich," with more than thirty different nations staking their claims to its various territories. The peoples who occupy these smaller Siberias are stouthearted and capable of enduring almost any imaginable hardship. More than 400 years ago, one of these peoples, like the Huns of old, chose to conquer and subdue the 200 or more Siberian indigenous tribes then in existence, and thus forever changed the demography of the subcontinent. Today, the aggregate population of native Siberians barely exceeds 4 percent of the total for the region, or approximately 1.3 million people.

Although "Greater Siberia" is many worlds, it is fundamentally two—a pair of enormous moieties, each more than two-thirds the size of the con-

1

terminous United States of America. Even though there is a compelling logic for considering them as separate units—as the Russians do—there is also a cogent argument for viewing them as a physical whole, as many Westerners do. As defined in this book, Greater Siberia consists of Siberia proper (Western and Eastern Siberia) plus the Russian Far East. (For the sake of geographic coherence, one might argue for the inclusion of the Urals provinces of Sverdlovsk, Chelyabinsk, and Kurgan, which would expand the region to the continental divide; but convention will not permit us to do this.) On this dual macrocosmic foundation, employing human and physical criteria, we can lay microcosmic brick upon brick—what I call the "little Siberias."

GREATER SIBERIA: RUSSIA'S "FOREIGN TERRITORY"

The Viewpoint

The basic theme of this book is that although the global economy has done without Siberia and can continue to do quite nicely without it, Siberia will languish in isolation from the global economy. Both inside and outside Russia, as Mark Bassin has astutely observed, Siberia traditionally has been considered *chuzhaya zemlya* (foreign territory).[1] Cycles of international interest and disinterest, which have stimulated or retarded regional development, have punctuated the history of Siberia. Although they are worlds apart from the rest of humanity, to flourish, the little Siberias must become an integral part of the global economy.

Western Siberia, Eastern Siberia, and *the Russian Far East* have become acceptable terms of reference in both hemispheres (see Map 1.1); however, these broad and general labels belie the extraordinary diversity that exists within the geography of the regions that they encompass. After six years of post-Soviet collapse, Siberia is no longer a unified whole. In reality, it has never been so. Instead, it always has been composed of numerous, dispersed fragments, held together only by tsarist autocratic rule and Soviet dictatorial terror. Without such glue, the little Siberias might have emerged much earlier. Already, Tyva (formerly Tuva) and Sakha/Yakutia (formerly Yakutia) have taken substantial strides toward economic if not social independence within the Russian Federation. Following their example, the tiny native populations of Chukotka, Khantia-Mansia, and Yamalia have aspired to liberate themselves from the clutches of the provincial authorities of Tyumen' and Magadan, respectively.

The non-Russian titular nationalities are not the only ones threatening to disrupt Moscow's 400-year reign over Siberia. Russian Siberians, too, have demanded regional control over their share of what Russians commonly refer to as "the periphery." For example, during the post-Soviet pe-

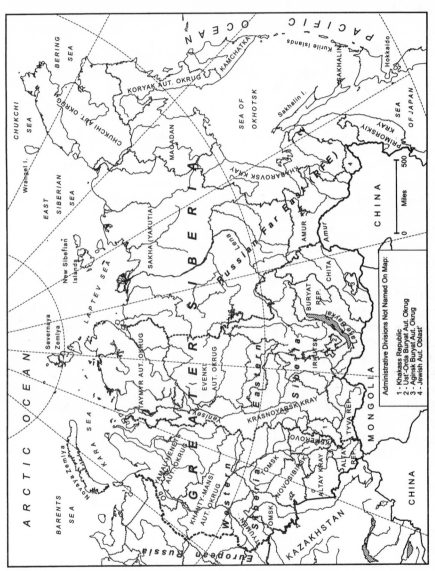

MAP 1.1 *Greater Siberia and the Little Siberias, 1998*

riod, developers of the oil and gas fields of Tyumen' and Sakhalin oblasts, the coal miners of the Kuzbas (Kemerovo oblast), and the regional governments of Irkutsk and Primor'ye have taken independent stands on many issues.

A Core and a Periphery

The Russian experience is a cogent example of a core-periphery relationship.[2] All countries have cultural and/or economic "cores," which have acquired competitive edges over their surroundings. More often than not, cores consist of a capital city and its immediate hinterland. Readily identifiable examples of such dominant urban systems are London and its sprawling suburbs, Paris and the Paris Basin, New York and "Megalopolis," and Moscow and Moscow oblast. As economic phenomena, cores' relationships with their environments may extend beyond the borders of their respective nation-states. Thus, in the contemporary global economy, the cores of the economically more developed countries largely control the fates of those that are less developed .

In the past, the relationships between cores and their surroundings were colonial in nature. While primary activities such as extractive industries and farming characterized the economies of the areas outside the core, described variously as "peripheries" or "semiperipheries,"[3] secondary and tertiary industries typified the cores. The noncores fed the voracious cores with cheap raw materials in exchange for expensive finished products, resulting in a wicked cycle of enrichment of the metropolis at the expense of the colony.[4] India's absorption into the British Empire, for instance, was very favorable to Greater London but extremely unfavorable to the "wonderful oriental gentle-subjects" in South Asia. "In the end, India, once a great cotton textile producer, exported only raw cotton to Britain, where it was turned into textile goods and sent back to India to be bought."[5]

Similarly, the autocrats and commissars of Moscow maintained a policy of economic hegemony over their vast backwaters in Siberia and Central Asia. Although modern Russia is at best semiperipheral within the global economy,[6] within the country, the "center," or Moscow and its environs, still reigns supreme over all other space. Russians perceive Moscow as having "everything," and for generations they have done almost "anything" to live there.

In contrast, Siberia is far removed from this fount of Russian development. Subjected to at least passive imperialism for most of its existence, Siberia has been, and is, at the mercy of the Center. Among the many moot definitions of the word *Sibir'* is "marshy forest."[7] From the very beginning of Mongol diffusion (see Chapter 3), therefore, Siberia was identified with its resource base. Even now, Russians view Siberia as a vast "larder" of raw materials, which historically they have exploited irrespective of the consequences.

THE PERIPHERY AS A RESOURCE FRONTIER

The establishment of the world economy between 1450 and the beginnings of the Industrial Revolution in the late 1700s ushered in an "Age of Exploration" not only of the world oceans but also of the great continental interiors. Before 1450, the races were essentially segregated worldwide: Caucasoids in Europe, North Africa, Southwest Asia, and northern India; Mongoloids in the rest of Asia, Madagascar, and the Americas; Negroids in Africa south of the Sahara and a few Pacific islands; and Australoids in Australia and southern India. Three centuries later, European Caucasoids dispersed white civilization to the Americas, Africa, and Oceania; the western hemisphere received boatloads of involuntary migrant Negroids; South Asians established markets in East and South Africa; and the Chinese developed Southeast Asia and Indonesia. Virtually all of these great movements occurred in part or in full via the sea lanes. One conspicuous exception was the expansion of Russians into northern Asia.

Many if not most of these human dispersals laid the groundwork for extensive colonial empires, within the frameworks of which the peripheries represented "resource frontiers." Not the least of these was Greater Siberia. Resource frontiers retreat in the face of expanding civilization. This was the case with the American West: Periphery became semiperiphery, and semiperiphery became part of the core. In Greater Siberia, however, the experience was different. Whereas the American West is no longer valued exclusively for its resources, Greater Siberia remains a salient example of a resource frontier.

Characteristics of Resource Frontiers

In his well-known case study of Venezuela, economist John Friedmann inventoried the characteristics of a resource frontier.[8] Based on Friedmann's criteria, Greater Siberia may be the world's quintessential example of this phenomenon.

According to Friedmann, *resource frontiers exist because of the finds of major resources, which are developed and supervised by an agency created in the core of the country.* The economy of Greater Siberia always has been based on the extraction of raw materials: furs, metals, trees, farm produce, or fossil fuels. Whether in St. Petersburg or Moscow, Russian authorities have dominated the region, and in Soviet times, they commanded it by means of bureaucratic institutions.

Resource frontiers are relatively remote from major centers of consumption, separated by vast expanses of wilderness. Even at its "gateways" (the Urals cities of Chelyabinsk and Yekaterinburg), Greater Siberia is a minimum of 1,750 kilometers (1,075 mi) from the core. Beyond the Urals, except along the Trans-Siberian Railroad, the bulk of the territory is wilderness. The arithmetic density of Greater Siberia is 2.5 persons per square kilometer (6.6 persons per square mile), which makes it more sparsely populated than Libya; moreover, when one considers that 80 percent of the population is concentrated in the southern 15 percent of the region, the northern 85 percent is more sparsely populated than Western Sahara![9]

The city is the civilizing agent: Resource frontiers are urban. Although Greater Siberia's overall urban share of 72.4 percent is slightly less than the proportion for the Russian Federation (73 percent), traditionally it has been ahead of the national average. The Russian Far East, at 76 percent urban, is well ahead of that mean, and Magadan and Sakhalin are the most urban provinces in the realm (see Chapter 2). Greater Siberia's settlement system includes 684 settlements of urban type, comprising 208 cities, 24 of which are large urban agglomerations.[10] Almost two of three Siberian residents live in a mere 52 cities.

The cities of the resource frontier perform only limited central-place functions because they are isolated; they are also specialized in maintaining the primary resource activity of the area. All except the very largest Siberian cities (Novosibirsk, Omsk, and Krasnoyarsk, for example) are limited in function. Crude frontier settlements, the only purpose of which is to shelter and feed miners and workers, support approximately half of the Siberian population. These settlements are almost always without even the most basic of necessities (such as toothpaste, soap, and detergents).[11]

The raison d'être of the resource frontier is exports, both regional and international. *Resource frontiers import almost everything they consume, while exporting all that they produce.* Greater Siberia has been the most important region for the production of Russian exports, and in the Soviet period, Siberia at times accounted for more than half of them.[12] The region imports 75 percent of all its machinery, while contributing only 7.4 percent of the total output of Russian machine building and metal fabrication. Less than 2 percent comes from Eastern Siberia and the Russian Far East. The latter have always relied on outside regions for 60 percent of their food.

The important export markets often will be foreign, and foreign interests will be committed to the development of the resources. Greater Siberia's share of Soviet exports soared from 18.6 percent in 1970 to 53 percent in 1985, the value exploding from $485 million to $11.2 billion, of which $9.7 billion derived from the sale of West Siberian oil and gas alone. This represented more than half of all Soviet receipts of hard currency.[13] Whenever possible during the Soviet period, foreign companies invested heavily in the development of Greater Siberia's oil and petrochemical resources. Since 1991, foreign enterprises have intensively sought toeholds in Asiatic Russian resource development projects.

Communities in resource frontiers usually reach their maximum size within a few years after the founding of the settlement. Only diversification of the economic base can assure their sustained growth and, therefore, their permanence. The cities of Greater Siberia typically grew very rapidly. The smaller ones maximized their populations within 15 years after their birth (Neryungri and Tynda, for instance). Novosibirsk acquired its millionth citizen within 60 years, faster than New York and Chicago. Very large Siberian cities, such as Novosibirsk, did diversify their economies and continued to attract residents.[14] During Soviet times, population increases also occurred as a result of governmental coercive policies.

The development of resource frontiers commonly is carried out as an integrated investment program under a single executive authority. Until the advent of *khozraschet* (cost accounting) and *samofinansirovaniye* (self-financing) in 1988, individual Siberian development programs were financed and supervised by departments within the Council of Ministers. In the post-Soviet world, Siberian authorities continue to seek the support of the core. Old habits are hard to break.

Resource frontiers are characterized by high transportation and labor costs, and subsidies and bonuses are encouraged. According to Leslie Dienes, in 1975 all twelve Siberian provinces east of the Yenisey River received "large, unreturned inflows of national income," and in six of the twelve, such inflows exceeded 700 million rubles.[15] Much of the subsidy shored up wages that were 1.2 to 3 times the average for the country. In a free market economy, transportation costs are always functions of distance and the number of transshipments (breaks-in-bulk). Lengths of haul of Siberian goods are 100 to 200 percent greater than the Russian average, and breaks-in-bulk are 2.7 times the mean.[16] For decades, the Soviet government subsidized the high costs of inshipments into Siberia so that it might benefit from the acquisition of low-cost bulk outshipments from the region. The Yeltsin government lifted the subsidies in the early 1990s. Freight rates since then have skyrocketed, and rail traffic has consistently been disrupted.[17]

Resource frontiers are long-term investments. Continuing insolvency—implying an endless stream of public income transfers to the region—would be a serious burden on the total national development effort and could be justified only with extreme difficulty in view of all other requirements. The controversy over whether to invest in Greater Siberia at the expense of the core and semiperiphery has been continuous since tsarist times. Under Brezhnev (1964–1982), authorities viewed Siberia as a valid long-term investment, or what John Hardt called a "frozen asset."[18] With Brezhnev at the helm, officials were commanded to absorb at least temporary losses on their investments in the periphery even as they reaped profits on their assets in the developed core and in foreign trade. The larder of raw materials was opened for the sake of the larder and not for short-term gain.[19] The economic approaches of first Gorbachev and then Yeltsin were more pragmatic and fiscally responsible than Brezhnev's, and concomitantly, more catastrophic for the economy of Greater Siberia.

Russia's Periphery: A Land of Contrast

Greater Siberia is a vast region of 12.8 million square kilometers (4.9 million mi^2), comprising three-fourths of Russia. It is one-third larger than the United States and one-fourth bigger than Canada, the second largest country in the world. The region's legendary dimensions stretch more than 5,000 kilometers (3,000 mi) from the Ural Mountains in the west to the Pacific Ocean in the east. From its borders with Kazakhstan, Mongolia, and China in the south to the Arctic Ocean in the north, it spans 40 degrees of latitude. Greater Siberia is so large that residents of the U.S. state of Maine are closer to Moscow than are Russian citizens in Primor'ye, on the Sea of Japan.

Greater Siberia is a paradox of positives and negatives. If its 30 to 35 million inhabitants were ever to exercise the unlikely scenario of secession from Russia, the territory they occupy would immediately become the largest and most sparsely populated nation-state, complete with the world's largest resource base. Simultaneously, it would contain the flattest and broadest plain (the West Siberian Lowland); the longest railroad (the Trans-Siberian); the largest peat bog (the Vasyugan'ye); five of the twelve longest rivers (the Ob', Yenisey, Irtysh, Amur, and Lena); the deepest lake (Baykal); the greatest expanse of coniferous forest (the taiga); and the largest reserves of fossil fuels (gas, coal, and oil).

Constraints to Development

Greater Siberia's superior size and endowment all too often are disadvantageous. Size dictates that most of the region is far from the sea and its moderating influences. Siberian climates are the most "continental" on Earth. The concept of continentality implies great ranges of temperature coupled with low average annual precipitation that peaks in summer rather than in spring. The northeastern part of the region experiences the coldest temperatures in the northern hemisphere, with onetime minima of -68° centigrade (-90° F) at Oymyakon and Verkhoyansk in Sakha (Yakutia). Six months later, the same places occasionally record maxima of 32° centigrade (90°F). The consequent difference, or range, of tempera-

tures is the widest on Earth, challenging human and technological tolerance to the extreme. The frigid, seven- to ten-month winters are combined
with the highest recorded air pressures (31.98 in) at Agata, deep in the
heart of Evenkia. The characteristic of subsiding air in the dominant winter season reduces annual precipitation to 10 centimeters (4 in) in the
Oymyakon-Verkhoyansk region, most of which falls in the brief high-sun
period. Thus, winters are not very snowy, and over most of Siberia the
snow that persists is shallow except where it lies in drifts. The lack of
snow, which is due to the continental effect, encourages the formation of
permafrost, which in combination with the long winter drought retards
the formation of soil. Adding insult to injury, the short, occasionally hot
Siberian summers encourage throngs of dreaded mosquitoes, gnats, and
black flies, which force human occupants to pray for the quick return of
winter.

Purely economic constraints enhance the physical disadvantages. Raw
materials, no matter how abundant, must be accessible enough for exploitation to be feasible. In Greater Siberia, supplies are far from consumers. Transportation systems are expensive to build, and once built,
the networks are difficult to maintain. Where Siberia is concerned, "quan-
tity" is hardly synonymous with "quality." The region is the planet's
quintessential example of geographic "too theory": too cold in winter; too
boggy in Western Siberia; too rugged in Eastern Siberia and the Russian
Far East; too dry most of the time in the majority of the region; too far
north, reducing the intensity of the sunlight and curtailing the length of
the growing season; too "bloody" full of sanguisugent insects in July and
August, at the peak of the harvest season; and ultimately, too far away
from almost everything and everyone.

Monotonous Diversity

Greater Siberia is northern Asia. In the west, it is tied to Europe by the
Ural Mountains, which like their Appalachian contemporaries, are now
low-lying nubbins of what were once mightier ranges. In the south, it is
flanked by the Kazakh Uplands and an extensive chain of diverse ranges
that include virtually all of Russia's highest mountains. The mountain
chain separates the region from Kazakhstan, Chinese Dzungaria, Outer
and Inner Mongolia, China's Northeast, and the Korean Peninsula. In the
Far East, Greater Siberia is bounded by the Chukchi and Kamchatka
peninsulas, the volcanic Kurile island arc, and the Pacific Ocean and its
extension, the Bering Sea. Siberia's mostly frozen northern coast is bor-
dered by arms of the Arctic Ocean: the Kara Sea, the Laptev Sea, the East
Siberian Sea, and the Chukchi Sea. In the extreme northeast, it is narrowly
divided from North America by the Bering Strait. Within these bound-

aries exist the predominantly low-lying plains of Western Siberia, the higher tablelands of Eastern Siberia, and the even higher mountains of the Russian Far East. Pockmarked with ecosystems of incredible beauty and variety, the intervening expanses are often enormous and tedious; thus, Greater Siberia, in my view, offers its visitors a spate of "monotonous diversity."

CONCLUSION

Greater Siberia is a massive storehouse of land and raw materials. As one of the world's least densely populated places, it is likely to remain peripheral to the global economy for some time to come. Because its raw materials are mostly inaccessible and expensive to market, the vast majority of Greater Siberia's resources will remain in reserve well into the next century.

As we have seen in this chapter, the region fully qualifies as a resource frontier. Whereas most of the planet's resource frontiers have retreated in the face of advancing civilizations, Greater Siberia continues to defy human aspirations because of almost "inhuman" constraints to development. As Anthony French of the University of London once observed, there are at least "two Siberias": one developed and hugging the Trans-Siberian Railroad, and another including everything else, mimicking a kind of "world wilderness area," reminiscent of the "boondocks" of Canada and Alaska. As frontiers increasingly are retreating before human technological expertise almost everywhere else on the globe, perhaps Greater Siberia should remain a wilderness.

The subtitle of this book, *Worlds Apart*, suggests the existence of more than two Siberias. These are the "little Siberias" that are shaped by factors of physical geography, ethnicity, and the provincial economy. In the chapters that follow, we shall focus our attention on them.

NOTES

1. Mark Bassin, "Russian Views of Siberia: Meeting Report," Xerox (Washington, D.C.: Kennan Institute for Advanced Russian Studies, The Wilson Center, December 12, 1988) and Mark Bassin, "Russia Between Europe and Asia: The Ideological Construction of Geographical Space," *Slavic Review*, Vol. 50, No. 3 (Spring 1991), pp. 1–17.

2. *Soviet Geography*, Vol. 30, No. 3 (March 1989), pp. 179–252; Immanuel Wallerstein, *The Modern World-System* (New York: Academic Press, 1974), and Immanuel Wallerstein, *The Modern World-System II* (New York: Academic Press, 1980).

3. "Peripheries" and "semiperipheries" are defined in accordance with their relative share of "peripheral processes," or what Alvin and Heidi Toffler have called "slow, first- or second-wave technologies." These are associated with low

wages and elemental occupance patterns. In time, peripheries may adopt enough core-like symptoms (high wages, "fast, third-wave technologies," and diversified production mixes) to become literal extensions of the core area, which Wallerstein (see above) calls the "semiperiphery." See Alvin Toffler, *The Third Wave* (New York: Bantam Books, 1981).

4. Peter J. Taylor, *Political Geography: World-Economy, Nation-State, and Locality* (London and New York: Longman, 1985), pp. 15–18.

5. Terry G. Jordan and Lester Rowntree, *The Human Mosaic: A Thematic Introduction to Cultural Geography* (San Francisco: Canfield Press, 1976), pp. 336–337.

6. In a 1996 study of "competitiveness" among the 46 economically most advanced countries, Russia ranked dead last on the basis of 244 criteria, such as economic strength, technology, financial services, international trade, governmental policy, administration, infrastructure, and skilled labor (International Institute for Development [IID], *World Competition Almanac* [Lausanne, Switzerland: IID, 1997]).

7. The origin of the Russian name for Siberia (Sibir') is debatable because it is confused with a multitude of myths and legends of Ugrian, Hunnic, and Mongolian origin. Perhaps the most commonly accepted today, because it best describes the nature of the region, is "sleeping land" (Mike Edwards, "Siberia in from the Cold," *National Geographic*, Vol. 177, No. 3 [March 1990], p. 10). Others identify it with the name of a sixteenth-century Tatar settlement, Sibir', near the site of contemporary Tobol'sk (James R. Gibson, *Feeding the Russian Fur Trade* [Madison, Wis.: University of Wisconsin Press, 1969], p. 4). Still others suggest that the word evolved from the Russian mispronunciation of the name of a fifth-century Western Siberian tribe called the *sabiri*, or *syvyry*. Another explanation is that the name derives from the Slavic word for north, or *sever*, which easily deteriorates into *siver*, which is very close to *Sibir'* (N. I. Mikhaylov, *Priroda Sibiri* [Moscow: Mysl', 1976], p. 3). A Hunnic, or Buryat, legend intimates that the name may be related to *Siber*, the legendary timber wolf or dog that rose miraculously out of the gelid waters of Lake Baykal (*Izvestiya*, January 19, 1979). Finally, the definition introduced in the text is Mongolian in derivation, being related to *siber*, or *siberi*—a marshland forest, or former oxbow lake (Leonid Shinkarev, *Sibir': Otkuda ona poshla i kuda ona idet* [Moscow: Sovetskaya Rossiya, 1978], p. 31).

8. John Friedmann, *Regional Development Policy: A Case of Venezuela* (Cambridge, Mass.: MIT Press, 1966), pp. 77–83.

9. *1997 World Population Data Sheet* (Washington, D.C.: Population Reference Bureau, 1997).

10. Gary Hausladen, "Siberian Urbanization Since Stalin," Xerox (Washington, D.C.: National Council for Soviet and East European Research, August 1990).

11. The situation has worsened since 1991. Even in Soviet times, these necessities had to be arduously imported across thousands of kilometers. Yakutia ranked last in the supply of consumer goods and services: In some places people waited months or "years" for the delivery of soap and toothpaste. Leslie Dienes, *Soviet Asia: Economic Development and National Policy Choices* (Boulder: Westview Press, 1987), p. 215.

12. A. Granberg and A. Rubensteyn, "Uchastiye Sibiri vo vneshneekonomicheskoy deyatel'nosti: problemy i perspektivy," *Vneshnyaya torgovlya*, No. 8 (1989), pp. 25–29.

13. M. J. Bradshaw, *Siberia at a Time of Change*, Economist Intelligence Unit, Special Report No. 2171 (London: EIU, 1992), p. 81.

14. The population of Novosibirsk grew by 95 percent between 1959 and 1985 (Hausladen, *Siberian Urbanization*).

15. Leslie Dienes, "Economic and Strategic Position of the Soviet Far East," *Soviet Economy*, Vol. 1, No. 1 (1985), p. 153.

16. An average of eight instead of three (A. G. Aganbegyan and V. P. Mozhin, eds., *BAM stroitel'stvo: Khozyaystvennoye osvoyeniye* [Moscow: Ekonomika, 1984], p. 217).

17. The scarcity of money has led to a catch-22: Government ministries cannot pay the mining companies. The mining companies cannot pay the freight rates. The railroad cannot pay for the electricity on the electrified lines, and the energy companies, out of sheer frustration, will not deliver the power, which shuts down movement on the rails ("Trans-Siberian Railroad Traffic Halted," *RFE/RL Newsline*, No. 71, Part 1 [11 July 1997], on-line posting at <http://citm1.met.fsu.edu/—glenn/russia/msg01288.html>).

18. John Hardt, "The Military-Economic Implications of Soviet Regional Policy," in *Regional Development in the USSR* (Newtonville, Mass.: Oriental Research Partners, 1979), p. 238.

19. G. A. Agranat and V. Loginov, "Ob osvoyenii severnykh territorii," *Kommunist*, No. 2 (1976), p. 47.

TWO

Greater Siberia: The Land and Its People

Cherish and protect your native country like the pupil of your eye.
—Ancient Sakha-Yakut proverb

INTRODUCTION

Although Greater Siberia is incredibly harsh to most members of the human race, to Siberian natives, such as the Sakha-Yakuts, it is a beloved place that must be cherished and protected. Massive even to the Russians, the region typically is subdivided into three macroregions, each of which is larger than the conterminous United States ("the lower 48"). Although there is some historical precedent for these subdivisions, they were established mostly for the convenience of Soviet economic planners (see Map 2.1).

WESTERN SIBERIA

The Land and Its Resources

Western Siberia is characterized by three physiographic provinces: the West Siberian Lowland, the Altay Mountains, and the Salair-Kuznetsk ranges. Among these, the lowland accounts for 80 percent of the territory.

No fewer than twenty major streams and hundreds of tributaries feed the West Siberian Lowland with sediments from the aforementioned highlands and the low-lying hummocks west of the Yenisey River and the Central Siberian Upland. By far the most important of these rivers, however, is the Ob', which traverses the plain entirely from its origin in the Altay to its destination in the linear gulf that bears its name. The fifth longest river in the world, the Ob' is joined midway by the ninth longest, the Irtysh, which originates in the Altay ranges of eastern Kazakhstan.

14

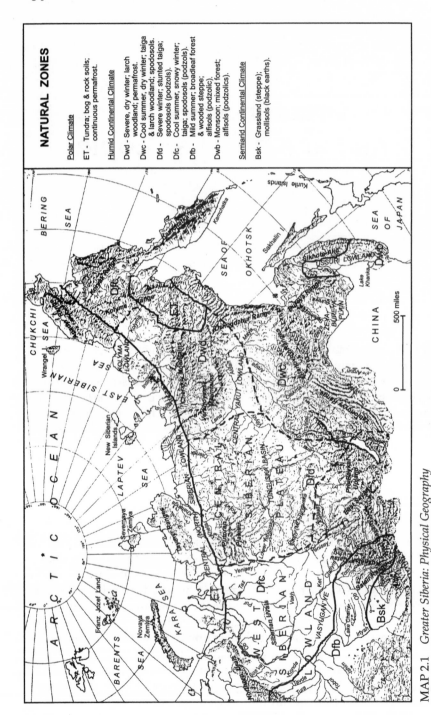

NATURAL ZONES

Polar Climate

ET - Tundra; bog & rock soils; continuous permafrost.

Humid Continental Climate

Dwd - Severe, dry winter; larch woodland; permafrost.
Dwc - Cool summer, dry winter; taiga & larch woodland; spodosols.
Dfd - Severe winter; stunted taiga; spodosols (podzols).
Dfc - Cool summer, snowy winter; taiga; spodosols (podzols).
Dfb - Mild summer; broadleaf forest & wooded steppe; alfisols (podzolic).
Dwb - Monsoon; mixed forest; alfisols (podzolics).

Semiarid Continental Climate

Bsk - Grassland (steppe); mollisols (black earths).

MAP 2.1 *Greater Siberia: Physical Geography*

SOURCES: The "Mountains and Plains" segment is adapted from original artwork by T. M. Oberlander in Paul E. Lydolph, *Geography of the USSR* (2d ed.; New York: John Wiley and Sons, 1964), inside front cover.

The Ob'-Irtysh system is fed in the west by the Sos'va, Konda, Tura, Iset', and Uy, each of which flows off the Urals; in the southwest by the Tobol and Ishim, which spring from high ground in Kazakhstan; in the southeast by the Katun' and Biya that converge to form the Ob' in the Altay; and by the Tom', which also flows out of the Altay to expose the famed seams of Russia's greatest operating coal field, the Kuznetsk Basin, or Kuzbas, between the Salair Ridge and the Kuznetsk Alatau. Finally, the slow-moving Chulym, Ket', Tym, and Vakh drain the gently sloping ground in the east.

For 1,600 kilometers (1,000 mi) from west to east and for 1,900 kilometers (1,200 mi) south to north, the West Siberian Lowland never exceeds an elevation of 180 meters (600 ft) above sea level. When its southern tributaries swell with meltwater in spring, the Ob' is still ice-dammed in the north. Floodwaters spread across the "pool table" that lies between the Ob' and Irtysh to create the massive Vasyugan'ye. For hundreds of millennia, the Vasyugan swamps have served as a catchment basin for microorganisms that have slowly decomposed into the Middle Ob' oil fields. In this hostile, watery environment, Ugrian Khants and Mansi and Samoyedic Nentsy and Sel'kups survived by fishing, trapping, and herding reindeer. The Ugrians, who are linguistic relatives of the Hungarian Magyars, led a limicolous existence, whereas the Nentsy, whose traditional dwelling is a portable teepee, led a nomadic life on the tundra.

During the past two million years, glaciation has been extensive in the northern third of the lowland. The glacial advances, which lasted tens of thousands of years, alternated with retreats of similar duration. The heavy glaciers helped to create a concave basement that filled with seawater in the warmer interglacial periods. (It is this concavity that partly explains the extensive spring and summer flooding of the lowland.[1]) The glaciers originated on Novaya Zemlya (an offshore extension of the Urals) and in the Byrranga-Putoran region east of the Yenisey River and advanced as far south as the Ob' and Irtysh junction. Just north of Khanty-Mansiysk, one of Russia's leading centers of oil field development, are the east-west morainal hillocks known collectively as the Sibirskiye Uvaly, or Siberian Ridges. Despite the modesty of their elevation, the hills serve as a sort of "subcontinental divide" between the north- and south-flowing river networks. As well known as the southern streams are for their association with petroleum, the north-flowing tributaries of the Nadym, Pur, and Taz rivers are famed for their roles in the exploration and development of natural gas: The Ob'-Taz depression is home to one-third of the planet's reserves.

In the south, the Ishim, Baraba, and Kulunda steppes, or grasslands, eventually merge with the foothills of the Altay Mountains. Rarely fluctuating in elevation and giving the illusion of a vast, quiet sea,[2] the steppes are hosts for the Trans-Siberian Railroad and its branch lines. Once exclusively blanketed with wildflowers, aspen, willows, and a sea of grass, the steppes, like the American Great Plains, have been put to the plow and now represent Russia's spring wheat belt. The West Siberian steppes also contain Greater Siberia's "lake district," with some lakes that are perennial, such as Lake Chany, and others that expand and shrink like Florida's Everglades, with the rise and fall of the water table. Many of the smelly, ephemeral lakes are rich in salts of both industrial and table varieties.[3] Since the thirteenth century, the grassy plains have been the homeland of the Turkicized Siberian Tatars, who chased the original Ugrian inhabitants into the Vasyugan'ye.

In the southeast, Western Siberia terminates in the Altay Mountains, replete with scenes similar to those found in the Colorado Rockies. Pushing 4,500 meters (14,600 ft), the highest peaks contain more than 750 glaciers that feed the Ob'-Irtysh system with meltwater.[4] The Altay of eastern Kazakhstan, the source of the Irtysh, is known as the Rudnyy Altay (the Ore-Bearing Altay) because of its abundant commercial deposits of copper, lead, zinc, and silver and its scattered outcrops of iron ore. The semi-nomadic Altay Turks have expertly ridden their Mongolian ponies in and out of these mountains for generations. In 1991, they audaciously seceded from Altay Kray and proclaimed their lofty homeland the Altay Republic.

The "gem" of the Altay region, however, is the Kuzbas. Here, the valley of the Tom' River is surrounded on three sides by extensions of the Altay: the Salair Ridge in the west, the Gornaya Shoriya (the Shor Mountains) in the south, and the Kuznetsk Alatau in the east. While the name Kuzbas is synonymous with coal, the Salair is identified with lead and zinc; the Gornaya Shoriya, with iron ore; and the Kuznetsk Alatau, with gold, manganese, mercury, and nephelite. The Shor Mountains are identified with another Turkic people, the Shor, who lead a quiet, sedentary existence.

Climates, Vegetation, and Soils

Although severe, the climates of Western Siberia are more moderate and generally moister than those farther east. The climates are arranged in latitudinal belts of varying widths. A narrow strip of semiarid continental (steppe) climate spills over into Western Siberia from Kazakhstan. This grades northward into a wider belt of humid continental climate in which the summers are relatively cool. The Trans-Siberian Railroad wends its way through this zone. The milder climates in turn merge northward with the humid continental, severe winter climate characteristic of most of Greater Siberia. Finally, along the northern fringe of the region, comprising most of the Yamal and Gydan peninsulas, are the polar climates.

As in the rest of Greater Siberia, here winter is the dominant season, with short, cool summers (four months or fewer) and very abrupt seasonal transitions. The growing season rarely exceeds 120 days per annum. Even in the more temperate zone of the Trans-Siberian Railroad, killing frosts might occur in any month except July. Farther north, no month is safe from their wrath. July temperatures average close to 20° centigrade (70° F) in Omsk, at latitude 55° N, gradually cooling to less than 10° centigrade (50° F) beyond the Arctic Circle (66.5° N), in the vicinity of the Gulf of Ob'. In Omsk, January averages –19° centigrade (–6° F), but onetime minima may plunge to as low as –50° centigrade (–58° F). Ironically, minimum temperatures at places like Surgut, in the Middle Ob' oil fields, and Salekhard, near the mouth of the same river, are not much colder, at –55° centigrade and –57° centigrade, respectively. The difference comes from the windchill factor, which accelerates dramatically near the Kara Sea. There the number of extremely windy days of 15 meters per second (30 mph) is nearly twice that in the Kulunda Steppe (84 days vs. 45 days). On or near the Gulf of Ob', windchills of –100° centigrade (–116° F) are not uncommon. In the southern steppes, winter winds of this velocity bring blizzards known as *burany* or *purgi*.[5]

Springs and falls are brief. In this regard, my autumn 1991 experience in the Kuzbas city of Kemerovo is particularly telling. I arrived in early September for a week-long conference arranged by the Siberian Academy of Sciences. During the drive from the airport to my hotel, I noticed that the leaves of the broadleaf deciduous trees were only beginning to change color. Seven days later, not only had the trees changed color but the true meaning of "fall" had been made abundantly clear: A literal leaf avalanche had tumbled off the trees in great spongy heaps within just a few days. By week's end, in mid-September, the trees were nearly bare, the temperatures had cooled dramatically, and it was apparent that the first snow was nigh.

In keeping with continentality, Western Siberia has a pronounced summer maximum of precipitation. At Omsk, 70 percent of it comes in the high-sun period (between April and September). Unfortunately, most of the region's rainfall typically arrives in the late summer and fall. This plays havoc with the wheat harvest, which must be carried out in two stages: One stage involves cutting and curing the grain; the other involves collecting and threshing it.[6]

Western Siberia bears the distinction of having more cyclonic weather than any other area in Russia. Although snow cover is shallow over most of Greater Siberia, because of the prevalence of winter cyclones in the valley of the Middle Yenisey, the depth of the snow there—at 30–60 inches per year—rivals that in the snowiest regions of Russia (the Central Urals and the Kola Peninsula). Moreover, the snow remains on the ground for more than 150 days. Because Western Siberia is the snowiest part of Greater Siberia, it lacks permafrost, except in the northernmost section of the Ob' basin. Summers are characterized by a dozen or more thunderstorms, one-third of them coming in July.

The climates condition the vegetation and soils of the region. Near the border between Russia and Kazakhstan, the semiarid continental climate yields steppe, or grassland, vegetation, the soils for which are typically black earths called chernozems. Because they are often associated with high water tables, however, West Siberian black earths are frequently saline or degraded.

Because wooden plows (*sokhi*) were no match for the deep sod of the Russian steppes, including those of Siberia, Siberians tended to occupy the cooler, wetter regions north of the grasslands until well into the nineteenth century. Here the grasslands were interspersed with copses of birch, aspen, and willow, creating an ecosystem known as wooded steppe. This was the favored zone of settlement in the early days of Russian migration into Siberia. In this area, the chernozems are less likely to be salinized, and they can be plowed more easily. Farther north, the humid continental, cool summer climate encourages a thin belt of continuous broadleaf forest. The tracks of the Trans-Siberian Railroad were laid along the southern flank of this forest. Slightly acidic, gray or brown forest soil characterizes this zone.

The broadleaf forests of the milder humid continental climates merge so swiftly with the taiga that there are few extensive stands of mixed forest (broadleaf-needleleaf woodland) in Western Siberia. Taiga, or northern coniferous forest, is typical of the humid continental, severe winter climate. Here marshlands hamper the continuity of these forests, which include stands of pine, true cedar, spruce, and fir. They also militate against the normal processes of soil formation, which usually yield highly acidic podzols. Instead, the soils of Western Siberia are commonly peat bogs and waterlogged clays.

With a growing season of fewer than 60 days, the polar climates support the simplest ecosystem on the planet, the tundra. The vegetation consists primarily of mosses, sedges, and lichens, one of the latter of which is reindeer moss (*Cladonia rangiferina*). The "polar" opposite of the tropical rain forest, the tundra often contains fewer than four species per square kilometer. As in the desert, there is little organic matter for the creation of topsoil; however, because no month averages temperatures above 10° centigrade (50° F), the consistently cool-to-cold weather actually preserves the potential humus. Combined with a high water table perched above permafrost, the climatic pattern results in bog-type earths and mechanically weathered rock materials.

The People

On January 1, 1993, Western Siberia recorded a population of 15.2 million, 10.8 million (71 percent) of whom lived in cities and 4.4 million (29 percent) of whom lived in rural areas. One of six persons resided in two cities: Novosibirsk (1.4 million) and Omsk (1.2 million). The rest of the population was unevenly distributed among the region's five oblasts (Kemerovo, Tyumen', Novosibirsk, Omsk, and Tomsk), the Altay republic and kray, and the autonomous okrugs of Khantia-Mansia and Yamalia. The most populous of these territorial units, Kemerovo oblast, had lost residents since 1991, as had Tyumen' and Tomsk oblasts. The declines were associated with the economic stagnation that had occurred in the extractive sectors of those provinces.[7]

No fewer than twenty of Greater Siberia's forty-five or more ethnic groups may be found in Western Siberia (see Map 2.2). Only seven of these groups—the Siberian Tatars, the Altay, the Khants, the Nentsy, the Shors, the Mansi, and the Sel'kups—were native to the region. These people were vastly outnumbered by *prishliye,* or nonnatives, such as Russians, nonnative Tatars, Ukrainians, Germans, and so on. In 1989, 85 percent of the population of Western Siberia was Russian, and native Siberians constituted only 1 percent.

EASTERN SIBERIA

The Land and Its Resources

The physiographic platform of Eastern Siberia is the Central Siberian Upland. A low north-south undulation divides the watersheds of Western Siberia from that of the Yenisey River and simultaneously defines the boundary of the latter with Eastern Siberia. For almost 2,000 kilometers (1,600 mi) the mighty Yenisey, which is a mere 200 kilometers (160 mi) east of that boundary, cuts a steep escarpment into the Central Siberian Upland. Representative of the Yenisey's right bank, the cliff reaches its highest elevations near where it and the river emerge from the Western Sayan Mountains in the Tyva Republic. Consisting of some of the planet's oldest rock, the upland is delimited in the north by the Byrranga Mountains, which form the Taymyr Peninsula, where barely 1,500 Samoyedic Nganasans and Entsy survive in their age-old way. In the south, a winding, linear basin separates the upland from the Western and Eastern Sayan Mountains. The Trans-Siberian Railroad runs within this natural trough between Krasnoyarsk and Irkutsk. Finally, the upland is bounded in the east by the Lake Baykal ranges (Pre-Baykalia) and the rippled terrain of Sakha (Yakutia).

The Central Siberian Upland is the source of several of the world's longest and most powerful tributaries: In the west, the three Tunguskas—the Upper Tunguska, or Angara; the Stony, or Mountain, Tunguska; and the Lower Tunguska—erode the plateau. In the north, the Kotuy-Khatanga system scours it. In the east, the Lena, the Vilyuy, the Olenek,

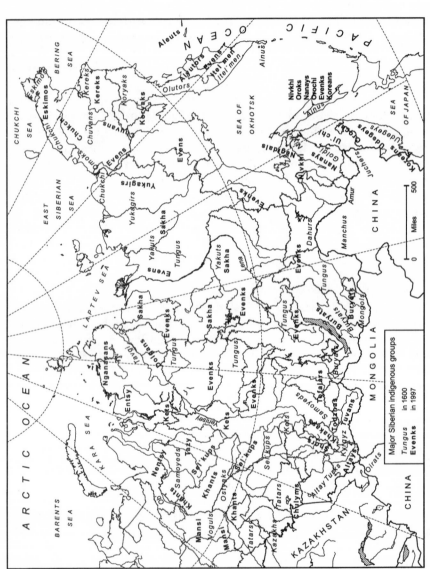

MAP 2.2 *Greater Siberia: Ethnic Groups*

SOURCES: Tochenov, *Atlas SSSR*, pp. 128–129; Forsyth, *A History of the Peoples of Siberia*, pp. 17, 24, 134, and 205; and Fondahl, "Siberia: Assimilation and Discontent," p. 191.

and the Anabar rivers attack it. Although the upland averages only 500 to 700 meters (1,600–2,300 ft) above sea level, the cumulative hydroelectric potential of these streams represents one-third of Russia's reserves, ranking first in the country.[8]

The upland is also home to some of the earth's most inaccessible humans. The Kets, for instance, who exist in scattered clusters in the basins of the Mountain Tunguska and Lower Tunguska rivers and on the Yenisey floodplain, barely exceed 1,000 individuals and speak a language as strange and as singular as they are. They live alongside the widely scattered Evenk people, whose autonomous okrug, Evenkia, dominates the upland. Ironically, fewer than 3,500 of the estimated 30,000 Evenks, who speak a variant of Tungus-Manchu, reside in Evenkia. More than half of them dwell in Sakha (Yakutia) and Buryatia.

A northeastern extension of the West Siberian Lowland, the North Siberian Lowland, divides the Putoran Plateau from Taymyria's Byrranga Mountains. The Putoran, which reaches elevations of 1,701 meters (5,528 ft), is an abruptly elevated mass that represents the last segment of the Yenisey escarpment. From its apex, rivers radiate outward like spokes of a wheel, including the Pyasino, the Kureyka, the Kotuy, and the Kheta, a left-bank tributary of the Khatanga. The Pyasino and Kheta basins of the North Siberian Lowland are home to about 4,800 of the 6,000 Dolgans, who, like the Sakha-Yakuts, speak a Turkic dialect.

The western edge of the Putoran Plateau fronts on the baleful settlement of Noril'sk, a city of 170,000 situated at 69° N. The unfortunate residents of Noril'sk, a former Stalinist slave-labor camp, mine and smelt copper, nickel, cobalt, platinum, and precious metals from the Putoran. These deposits, in combination with nearby coal fields (only 20 miles distant), spurred the development of the world's most isolated industrial complex, including not only Noril'sk, but also nearby Talnakh and the Yenisey River port of Dudinka. In terms of per capita emissions, Noril'sk is also the planet's most polluted place, easily outdistancing the statistics for smog-choked Mexico City and São Paulo. Moreover, since most of Noril'sk's atmospheric excreta is sulfur dioxide, the city is far deadlier than others.[9]

In terms of raw materials, Eastern Siberia is a "sleeping land." Between the Kuzbas and Lake Baykal along the Trans-Siberian Railroad, in the Kansk-Achinsk and Irkutsk basins, are active strip mines that yield low-quality soft coals. North of these accessible deposits, however, lie the Tungus, Tunguska, and Taymyr basins, which contain more than half of Russia's undeveloped coal resources. When, and if, the world's fossil fuels are exhausted, the last to go will be the coal of the Tungus Basin. The Angara watershed is loaded with mostly undeveloped ferrous, nonferrous, and precious metals. Arranged like beads along the river are iron ore and alumina-bearing deposits. Oil and gas have been discovered north of Irkutsk, in the Bratsk area, along the Mountain Tunguska, and in the North Siberian Lowland, but few of these fields are actually producing.

Unlike Western Siberia, which is literally awash in lakes and marshes, Eastern Siberia is a massive, efficiently drained tableland that is void of major lakes, save one. That single exception is, by volume, the greatest freshwater lake in the world. It is also unequivocally the deepest and oldest. Lake Baykal, which is no younger than 20 million years—an average lake's life span is 15 million—is at its deepest 2,063 meters (5,715 ft) and contains more potable water than all five North American Great Lakes combined. Belgium-sized in area, the crescent-shaped Baykal is not particularly impressive from a bird's-eye view; but what it lacks in the horizontal plane it makes up in the vertical. This deep lake contains more than 80 percent of Russia's, and 20 percent of the world's, drinkable water. Similar to the lakes of East Africa, Baykal occupies a trench, or a rift in the earth's surface. This rift is currently increasing at the speed of a fingernail's growth; thus, Baykal is gradually becoming even wider and deeper.

Hydrologists estimate that if Baykal's cup were empty, it would take all the world's rivers an entire year to refill it. Baykal is not empty, however: It continuously receives the waters of 336 streams and is drained by only one, the Angara. If the tap were ever turned off, the Angara would empty Baykal in 305 years. In other words, had this hypothetical process begun during the reign of Peter the Great (1689–1725), the lake would be dry now.[10] That would be a shame, for Baykal's water is so unusually pure that under sunny skies, a visitor can espy a silver coin at a depth of 40 meters (120 ft) below the lake's surface. Only the Sargasso Sea boasts greater translucency.

As long as it is not covered by snow, the lake is just as translucent in early January. It remains solidly frozen until May and obtains a maximum ice thickness of 2 meters (6 ft). The great thickness of Baykal's ice has inspired myths surrounding the lake's capability of supporting early Trans-Siberian Railroad trains. Before the construction of the first railway loop around the lake's southern tip (1901–1904), passengers and rolling stock were ferried across Baykal by two British-built icebreaking train ferries. In the severest of winters, the icebreakers became ice-bound. Such was the winter of 1903–1904, when in February the Japanese launched their surprise attack on the Russian fleet at Port Arthur. For several years before the outbreak of the Russo-Japanese War (1904–1905), the Russian railway ministry toyed with the idea of laying a temporary track across the ice of Baykal, which that winter was at maximum thickness. Using long sleepers to spread the load, the toying finally became reality: The soldiers cautiously rolled a test locomotive onto the track, when suddenly, the ice—weakened by a warm spring beneath the surface—creaked, popped, and violently cracked. The test engine plunged to the bottom, leaving in its wake a jagged, 2-meter rift in the ice that ultimately spread more than 22 kilometers (14 mi) across the otherwise frozen lake. Thereafter, engines were dismantled, and together with the component parts, were loaded onto flatcars, which "were dragged across the ice by teams of men and horses."[11] What a way to win a war! (Needless to say, they did not.)

The Pre-Baykal and Transbaykal ranges manifest steep shorelines west and east of the lake, respectively. During the 1970s and 1980s, in association with the planning and construction of the Baykal-Amur Main Line rail system, or BAM, which passes through them, these ranges became veritable household words in the Soviet Union. In addition to their scenic and recreational value, the highlands contain rich deposits of titanium, lead, zinc, graphite, and nephelite, many of which were exposed and polished by glaciation in the past 2 million years. Lake Baykal and its ranges are the homelands of the Buryat nation, a Mongol-speaking Buddhist people who live both west and east of the lake. The largest Siberian native minority, numbering more than 400,000, the Buryats proclaimed their ASSR a full-fledged republic in 1991. They and the Evenks are longtime neighbors.

The mountains of the south (Western and Eastern Sayans, Tannu-Ola, and Yablonovyy) are older and higher than the Baykal ranges. In the west, the Sayans trap a series of steppe basins. Because of their isolation and singularity, the basins were appealing sites for early settlement (see Chapter 3). In addition to the strategic value of the basins, being steppes, their soils were suitable for Neolithic farming.

The most fertile of the lowlands is the Minusinsk Basin. Triangular-shaped and hemmed in by the Western and Eastern Sayans, the basin is noted for its rich, black, loamy soils. Within its fertile confines live the Khakass, a group of northeastern Turks, who established a republic there in 1991. East of Khakassia, in the Biryusa-Uda valleys, exists another Turkic tribe, the Tofalars, who rank among Siberia's smallest ethnic groups. Likewise, south of the Minusinsk Basin, the Tyvan people occupy three isolated lowlands between the Sayans to the north and the Tannu-Olas to the south. The Tyvans (formerly Tuvans), who represent one of only two groups of native Siberians to boast a clear majority within their homeland (the other being the Aga-Buryats), are the titular population of the Tyva Republic. Their semiarid capital, Kyzyl, proudly lays claim to the "center of Asia."[12] Here the Tyvans mine coal, asbestos, and cobalt.

South and east of Lake Baykal is the Yablonovyy Range, which forms a watershed between Lake Baykal and the tributaries of the Amur River. Contiguous with Outer Mongolia in the west and Inner Mongolia in the east, the Yablonovyys are rich in steam coal, rare earths, molybdenum, tungsten, and gold.

The Yablonovyys join the rugged highlands of Transbaykalia in the north and originate the generally north-flowing tributaries of the Vitim River, a major tributary of the Lena network. One of the rivers, the Upper Angara, flows against the grain into the northern tip of Lake Baykal. Together these two opposing systems carve the western end of the Stanovoy Range. They occupy and erode a series of faulted lowlands that are extensions of the same scar that holds Lake Baykal. The resulting escarpments expose a vast array of minerals, along which passes the BAM railway.[13]

Climates, Vegetation, and Soils

Although there are subtle climatic variations associated with the evenness of the annual distribution of precipitation and with extremely localized weather patterns, the climate of Eastern Siberia is quite simple. Located far from the moderation of ice-free seas, the region bears a regime that is even more continental than that of Western Siberia, intensifying to the extreme those aforementioned characteristics of continentality (great ranges of temperature, low annual precipitation, and summer-peak rainfall). The dominance of winter is overwhelming: On the Taymyr Peninsula, the Samoyeds battle against 300 days of frost. Even in southerly Kyzyl, Tyvans weather more than 160 days with average temperatures below the freezing point. Springs and autumns are even more abbreviated than they are in Western Siberia, and temperatures average above 10° centigrade (50° F) for three months or fewer during the year, the latter being the season called summer. Winters are dry in the south and drier in the north and northeast because of a persistent high pressure cell known as the Asiatic Maximum, often misnamed the "Siberian High." This winter-only phenomenon centers on Mongolia and stretches northeastward deep into Sakha (Yakutia). The snow cover here is Russia's shallowest, and, because of that fact, Eastern Siberia's permafrost is the country's deepest and most extensive. Precipitation rarely exceeds 400 millimeters (15 in), with 75 percent falling in the high-sun period, usually peaking after July. The growing season lasts fewer than 110 days, and frost can occur in any month. As in Western Siberia, the polar climates of the north experience a growing season of no more than 60 days. These harsh tundras evidence the coldest windchills outside of the Antarctic continent (−150° C).

The simple climate yields an even simpler vegetational complex. Although there are sheltered steppes in the isolated basins of the south, virtually all of Eastern Siberia, except the tundras of the Putoran and Taymyr, is blanketed in taiga. In 1990, Eastern Siberia was the Soviet Union's leading supplier of commercial timber, yielding more than one-fifth of the harvest. Most of it came from the forest of pine, stone pine, spruce, and fir that line the Trans-Siberian and BAM railroads. Most of the region, however, is covered with noncommercial stands of larch—a species of tamarack that loses its needles in winter. Because of its shallow, spreading root system, the larch is the only conifer species that grows well on permafrost, which underlies 95 percent of Eastern Siberia in one form or another. Without larch, most of the region's taiga would have no trees at all.

Permafrost, or permanently frozen ground, with or without underground ice, is more important than climate and vegetation in determining the nature of the soils of Eastern Siberia. Because permafrost is impenetrable and thaws from less than one meter in the Taymyr tundra to three meters in the isolated steppes of the south, the vast majority of Eastern Siberia has no true soil, or solum. "Soils" are mostly waterlogged organic detritus and weathered bedrock. The solum that exists is either the highly acidic podzols (spodosols) of the taiga or the loamy chernozems (mollisols) of the isolated steppes.

The People

On January 1, 1993, 9.2 million people lived in Eastern Siberia. Of these, 6.6 million (71 percent) were city dwellers and 2.7 million (29 percent) were villagers and farmers.[14] These residents were found in three republics (Buryatia, Tyva, and Khakassia), one kray (Krasnoyarsk), two oblasts (Irkutsk and Chita), and four autonomous okrugs (Dolgano-Nenetsia, Evenkia, Ust'-Orda Buryatia, and Aga-Buryatia). Almost two of three Eastern Siberians lived in Krasnoyarsk kray and Irkutsk oblast. One of six persons lived in the cities of Krasnoyarsk (919,000) and Irkutsk (635,000) alone.

Eastern Siberia comprises approximately twenty of Greater Siberia's forty-five or so ethnic groups. Eleven groups are native to the region, the most numerous of whom are the Buryats, Tyvans, Khakass, Evenks, and Dolgans. Six others number fewer than 1,500 individuals per group. More than 83 percent of the total population of the region is Russian, whereas native groups account for 8 percent.

THE RUSSIAN FAR EAST

The Land and Its Resources

The western borders of Sakha (Yakutia) and Chita oblast arbitrarily divide the Russian Far East from Eastern Siberia. For decades, Russian geographers and government officials have bickered about the landmarks that separate the two regions.[15] The latest debate took place in the early 1960s, when Yakutia [now Sakha (Yakutia)] was transferred to the Soviet (now Russian) Far East.

Bearing some of the earth's oldest and richest rocks, the Russian Far East boasts 99 percent of Russia's current diamond output; 90 percent of its gold; virtually all of its tin, tungsten, and molybdenum; all of its lithium; probably all of its mercury and antimony; much of its beryllium; and a majority of its lead and zinc reserves. Although lacking in iron ore, the region is rich in coal resources, especially in the Lena Basin. Still relatively unexplored are the petroleum and natural gas resources of the Lena-Tunguska, Anadyr', and Sakhalin basins.

From the 1930s to his death in 1953, Joseph Stalin sent hundreds of thousands of political prisoners to mine these minerals, usually to *their* deaths. The most likely destinations of these poor souls were gold-rich, but unspeakably harsh, Yakutia and the Kolyma and Anadyr' uplands. Farther northeast, where mercury and tin are mined, is the Chukchi Peninsula, the home of a Paleo-Asiatic people who resemble the Alaskan Eskimo. Often the objects of lowbrow Russian humor, the Chukchi have been able to expand their political autonomy during the post-Soviet period. Moreover, since the collapse of the USSR, Russian Eskimos who live on the coast of Chukotka periodically have exchanged visits with their relatives in Alaska.

The Stanovoy Mountains divide northeast from southeast Siberia. The easternmost Stanovoys bend sharply northeastward to join the Dzhugdzhur Range, which dips steeply into the Sea of Okhotsk. In the north, the Lena River makes a sweeping northwesterly turn through the Yakut Lowland, the traditional hearth of the Turkic Sakha, or Yakut, people. In this remote segment of the planet, the now sedentary Sakha-Yakuts have raised the earth's most hardy breeds of horse and cattle for centuries. Separating them from the Even and Chukchi people in the northeast are the crescentic ranges of the Verkhoyansk and Cherskiy.

In the south, the less lofty Sikhote-Alin' is flanked in the west by the Ussuri-Khanka Plain, which begins at the North Korean border and stretches along Russia's once hostile eastern perimeter with China to the expansive Amur River lowland near Khabarovsk. The Bureya and Turana mountains separate the Amur Basin from the Zeya-Bureya Plain. Unlike the soggy, flood-prone Amur Valley, the Zeya-Bureya region is suitable for diversified farming, including the growing of most of Russia's soybeans. Early Cossack explorers Yerofey Khabarov and Vasiliy Poyarkov sought to assimilate and subdue Amuria and neighboring Dauria in order to obtain food and gold for early Russian expansion. Their cruel, sadistic actions have been retold in the oral histories of the Amur river natives (the modern Nanays, Udegeys, Ul'chi, Orochi, Negidals, and Nivkhi) for more than 200 years.

The Pacific coast of Russia, inclusive of Sakhalin and the Kurile Islands, is on the leading edge of the so-called ring of fire and subject to earthquakes and volcanic eruptions. The Kamchatka Peninsula comprises 120 volcanoes, 23 of which are active. One of these is Russia's highest mountain, Mt. Klyuchevskaya, at 4,750 meters (15,438 ft). In simple terms, the Pacific Ocean basin is gradually sliding beneath the eastern edge of Eurasia, inducing earthquakes, then melting and rising to the surface in the form of lava. Molten rock from the basin has created and continues to feed the volcanoes of Kamchatka and the Kuriles (the name of the latter derives from the Russian verb *kurit'* [to smoke]). Russia's only geothermal electric plant is on Kamchatka. Except for the geothermal power potential and the fossil fuels of Sakhalin, the only commercial resources so far extracted have been gold and sulfur. Here, in this fiery world, dwell 7,000 Koryaks, 1,400 Itel'men, and offshore, on the Commander Islands, 600 Aleuts. There also might yet be a few Ainu and Koreans living on the southern Kuriles (Iturup and Kunashiri) opposite Hokkaido, the northernmost island of Japan.

In keeping with this naturally violent world, the region has had a tumultuous political past. In the last two weeks of World War II, the Russians occupied the southernmost Kurile Islands, including Iturup, Kunashiri, Shikotan, and the Habomai group. The invasion violated the conditions of a Russo-Japanese neutrality pact that representatives of both nations had signed earlier in the war. To the Russians, the islands represent the spoils of war. To the Japanese, the "northern territories" represent an emotionally charged breach of contract. For both countries, the value of the islands is chiefly symbolic: Apart from their strategic location (at the head of the Sea of Okhotsk) and the rich salmon fishing grounds surrounding them, the islands conceal no treasure trove of raw materials.

Ironically, Sakhalin Island, which is no longer in dispute between Russia and Japan, is far more valuable. The sediments of northern Sakhalin—which was once the location of the Amur River delta—are recent, porous, and permeable, and often contain oil and gas. No fewer than 50 onshore and offshore oil and gas wells have been drilled there since 1900. Closer to the mountainous core of the island, in central and southern Sakhalin, coal is extracted from a half-dozen sites. Sakhalin is home to 2,000 Nivkhi, a Paleo-Asiatic group, and a few hundred Tungus-Manchus: the Orochi (212), the Nanays (173), and the Oroks (129). All except the Oroks are more numerous in the Amur Basin than on the island. The Russianized urban Koreans living on the island, who are estimated to number about 40,000, are the offspring of an equal number of slave laborers imported by the Japanese to mine coal when both Korea and south Sakhalin (Karafuto) belonged to Japan. The Japanese killed 20,000 of the émigrés before the end of World War II. Only 1,000 of the original arrivals have survived.

Climates, Soils, and Vegetation

Continentality culminates in the northern part of the Russian Far East. Nowhere on Earth are the annual ranges of temperature so extreme and the mean winter air pressures so high as they are in Sakha (Yakutia). With the exceptions of Chukotka, Kamchatka, Sakhalin, and the Kuriles, which exhibit "evenly distributed" patterns of precipitation, all of the climates of the Russian Far East are distinctly monsoonal. The long winters are particularly dry and the brief summers are extremely wet, with 75 percent of the precipitation falling in the high-sun period. Coastal areas are subject to high winds throughout the year and to occasional typhoons (hurricanes) between July and October. Peak precipitation also typically occurs in those months. The extreme southeast enjoys the mildest climates, with four months of balmy, often cloudy summers; but midwinters in Khabarovsk on the Amur River are colder than they are in Omsk in Western Siberia. Winters elsewhere, except for southeastern Kamchatka, which is exposed to the ice-free Pacific Ocean, experience temperatures of –30° centigrade (–22° F) or less at least once in winter. Near the Korean border, the port of Vladivostok averages winter temperatures that are lower than those in Moscow, which lies twelve degrees farther north. Although shallow and breakable, shorefast ice plagues Vladivostok's Peter the Great Bay for at least three months each year. The only places where the growing season exceeds 120 days are the Zeya-Bureya and Ussuri plains.

Except for the tundra and the mixed forests of the Amur River Basin and Primor'ye, all of the Russian Far East is a larch woodland mixed with cedar scrub. As in Western and Eastern Siberia, the tundra here is found along the Arctic coast and at higher elevations associated with summer averages of less than 10° centigrade (50° F). Amuria and the lowlands and foothills of the Sikhote-Alin' support the only true mixed (broadleaf deciduous-conifer) forest in Greater Siberia. Some species are extremely exotic, such as the Amur cork, the Amur lilac, Asian bird cherry, various maples, wild apple and pear, and a host of lianas. The fabled ginseng root also grows there.

The tundra and taiga soils here are the same as those in Eastern Siberia. The mixed forest soils of the southeast, however, are less acidic, brown forest varieties (alfisols).

The People

Predictably, the population of the Russian Far East has declined since 1991. By January 1, 1993, it had fallen from 8.1 million to 7.9 million people, or by 157,000 residents. Although every province, except Primor'ye kray, experienced a drop in population, the worst deficits understandably occurred among nonnatives who had been reluctant residents of the harshest regions (Sakha [Yakutia], Chukotka, and Kamchatka). The Russian Far East contains the Sakha-Yakut Republic; two "independent" autonomous okrugs (Jewish and Chukchi, respectively); two krays (Primorskiy and Khabarovsk); four oblasts (Amur, Kamchatka, Magadan, and Sakhalin); and one "dependent" autonomous okrug (Koryak, a sub-unit of Kamchatka oblast). Almost 77 percent of the residents live in the provinces of Primor'ye, Khabarovsk, Sakha (Yakutia), and Amuria. The Russian Far East is Russia's most urban region, with 76 percent of the people living in cities. Magadan and Sakhalin, at more than 85 percent, are the *most* urban provinces in Russia, and Koryakia ranks among the least (37 percent). The only cities with more than 500,000 residents, however, are Vladivostok (643,000) and Khabarovsk (612,000).

At least twenty-three of Greater Siberia's forty-five different ethnic groups are found in the Russian Far East. Not only does this represent the largest inventory of native minorities in Greater Siberia, at more than 550,000 individuals, it is also the greatest proportion (7 percent). Sakha-Yakuts compose the largest group, with 380,000 people, or 69 percent of all native Russian far easterners. Present also are all eight subfamilies of the Tungus-Manchu languages. These make up 10 percent of the region's ethnic minorities, including the Evenk and Even (in the northeast) and the Amur River peoples. The remaining share of 21 percent comprises nine other groups that occupy the region's Pacific coast. These are the Eskimo-Aleuts, the Chukchi-Kamchatkans (Koryaks and Itel'men), the Koreans, the Nivkhi, the Yukagirs, and possibly the Ainu. Four of five inhabitants of the Russian Far East are Russians. Historically, Ukrainians have represented another sizable nonnative minority, living primarily in Primor'ye.

CONCLUSION

Greater Siberia is composed of three macroregions: Western Siberia, Eastern Siberia, and the Russian Far East. Although designed to facilitate Soviet central planning, these regions' physical and human geographies are sufficiently distinctive to merit their formal differentiation, as I have tried to show briefly here. The following two chapters will cover key issues and concepts in the historical development and cultural geography of Greater Siberia up to the Bolshevik Revolution in 1917.

NOTES

1. Paul E. Lydolph, *Geography of the USSR* (3d ed.; New York: Jóhn Wiley & Sons, 1977), p. 370; and S. P. Suslov, *Physical Geography of Asiatic Russia* (San Francisco: W. H. Freeman and Co., 1961), pp. 3–6.

2. Eric Newby, *The Big Red Train Ride* (New York: St. Martin's Press, 1978), pp. 104–105.

3. Some of the ephemeral lakes, called *sors*, reek of "rotten eggs" and are fouled with bird guano (M. I. Pomus, ed., *Rossiyskaya Federatsiya: Zapadnaya Sibir'*, in the

series *Sovetskiy Soyuz,* ed. S. V. Kolesnik [22 vols.; Moscow: Mysl', 1971], pp. 17–25).

4. V. V. Tochenov et al., *Atlas SSSR* (Moscow: Glavnoye upravleniye geodezii i kartografii pri Sovete Ministrov SSSR, 1983), p. 86.

5. Lydolph, *Geography of the USSR* (3d ed.), pp. 376–377; Paul E. Lydolph, *Climates of the Soviet Union,* Vol. 7 of *World Survey of Climatology,* ed. H. E. Landsberg (13 vols.; New York: Elsevier Scientific Publishing Company, 1977), p. 400.

6. Lydolph, *Geography of the USSR* (3d ed.), p. 378.

7. Goskomstat Rossii, *Rossiyskaya federatsiya v 1992 godu* (Moscow: Respublikanskiy informatsionno-izdatel'skiy tsentr, 1993), pp. 91–92. The depressed economic sectors were coal mining and petroleum extraction.

8. Victor P. Petrov, *Geography of the Soviet Union: Electric Power* (Washington, D.C.: Victor Kamkin, 1959), p. 4. At the time, "Eastern Siberia" also included Yakutia and the Lena Basin, comprising altogether 41.4 percent of total Soviet potential.

9. Victor L. Mote, *An Industrial Atlas of the Soviet Successor States* (Houston, Texas: Industrial Information Resources, 1984), p. I-4.

10. L. Rossolimo, *Baykal* (Irkutsk: Vostochno-Sibirskoye knizhnoye izd., 1971), p. 63; and Yu. B. Khromov and V. A. Klyushin, *Organizatsiya zon otdykha i turizma na poberezh'ye Baykala* (Moscow: Stroyizdat, 1976), p. 3.

11. Newby, *The Big Red Train Ride,* pp. 183–184.

12. Harmon Tupper, *To the Great Ocean* (Boston: Little, Brown & Co., 1965), p. 221.

13. Theodore Shabad and Victor L. Mote, *Gateway to Siberian Resources (the BAM)* (New York: John Wiley & Sons, 1977), p. 71; and Victor L. Mote, "The Baikal-Amur Mainline and Its Implications for the Pacific Basin," in *Soviet Natural Resources in the World Economy,* ed. Robert G. Jensen, Theodore Shabad, and Arthur W. Wright (Chicago: University of Chicago Press, 1983), p. 149.

14. Goskomstat Rossii, *Rossiyskaya federatsiya v 1992 godu,* pp. 92–95.

15. N. I. Mikhaylov, *Priroda Sibiri* (Moscow: Mysl', 1976), pp. 3–4.

THREE

The Little Siberians:
On the Planet's Periphery

The spoken word will freeze in the air.
—**Buryat saying**

Why did you discover it, this cursed land of Siberia, Yermak?
—**Nikolay Nekrasov**

INTRODUCTION

Like provincial minorities everywhere, the "little Siberians" are wary of interlopers—a reaction kindled by centuries of untoward experiences on the margins of the earth. Outsiders have disrupted, if not crushed, their fey existence. Before the arrival of the Russians, more than 200 native tribes vied for territory in Greater Siberia. Intertribal warfare, based on the use of simple weapons (spears, knives, bows and arrows, and so on), took place. Occasionally, large confederations, such as those of the Huns, Avars, and Mongol-Tatars, rose up, expanding the territories under dispute and raising the stakes. Only the Russians, however, came to stay: The Russians exploited the intertribal animosities to their advantage, reorganized life in Greater Siberia, and began a four-hundred-year-long process of subjugation and assimilation.

THE PEOPLING OF SIBERIA

Most archeologists contend that the people of the Middle Paleolithic era (100,000–38,000 years before the present [B.P.]) strove to avoid the harsh continental climates of northern Asia.[1] Although they left no physical evidence east of Uzbekistan, a few Neanderthal bands may have roamed across southern Siberia, which during the last glacial advance was a

31

partly wooded tundra instead of taiga, as much of it is today. Ahead of them, both north and east, were bustling herds of horses, bison, and woolly mammoths, which might have lured Neanderthal hunters to the threshold of North America, if not onto the continent proper.

Despite the absence of physical evidence of Neanderthals in Siberia, they seem to have left "cultural" vestiges. Modern Yukagirs, for instance, hunt reindeer in Neanderthal-sized bands by stalking them for miles on end. After the men kill the animal, the women carry the carcass back to the base camp—an assumed Neanderthal trait. The Yukagirs and other Siberian natives eat frozen berries in presumed Neanderthal fashion. The shamanistic worship of the bear, which may have originated with Neanderthal adoration of the cave bear, remains popular among the Ugrians, Ainu, and other native ethnic groups.[2]

Although humans (*Homo erectus*) may have been present in the Russian Far East as early as 300,000 B.P., the oldest remains found to date in Greater Siberia were uncovered in the Diring-Yuryakh Gorge, located 145 kilometers (90 mi) south of Yakutsk, in the Lena River basin. The earliest, accurately dated physical evidence for human settlement there does not predate 35,000 B.P. (Upper Paleolithic).[3] Thus, Neanderthals, who reached a dead end circa 30,000 B.P., would have had five millennia to work their magic in Siberia. The only other evidence of early humans in the region before 20,000 B.P. is associated with *Homo sapiens sapiens*, or modern man. This includes discoveries at Rubtsovsk, in the Kulunda Steppe (see Chapter 2); in caves in the neighboring Altay Mountains; and near Vladivostok.[4]

Most of the human evidence in Greater Siberia dates from times more recent than 20,000 B.P. Cro-Magnons, not Neanderthals, crossed the Bering Strait into North America and into Japan via Sakhalin and Hokkaido because the sea level was so low (-100 m) that it exposed dry "land bridges." Physical evidence of human settlement in Greater Siberia before the Mesolithic (12,000–10,000 B.P.) includes whole settlements (Mal'ta and Buret' in the Angara Basin), Venus figurines, weapons, leathercraft tools, cave art and petroglyphs, food storage vaults, graves, and funerary gifts. The clothing and domiciles were very similar to those used by eighteenth- and nineteenth-century Chukchi and Eskimos.[5] Accordingly, at the end of the last glacial advance (10,000 B.P.), the roots of culture had taken hold in faraway, frigid Siberia.

ETHNOGRAPHY BEFORE THE RUSSIANS

The Mesolithic: The Dawn of "Race"

During the Mesolithic era (12,000–10,000 B.P.), the climate changed. The weather became warmer and wetter. The retreating ice sheets permitted the expansion of new vegetational zones: Where there had been tundra and grass, new forests emerged. The new vegetation attracted fresh species of smaller animals. It was a timely event. Paleolithic hunters had placed many of the giant species of the tundra on the brink of extinction; now nature conspired with them to finish the task. The great woolly mammoth, rhinoceros, cave bear, and Eurasian bison were lost forever, and with their extinction, stocks of meat reached an all-time low. In the new environments, Mesolithic Siberians adopted a nomadic way of life, hunting the smaller, often quicker, wildlife (reindeer, horses, and wild oxen). In place of semipermanent pit houses, they resorted to collapsible wigwams similar to those of the modern Tungus and Nentsy, not to mention the Canadian and Plains Indians. "Villages" became fleeting base camps.

The Upper Paleolithic and Mesolithic eras were the settings for the emergence of the basic racial stocks worldwide. Paleolithic Siberians might have been in contact with Europeans, or might even have had European roots. The thousands of years and miles, however, must have been instrumental in the eventual development of the physiological traits that came to differentiate European Caucasoids from Asiatic Mongoloids.[6] Physical anthropologists note that human physical distinctions, including aspects characterized as "race" or racial subtype, are the products of genetic evolution fixed over long periods of time by means of geographical isolation, social selection, and natural selection. Among these factors, isolation was most instrumental in shaping the physiology of Mesolithic Siberians.

Mongoloid physical types arose in eastern and central Asia as early as 21,000 B.P. By the Mesolithic era, a Mongoloid physiological realm that eventually would be identified with the Altaic cultural-linguistic group stretched from the Middle Yenisey River to Lake Baykal, inclusive of Mongolia. Ironically, the Altay Mountains themselves, along with the proximal Minusinsk Basin (see Chapter 2), were distinguished by the dominance of Europoid, not Mongoloid, anthropological types.

The Siberian Neolithic

The Agricultural Revolution came late to Greater Siberia. The domestication of plants and animals, which characterizes the Neolithic, or New Stone Age, did not arrive there until 3000 B.C. Apart from the domestication of the dog and widespread fishing with harpoons and hooks, "Neolithic" Siberians continued to subsist on hunting and gathering for five millennia after the beginning of the Middle Eastern Neolithic (10,000 B.P.). The venerable harpoon, used by Eskimos to spear fish and seagoing mammals well into the twentieth century, was also employed by the ancestors of the Evens, Evenks, Nentsy, and Koryaks.

The first manifestation of agriculture in Greater Siberia, pastoralism, was associated with the introduction of copper tools at the end of Europe's Chalcolithic, or Cupric Stone Age. Around 5,000 B.P., the first major Siberian civilization, the Afanas'yevo culture, arose in the Kuznetsk and Minusinsk basins. The Afanas'yevans were not only Siberia's first coppersmiths but also the region's earliest true pastoralists, herding sheep, horses, and cows. Racially Europoid, they traded actively with the peoples of Central Asia and those as far west as the Volga River.

Approximately 3,500 B.P., the Andronovian culture supplanted the Afanas'yevan. The Andronovians mined not only copper and gold but also tin along the upper Irtysh River. Copper and tin, at a 10:1 ratio, are the primary ingredients in bronze.

The Bronze Age

With the manufacture of bronze, Siberians finally caught up with the technological advances that had prevailed in Southwest Asia and Europe for several millennia. The Andronovians, who ranged from the Tobol River in the west to the Minusinsk Basin in the east, were farmers as well as pastoralists. Living in wood-sod houses, they were sedentary wheat farmers who used bronze scythes to harvest their crops. They bartered with the Ural-Volga people in the west and the Chinese in the southeast (Photo 3.1).

The Andronovians survived peacefully until 1200 B.C., when their homeland in the Minusinsk Basin was invaded by half-caste Karasuk nomadic warriors. The Karasuks were classic pastoralists who raised camels as well as horses, cows, sheep, and goats. Extremely mobile, the Karasuks roamed the vast countryside between the Urals and Yakutia. Like itinerant peddlers, wherever they went, they exchanged copper and bronze artifacts for local raw materials and folk art. Karasuk art, itself, reflected the influence of the Chinese, who had mingled with the Afanas'yevans and Andronovians in the Minusinsk Basin for several thousand years. To modern Buryatia, the Karasuks diffused goods that the Chinese had acquired from places as far away as Japan and the Moluccas. They also introduced Chinese calligraphy and bronze metallurgy to the Mongoloid peoples of Lake Baykal and Yakutia.

By 1000 B.C., the racial composition of Siberia consisted of Andronovian Europoids in the steppes of Western Siberia and in the Altay; half-caste Karasuks, who wandered far and wide from their Minusinsk homeland; and purely Mongoloid peoples in Eastern Siberia and the Russian Far East. The peoples of the Ob' Basin, who resided between the swamps and the steppe-dwelling Andronovians, already bore the ornamentation that is still worn by modern Khants and Mansi. The natives of Transbaykalia resembled modern Tungus and Yukagirs, who were far more numerous and widespread than they are today. Paleo-Asiatic peoples including Yukagirs, Itel'men, Chukchi, Chuvans, Koryaks, and so on, lived in what is now Sakha (Yakutia). And the Amur River cultures, the ancestors of the contemporary Nivkhi (another Paleo-Asiatic group), Nanays, Udegeys, and so forth, were strongly influenced by the Chinese.[7]

Approximately 3,000 B.P., Tagarian pastoralists began to supplant the migratory Karasuks in both the Minusinsk and Ob' regions. Sedentary Tagarian farmers built permanent log houses, used sophisticated irrigation canals, and tilled the land with hoes. The Tagarians of the Kulunda Steppes were in contact with Iranian Scythians who

PHOTO 3.1   *Bust of Andronovian woman ca. 2000 B.C.* SOURCE: *G.S. Martynova, curator of the Museum of the Tomskaya Pisanitsa, in Kemerovo.*

lived nearby, in Turkestan. Through them, other Siberian groups learned to domesticate the horse, and later, to mold iron.[8]

Eventually, the powerful Scythians, who are far better known for their activities in Ukraine than in Asia, established an empire of "vast steppe-land and wooded steppe that stretched from the Amur and the Huang He (Yellow River) in the east to the Caspian and Black seas in the west."[9] Scythian influence in Siberia is less known; but recently unearthed tombs in the Altay Mountains indicate it was once a force to be reckoned with.[10] As natural refrigerators, the graves preserved the remains of Scythian chieftains as well as their horses, chariots, and material wealth, including humankind's oldest surviving tapestries. Although the majority of individuals buried in the Scythian tombs were of Europoid stock, a few were Mongoloid, indicating that they perpetuated the Karasuk tradition of maintaining contact with the Chinese.

At the same time that Scythian dominance was weakening in the west and was being replaced by that of the Turkestan-dwelling Sarmatians, in the east the Scythians gradually were superseded by the Huns. Around the time of Christ, dual-race Tashtyks inhabited the Minusinsk Basin con-

PHOTO 3.2 *Man of mixed race, Baraba Steppe, near the time of Christ.* SOURCE: *G. S. Martynova, curator of the Museum of the Tomskaya Pisanitsa, in Kemerovo.*

temporaneously with the Yenisey Kyrgyz, direct ancestors of the modern Kyrgyz people who live in the Tyan' Shan' Mountains far to the southwest. Mixing farming with pastoralism, like the Andronovians and Karasuks before them, the Tashtyks diversified their occupance by breeding domesticated reindeer. They also diffused into the Kuznetsk Basin. In contact with the Chinese and Huns, the Tashtyks were fond of silk fabrics, dwelled in Chinese-style structures supported by massive beams, and cremated their dead.[11] The Altay-Sayan crossroads at the time, therefore, consisted of Scythians and Sarmatians in the west and southwest, Huns in the east, and Chinese in the south. The vestigial art, technology, and physiology of the people reflect this cultural mosaic. Their art, in fact, in modified form, persists to this day as the folk art of the Kyrgyz of Central Asia, the Kazakhs, and the Altays (Photo 3.2).

Iron Age Huns and Avars

The Huns are intriguing not only because of their notoriously hawkish history, but also because of their place as middlemen between Mongol and Turkic ethnicity. The few Hunnic phrases that survive closely resemble their counterparts in the Turkic language. Yet, the name "Hun" is a Mongol word (*khun*) that means "man." This strengthens the pan-Turkic contention that Turks, Huns, Mongols, and even Iranians are all "Turks."

Long associated with Attila's invasion of Europe in the fifth century A.D., the Hsiung-nu people, or Huns, were the bane of Chinese existence. The bulk of the Great Wall was built and rebuilt (300–100 B.C.) to discourage the invasions of barbarian Huns.[12] The Huns were primarily pastoral nomads, but they also learned (from the Chinese) to raise millet. Along with millet, they consumed meat, mare's milk, and cheese—still the typical diet of their nomadic progeny today. Even before Attila's outburst, the

Huns ranged as far north as Transbaykalia, forcing northward migrations of Mongol Buryats and Turkic Uygurs. Although the Chinese ultimately routed the eastern Huns, the main body moved inexorably westward like a plague of locusts, provoking mass migrations all over the Eurasian plains.

Within 100 years after Attila's famous assault on the Roman Empire, Avars split the unified Turkic empire into two large confederacies. One of these was established south of Lake Baykal. Consisting of Kyrgyz and Uygurs, the Baykal confederacy traded with the ancestors of the forest-dwelling Tofalars and Sakhalars. The descendants of the Sakhalars were driven later by the Buryats northward into the Lena River valley, where ultimately they would become Sakha-Yakuts. In the process, the once widespread Yukagirs were forced by the Sakhalars into their now isolated homeland between the mouths of the Indigirka and Kolyma rivers.

If the proto-Koryaks and Eskimos were isolated from all this in the northeast, then so were the Ob' River peoples. Huns, Avars, and Kipchak Turks could ravage the steppes on horseback but not the Vasyugan swamps. It was to the Vasyugan that the former occupants of the steppes retreated during Attila's assault on Europe. Protected by the Vasyugan moat, the Ostyaks (Khants) and Voguls (Mansi) developed a mostly hunting and fishing culture. Left behind by the Khants and Mansi were their linguistic relatives, the Magyars, who took refuge in the southern Urals, and later, the middle Volga region. In A.D. 874, the Magyars borrowed some of the Kipchaks' warlike proclivities and marauded their way onto the Hungarian Plain.

At the end of the first millennium A.D., the Middle Ob' region had become the homeland of Uralic Ugrians. Not long afterward, Uralic Samoyeds (Nentsy, Entsy, Sel'kups, and Nganasans) diffused across the West Siberian Lowland from the Altay-Sayan region. It was these peoples who introduced reindeer herding to the tundras of the Far North.

The origin of the Tungus language, a third branch of Altaic, is less certain. A plausible argument asserts that the Tungus emerged from Heilongjiang (Manchuria), where a number of them still live, in approximately 4,000 B.P. Once in Siberia, they learned reindeer breeding from their Uralic and Turkic neighbors. They dispersed gradually and randomly across the Central Siberian Upland and into the Amur Basin.

The Last Migrations: The Mongol-Tatars

Genghis Khan, who was born around 1167 in the Greater Khingan Mountains of contemporary Inner Mongolia, did not live to see his Mongol army's greatest triumphs in China and Europe, including most of what would become Russia. That glory would accrue to his grandson, Batu, son of his eldest son, Juchi. Before he died in 1227, the patriarch divided his conquests among his four sons. The lands west of the Ob'-Irtysh system and north of Khorezm were to go to Juchi, who also died before he could benefit from the inheritance. Batu's expanded version of the territory would become known as the Golden, or Great, Horde.[13]

From the time that Batu and his 150,000 Mongols, Tatars, and other subgroups invaded it in 1236, Western Siberia became associated with the Great Horde. With the passage of time the huge territory became rife with mismanagement. In 1307, it was subdivided into the Kok, or Blue, Horde west of the Volga and the Ak, or White, Horde in Siberia.[14] Thereafter, wrecked by politics, invasions, Muscovite ascension, and the collapse of the Silk Route, the Great Horde fissiparated into the Crimean, Astrakhan', Kazan', and Siberian khanates.

The Siberian Tatars

Before the Mongol invasion, virtually the only permanent inhabitants of the later Siberian Khanate were Ugrians and Samoyeds who lived in the swamps or forests. Kipchak Turks occupied the steppes. The Mongols set the Kipchaks in motion. Those caught up in the movement, ranging from natives to newcomers, ultimately were Turkicized. A few of the Tatars who arrived with Batu occupied the Tura River valley, coexisting there with the Ugrians. The majority dwelled in the West Siberian and Turkestani steppes along the Tobol, Ishim, and Irtysh rivers.

Racially mixed, as Tatars are today, all of these people became known as the "Siberian Tatars." Although many became sedentary farmers, all remained equestrians. They were skilled in handicrafts and actively traded with the Central Asians and Chinese.[15] After 1480, these people—nomads, farmers, and merchants—became subjects of the Siberian Khanate.[16]

The first capital of the Siberian Khanate, indeed of Siberia, was a small settlement on the Tura River near what is known today as Tyumen'. Some twenty years later, Isker, later named Sibir' (Siberia), became the capital by virtue of its better site, atop one of the highest promontories along the Irtysh River. Approximately 15 kilometers (10 mi) north of the site is the modern city of Tobol'sk.

For more than a century, the Siberian Khanate had to contend with the growing influence of the grand princes of Muscovy, who aspired to collect the *yasak* (fur tribute) from the Siberian Tatars much as they were doing from the Ugrians and Samoyeds. For a while, the Muscovites were successful; but in 1571, the tax came to an abrupt end.

The repudiation came on the orders of a fiery new leader, who as if to mock the first "tsar of all the Russias," Ivan IV, proclaimed himself

Kuchum Khan, "Lord of the Tura, Irtysh, Tobol, and Baraba Tatars."[17] Ivan IV, or Ivan the Terrible, in fact, was more interested in subjugating the Baltic Livonians (coastal Estonia) than the peoples of the Siberian Khanate. Encouraged by Ivan's disinterest, the precocious Kuchum routed the army of the military governor of Perm' Province.

Kuchum's victory naturally struck fear into the hearts of the residents of the province, especially those of the Stroganov family. Ivan had granted the Stroganovs, who had made their fortune as merchants and industrialists, vast tracts of land, newly acquired from the vanquished Kazan' Tatars, just west of the Ural Mountains. The family in turn had leased their land to brave pioneer settlers—a privilege that afforded the pioneers freedom from taxation and tariffs. During the early part of Ivan's reign the pioneers advanced the frontier across the Kama, which enabled the Stroganov family to begin to mine the salt of Berezniki and Solikamsk. Each time the frontier was peeled back, new garrisons of Muscovite troops had to be summoned to maintain a new skirmish line. Gradually this process placed a strain on the reserves of the Muscovite army.

Until Kuchum's violent acts in 1572 and 1573, the relationship between the family and the Siberian Tatars had been cordial. Sensitive to Ivan's needs on the western front, the Stroganovs beseeched the tsar to permit them to hire Cossack mercenaries to protect them from Kuchum's raiders. The tsar granted their request without hesitation.

RUSSIANS IN SIBERIA

Between 1582 and 1953, the name Siberia was synonymous with the decimation of native populations and their cultures. At the time of the Russian conquest, the region was homeland to an estimated 230,000 people. These included 50,000 Turks, more than half of whom were Sakha-Yakuts; 37,000 Mongols, 75 percent of whom were Buryats; 36,000 northern Tungus (Evens and Evenks); 35,000 northeastern Paleo-Asiatics (Chukchi, Chuvans, Koryaks, Itel'men, Nivkhi, and 5,000 Yukagirs); 4,000 Eskimo-Aleuts; 18,000 Ugrians; 14,000 northern Samoyeds; 5,600 Kets; and several thousand southern Tungus, Manchus, and Ainus. In their subsequent century-long march to the Pacific, the Russians encountered no fewer than 120 "languages" and dozens more dialects.[18] In modern Siberia, there may be as many as 35 extant native languages and 14 to 18 dialects. Since the 1600s, nine Samoyedic and Kettic "languages" have become extinct. The 75 or more other ethnicities have vanished without a trace.

Russians first crossed the Urals in the ninth century. They came from Novgorod in search of fish, salt, freshwater pearls, walrus tusks, and furs for European consumers. The quest for "soft gold," or furs, drove the Novgorodians to plunder one region after another, until in Yugra, near the mouth of the Ob', they came into contact with the Nentsy and Ostyaks (Khants) in 1079.[19] By the fifteenth century, the Hanseatic League, of which Novgorod was part, began to flounder, and Novgorod's economic strength waned with it. Yugra was there for the taking.

Novgorod's descent was countered by the ascent of the Muscovites, who established their own trade relations with the Nentsy and Ugrians as early as 1465, six years before they subdued the Hansa partner.[20] By 1502, Muscovy firmly grasped the lands of the Lower Ob', and the Ugrians began to pay a fur tribute to "the Center"—80 years before the formal "conquest of Siberia."[21]

The Conquest of Siberia

Motivated by fur fever, Russians reached the Sea of Okhotsk and the Bering Straits within seventy years after their initial hostile engagement with the Siberian Tatars (1581–1648). Economic historian Peter Lyashchenko described the process of rolling back the Siberian frontier in four stages. The point men in the process were Cossacks (who were often brigands), fur traders, and other adventurers, who randomly and sometimes unwittingly gathered information about the new region. They fought the natives, but often with native assistance: Cossacks and Khants subdued the Nentsy and Mansi; Yukagirs and Cossacks battled the Chukchi; and the newcomers and Evenks together subjugated the Buryats. The second stage included the actions of troop commanders, soldiers, and other Cossacks, who built structures for the proper administration of the frontier (blockhouses, prisons, and so on); exacted fur tribute from the native population; and regularly patrolled the fortified lines that determined the leading edge of settlement. After the area was secured militarily, civilian governors and their assistants arrived to administer and consolidate it for the Muscovite tsar. They also laid claim to any known important mineral deposits in the name of the autocrat. During this third st:.ge, also, merchants and traders ventured in to barter peacefully with the indigenous tribes. Lyashchenko's last stage was characterized by detailed exploration, consolidation of the holdings, and assimilation of the natives. Cajoled with gifts, promises, and vodka, the indigenes not only conveyed fur tribute but also declared themselves loyal subjects of the tsar.[22]

The First Point Man: Yermak.　During the reign of Ivan IV (1530–1584), thousands of refugees fled to the frontier from Muscovy and the various steppe hordes. They soon formed multiethnic bands of freemen known as Cossacks. After Ivan's armies defeated the Astrakhan' Tatars in 1556, the Russians tried to consolidate their lands along the Volga to preserve the valuable horse trade between Central Asia and Muscovy. Swearing allegiance to no living authority, some of the Cossacks raided Volga river-boats that were laden with horses destined for Livonia. One of the raiders was a celebrated fugitive named Vasiliy Timofeyevich Alenin, who had been born on a tributary of the Kama River in the Ural Mountains. A fur trapper turned brigand, Alenin soon attracted a loyal band of Don and Volga Cossacks, who in classic fashion rechristened him "Yermak," or "millstone."[23] A kind of Robin Hood, Yermak soon had a heavy price on his head.

The Stroganovs maintained friendly relations with the Volga Cossacks because of their extensive knowledge of the Kama watershed.[24] In the late 1570s, with the tsar's troops in hot pursuit, Yermak and his band of 500 took refuge in the Kama River forests owned by the Stroganovs. The family hired him to fight Kuchum Khan.[25]

In 1581 or 1582, Yermak's band, now swollen to 1,650 well-armed Cossacks, descended into the Tura River country to confront the enemy. Equipped with muskets and armor, they easily outgunned a ragtag army of Tatars, Ostyaks, and Voguls armed with swords, lances, and bows and arrows, near Tyumen'. By midsummer, at the cost of perhaps one-third of his men, Yermak had routed Kuchum's armies no fewer than three times, but never the khan himself. Finally on October 23, Yermak faced Kuchum directly, in the Battle of Sibir' (the settlement, not the region). Yermak won a Pyrrhic victory, losing 100 more men, but Kuchum and the remnants of his garrison escaped to the southern steppes.

The tsar was delighted, granting full amnesty to Yermak and his vestigial army. He sent gifts, one of them a heavy breastplate bearing the imperial coat of arms, for Yermak. For the next two years, the Cossacks collected tribute in sable skins. As he consolidated and administered Kuchum's khanate, Yermak had to cope with the disaffection of the locals and incessant raids by the remnant Tatars. Finally, in August 1584 (or 1585), the Cossack leader learned that Kuchum had raided a caravan from Bukhara and was hiding upriver on the Irtysh. Kuchum watched as Yermak's party floated up the Irtysh and encamped on a small island. Kuchum's army fell upon the sleeping Cossacks, killing all but one. Legend has it that Yermak tried to swim for shore but was drowned by the weight of the very breastplate that he had received from Ivan. Ironically, the tsar himself had died five months earlier, little realizing that Yermak had opened the way to a region that would become the richest ever won in Russian history (Map 3.1).

From Yermak to Peter: Point Men and Administrators.   The collapse of the Siberian Khanate unlocked the doors to the rest of Greater Siberia. The rapidity with which the Russians traversed it is astounding. A mere 66 years separated Yermak's capture of Sibir' (ca. 1582) and Dezhnev's navi-

42

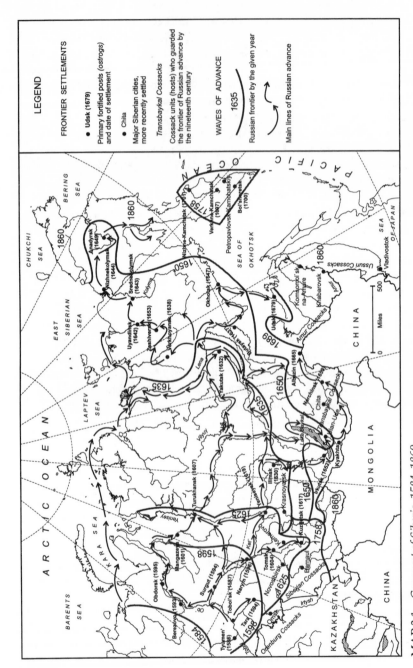

MAP 3.1 *Conquest of Siberia, 1584–1860*
SOURCES: Forsyth (1992), *A History of the Peoples of Siberia*, p. 102; and Gibson (1969), *Feeding the Russian Fur Trade*, pp. 6–7.

gation of the Bering Strait (1648). Trappers and traders led the way along a remarkable interlocking system of rivers and portages. In the early 1600s, the Russians consolidated their winnings in the Ob'-Irtysh basin. In the 1620s, they took the Yenisey and the Tunguskas. In the 1640s, they had navigated the lengths of the Lena, Amur, Indigirka, Kolyma, and Anadyr' systems. And by 1650, they had crisscrossed the Lake Baykal region. They had met surprisingly little resistance along the way.

The fortified lines erected in the wake of the trailblazing explorers and venturesome fur trappers ensured the safety of the Russian advance from the dreaded steppe nomads of Mongol and Turkic descent. For this reason also, Russian settlements remained confined to the forests throughout the 1600s.[26] Whether it was the enduring memories of Attila and Batu that kept the Russians at bay or something entirely different, the decision was good for the fur trade. The taiga of the 1600s teemed with fox, squirrel, ermine, and the softest gold of all—sable, the most prized commodity at the Leipzig fur market. In the forests the newcomers met only occasional resistance to their tribute-taking, the most noteworthy of which came from the Nentsy and Mansi. The Russians strove to avoid the grasslands, where the few skirmishes they had with the Khakass, Buryats, and Kyrgyz were more violent; thus, they selected a northward and eastward path, the path of least resistance. Along the way, only the Evenks and Evens dared to defy the Russians, until they reached the far northeast in the 1700s. There they encountered surprisingly fierce intransigence from the Itel'men and Chukchi, the latter of whom persisted as an independent nation until the 1800s.[27] Stiffest of all was the opposition exerted by the Amur River peoples. Nevertheless, replicating the four-stage Lyashchenko model, by 1662, Greater Siberia had a Russian population of 70,000, out of a total of 288,000 people.[28]

Intense loneliness, hunger, disease, and the occasional hostilities wore on the explorers. They were lonely not only because there was only one native per 40 square kilometers (15.44 mi[2]) but also because their own numbers were usually fewer than 100 men.[29] During his 1643–1646 expedition to the Amur, the nefarious Vasiliy Poyarkov, "a man too cruel even for Cossacks," began with 132 followers and returned with 60. He lost 40 to starvation and sickness—with many of the survivors resorting to cannibalism—and another 32 to battles with the hostile Tungus-Manchus. Poyarkov, like many of his contemporaries, departed with the mistaken notion that he would gather provisions along the way, and ended up eating "grass and roots."[30] Eventually, the demand for plowland became as important as the desire for furs in the Russians' expansion to the Pacific.

Despite these associated hazards, by 1700, no fewer than thirty-seven significant Siberian expeditions had been carried out by simple, often illiterate men, some of whom were even criminals. In the process, they proved themselves both saints and sinners. Having, as saints, uncovered a wealth of knowledge about geography, flora, fauna, and crude ethnographies, as sinners, they hunted furbearing animals to near extinction and practiced genocide on the indigenes.[31]

Following the Cossack point men, the *voyevody* (military governors) arrived to administer the regions in the name of the tsar. Most governed with honor. The exceptions, so-called Siberian satraps, deliberately set out to get as rich as possible by whatever means necessary. In short order, they became very powerful within their fiefs, setting a precedent that is true of a few of today's Siberian governors. The satraps took native leaders hostage to guarantee payment of tribute. Khabarov in Amuria and Pavlutskiy in Chukotka used excessive, cruel methods to subjugate and eventually devastate the indigenes. Natives who rose up in anger suffered wholesale pogroms.

Only two far eastern powers, China and Japan, were strong enough to have countered the Russian advance into Greater Siberia; but in the early 1600s, both maintained passive foreign policies. In fact, until Khabarov set up house in Amuria (ca. 1650), the Chinese were more worried about domestic matters than they were about a few "Russian barbarians." Even barbarians can venture too far, however. With memories of Poyarkov's cruelties fresh in their minds, the Amur tribes did not roll out the red carpet for his fellow Cossack, Yerofey Khabarov. In response, Khabarov destroyed, looted, and murdered, in exploits so heinous that they were not forgotten for 200 years. In one of many instances, he seized 350 livestock, 243 women, and 118 children, allegedly roasting the children "on gridirons formed by the bodies of their parents."[32] These horrors forced China and Russia to the "dagger's edge." The Treaty of Nerchinsk in 1689 finally resolved the borderlands issue, forcing the Russians to withdraw from the lands east of the Stanovoy Mountains and north of the Amur River. The treaty created a buffer zone between the two rivals that successfully safeguarded their interrelationship along the Amur for 170 years.

Post-Petrine Siberia: Colonization and Consolidation.   The reign of Peter the Great (1682–1725) was a period of further expansion. Imperial Russia began with Peter, even though most of the empire was already under Russian control when he came to power. Best known for his accomplishments in Europe, the tsar also made strides in Asia. During his reign, Russia acquired the Kamchatka and the Altay-Sayan region and laid the foundations for Bering's expeditions to North America.[33] More importantly, Petrine Russia marked the beginning of the settlement of Greater Siberia, although the mass migrations of *prishliye* (newcomers) would not occur until the 1880s.

Midway through Peter's reign (1710), the total Russian population included more than 300,000 persons, with 247,000 in Western Siberia and 66,000 in Eastern Siberia. The Nerchinsk Treaty's restrictions ruled out settlement in the Russian Far East, where the few newcomers and natives were no more than 50,000. Ninety percent of the migrants had come voluntarily, even though the Romanov Code of Laws, permitting compulsory settlement or banishment to Siberia, had been in effect for sixty years.[34] By 1719, the ratio of Russians to native Siberians had reached 70:30, which represented a 230-percent Russian increase in only 57 years.

During the eighteenth century, Greater Siberia's population expanded two and a half times. By 1795, there were 1.2 million people, 783,000 of whom were Russians, including a maximum of 35,000 exiles and their families. Approximately 56 percent resided in Western Siberia and 44 percent in Eastern Siberia. Again, the Nerchinsk Treaty stifled development of the Russian Far East, although the population of the region was probably between 50,000 and 100,000. Migration continued to be slow, and most of the growth came from natural increase among both newcomers and indigenes; the ratio of Russians to natives, in fact, remained the same throughout the century (70:30).[35]

Through 1858, natural increase continued to power Siberian population growth, which was proportionally greater than that anywhere else in the empire. From 1795 to 1858, almost three-fourths of the growth came as a result of natural increase. The relatively high birth rates and low death rates have been explained as a consequence of the absence of serfdom, abundant land and resources, lack of suffering during the Napoleonic wars, and the infrequency of crop failures and epidemics.[36] Thus, of the 700,000 persons added to the Siberian population between 1795 and 1815, only 5 percent accrued from migration (mechanical increase), and all of the new migrants were exiles.

The scarcest commodity in Siberia's rapidly growing frontier was labor, and mechanical increase became more important between 1816 and 1834, accounting for one-third of the population growth. Compulsory migration was the most expedient means of satisfying the shortage, and during this period, exiles outnumbered voluntary migrants by seven to one.[37] Between 1835 and 1850—and for the first time since the 1600s—mechanical increase exceeded natural increase. In that period, 140,000 individuals, or 60 percent of all migrants, were exiled to Siberia. Practically all of them traversed the 2,000- to 3,000-kilometer distance to the royal gold and silver mines in the Sayan and Yablonovyy ranges on foot and in leg irons. The growing number of voluntary and runaway migrants settled in the steppe lands of Western Siberia.

Before the Treaty of Peking (1860), under the terms of which Russia acquired Amuria and Primor'ye, the population of the Russian Far East remained small. By 1858, 3 million people lived in Siberia: 1.7 million in Western Siberia, and 1.3 million in Eastern Siberia. Several important demographic changes had occurred. First, natural increase had reasserted itself, accounting for two-thirds of the population growth. Second, the 110,000 in-migrants were about equally divided between compulsory and voluntary migrants. Third, Siberia surpassed New Russia and the North Caucasus as the empire's most important frontier of settlement. Fourth, in violation of the Treaty of Nerchinsk, Russians once again penetrated Amuria.

Murav'yev: A Man Named Amurskiy. The Treaty of Nerchinsk worked because the Manchus maintained absolute dominion over Amuria, decapitating any Russian whom they caught trespassing. Those who chose this fate were usually desperate runaway exiles, compulsive adventurers, or idealistic naturalists. The Opium Wars (1839–1842) between Great Britain and China revealed considerable administrative weakness in the Manchu Dynasty. Moreover, the jingoism that preceded the Crimean War (1853–1855) infected Russians and British alike. Suspicious of British and French intentions in China, including the Amur-Ussuri Basin, Nicholas I appointed a 38-year-old general, N. N. Murav'yev, to serve as governor-general of Eastern Siberia.

Keenly aware of the tsarist regime's dread of potential geopolitical decline and dismemberment, Murav'yev began to toy with St. Petersburg's fear of Siberian separatism as soon as he arrived in Irkutsk, in 1847. The decline of the Russian-America Company, which at one time had staked claims to Alaska, Hawaii, and much of the Pacific Coast of North America, forced the regime to reorient its geopolitical interests to its own backyard.[38] In that backyard was long neglected Amuria. Murav'yev contended that without command of the Amur, Russian development of Eastern Siberia would remain at an impasse; and that unless Russia annexed Amuria, Eastern Siberians might have to absorb the region on their own, lest the British and French take it.

Not without his critics, who argued that the opening up of Amuria would only expose Siberians to greater contact with foreigners and therefore with separatist ideas, Murav'yev ordered immediate exploration of the Sea of Okhotsk and the mouth of the Amur. He himself set sail for Petropavlovsk-Kamchatskiy. Around the same time, Admiral Nevel'skoy discovered that Sakhalin was an island, not a peninsula.

When they unfurled a Russian flag at the mouth of the Amur and christened the site Nikolayevsk in the tsar's honor, Nevel'skoy and Murav'yev aroused a storm of protest from critics who argued that the act flagrantly violated the Treaty of Nerchinsk. A possible war with China, they feared, would lead to the loss of Siberia and a disintegration of the empire. Count

Nesselrode, the Russian minister of defense, feared that this stunt would disrupt the lucrative Russo-Chinese border trade and demanded an immediate closure of the base; but Murav'yev had the total support of the militant tsar, who declared, "Where once the Russian flag is hoisted, it must never be lowered."[39]

Royal sanction in pocket, Murav'yev established military posts at a number of strategic locations between Lake Baykal and Sakhalin Island; built an ironworks at Petrovsk-Zabaykal'skiy; developed an Amur militia; and agreed to the Treaty of Shimoda, which gave Japan the Kuriles south of Urup (the Northern Territories) in exchange for joint administration of Sakhalin. After 1850, Russians built blockhouses, trading posts, and whole settlements in Amuria. The Petrovsk factory (Petrovskiy zavod) built the first Russian steamer in Siberia, the Argun'. With the outbreak of the Crimean War, Murav'yev boldly sailed down the Amur at the head of a mighty Russian flotilla—a show of force against a potential Anglo-French attack. Under his charismatic leadership, Russian forces warded off the enemy at Petropavlovsk-Kamchatskiy and quelled a would-be invasion near the mouth of the Amur River. Thus, while tsarist troops lost the Crimean War, they celebrated victory in the Far East.

After the war, at Murav'yev's insistence, Russians and their livestock spilled into Amuria. Sakhalin's coal deposits were geologically established. Khabarovsk and Blagoveshchensk were founded. Inspired by the ideas of an American businessman, Murav'yev even urged Nicholas to build a steam railway from Chita to Irkutsk.[40] Finally, in spring 1858, with no further room to maneuver, the Chinese signed the Treaty of Aigun', which gave the Russians all territories north of a line drawn between Khabarovsk and the Tatar Strait. A genuine hero in a defeated nation craving heroes, Murav'yev's crowning moment came when the tsar honored him with the title of Count of Amuria (thereby adding the descriptive "Amurskiy" to Murav'yev's last name).

In 1859, the British and French again threatened to attack the Manchus. Russians served as mediators and "saved" the dynasty from embarrassment, if not defeat. Some would say "in gratitude," the Chinese signed the Treaty of Peking in November 1860. Not only did the pact validate the Treaty of Aigun, it also ceded Primor'ye to Russia. With Primor'ye, Russians acquired the excellent harbor of Vladivostok, a port that Murav'yev claimed for the crown that summer. With the exception of some fine tuning in the extreme southeast (Sakhalin, the Kuriles, and along the Mongolian border), the Russian Far East took the shape that it has today.

Count Murav'yev-Amurskiy fell from grace in 1861. Because he had dared to muse about a "United States of Siberia, federated with the United States of America," rumors flew that he was ready to proclaim himself a "Siberian tsar." Suffering from liver disease, he retired to St. Petersburg, where he was often criticized for his liberal views about the emancipation of the peasantry. He emigrated to Paris and died there in 1881. Originally interred in Montmartre, Murav'yev-Amurskiy's ashes were returned to Vladivostok in 1991.[41]

The Great Siberian Migration and the Trans-Siberian Railroad

Tsarist migration policies did not change abruptly after the emancipation of the serfs (1861). Until 1867, peasants could not leave the commune until they had liquidated their mortgages. After that year, they could migrate at their own expense, but only if they owned land at their destination. The policy hardly encouraged migration to Greater Siberia: Between 1859 and 1870, only 130,000 immigrants, 55 percent of whom were exiles, settled in any part of the region.

The Russian Far East was a separate issue. Alexander II hoped to quickly consolidate his new holdings, and he approved a law that gave far eastern migrants the right to free homestead on state land for temporary use or private ownership. The tsar even agreed to grant parcels on the right bank of the Ussuri to groups of fifteen or more families "in perpetuity." Additionally, far easterners were exempt from military service and taxes. There was one drawback: Peasants had to arrange passage to the region, which was 10,000 kilometers (6,000 mi) away, without state assistance. Consequently, of those who tried between 1866 and 1871, less than one-third ever arrived. Most gave up and stayed in Western or Eastern Siberia.

Tsarist migration policy continued to flounder through 1890. Between 1870 and 1879, only 14,000 hardy souls reached the Russian Far East. Many of these were gold miners. A mere 135,000 migrated to Western and Eastern Siberia. Of the 135,000 who went to those regions, only 30,000 moved voluntarily. Although the 1880s saw further action to encourage the migration of peasants with and without means, the long, hazardous journey discouraged the movement. On the advice of Primor'ye's governor-general, after 1883, poor peasants from Ukraine were allowed to migrate to the Russian Far East by sea for the first time. In the first two years, however, only 5,000 bravely weathered the long voyage from Odessa to Vladivostok. All told, exclusive of 100,000 exiles, 200,000 peasants migrated to Greater Siberia between 1882 and 1890.[42] By the end of the 1880s, officials recognized that manipulation of migration policy alone, without improving transportation to the frontier of settlement, would fail to increase the numbers of migrants.

The Influence of the Trans-Siberian Railroad. The construction of the Trans-Siberian Railroad came at the end of the era of great transcontinental railway building, which began in North America in the 1860s. The delay was the result of the late arrival of the Industrial Revolution in Russia, the fiscal conservatism of tsarist officials, the lack of entrepreneurial spirit among the tsar's subjects, and Siberia's massive size and physical constraints.

Between the time Murav'yev urged Alexander II to lay tracks between Chita and Irkutsk (1857) and 1891, foreigners and Russians alike proposed dozens of alternative routes for a trans-Siberian trunk line. A few of these proposals came from Siberian provincial authorities who hoped the iron horse would bring prosperity to their newly settled provinces and hinterlands, but the majority originated in the halls of government. The latter were fueled by exaggerated fears of the Chinese, who were rumored to be building a trans-Manchurian railway, in collusion with the British and others, that would be used to reannex Amuria and Primor'ye. Tsarist military officers increasingly saw Manchuria as an extension of Russia, and any trans-Siberian railway had to have a strategic thrust to counter not only the Manchus but also the Japanese.[43]

In time, arguments boiled down to the ideas of two high-ranking men: A. A. Abaza, Minister of Finance, and Konstantin Pos'yet, Minister of Communications. Abaza was against state deficit spending and contended that any and all railway schemes should be assured of financial success. He favored building trunk lines in European Russia rather than in Siberia. Pos'yet defended the transcontinental line because railroads create capital, eventually pay for themselves, and stimulate sociopolitical and economic benefits. This dichotomy between persons favoring western investment and those supporting eastern investment would continue well into the next century. Ironically, Alexander III—who was generally a reactionary ruler—ultimately approved Pos'yet's notions and his choice of the route of the Trans-Siberian Railroad, on March 29, 1891.

The Colonizers: Witte and Kulomzin. Interestingly, except for a small gulf and town in southwestern Primor'ye named in his honor, Pos'yet is mostly forgotten. In fact, one of his supporters, Sergey Witte (1849–1915), is now recognized as "the leading spirit and force behind the construction of the Trans-Siberian Railroad." One of the true giants of his age, Witte was a maelstrom of contradictions. An instinctive entrepreneur who no doubt would have flourished as a capitalist, he was a pragmatist and patriot who desired to strengthen Russia, to preserve the autocracy, and to glorify the monarch. As finance minister (1892–1903) he opposed private enterprise, entrepreneurship in general, and the privatization of Russian railroads in particular. Yet, during his tenure, Russian capitalism experienced unprecedented growth. Superficially a pro-Western "Atlanticist," in his soul Witte was a zealous Slavophile and an "Orientalist," who saw the Trans-Siberian Railroad as a means for Russia to repudiate its "colonial" association with Europe and to tie itself commercially to Asia. To Witte, landlocked Russia could rely on its railways in the same way that maritime Europe depended upon navies.

Geopolitics entered into the picture in another way. Russia's demoralizing defeat in the Russo-Japanese War (1904–1905) undermined the autocracy and forced it to accede to democratic reforms. Witte, as prime minister, represented Russia in negotiating the Treaty of Portsmouth, which formally ended the conflict. The nationalist press demanded revenge and raised the specter of the Yellow Peril. Until then, Primor'ye and Transbaykalia had been linked by the Chinese Eastern Railway, which ran across Manchuria, from Chita to Vladivostok. As a consequence of the Japanese victory, Russia lost the southern branch of this railway, Port Arthur and Dal'niy in China, and the southern half of Sakhalin. At the insistence of the nationalists and against the fiscally sound advice (and oriental sympathies) of Witte, the Amur branch of the Trans-Siberian Railroad was built entirely on Russian soil around the great bend of the river. This created a buffer between Russia and Manchuria, and accordingly, the Chinese and Japanese.

If Witte was the "spirit," Anatoliy Kulomzin (1838–1924) was the "sweat and blood" behind the construction of the Trans-Siberian Railroad and subsequent Siberian colonization. In 1892, Witte appointed Kulomzin to lead the Committee of the Siberian Railroad, but this task drew him into a host of secondary activities: inland waterways, industrial development, and most important, peasant resettlement. Historian Steven Marks believes that Kulomzin's accomplishments in Greater Siberia give him the same stature as Lord Curzon, viceroy of India, and Cecil Rhodes in South Africa, as one of the great colonizers of the past two centuries.[44] Although Kulomzin had many obligations, his primary purpose was to strengthen the core's control over the periphery. To do this, he aspired to facilitate the mass migration of millions of land-starved European Russians to "civilize" land-rich, people-poor Greater Siberia. Although he failed in homogenizing Siberian society to the favor of European Russians, Kulomzin managed to lay the basis for future Siberian regional development.

The Consequences of the Railway.   From the time the Tsarevich Nicholas christened it in Vladivostok in 1891 to the completion of the Amur River Bridge at Khabarovsk in 1916, the Trans-Siberian Railroad was mired in controversy. A technological marvel at the time, the railway was criticized blatantly as a "monument to bungling."[45] Its critics had a point. The rails and sleepers were too light, inducing frequent derailments. The wooden bridges were flimsy. What the workers, many of them unskilled prisoners, lacked in knowledge about ballast- and track-laying, they made up for in their ken of sabotage (after all, they were mostly prisoners!). The total cost of the project in 1916 U.S. dollars is estimated to have been between $770 million and $1 billion, or approximately one-fifth of the existing Russian national debt. During its construction, there can be no doubt that the Trans-Siberian Railroad was a serious drain on the tsarist economy, and later, the war effort. Despite the criticism, the Trans-Siberian more than paid for itself during the subsequent century. Indeed, it would be hard to imagine Greater Siberia without it. It has become the veritable symbol (and unifier) of the region.

The effects of the railway were immediate: The average annual number of migrants to Greater Siberia was 46,000 between 1871 and 1896; the number soared to 88,000 per annum between 1896 and 1904, and to 174,000 between 1905 and 1914.[46] Between 1897 and 1916, a total of 2.5 million peasants migrated to Greater Siberia, or 57 percent of everyone who had immigrated to the region after 1796. Of these 2.5 million settlers, two out of three ended up in Western Siberia—the vast majority, or 1.5 million, in Tomsk province alone.[47]

CONCLUSION

After three centuries of perpetual Russian advance, the frontier of tsarist settlement had attained its "manifest destiny": the Pacific and Arctic oceans and some of their islands; and the current borders of the United States, Japan, China, and Mongolia—that is, the whole of Greater Siberia.[48] By the beginning of the twentieth century, the region was overwhelmingly Russian, 78 percent. The native population was the next largest group, accounting for slightly less than 10 percent of Siberians. Ukrainians (primarily in the Russian Far East) came next, with 4 percent. The remaining 8 percent was composed of other groups, including Belorussians (in Eastern Siberia), Germans, Tatars, Chuvash, and Mordvins.

At the time of the Bolshevik Revolution, 10.7 million people resided in Greater Siberia. This population was the youngest and the fastest growing in the Russian Empire. Between 1896 and 1917, Greater Siberia's population climbed by 85 percent, compared to a 40 percent increase in the empire as a whole. Thanks to the plowing of virgin chernozems in Western Siberia, it had become one of the country's major agricultural areas. Overall, its sown area had more than doubled since 1895. Its butter industry, which, by 1917, comprised more than 4,000 individual creameries, provided exports to foreign markets that were second only to those of Denmark.[49] Flour mills had blossomed in Omsk, Novonikolayevsk (Novosibirsk), Barnaul, Biysk, and Blagoveshchensk. Western Siberian railheads often had stockyards and slaughterhouses. Almost every major town on the Trans-Siberian Railroad had its own sawmills. Yet despite this progress, only 11.3 percent of the region's population was urban, and as of 1908, a mere 0.2 percent of the people worked in Siberian factories—from which, in 1917, came only about 2 percent of the empire's gross industrial product. Grain processing contributed more than 75 percent of that fraction. Meat processing provided 4 percent, metallurgy (at Petrovsk-Zabaykal'skiy) added 6 percent, and sawmilling produced 3 percent.[50]

NOTES

1. Richard G. Klein, *The Human Career* (Chicago: University of Chicago Press, 1989), p. 388; and Andrew Sherrat, ed., *The Cambridge Encyclopedia of Archeology* (New York: Crown Publishers, 1980), p. 94. An interesting counterargument was proposed in 1990 by Siberian anthropologist Yuriy Mochanov, who believes that humans have occupied Siberia for at least two million years (*Nauka v Sibiri*, No. 12 [March 1991]).

2. Marjorie Mandelstam Balzer, *Russian Traditional Culture: Religion, Gender, and Customary Law* (Armonk, N.Y: M. E. Sharpe, 1992), pp. 48–70; and George Constable, *The Neanderthals* (New York: Time-Life Books, 1974), pp. 58, 79, and 112. I wish to thank Dr. Balzer, who kindly made me aware of several references on Siberian minorities.

3. John Stephan, *The Russian Far East: A History* (Stanford: Stanford University Press, 1995), p. 12. The May 1997 issue of *National Geographic* reveals no evidence for *Homo erectus* farther north than Beijing (Rick Gore, "The Dawn of Humans," *National Geographic*, Vol. 191, No. 5 [May 1997], p. 89). Soil analysis at Diring-Yuryakh suggests that the stone tools found there are around 500,000 years old. More conservative estimates intimate 50,000 years in age, both "significantly older than any other Siberian site" (B. Bower, "Siberian Site Cedes Stone-Age Surprise," *Science News*, Vol. 145, No. 6 [February 5, 1994], p. 84).

4. Chester S. Chard, "Archeology in the Soviet Union," *Science*, Vol. 163 (February 21, 1969), p. 778; and M. I. Pomus, ed., *Rossiyskaya Federatsiya: Zapadnaya Sibir'*, in *Sovetskiy Soyuz*, ed. S. V. Kolesnik (22 vols.; Moscow: Mysl', 1971), pp. 17–25.

5. A. P. Okladnikov, ed., *Drevnyaya Sibir'*, Vol. 1 of *Istoriya Sibir'*, ed. A. P. Okladnikov (5 vols.; Leningrad: Nauka, 1968), p. 44; V. V. Pokshishevskiy, ed., *Rossiyskaya federatsiya: Vostochnaya Sibir'*, in *Sovetskiy Soyuz*, ed. S. V. Kolesnik (22 vols.; Moscow: Mysl', 1969), p. 81; M. G. Levin and L. P. Potapov, eds., *The Peoples of Siberia* (Chicago: University of Chicago Press, 1964), p. 17; to compare artifacts, see also M. G. Levin and L. P. Potapov, eds., *Istoriko-etnograficheskiy atlas Sibiri* (Moscow-Leningrad: Akademiya nauk SSSR, 1961).

6. Joseph Bixby Hoyt, *Man and the Earth* (3d ed.; Englewood Cliffs, N.J.: Prentice-Hall, 1973), pp. 3–5.

7. Levin and Potapov, *The Peoples of Siberia*, pp. 37–60.

8. Iranian Scythians, whose native land was Turkestan, used the horse and composite bow to sack Assyria and to move from there into the Pontic Steppes (modern Ukraine), initiating two thousand years of *Völkerwanderung* (migration). "Before 2000 B.C., the horse of the Old World was a poor thing, valued by humans as meat rather than a mount, too weak in the back to be ridden at all" (John Kee-

gan, *Fields of Battle* [New York: A. A. Knopf, 1995], p. 170). I wish to thank Dr. Harry Walsh for calling this reference to my attention.

9. Levin and Potapov, *The Peoples of Siberia*, pp. 59–60.

10. Between 1947 and 1949, Soviet archeologists unearthed six Scythian tombs at Pazyryk, near Lake Teletskoye in the Altay Mountains (M. I. Artamonov, "Frozen Tombs of the Scythians," *Scientific American*, May 1965, pp. 101–109; and Nataliya Polosmak, "A Mummy Unearthed from the Pastures of Heaven," *National Geographic*, Vol. 186, No. 4 [October 1994], pp. 80–103).

11. Interview with G. S. Martynova, curator of the Museum of the Scientific Preserve, *Tomskaya Pisanitsa*, Kemerovo, West Siberia, September 16, 1991. Dr. Martynova is the world's leading authority on Tashtyk culture. A few dozen kilometers downstream from Kemerovo, along the right bank of the Tom' River, stands a rock face with 280 petroglyphs, illustrating 4,000 years of history beginning with the Afanas'yevans and ending with the Tashtyks (A. I. Martynova, *Pisanitsa na Tomi* [Kemerovo: Kemerovskoye knizhnoye izd., 1988], pp. 3–55).

12. Karl H. Menges, *An Outline of the Early History and Migrations of the Slavs* (New York: Columbia University Press, 1953), p. 12; and Geoffrey Barraclough, ed., *The Times Atlas of World History* (6th ed.; Maplewood, N.J.: Hammond, 1984), pp. 80–81.

13. V. I. Ogorodnikov, *Ocherk istorii Sibiri do nachala XIX stol.* (Irkutsk: Tir. shtaba voyennogo okruga, 1920), p. 145.

14. B. D. Grekov and A. Yu. Yakubovskiy, *Zolotaya Orda i yeye padeniye* (Moscow-Leningrad: Akademiya nauk SSSR, 1950), p. 261.

15. M. V. Fekhner, *Torgovlya russkogo gosudarstva so stranami vostoka v XVI veke* (Moscow: Izd. Gos. istoricheskogo muzeya, 1952), p. 17.

16. R. M. Kabo, *Goroda Zapadnoy Sibiri* (Moscow: Gos. izd. geograficheskoy literatury, 1949), p. 18; and G. F. Miller, *Istorii Sibiri* (Moscow-Leningrad: Akademiya nauk SSSR, 1937).

17. V. K. Andreyevich, *Istoriya Sibiri* (St. Petersburg: Tir. B. B. Komarova, 1889), p. 6; and V. I. Sergeyev, "K voprosu o pokhode v Sibir' druzhiny Yermaka," *Voprosy istorii*, No. 1 (January 1959), p. 121.

18. V. I. Shunkov, ed., *Sibir' v sostave feodal'noy Rossii*, Vol. 2 of *Istoriya Sibiri*, ed. A. P. Okladnikov (5 vols.; Leningrad: Nauka, 1968), pp. 55–56. The language estimates come from James Forsyth, *A History of the Peoples of Siberia* (Cambridge: Cambridge University Press, 1992), p. 10.

19. James R. Gibson, "The Rush to Meet the Sun: An Essay on Russian Eastward Expansion," *Siberica*, Vol. 1, No. 1 (Summer 1990), p. 70; Alan Wood, ed., *Siberia: Problems and Prospects for Regional Development* (London: Croom Helm, 1987), p. 37; D-R.R.I. Gavelka, "Severo-vostochnyy morskoy put' k baseynu Ob'-Irtysha," *Vol'naya Sibir'*, No. 1 (1926), p. 111; S. V. Bakhrushin, *Ocherk po istorii kolonizatsii Siberi v XVI i XVII vv.*, Vol. 3 of *Nauchnyye trudy* (Moscow: Akademiya nauk SSSR, 1955), p. 74; and L. N. Yegorova, et al., eds., *Atlas istorii SSSR*, Pt. 1 (3 pts.; Moscow: Min. Geologii i okhrany nedr SSSR, 1960), pp. 8–9. "Siberian Lands" are first mentioned in the Russian chronicles of 1407.

20. Muscovy conquered Novgorod in 1471 (L. Ye. Iofa, *Goroda Urala* [Moscow: Akademiya nauk SSSR, 1951], p. 47). Fondahl notes that hostile acts by the Nentsy drove the Russians southward, into Ostyak-Vogul (Khanty-Mansi) territory, at the

end of the fifteenth century (see Gail Fondahl, "Siberia: Native Peoples and New-comers in Collision," in *Nations and Politics in the Soviet Successor States*, eds. Ian Bremmer and Ray Taras [London: Cambridge University Press, 1993], p. 481).

21. V. K. Andreyevich, *Istoriya Sibiri* (St. Petersburg: Tir. V. V. Komarova, 1889), p. 2.

22. Peter I. Lyashchenko, *History of the National Economy of Russia to the 1917 Revolution* (New York: Macmillan, 1949), pp. 237–241; and V. V. Sapozhnikov and N. A. Gavrilov, "Zemli Kabineta Yego Velichestva," in *Aziatskaya Rossiya* Vol. 1 (3 vols.; St. Petersburg: Izd. Pereselencheskogo upravleniya glavnogo upravleniya zemleustroystva i zemledeliya [hereafter PUGUZZ], 1914), pp. 388–439. Quoting George Lantzeff, Fondahl has described how Russians used intertribal rivalries to assist them in turning back the frontier (see Fondahl, "Siberia: Native Peoples," p. 481).

23. A. Boronikhin, "K biografii Yermaka," *Voprosy istorii*, No. 10 (October 1946), p. 99; and Edward Louis Keenan, "Muscovy and Kazan': Some Introductory Remarks on the Patterns of Steppe Diplomacy," *Slavic Review*, Vol. 26, No. 4 (December 1967), p. 552. During this time, Muscovy typically bought 30,000 to 40,000 Nogay horses per year for use in its wars against the Swedes.

24. S. M. Seredonin, "Zavoyevaniye Aziatskoy Rossii," in *Aziatskaya Rossiya*, Vol. 1 (3 vols.; St. Petersburg: PUGUZZ, 1914), p. 7. They had hiding places in the Kama Basin.

25. V. I. Sergeyev, "K voprosu o pokhode v Sibir' druzhiny Yermaka," *Voprosy istorii*, No. 1 (January 1959), pp. 122–124; R. G. Skrynnikov, "Podgotovka i nachalo Sibirskoy ekspeditsii Yermaka," *Voprosy istorii*, No. 8 (August 1979), pp. 44–56; and *Sibirskaya gazeta*, December 10–16, 1990. These citations clearly reveal the broad disagreement over dates, places, and true identities associated with the Yermak legend.

26. Basil Dmytryshin, "Russian Expansion to the Pacific, 1580–1700: A Historiographical Review," *Sibirica*, Vol. 1, No. 1 (Summer 1990), p. 7; and James R. Gibson, *Feeding the Russian Fur Trade* (Madison: University of Wisconsin Press, 1969), p. 8.

27. P. A. Slovtsov, "Istoricheskoye obozreniye Sibiri," *Sibirskiye ogni*, No. 1 (1991), p. 102; and Fondahl, "Siberia: Native Peoples," p. 481.

28. Lyashchenko, *History of the National Economy*, p. 241.

29. G. A. Leont'yeva, *Zemleprokhodets Yerofey Pavlovich Khabarov* (Moscow: Prosveshcheniye, 1991), pp. 3–15. Vasil'yev explored the Vilyuy with 50 men; Perfil'yev, the Angara and Lena with 36; Moskvitin, the Sea of Okhotsk with 21; and Bakhtyarov, the Vitim with 55.

30. *Ibid.*, p. 14. The description is Newby's. Poyarkov "plundered and betrayed to an unspeakable degree, with the result that the natives fled at the approach of other Russians" (see Eric Newby, *The Big Red Train Ride* [New York: St. Martin's, 1978], p. 162).

31. Dmytryshin, "Russian Expansion to the Pacific," p. 9.

32. Harmon Tupper, *To the Great Ocean* (Boston: Little, Brown & Company, 1965), p. 29.

33. Gary Hausladen, "Russian Siberia: An Integrative Approach," *Soviet Geography* (Chicago: University of Chicago Press, 1956), p. 234.

34. Shunkov, *Sibir' v sostave*, p. 55; and Alan Wood, "Siberian Exile in the Eighteenth Century," *Sibirica*, Vol. 1, No. 1 (Summer 1990), p. 42.

35. V. M. Kabuzan, "The Settlement of Siberia and the Far East from the Late 18th to the Early 20th Century (1795–1917)," *Soviet Geography*, Vol. 32, No. 9 (November 1991), p. 617; and V. Z. Drobizhev, I. D. Koval'chenko, and A. V. Murav'yev, *Istoricheskaya geografiya SSSR* (Moscow: Vysshaya shkola, 1973), pp. 186–193.

36. Kabuzan, "The Settlement of Siberia," p. 617.

37. *Ibid.,* pp. 620–621.

38. Mark Bassin, "The Russian Geographical Society, the 'Amur Epoch,' and the Great Siberian Expedition, 1855–1863," *Annals of the Association of American Geographers*, Vol. 73, No. 2 (March 1983), pp. 240–256; and N. Bolkhovitinov, "Kak prodali Alyasku," *Mezhdunarodnaya zhizn'*, No. 7 (1988), pp. 120–131.

39. Tupper, *To the Great Ocean*, p. 33.

40. The promoter was P. M. Collins, who visited Amuria in 1857 (Steven G. Marks, *Road to Power: The Trans-Siberian Railroad and the Colonization of Asian Russia, 1850–1917* [Ithaca, N.Y.: Cornell University Press, 1991], p. 32).

41. John J. Stephan, *The Russian Far East: A History* (Stanford: Stanford University Press, 1995), p. 327. Historical geographer Mark Bassin views Murav'yev much less as a hero than as a pragmatic opportunist whose ideas shifted with the political winds (personal conversation with Mark Bassin, January 22, 1992). In 1847–1850, the Count was against separatism; yet, on the eve of the coronation of reformist Tsar Alexander II, Murav'yev favored decentralization and openly entertained the idea of an independent Siberia (Peter Kropotkin, *Memoirs of a Revolutionist*, Vol. 1 [2 vols.; New York: Houghton, Mifflin & Co., 1899], p. 198).

42. Kabuzan, "The Settlement of Siberia," pp. 623–625, and "Sibirskaya zheleznaya doroga," *Entsiklopedicheskiy slovar'*, Vol. 58 (1900), p. 738. The government was especially generous to peasants with means (later to be called *kulaki*). After 1889, such male migrants to Western Siberia obtained 41 acres of state land in exchange for the payment of property taxes. Those who did this were exempt from other taxes and military service for three years. They also received reduced railway and steamer fares, cheap food, medical care, and a loan of between 30 and 100 rubles that would be repaid without interest over the next decade (Donald W. Treadgold, *The Great Siberian Migration* [Princeton: Princeton University Press, 1957], p. 27).

43. Marks, *Road to Power*, pp. 35–46; David N. Collins, "Plans for Railway Development in Siberia, 1857–1890, and Tsarist Colonialism," *Siberica* Vol. 1, No. 2 (Winter 1990–1991), pp. 128–150; and V. P. Semenov-Tyan'-Shanskiy, *Zapadnaya Sibir'*, Vol. 16 of *Polnoye geograficheskoye opisaniye nashego otechestvo* (19 vols.; St. Petersburg: Izd. A. F. Devriyena, 1907), pp. 366–370. One of the proposals urged the laying of track north of Lake Baykal over the route of the Baykal-Amur Mainline (1974–1985), which is a shorter route to the Pacific; but the presence of permafrost in that region ultimately defeated that alternative (see Akademiya Nauk SSSR, Komissiya po problemam Severa, *Letopis' Severa* [Moscow: Geografgiz, 1957], p. 202).

44. For excellent coverage of Witte's career, see Marks, *The Road to Power*, pp. 117–143. For his examination of Kulomzin, see Steven G. Marks, "Conquering the

Great East," in *Rediscovering Russia in Asia: Siberia and the Russian Far East*, eds. Stephen Kotkin and David Wolff (Armonk, N.Y.: M. E. Sharpe, 1995), pp. 23–39. For circumstances surrounding the Russo-Japanese War and the Chinese Eastern Railway, see F. A. Kudryavtsev, ed., *Sibir' v epokhu kapitalizma*, Vol. 3 of *Istoriya Sibiri*, ed. A. P. Okladnikov (5 vols.; Leningrad: Nauka, 1968), p. 286; V. N. Vartanov et al., *Konflikt na KVZhD* (Khabarovsk: Khabarovskoye knizhnoye izdatel'stvo, 1989), pp. 5–16; and Paul Goble's remarks in "Panel on Siberia: Economic and Territorial Issues," *Soviet Geography*, Vol. 32, No. 6 (June 1991), p. 369.

45. Marks, *The Road to Power*, p. 191; and Kudryavtsev, *Sibir' v epokhu*, p. 177.

46. L. F. Sklyarov, *Pereseleniye i zemleustroystvo v Sibiri v gody Stolypinskoy reformy* (Leningrad: Institut imeni Gertsena, 1962), pp. 450–453.

47. Kabuzan, "The Settlement of Siberia," p. 629.

48. Southern Sakhalin and the still controversial southern Kuriles, or "Northern Territories," were added in 1945. For an encapsulation, see Japanese Ministry of Foreign Affairs, *Japan's Northern Territories* (Tokyo: Foreign Office, 1987). Tuva (now Tyva) became a protectorate in 1911 and a part of the USSR in 1944.

49. Victor L. Mote, "The Chelyabinsk Grain Tariff and the Rise of the Siberian Butter Industry," *Slavic Review*, Vol. 35, No. 2 (Summer 1976), pp. 304–317. See also A. A. Kallantar', "Molochnoye khozyaystvo," in *Aziatskaya Rossiya*, Vol. 2 (3 vols; St. Petersburg: PUGUZZ, 1914), p. 332; and L. M. Goryushkin, *Sibirskoye krest' yanstvo na rubezhe dvukh vekov* (Novosibirsk: Nauka, 1967), p. 162.

50. M. B. Vol'f, *Geograficheskoye razmeshcheniye russkoy promyshlennosti* (Moscow-Leningrad: Gosudarstvennoye izdatel'stvo, 1927), p. 21; and R. S. Livshits, *Ocherki po razmeshcheniyu promyshlennosti SSSR* (Moscow-Leningrad: Gosudarstvennoye izdatel'stvo politicheskoy literatury, 1954), p. 88.

FOUR

Regionalism, Separatism, and Russification Before the Revolution

Nothing on earth compares to Siberia. She probably could exist as a planet on her own. She has everything that a planet needs . . . on land, underground, and in the air. Her very existence is so omnifarious and multifaceted that it is impossible to epitomize her with known concepts.

—Valentin Rasputin, Siberian writer

THE BIRTH OF A REGION

Historical geographer Mark Bassin has observed that "Russian views of Siberia were examples of the same sort of 'imaginative geography' that resulted from European attempts to depict and understand the non-European world as a whole." Siberia as a region, in Bassin's view, was "invented" in the nineteenth century as a focus of four enduring themes: (1) Siberia as a typical colony, or as a source of furs and precious metals and a desolate repository for "undesirables"; (2) Siberia as a fount of democratic and egalitarian idealism; (3) Siberia as a romantic, inspirational ideal for the Russian nation as a whole; and (4) Siberia as an independent political entity.[1]

Colonial Siberia

Until the twentieth century, Greater Siberia was not commonly regarded as an organic part of Russia. During the 1600s, Muscovites subdivided the territory into competing military fiefdoms to discourage unity and the possibility of a challenge to the tsar from a charismatic Siberian viceroy. In his role as Siberian governor-general between 1819 and 1821, political reformer Mikhail Speransky aspired to make the region an integral part of Russia. Yet this did little to allay the fears of tsarist officials: Even as late as 1861, officials in St. Petersburg suspected Murav'yev-Amurskiy of sedition (see Chapter 3). Throughout the remainder of the nineteenth century, authorities treated Greater Siberia as Russia's by-blow.

Greater Siberia and "Soft Gold."   When someone writes the ultimate economic history of Siberia, "gold" will hold a prominent place—that is, soft gold (furs), solid gold (metals), dry gold (grain), creamery gold (butter), and black and blue gold (oil and gas). Without question, mercantilism perfused the region between 1600 and 1800.[2] From the standpoint of those in the Russian core, the Siberian periphery existed to fill the coffers of Moscow or St. Petersburg. Whether soft or solid gold, the wealth of the periphery was extracted to enrich the autocrat either as domestic product or as a source of foreign exchange.

In the 1600s, one-tenth of Russia's state income came from sales of fur from Greater Siberia.[3] According to Fisher, two black fox skins in the 1620s could "fetch" 50 acres of land, a cabin, 5 horses, 10 head of cattle, 20 sheep, several dozen fowl, and still leave change.[4] Such incentives encouraged the depletion of Western Siberia's stock of furbearing animals by 1650, and that of Eastern Siberia by 1700. By the latter date, three-fourths of Greater Siberia's total fur resources were gone. Bassin has argued that the tsars approved the Treaty of Nerchinsk primarily because they deemed Amuria barren of fur (and food).[5] For 200 years, under the treaty, Russians cleverly substituted otter pelts from North America for the sable skins of Amuria, and in the process, salvaged Sino-Russian commercial relations.

Greater Siberia and Solid Gold.   As the fur trade diminished, the relative importance of metals ascended. As early as the 1600s, Muscovy ordered its expeditions to be on the lookout not only for sable skins but also for sources of silver, gold, copper, and lead. By 1700, large silver mines and smelters were on stream at Kolyvan in the Altay region and Nerchinsk in the Yablonovyy district.

Between 1728 and 1745, the Altay enterprises belonged to the Demidov family, the patriarch of which had made his fortune at Russia's very first iron works, in Tula. In 1702, Peter the Great gave the Demidovs rights to develop a new metallurgical combine in the Ural Mountains. The family ultimately owned 40 iron and copper smelters in the Urals alone. A quarter century later, the Demidovs obtained the rights to the silver and gold mines at Kolyvan, Zmeinogorsk, and Salair in the Altay-Salair ranges. When the patriarch died in 1745, the family's Altay holdings reverted to the imperial family.[6]

Gold fever nourished the flood of exiles into Eastern Siberia. Simultaneously, the tsars began to show much more interest in the Greater Siberia region. Authorities began to refer to the region as "El Dorado," "California," or more prosaically, a "gold mine." Apart from the Demidovs' holdings, other aristocratic families also owned gold mines, and their aggregate investments in Siberia decidedly influenced the development of government policy.[7] As a token of gratitude, the tsar allowed the aristocrats to employ imperial factory serfs in their mines (and factories), until Murav'yev liberated these serfs in the 1850s.[8]

Between 1830 and 1850, gold output from Greater Siberia increased 250-fold. Accounting for 11 percent of Russia's gold production in the former year, the region's share rose to 71 percent by the end of the period. Two-thirds came from Yenisey River placer deposits. Later, the focus would shift to the Lena Basin, and later still, to the notorious Kolyma.[9] By midcentury, only 9 percent of Siberia's production came from the old metal mines in the Altay and at Nerchinsk. Revenues from gold mining, however, never equaled those from sales of "soft gold" during its heyday.

Creamery Gold for Dry Gold.   From 1894 to 1917, Siberia became renowned for a most unlikely product: butter. With the tsar's approval of construction of the Trans-Siberian Railroad, the commercial estate owners in European Russia prevailed on the crown to protect them from what they feared would be a flood of grain from Western Siberia. The government responded with the imposition of the "Chelyabinsk Tariff Break," whereby Siberian grain would be penalized by a second acceleration of the freight rate structure, which normally decreased with distance. Rates would rise initially on shipments from eastern points of origin to Chelyabinsk, and would rise again on shipments from Chelyabinsk to western destinations. Siberia's "dry gold" could no longer compete on the domestic market, because of the excessive transportation costs. The policy of regional protectionism compelled Siberians to find new sources of earning power. They found it in their dairy cows, a unique breed that yielded high-fat milk.

With the arrival of the Trans-Siberian Railroad, buttermaking diffused from a single creamery established in the Kurgan Steppe in 1894 to more than 2,000 in 1913. Soon, because of the high butterfat content of the milk and the relatively low labor costs, Siberian butter became the cheapest competitor on the international market. This was true even after the addition of the costs of transportation to the commodity's principal buyers in Britain and Germany. It was said to be the only butter that the European working man could afford. The success of the industry was so great that Prime Minister Stolypin was quoted as saying, "Siberian butter production yields twice as much gold as the whole of the Siberian gold industry."[10]

The gradual lifting of the Chelyabinsk Tariff Break (1910–1913) encouraged a twofold jump in Siberian grain shipments to the west. Much of the produce, especially durum wheat, was destined for foreign markets, where it was processed into pasta. Interrupted by the war, revolution, and civil disturbances, the trade was renewed during the New Economic Policy (NEP), which was in force between 1921 and 1928. Under the NEP, Siberians produced huge, nationally important grain surpluses, three-fourths of which was spring wheat. At the peak of its hard currency earning potential (1926–1927), Siberian "dry gold" represented 35 percent of all Soviet wheat exports and 23 percent of the value of the exports of all grain. It also accounted for half of the total increase of foreign exchange earnings in 1927.[11] Thus, together with revived butter shipments, Siberian grain exports became an important source of hard currency for the Bolsheviks, precisely at the time they intended to launch their policies of collectivization and industrialization.

Black and Blue Gold.   More will be said about this subject in later chapters. Here I simply want to indicate that the exploitation of Siberian oil and gas as primary sources of foreign exchange income since the 1960s perpetuates the long-established tradition of using Siberia as a resource frontier and colony. Because of the rapid increase of oil and gas extraction in the Middle and Lower Ob', Greater Siberia's share of Soviet exports exploded from less than 20 percent in 1970 to more than 50 percent in 1985, the first year of Gorbachev's tenure. Oil and gas exports alone accounted for 87 percent of Greater Siberia's contribution. Residents of the periphery, both then and now, typically complain that the benefits accrued from the sales of their hydrocarbons are radically skewed in favor of the core. That is, very little of the hard currency accumulated from the trade of these commodities returns to the regions of origin. Note that this is not a novel complaint: It has been registered throughout the "colonial" period—the period of Russian and Soviet domination.

Greater Siberia as an Outback and Fount of Democracy

The title of this section may seem paradoxical; yet it is precisely the habit of using Siberia as a place of exile, particularly political exile, that engendered the democratic traditions of the region. During the early nineteenth century, the colonial perception of Greater Siberia was supplemented by an image that unfortunately has been more enduring. A region that had been variously described as "our Peru," "our Mexico," a "Russian Brazil," or even "our East India" was now identified as Count Nesselrode's "deep net" for criminals.[12] The fabulous bounties of soft and solid gold could not dampen the growing sympathy for the notion that Greater Siberia was a frozen outback suitable for habitation by none but the dregs of society.

Among Westerners, this perception of Greater Siberia has prevailed. As we have seen, however, the majority of Siberians—even before the great migration associated with the completion of the Trans-Siberian Railroad—were not exiles. In fact, between 1867 and 1896, mechanical increase was 1.2 million persons, the majority of whom were exiles; but these were more than offset by the 1.6 million people who accrued to the population by natural means. The number of exiles, 99 percent of whom were criminals rather than political prisoners, only occasionally exceeded 10 percent of the total population.[13]

The image of Siberia as an outback for exiles survives despite the facts, because of the notoriety attached to the region by the memoirs of political prisoners, including disgraced courtiers, high-ranking officials, rebel militiamen, religious dissenters (Old Believers), national minorities, and prisoners of war. Among the best known was Archpriest Avvakum, whose vivid description of his ten-year exile (1653–1664) remains a Russian literary classic; Abram Hannibal, Pushkin's African ancestor, who was exiled to Siberia between 1727 and 1731; and Alexander Radishchev, who was sentenced to a ten-year exile, beginning in 1790, for writing his scandalous tale of *A Journey from St. Petersburg to Moscow*.

This image also was fostered in part by the Decembrist Revolt of December 14, 1825, and its aftermath. The participants in the insurrection were primarily young Russian and Polish intellectuals of the imperial officer corps who had been exposed to the democratic revolutions of the radical Whigs of Europe and the United States. To the Decembrists, autocracy was arbitrary, capricious, and cruel, and it had to be changed. Of the 126 who were arraigned for sedition, five were hanged and the remainder were banished for life to Greater Siberia.[14] Some of the banished, like N. V. Basargin and Artamon Murav'yev, believed their lives were over.[15]

As they plunged into the deep net, the Decembrists not only maintained their convictions but also—greatly impressed by the singularity of Siberia and the Siberians—began actively to propagate those convictions. To the Decembrists, the Siberians were freer, cleverer, better educated, more humane, and more egalitarian than other Russian peasants. They likened Siberia to the United States in that it had become a safe haven for religious and political dissenters, some of whom—like the Old Believers and Dukhobors—had preceded the Decembrists into exile.

Wherever they were or went in Greater Siberia, the Decembrists and their wives served as intellectual magnets in their communities. Because they were so widely dispersed—the senior officers to the "more interesting" sites in southern Siberia and the junior officers to the "wildest and most remote corners"—they could impart a cultural catechism to the

Siberian population that belied the possibilities inherent in their numbers alone. Gradually, Siberia became for the Decembrists a second motherland. Forbidden to engage in politics, they rallied to cultural and economic causes. They taught school, practiced agronomy, and introduced the rudiments of medical care. In the towns and cities, such as Irkutsk, they created social circles, set up libraries, and gave public lectures. They founded some of the first Siberian newspapers and even tinkered with the mechanics of public administration. These and other activities were carried out in a Greater Siberia with a population of between 2 and 3 million persons during the Decembrists' three decades of banishment. Few Siberians, if any, were ignorant of their presence.

The Decembrists were not separatists, nor did they urge Siberians to follow the example of any other world culture, including that of the United States. Although they had suffered terribly at the hands of the autocrat, they remained faithful to Russia even as an imperial entity. That entity, in their view, *included Siberia.* They wanted to transform all of Russia, embracing Siberia too, into a democratic realm in which all citizens would have equal opportunity to experience freedom and liberty. Concerning Greater Siberia alone, the Decembrists hoped for the destruction of the colonial yoke, the establishment of self-governance, the reorganization of the administrative framework, and the creation of a responsible judiciary. They argued for a continuation of the cultural and economic improvements that they themselves had begun. They contended that a Siberian industrial revolution would occur only when both Russians and Siberians appreciated the value of the natural resource base. In support of such an economy, they envisioned a network of railways and a great Pacific commercial fleet.

Siberia as a Romantic Inspiration

While the Decembrists were accepting their various fates in Nesselrode's deep net, yet another perception of Siberia emerged on the wings of Russian nationalism. In the first half of the nineteenth century, a plurality if not a majority of Russian intellectuals rejected the Westernization (or Europeanization) of their country and stressed "Russian national exclusivity independent of Europe."[16] Glorification of Russia naturally meant the glorification of its regions, by far the most conspicuous of which was Greater Siberia. Soon Yermak's conquest of the Siberian Tatars was being compared to the European discovery of the New World. Territorial expansion and all the attendant events were vaunted as sacred acts carried out by self-sacrificing, patriotic sons of the motherland. Pulp novels and short stories glorified the heroic exploits of the righteous Orthodox Cossacks against the pagan Siberian savages. Even Pushkin aspired to write a

Siberian epic based on his correspondence with his Decembrist friend, V. K. Kyukhel'bekker ("Kyukhlya").

As Slavophilism gathered steam nationwide, the perception of Siberia as a brooding, frozen wasteland unfit for civilized people gradually shifted to an almost Elysian image. Siberia as outback became Siberia the bountiful, the beautiful, the wise. After more than two centuries, Siberia finally was *also* Russian land (see the epigraph to Chapter 1).

In association with this change of opinion, possibly the loftiest of encomia came from someone who never came closer to Siberia than Vyatka (Kirov), several hundred miles west, not east, of the Urals. Alexander Herzen (1812–1870) extolled the virtues of the "unspoiled" common folk of Siberia: a new people, a healthy people, a free and equal people, filled with "the energy, dynamism, and plasticity of youth." It was Herzen who envisioned Siberia as Russia's future and the Pacific Ocean as the future Mediterranean. The settlement of Siberia, he said, was the Russian version of the settlement of North America, and he praised the "civilizing" aspects of both great movements. In the end, from his catbird's seat in Europe, he dared to condone P. A. Slovtsov's notion of a liberated, independent Siberia, a territory internally cohesive and distinct from the Russian core.[17]

Siberian Regionalism: Siberia as an Independent Political Entity

The reactionary Tsar Alexander III (1881–1894) took the throne during the tricentennial of Yermak's conquest. Siberian *oblastnichestvo* (regionalism) was in full bloom, and Siberian development was a major public issue.[18] In full flower as well was the debate over the financing of the Trans-Siberian Railroad and overall migration policy (see Chapter 3). All of the key players in the struggle were aware of the implications of Siberian regionalism, even if they misunderstood its true intentions.

Time and distance are the handmaidens of cultural distinction. This fact was not lost on Siberia's governors and petty officials, who often acted as independent viceroys. Even the autocrat got into the act in the 1760s, when Catherine the Great established the *Sibirskoye tsarstvo* (Siberian kingdom). The "enlightened" Catherine looked upon Siberia as a self-supporting dominion of Russia, complete with its own currency. The "kingdom" was repudiated in 1781, however, and thereafter no tsar ever again officially entertained the concept of an independent Siberia.

The intellectual wellspring of Siberian regionalism was the notion of "Siberian patriotism" espoused by an Orthodox priest named P. A. Slovtsov (1767–1841). The voluntary migration of hordes of oppressed masses from the injustices of tsarist tyranny to Greater Siberia was the source of Slovtsov's ideas. His message of an exclusive Siberia and Siberians sent shivers up the spines of conservative authorities in St. Petersburg, who by 1859 were well aware of the Siberian student movement in the capital itself. Colored by their fears of communism and other revolutionary movements in Russia, Siberian regionalism seemed to them only the latest variant of radical separatist conspiracy. Adding fuel to the fire, the radicals Mikhail Bakunin and M. V. Butashevich-Petrashevskiy openly supported liberation and total self-government in Siberia: The moderate philosophies of Slovtsov, the Decembrists, and Herzen were one thing; the wilder notions of Bakunin and Butashevich-Petrashevskiy were quite another! In 1860, for example, Bakunin wrote a letter to Herzen from Irkutsk in which he declared that Siberia's secession from Russia was then just a matter of time.[19]

From its beginnings in the late 1850s to its demise in the 1920s, Siberian regionalism was also fostered by the intellects and scholarship of two other men: N. M. Yadrintsev (1842–1894) and G. N. Potanin (1835–1920). They, in turn, had been inspired in part by the federalist ideas of A. P. Shchapov, a half-Buryat native of Irkutsk province. Until his death, Yadrintsev was the leading authority on Siberia. In his best known work, *Sibir' kak koloniya* (Siberia as a Colony), Yadrintsev depicted Siberians as colonists with interests worlds apart from those of Russians living in the European Russian core. In his opinion, Siberians were distinctive enough to merit consideration as a separate ethnicity: one of mixed Russian and native heritage that was much better adapted to cope with austere physical conditions. Siberians were liberty-loving "individuals" who could barely remember their Russian pasts, and most of them regarded European Russians as contemptible foreigners. Of course, many migrants to Siberia, and all of the indigenes, were non-Russians.

Yadrintsev's Siberia was singular and pure, an isolated agricultural colony that in many ways was closer to the Americas and Asia than to the Russian core. It had the potential to become a new nation. Yadrintsev disdained St. Petersburg's systematic "fleecing" of Siberia's resources and mourned the periphery's total dependence on the gratuity of European Russian manufacturers.[20] Heralding modern conservation movements, Yadrintsev characterized the crown's colonial policies as a "plundering of our natural wealth and the destruction of our forests."[21]

Yadrintsev's criticism also extended to the omnipresent political corruption and the violation of civil liberties and rights: The strongly centralized administrative hierarchy, in his opinion, was deliberately designed to stifle local initiative and self-government. Yadrintsev died before the Russian *zemstvo* (local council) reached Siberia (1897); and the variant that eventually arrived, unlike its counterparts elsewhere in the empire, lacked the power to conduct trial by jury. Meanwhile, the region was being run by bribe takers and embezzlers (Slovtsov's "Siberian satraps"). If and when such speculators were caught red-handed, they were merely slapped on the wrist and reassigned to perpetuate their malfeasance elsewhere in Greater Siberia.

Embittered by the widespread corruption in the "colony," Yadrintsev and Potanin beseeched Siberian patriots to consider the establishment of an economically independent democratic republic. In the 1860s, the scholars demanded an end to the region's economic dependence on European Russia; the abrogation of the exile system, which was nothing more than glossed-over serfdom; the creation and enhancement of a Siberian intelligentsia to serve as the cultural cynosure of the new democratic republic; and the founding of a Siberian university. (Of these demands, only the last was fulfilled: Tomsk University was founded in 1888.) About the same time, the pair teamed up with historian S. S. Shashkov to charter the "Siberian Independence Society." The trio called for the immediate "separation of Siberia from Russia and its establishment as a republic composed of federated states similar to those of North America."[22]

The tsarist government did not take these words kindly. In 1865, Yadrintsev and Potanin, among other regionalists from Omsk and Tomsk, were jailed as "separatists" who had plotted to create an American-style republic in Siberia. The fears were further augmented in 1866, during a futile uprising of Polish political exiles near Lake Baykal. The insurgents hoped to free the exiled pamphleteer N. G. Chernyshevskiy, author of *Chto delat'?* (What Is to Be Done?), and to make him president of a Siberian Republic tentatively named *Svobodoslaviya* (Freedom's Glory). The rebellion had little popular support and died aborning,[23] and so did the modest radicalism of intellectuals like Yadrintsev and Potanin. At his trial, like Simon Peter, Potanin denied at least three times that political separatism was ever a part of the regionalists' platform.[24]

Even though it was a politically limited intellectual movement and not very dangerous, Siberian regionalism thus received negative publicity as early as 1865. Not all Siberian intellectuals, in fact, and virtually none of the masses, supported Yadrintsev and Potanin. A motley assortment of pro-Russian conservative intellectuals, populists, local bureaucrats, and Marxist revolutionaries stifled the regionalists well into the twentieth century. These individuals, whom Allison has referred to as "centralists," vilified Yadrintsev's newspaper *Vostochnoye obozreniye* (Eastern Review) as the voice of separatists and revolutionaries. Enhancing the cause of the centralists were rumors of Russian Siberians beginning to eat like Eskimos and Chukchis learning to speak English from their encounters with American whalers.[25]

Regionalism in the Russian Far East. Regional consciousness in the Russian Far East was distinct from that in the rest of Greater Siberia. Its acquisition was both belated and prolonged. Between 1880 and 1917, the region was an "ethnic bazaar" containing immigrants, mostly from Ukraine; old settler descendants of Murav'yev's Transbaykal, Amur, and Ussuri Cossack Hosts; Koreans; Japanese; religious dissenters; and myriad travelers. Few people in this emporium of strangers ever identified strongly with Mother Russia. When in 1885 a Chinese traveler observed that far easterners would rather surrender St. Petersburg than relinquish Vladivostok, he was merely acknowledging that half of Vladivostok's civilian residents were Chinese.

Stephan has identified three factors that inspired far eastern regionalism: distinctive migrants of Russian, Ukrainian, and Baltic heritage; its own administrative identity after 1884; and the establishment of intellectual circles in the larger far eastern cities.[26] Helping to mold the regional consciousness in the Russian Far East was the fear not only of the formidable Japanese militarists but also of the slumbering Chinese millions. The crown's putative dearth of concern for the region also proffered little comfort to residents: After 1909, the regime appeared to be more interested in taxing goods sent through Siberia's ports than in the welfare of Siberians. The fact that the region had little or no voice in the national Duma was reminiscent of colonial America's "taxation without representation." Between 1917 and 1922, the same inhabitants were either cut off or veritably autonomous from the center, and further original experiences were engendered by the short-lived Far Eastern Republic (see Chapter 5).

RUSSIFICATION AND THE SIBERIANS BEFORE 1917

No friend of liberals, Alexander III strove to nip "separatism" and foreign influences in the bud by reorganizing the administrative structure of Greater Siberia. The reorganization was carried out in accordance with the rigid administrative hierarchy of European Russia; thus, Siberia was to be integrated into the realm and Russified. "By 1887, the very name of Siberia was no longer used as an administrative term."[27] The policy of "divide and conquer," which Stalin used so effectively a half century later, had a precedent in the tsar's dealings with the periphery.

The crown's instrument of integration and Russification was to be the Trans-Siberian Railroad, and the taskmasters were Witte and Kulomzin. The majority of Siberian regionalists wanted to develop their economy slowly, without the diseconomies of rapid progress. They understood the benefits of the railway but were suspicious of what it might do to Siberian unity and traditional culture. Potanin, for example, believed that Greater Siberia needed more people, factories, and civil rights *before* it needed a railroad.

Ironically, conservatives in St. Petersburg who previously had "railed" against the Trans-Siberian Railroad suddenly became champions of the iron horse when confronted with the prospect of Siberian "separatism."[28] Kulomzin, for example, hoped to quash the centrifugal forces by filling Greater Siberia's huge voids with hordes of peasants from European Russia, thereby creating a Russian "melting pot." According to Marks, despite his altruism in other matters, Kulomzin was, like Witte, a Russian patriot, and showed obvious disdain for Greater Siberia's "motley mixture" of ethnicities and beliefs. The salmagundi that he hoped to transform into a purée of blond, blue-eyed Russians included Orthodox Russians; sectarians, comprising Old Believers, Skoptsy, and Dukhobor-Molokans; Muslim Kazakhs and Tatars; Buddhist Buryats; and shamanist Ugrians, Tungus-Manchus, and Paleo-Asians.[29] The homogenization of the Siberian population would create the foundations for more effective socioeconomic relations and counter the Yellow Peril that lay to the south and east, in China and Japan.

The Russian Siberians: European Born, Siberian by Choice

Many factors conspired to attract migrants to Greater Siberia. The majority of settlers were pushed out of the west by overcrowding and a lack of land and pulled eastward by the promise of land and liberty. As Treadgold observed in 1957, settlers in Siberia found "more of both [of the latter pair] than they had ever known."[30] Abandoning the security of the peasant commune in which they had been born and bred to risk everything for an unknown land thousands of miles away was the most important decision potential migrants would ever make. The new Siberians soon learned that *Bog vysoko, a tsar' daleko* (God is on high, and the tsar is far away); that they could bend the law and local officials to suit their needs; and that they might even evade the hand of government altogether. Having successfully survived the Siberian migration, how could they feel inferior to anyone ever again? How could they not be proud to be Siberians?

Many were proud enough to intermarry with other Siberian peoples and groups. From the beginning of Siberian settlement, Russian women were in short supply. A few were imported for the specific purpose of marriage. Most Russian male settlers, however, had either to content themselves with celibacy or to wed indigenous women. Conditions at times became so desperate that native women were enslaved or purchased as concubines or wives. In the beginning, Ugrian women were the most vulnerable to these practices, due to their proximity. Half-breeds were common throughout Greater Siberia. By 1900, a large proportion of the "Russian" population of Western Siberia was actually made up of hybrid Slavs and Tatars. In Eastern Siberia, Russian immigrants readily married Buryats and bore swarthy children with dark eyes (with or without the epicanthic fold). The half-caste offspring were numerous enough to be given the ethnic distinction *Karymy*. Likewise, the unions of Russians and Yakuts often resulted in children who spoke Yakut but who were Russian in almost every other way.[31] Miscegenation was not unique to Russians and natives: Eastern Slavs (Russians, Belorussians, and Ukrainians) from various European provinces lived side by side and often intermarried.

The cohabitation disturbed Kulomzin, who called Siberian villages "veritable ethnographic exhibitions." Native and Russian villages were never far from one another, but sometimes they were a proverbial ethnic mosaic.[32] In a single settlement in Tobol'sk province, Kulomzin found an ethnic farrago of Russians, Ukrainians, Belorussians, Maris, Komis, and Chuvash. He worried that such mixtures would lead to problems of tax collection and other administrative difficulties. The ethnic diversity of the Siberian village naturally led to peculiar Russian dialects, including different words and pronunciations, idiosyncratic slang, and shifting emphases, for example, *doch-KA* in lieu of *DOCH-ka* (daughter).

Although Kulomzin did not condone the Russification of venerable cultures such as those of the Poles, Finns, and Armenians, he had no qualms about the assimilation of undesirables, such as Muslim Kazakhs and Tatars and Buddhist Buryats. His settlement policy, therefore, was aimed at overwhelming ethnic groups such as these with waves of Russian immigrants.

Sectarians and Jews: Outsiders in the Outback

The Great Schism that occurred with the introduction of new liturgical forms into the Russian Orthodox service in the 1650s divided the faithful into two groups: the loyal majority, who agreed with the changes, and a minority of "Old Believers," or "sectarians," who wished to maintain the old rites. Severely persecuted by the Muscovite government—particularly in Arkhangel'sk province, where the tsars had imprisoned their leader and martyr, Archpriest Avvakum, among the Samoyeds—the Old Believers finally crossed the Urals into Siberia. One group was deported to the Altay, to provide labor and agricultural support for the Kolyvan mines (see Chapter 3). Another group migrated to the Central Siberian Upland and Transbaykalia and dwelt peacefully there, hunting, gathering, and fishing among the Tungus and Buryats. Although the Old Believers kept strictly to themselves through the 1905 Revolution, a few Tungus admired the sect enough to become adherents.[33] By 1880, Old Believers formed the majority of the population of Amuria, "which had more religious sectarians than any other province in Russia."[34] Others lived in the Sikhote-Alin Mountains and on the Lake Khanka plain in southern Primor'ye. German Mennonites and Baptists also wisely settled in the relatively fertile Zeya-Bureya Plain.

In the 1700s, other religious dissenters, such as the Skoptsy and Dukhobors, were deported to Siberia. The Skoptsy (from a word meaning "eunuch"), who practiced sexual abstinence and self-castration, were banished to Yakutia, where, despite the harsh climate, they developed homesteads that became models for the native peoples. The Dukhobors, or "soul strugglers," stressed the supreme authority of inner experience and believed that their leaders embodied the spirit of God. The Dukhobors and their offshoot, the Molokans, who drank milk during Lent, had farms in the vicinity of Blagoveshchensk, in Amuria. The Molokans led sober, abstinent lives similar to those of the Mormons of Utah. Their orderly houses and fields contrasted sharply with those of their Cossack neighbors. By the end of the nineteenth century, they had more farm machinery per capita than any other people in the Russian Empire. Frugal and savvy in business as well as in agriculture, the Molokans eventually owned flour mills and steamship lines in the Russian Far East.[35]

Before 1830, Jews came to Greater Siberia only as convicts and exiles. For a short time, during the reign of Nicholas I, they were allowed to homestead in the region, but later the policy was reversed as they were increasingly confined to the Pale of Settlement in western Russia. Despite these constraints, by 1900, approximately 35,000 Jews lived in Siberia, the majority employed as merchants in towns and cities such as Tobol'sk, Omsk, Tomsk, Irkutsk, and Chita.[36]

Muslims, Buddhists, and Shamanists

The nineteenth century was a disaster for the indigenous peoples of Greater Siberia. Nomadic groups and shifting bands were sedentarized in Russian-style communes. As newly settled people, ethnic groups such as the Khakass, Buryats, Evens, and Kets were now subject to the poll tax, which represented as much as a tenfold increase over their previous tribute in furs. Tribal headmen or chiefs, whom the Russians had bribed, were only too willing to collect the taxes, which steadily impoverished and demoralized their subjects until the poll tax was abolished in 1900s. With the spread of poverty, their minions became vulnerable to communicable and venereal diseases: Syphilis, for example, plagued the Samoyeds, Ugrians, and Yukagirs. Typhus, scurvy, and tuberculosis also abounded among them. Indigenes who had not been Russianized (that is, exposed to Russian ways) were extremely rare by 1900. The 1800s proved to be a century of precipitous decline, if not extinction, for many Siberian native groups, including the Yukagirs, Itel'men, Kets, Sel'kups, and Nganasans. By 1917, the populations of the Ugrians, Evenks, and Nanays had fallen by more than one-third since their first contact with the Russians. In contrast, the Buryats,

Yakuts, Nentsy, and Entsy experienced substantial growth. While in 1800 the native peoples totaled 200,000 persons, in 1900, they numbered 800,000, two-thirds of whom were either Buryat or Yakut.

With the exception of a forty-two-year period of religious tolerance under Catherine the Great and Alexander I (1773–1815), the autocracy aspired to convert all of these people to the "one true faith," Russian Orthodoxy. Virtually all Siberian minorities, at one time or another, were exposed to missionaries. To many, among them the Ugrians, Buryats, and Yakuts, the effects of Orthodox baptism were evanescent or syncretic: These individuals were superficially Orthodox but internally shamanist. Other cultural differences also remained: For example, Buryats spoke Russian in the street but Buryat in the yurt.

Although they had been under Russian rule since the 1630s, Yakuts likewise were Christians "in name only." Yet, nursing the ambition of joining the Russian gentry—an aspiration that was unique among Siberian minorities—Yakuts preferred Russian names and patronymics to their native Turkic ones. As long as they delivered the tsar's fur tribute on time, they usually were left to their own devices. Through the turn of the century, the Russification effort was weak in Yakutia. In fact, the few Russian colonists who settled there commonly spoke Yakut, often to the extent that they forgot their native language. Despite their seeming liberty, however, the Yakuts were a conquered people. In 1906, the Yakut Union, a national front organization, challenged the Russians to return all the Yakut lands in their possession and exhorted them to appoint only Yakuts to local law-enforcement agencies. Tsarist authorities soon arrested the ringleaders, but the Yakut people perpetuated their revolutionary movement until 1923.[37]

Islam had come to Siberia and the Middle Volga region via Central Asia in the tenth century. After the Mongol invasion, Russians tended to call all Muslims Tatars.[38] The vanquished Siberian Tatars were Muslims, as were their admixture, the Caucasoid Volga Bulgars from Kazan' province. By 1900, almost 70,000 Tatars dwelled in Greater Siberia. Approximately 30,000 of them were Volga Tatars, the sons and daughters of exiles or voluntary migrants who had settled in the region since the 1600s. Because they were coreligionists, Tatars readily intermarried with their Siberian compatriots and the northern Kazakhs, who were known as "the Kyrgyz of the steppes." After 1755, the tsars actually condoned Islam among these peoples, even permitting the construction of mosques. The greatest concentration of practicing Muslims resided in small, strictly segregated villages in Tobol'sk province. Those who lived together with the Russians, however, were Russified, even to the point of losing their native tongue. Although most Tatars were destitute by 1900, the more successful worked as hired laborers, carters, craftsmen, and merchants specializing in grain and salt processing or leathercraft. Like the Jews, Tatars were chiefly townsfolk, residing not only in Tobol'sk, but also Tyumen', Tomsk, and Irkutsk provinces. Others lived in the Baraba Steppe, Transbaykalia, and in rural Yakutia.

Shamanism, the idea that natural spirits can possess human beings and that tribal holy men (shamans) can control them, was the foundation on which rested the beliefs of virtually all the tribes of Greater Siberia until the arrival of Orthodoxy. Buryats, both west and east of Lake Baykal, were shamanists until 1710, when they fell prey to Tibetan and Mongolian Buddhist missionaries of the Yellow Hat sect. The natural spirits of the shamans now became Lamaist protector deities. Lamaism enjoyed enormous popularity among Buryats, and until 1825, the crown tolerated it in order to curry favor with clan rulers, or *noyons*. Thus, Russian religious tolerance was more duplicitous than altruistic. In the 1760s, to discourage Buryat contacts with foreign undesirables in Mongolia and Tibet, Russian authorities condoned an autonomous Lamaist church in Buryatia. Tsarist officials gave some of the *noyons* gentry status, whereupon the clan leaders began to copy their corrupt Russian exemplars by greedily arrogating the best lands of their subjects. Occasionally, the duplicity went the other way, when particularly corrupt Buryat chiefs became Christians less to prove their loyalty to the tsars than to maintain their considerable wealth.

Unlike their brothers west of Lake Baykal, who took up sedentary farming under Russian influence in the early 1800s, the Buryats of Transbaykalia retained a purely pastoral economy through the 1920s. Before 1850, they remained nomads, rearing cattle, sheep, goats, and Bactrian camels, and driving or following their herds over vast distances. Under Russian influence, their nomadic ways became more systematic, and by 1900, the migrations occurred only twice yearly, from winter camps to summer camps and back again.

By the 1830s, Buddhism was practically universal throughout Buryatia. Although Russian authorities became increasingly intolerant of Buddhism, one in five Buryat males was a Buddhist lama. In midcentury, Murav'yev placed limits on the number of lamas and forbade the construction of new monasteries. Wholesale Russification was pursued during the reign of Alexander III, when monasteries were burned and Buddhists were caned by Russian police until they converted to Orthodoxy. After 1905, religious tolerance was reimposed, and the new converts became Buddhists again. By then, Buryat intellectuals were permitted to make regular pilgrimages to Mongolia, where they picked up the idea of creating a "Pan-Mongolian" state. By 1917, Buryat Buddhism was clearly international in orientation, and the intelligent Buryats were the only Siberian indigenes with their own written language.[39]

Despite his avowed aim of Russifying the Buryats, Kulomzin had to admit that they were a "likable and attractive" people, whose penchant for beauty and sobriety contrasted sharply with the crudity and drunkenness of his Russian compatriots. He openly wondered whether "Mongolian civilization would prove sturdier than Slavic."[40]

CHANGES IN THE INDIGENOUS PEOPLE ON THE EVE OF THE SOVIET PERIOD

During the expansionist period, tsars demanded that their henchmen do nothing more than guarantee the uninterrupted flow of revenue from Siberia to the core. The crown frequently denounced the exploitation of native peoples and the use of force against them. Though "far away," the autocrats desired to protect the indigenes. They tried to achieve this by authorizing laws to keep native peoples and Russians separate from each other, but the laws were unenforceable and abortive. In Siberia, the tsar's "Siberian satraps" often simply ignored such decrees, and Cossacks and military men continued to rape and pillage the autochthonous peoples.

By 1917, the lifestyles of almost all native Siberians, particularly those who were in constant contact with the *prishliye*, had undergone significant changes. Virtually all of them, except a share of the Siberian Tatars, had qualified as nomads before the advent of Yermak. In the early 1900s, those who had been nomadic were at least seminomadic, and those who had been seminomadic were sedentary. Previously nomadic peoples, such as the Khakass (who loathed the Russians), Buryats, and Yakuts, were quite sedentary for the reasons given above. The Russians living nearby used the indigenes as hired hands. They also adopted indigenes' styles of dress, learned their methods of survival, and incorporated many of their words in everyday Russian speech. In turn, the natives began to wear Russian clothing, to use Russian tools, and to speak the Russian language, albeit with mistakes and an accent.

Yet, large numbers of people still pursued traditional ways of life: nomadism or wandering, supplemented with fishing and hunting. Reindeer herding was (and still is) a major occupation for at least eighteen of the groups. The animal was raised for its highly nutritious meat, for draft, and for human transport. Eleven groups actually saddled and rode reindeer, the most famous being the Tungus (Evenks, Evens, and Negidals). The Turkic Tuvans and Tofalars, like the Evenks, also rode and packed their animals. Eight other groups—the Evens, Negidals, Oroks, reindeer Yakuts, Yukagirs, Chukchis, Koryaks, and Dolgans—not only rode and packed but also harnessed their reindeer to sleds of various shapes and sizes. The Uralic and Ket peoples used reindeer exclusively for drawing sleds.

Most of the same groups were also skilled with dogsleds. In Western Siberia, the Nentsy and the Ugrians (Khants and Mansi) were joined in this practice by the Old Russian settlers who lived in the vicinity of the Yamal, Gydan, and Taymyr peninsulas. In the Russian Far East, Old Russian settlers living in the Arctic and along the Sea of Okhotsk learned dogsledding from neighboring Itel'men, Koryaks, coastal Chukchi, and Eskimos. Sled dogs also were used among the Udegeys, Nivkhi, and Nanays in the Amur River Basin.

Still others raised horses for riding and draft purposes. The ordinarily hardy Yakut horse became famous during Robert Falcon Scott's ill-fated expedition to Antarctica, where all of the horses froze to death (as did Scott). In Sakha (Yakutia), however, the animal can remain unsheltered even during the dead of winter, scratching out meager pasturage beneath the shallow snow cover. Horses were husbanded and expertly ridden by the Transbaykalian Buryats, the northern Kazakhs, the Altays, the Old Settler Cossacks, and the Horse Tungus of the Amur Basin. Many early tourists traveling on the Trans-Siberian Railroad recalled being entertained by the innocent "raids" of mounted northern Kazakhs, whom they called "Kyrgyz."

Apart from draft animals, transportation was typical of subarctic peoples found elsewhere in the northern hemisphere. All the native groups skied or used snowshoes in winter. These varied in style among the indigenes, so that an experienced ethnographer could associate the artifact with the maker. Living along rivers, oceans, or seas, practically all of the Siberian natives made their own boats: kayaks among the Chukchi, the Eskimos, and the Itel'men; sailing craft among the Chukchi and the Evenks; and dugouts and canoes of all sizes and shapes among the others.

Native housing and clothing were simple, practical, and made from natural materials. Twelve groups, primarily the reindeer herders, used portable modified wigwams, the most notable of which were those of the Samoyeds, Ugrians, Turks, and Tungus. As Mongols, the Aga-Buryats lived in yurts until the 1950s, but the western and Transbaykalian Buryats increasingly built rectangular log cabins, usually with a sod roof. Earth houses, both sunken and semi-sunken, were favored among the Khants, the Sel'kups, the Kets, the Evenks, the Nanays, and the Nivkhi, whereas the Baraba Tatars and Dolgans preferred sodhouses. The dwellings took many shapes—A-frames, multiangular, circular, arched, and so forth— and groups typically had more than one characteristic style. Yakuts, for example, lived in adobe houses, square frame houses, wigwams, A-frames, log houses, and lean-tos.

At the time of the Revolution, typical native clothing was made of hides, furs, down, or even fishskin. In winter, the indigenes wore seamless, buttonless, wrapover fur coats of reindeer hide, often lined with squirrel or rabbit fur or the down of ducks, geese, or loons. No part of the hunter's or trapper's kill was discarded. The Amur River peoples, who made their living by fishing or hunting sea mammals, even wore cured fishskins as their outer garments.[41]

CONCLUSION

Like the American West, with its images of abundance, plains, deserts, cowboys, and hostile Indians, the name "Siberia" engenders a phantasmagoria of perceptions. As a resource-laden periphery, it began as a colony, but it soon became a vast prison for criminal and political castoffs of the core. Ironically, the exile system helped to create still another image of Siberia: a fount of hope and inspiration for freedom-loving doers and thinkers, who ranged from landlordless peasants to intellectual Decembrists. From here, it was a quick intellectual jump to the romantic idealization of Siberia as the wild, rugged, and beautiful East, filled with glorious legends of brave or fallen Russian heroes. Finally, on the heels of the Decembrists, the Siberian regionalists took the perception one step further, contending that Siberia, because of the distinctiveness of the land and its people, was a prime candidate for regional autonomy.

At almost every turn, the autonomy movements of the periphery were countervailed by the power of the core. Nevertheless, the Siberians of 1917 were different from those of 1717. Irrespective of their greater numbers, they reflected greater individuality. Having endured the throes of migration, the shackles of exile, the effects of miscegenation, and the Russification efforts, new and old Siberians defied, and sometimes even mocked, the conformity of European Russia. The native minorities struggled to maintain their traditions in the face of an avalanche of Slavic settlers, while within a generation after their arrival in the periphery, newcomers learned to appreciate their new lives in isolation from the core. By the time of the Revolution, the relationship between core and periphery had become an "us versus them" situation. Yet, few Siberians were true separatists; rather, they hoped to maintain, within a tolerant Russian motherland, the things that made them distinctive—their free, pioneering spirit, their hodgepodge ethnicity, their idiosyncratic behavior and speech, and their love of nature. To the extent that there was any democracy in the Russian Empire, it existed in Greater Siberia.

NOTES

1. Mark Bassin, "Inventing Siberia: Visions of the Russian East in the Early Nineteenth Century," *American Historical Review*, Vol. 96, No. 3 (June 1991), p. 792. The first part of this chapter is modeled on concepts and ideas previously explored by Professor Bassin. Accordingly, I am deeply indebted to him for his support and encouragement.

2. See Bassin's commentary in "Panel on Siberia: Economic and Territorial Issues," *Soviet Geography*, Vol. 32, No. 6 (June 1991), p. 366. Mercantilism encouraged the maintenance of trade surpluses and the hoarding of precious metals such as gold and silver.

3. James R. Gibson, *Feeding the Russian Fur Trade* (Madison: University of Wisconsin Press, 1969), p. 25. In the 1640s alone, the share was one-third (Bassin, "Inventing Siberia," p. 767).

4. Raymond H. Fisher, *The Russian Fur Trade* (Berkeley: University of California Press, 1943), p. 29.

5. Mark Bassin, "Expansion and Colonialism on the Eastern Frontier: Views of Siberia and the Far East in Pre-Petrine Russia," *Journal of Historical Geography*, Vol. 14, No. 1 (1988), p. 11.

6. "Demidovy," *Bol'shaya Sovetskaya entsiklopediya*, 1972, Vol. 8, p. 72. The Demidovs maintained their Urals possessions, albeit in greatly diminished form, until the early twentieth century.

7. Steven G. Marks, *The Road to Power: The Trans-Siberian Railroad and the Colonization of Asian Russia, 1850–1917* (Ithaca, N.Y.: Cornell University Press, 1991), p. 48.

8. The Demidovs, for instance, employed 38,000 male factory serfs at one time ("Demidovy," p. 72). Former serfs in Greater Siberia would become the Transbaykal Cossacks, and still later, the Amur and Ussuri Cossacks.

9. Robert Conquest, *Kolyma* (London: Macmillan, 1978), pp. 38–39. Gold in the Kolyma Basin appears to have been discovered by a fugitive convict named Boriska in 1910.

10. James Hughes, *Stalin, Siberia, and the New Economic Policy* (Cambridge: Cambridge University Press, 1991), pp. 19–20. The best coverage of the Siberian butter industry to date is L. M. Goryushkin, *Sibirskoye krest'yanstvo na rubezhe dvukh vekov* (Novosibirsk: Nauka, 1967).

11. Hughes, *Stalin, Siberia and the NEP*, p. 23.

12. Bassin, "Inventing Siberia," pp. 770 and 774.

13. George Kennan, *Siberia and the Exile System* (2d ed. abridged; Chicago: University of Chicago Press, 1958), p. 26; F. A. Kudryavtsev, ed., *Sibir' v epokhu kapitalizma*, Vol. 3 of *Istoriya Sibiri*, ed. A. P. Okladnikov (5 vols.; Leningrad: Nauka, 1968), p. 75; and Alan Wood, "Settlement and Unsettlement: Massive Criminal Exile to Siberia in Tsarist Russia" (paper presented at the conference on "The Development of Siberian Territories: Historical and Economic Aspects," Kemerovo, USSR, September 1991), p. 4. Elsewhere, Wood has colorfully noted that the habit of sending undesirables to Siberia began in 1582, almost seventy years before official tsarist sanction in 1649 (see "Sex and Violence in Siberia: Aspects of the Tsarist Exile System," in *Siberia: Two Historical Perspectives* [London: School of Slavonic and East European Studies, 1984], p. 23). The 1662 census revealed that exiles accounted for about 10 percent of the population (p. 25).

14. Glynn Barrat, *Voices in Exile: The Decembrist Memoirs* (Montreal and London: McGill-Queen's University Press, 1974), p. 2; and Michael T. Florinsky, *Russia: A History and Interpretation in Two Volumes*, Vol. 2 (New York: Macmillan, 1964), p. 751.

15. Anatole Mazour, *The First Russian Revolution, 1825* (Stanford: Stanford University Press, 1977), p. 222.

16. Bassin, "Inventing Siberia," p. 779; see also Mark Bassin, "Russia Between Europe and Asia: The Ideological Construction of Geographical Space," *Slavic Review*, Vol. 50, No. 1 (Spring 1991), pp. 9–13.

17. Bassin, "Inventing Siberia," pp. 784–787, 790–791. "Siberian historian" Slovtsov is considered "the first patriot of Siberia" (Valentin Rasputin, *Sibir', Sibir'* . . . [Moscow: Molodaya gvardiya, 1991], p. 53).

18. Marks, *The Road to Power*, p. 49. Siberian regionalism was primarily an intellectual movement. According to Pereira, who quotes Baron A. P. Budberg, dated November 10, 1930: "It is doubtful whether genuine Siberians ever heard much about the inflated 'Siberian separatism.' [However,] they hated the Metropolis [or Core] but did not go beyond the hating. All the higher-flown variations were produced in intellectual circles, infinitely remote from the real life of the people" (N.G.O. Pereira, "Regional Consciousness in Siberia Before and After October 1917," *Canadian Slavonic Papers*, Vol. 30, No. 1 [March 1988], pp. 128–129).

19. L. M. Goryushkin, "Late-Nineteenth- and Early-Twentieth-Century Siberian Regionalists' Views on the Economic Independence of Siberia," *Siberica*, Vol. 1, No. 2 (Winter 1990–1991), pp. 80–81; Anthony P. Allison, "Siberian Regionalism in Revolution and Civil War, 1917–1920," *Sibirica*, Vol. 1, No. 1 (Summer 1990), p. 79. The Bakunin reference is in John J. Stephan, "Far Eastern Conspiracies? Russian Separatism on the Pacific," *Australian Slavonic and East European Studies*, Vol. 4, Nos. 1–2 (1990), p. 137.

20. Goryushkin, "Late-Nineteenth- and Early-Twentieth-Century . . . ," pp. 155–157.

21. *Ibid.*, p. 160. Yadrintsev was a contemporary of Americans George Perkins Marsh and John Muir, who today are looked upon as founders of the preservationist movement.

22. *Ibid.*, pp. 161–162; and Pereira, "Regional Consciousness in Siberia," p. 112.

23. Alan Wood, ed., *Siberia: Problems and Prospects for Regional Development* (London: Croom Helm, 1987), p. 54.

24. Kudryavtsev, *Sibir' v epokhu*, p. 142. Between 1883 and 1886, one last revolutionary outburst took place among a group of regionalists, which established the fleeting, quasi-independent Zhetuginskiy Republic near the border with China (Paul Goble, in "Panel on Siberia," p. 369).

25. Allison, "Siberian Regionalism," p. 80; Marks, *Road to Power*, p. 52.

26. Stephan, "Far Eastern Conspiracies?" pp. 137–139.

27. *Ibid.*, p. 53. For thorough treatments of Siberian administrative-territorial history, see "Administrativnoye deleniye," *Sibirskaya Sovetskaya entsiklopediya*, 1929, Vol. 1, pp. 20–22; and Treadgold, *The Great Siberian Migration*, pp. 19–23, 263–265.

28. Marks, *Road to Power*, pp. 86–92.

29. Marks, "Conquering the Great East," p. 52.

30. Treadgold, *The Great Siberian Migration*, p. 239.

31. *Ibid.*, p. 241; and James Forsyth, *A History of the Peoples of Siberia* (Cambridge: Cambridge University Press, 1992), pp. 163, 198. Chekhov did not even recognize the settlers of the Amur Basin as Russians. In his words, he might just as well have been in "Patagonia or Texas" (quoted in Forsyth, *ibid.*, p. 198). For an explicit description of the female shortage, read Wood, "Sex and Violence," pp. 38–42.

32. Marks, "Conquering the Great East," p. 34; and Gail Fondahl, "Siberia: Native Peoples and Newcomers in Collision," in *Nations and Politics in the Soviet Successor States*, eds. Ian Bremmer and Ray Taras (London: Cambridge University Press, 1993), p. 483.

33. Forsyth, *A History of the Peoples of Siberia*, pp. 44 and 250; and Boris Ivanov, "Siberian Old Believers," *Soviet Life*, No. 6 (June 1991), pp. 14–19. After 1907, Old Believers were allowed to observe their holidays and to establish religious communities. They were severely persecuted under Stalin, and many were sent into forced labor. Others fled deeper into the Siberian taiga, or to the Americas. In the 1950s, they were permitted to return to their native villages.

34. John J. Stephan, *The Russian Far East: A History* (Stanford: Stanford University Press, 1994), pp. 67–68.

35. *Ibid.*

36. Forsyth, *A History of the Peoples of Siberia*, p. 196.

37. Nikolay Ushakov, "The Origins of the Yakuts," *Yakutia: Frozen Gem of the USSR*, 1978. Available on-line at <http://www.maximov.com/Russia/Sakha/yakutia_past.html#origins> (28 September 1997).

38. Richard V. Weekes, ed., *Muslim Peoples: A World Ethnographic Survey*, Vol. 1 (2 vols.; Westport, Conn.: Greenwood, 1984), p. 758.

39. Forsyth, *A History of the Peoples of Siberia*, pp. 150, 156, and 168–174; see also Fondahl, "Siberia: Native Peoples," pp. 477–510; and Caroline Humphrey, "Buryats," in *The Nationalities Question in the Soviet Union*, ed. Graham Smith (London: Longman, 1992), pp. 290–303.

40. Marks, "Conquering the Great East," p. 34.

41. This section is based primarily on material from M. G. Levin and L. P. Potapov, eds., *Istoriko-etnograficheskiy atlas Sibiri* (Moscow-Leningrad: Akademiya nauk SSSR, 1961), numerous pages; and Fondahl, "Siberia: Native Peoples," pp. 480–484. For information on the "Fishskin Tatars," see Forsyth, *A History of the Peoples of Siberia*, p. 210.

FIVE

Revolution, Civil War, and Stalinism in Greater Siberia

Siberians have a different spirit than do the European Russians. They very much prize their individuality and will fight hard to keep it.
—**Mark Sergey, Siberian poet**

We want Bolshevism, but not Communism.
—**Anonymous Siberians (early 1920s)**

REGIONALISTS AND REVOLUTIONARIES

After Yadrintsev's death in 1894, Potanin became the undisputed leader of Siberian regionalism. Twenty years later, in the last decade of his life (1910–1920), he was widely described as the "father of Siberia" and as an "otherworldly fellow" (*bozhiy chelovek*). But Potanin's shining hour came when he was already past seventy and the forces of Russian history were clearly at odds with the abilities of any individual—even one thought to possess special wisdom. In the words of Anthony Allison: "Before 1917, the debate between centralists and regionalists was carried out in newspapers, intellectual circles, and duma committees. During the Russian Revolution and Civil War, this debate became an outright political and military struggle for the control of Siberia. Thus, the final and most dramatic chapter in the history of Siberian regionalism began in the gathering chaos of early 1917."[1]

The events of 1917 were rooted in those of 1905. The Russo-Japanese War—to that time, the bloodiest in history—had unmasked Russia's inability to supply and defend its massive eastern flank. Although members of the royal family and the nationalist press demanded revenge, urban Russians showed indifference to the loss. The usually compliant rural folk, however, whom the revolutionaries had been wooing for more than

50 years, took advantage of the aristocracy's melancholy by burning the estates of absentee landowners. In Siberia, armed revolts occurred in Krasnoyarsk, Chita, Vladivostok, and other towns.

These events persuaded the Siberian regionalists to proclaim their support for a constitutional democracy and the observance of basic human rights at the national level, and the establishment of their own Siberian duma at the local level.[2] Their notions were openly confederative: The regional government would be strong and the national one would be weak. They envisioned their Siberian duma in control of the regional economy, the budget, education, social programs, property rights, and resource use. In mirror image to the Tenth Amendment to the U.S. Constitution, all powers not vested in the Siberian duma were to be reserved for the national government. These sentiments were reinforced by a declaration that the new Siberia would be a separate, self-governing community *within* Russia. Thus, in 1905, Siberian regionalists clearly desired a Russian dominion similar to that of Canada, in which the provinces (or regions) were politically powerful.

The confederation was stillborn: With the establishment of the All-Russian Duma in St. Petersburg and without a party of their own, the Siberian regionalists became loosely allied with Kerenskiy's Constitutional Democrats (Kadets). Like the Kadets, they were neither very numerous nor well organized, which was not the case with Siberia's Social Revolutionaries (SRs). The SRs, who far outnumbered the Bolsheviks in every province of Greater Siberia except Krasnoyarsk, dominated the countryside, the towns and cities, and the local economy. Unlike the Kadets, who tended to favor a unitary state, the SRs supported the concept of U.S.-style federalism for Russia. Although the majority of Siberian regionalists still favored a "looser lead," in the heady days of 1917, they shifted their loyalty to the SRs.

In May 1917, the Siberian regionalists organized a Provincial People's Assembly that met in Tomsk. The delegates unanimously approved a declaration stipulating the right to self-government, the creation of a Siberian duma, and the subordination of Siberia to Russian laws in affairs of state. They appointed an executive committee to organize a congressional assembly that would convene three months later. The delegates approved a white-and-green Siberian flag, representing the region's snows and forests. Finally, the executive committee selected the octogenarian G. N. Potanin to be its congressional leader.

The August "congress" met again in Tomsk and was so poorly attended that Potanin downgraded it to the status of "conference." A conference was what it was, serving mainly as a podium for the delivery of reports on the status of the Siberian economy. The most important outcome of the meeting was the proclamation to hold still another meeting in October.

With Lenin's Bolshevik Revolution less than one week away, the First Siberian Regional Congress attracted twice as many delegates from all over Greater Siberia, including the representatives of ethnic minorities. More than half of the 87 delegates were SRs and SR sympathizers, 25 were Social Democrats (SDs), 3 were Kadets, and 20 were nonpartisans. Factionalism destroyed the congress, the specific duty of which was to set up the framework and standing committees of the regional government. The SDs walked out because the cadre of congressional delegates was "too bourgeois" for them. The trio of Kadets also departed, because the congress was "too leftist" for them. The remaining delegation was so unruly that by the time the congress adjourned, only 25 loyal SRs and regionalists remained.

When the Bolshevik Revolution did occur, the Siberian regionalists were divided into two camps: one headed by Potanin, who believed that the regional government should recognize the suffrage of *all* social classes, and another led by Odessa-born SR Peter Derber, who wanted suffrage to comprise socialists only. With the Bolsheviks in power in St. Petersburg, Potanin's Tomsk-based executive committee called for the convocation of the long-awaited Siberian Regional Duma in January 1918. In reaction, the more numerous SR regionalists, supporting Derber's notions, forced the resignation of Potanin, who accused them of exclusivism.[3]

The Siberian duma never met in full session. In late January 1918, as duma members tried to convene their legislature in Tomsk, the Bolsheviks arrested 60 of the 100 would-be representatives. The 40 who escaped formed a new executive committee, swearing allegiance to the "Provisional Government of Autonomous Siberia" and to Derber as head of state.[4] Shortly afterward, Derber and a motley crew of 20 loyalists fled to Harbin, where he was "inaugurated" in a railway car supplied by General D. L. Horvath, the General Manager of the Chinese Eastern Railway (CER), who also aspired to Siberian leadership.

SIBERIA IN THE CIVIL WAR

By February 1918, the Bolsheviks were present in almost every Siberian province. This did not mean, however, that they had a broad base of support in the region. Lenin-sanctioned land seizures were not a high priority for the comparatively prosperous, landlordless Siberian peasant.[5] Although Siberians would later react violently to Bolshevik leveling and forced requisition policies, they were initially apathetic to the takeover. Lenin's party was not yet strong enough to matter in the region.

The treaty of Brest-Litovsk, which brought an end to Russia's involvement in World War I on March 3, 1918, inspired three, possibly four, anti-

Bolshevik governments in Siberia: those of Derber, Horvath, a cruel and unruly Cossack named Grigoriy Semenov, and—waiting in the wings— Admiral Alexander Kolchak. The half-Buryat Semenov ruled Irkutsk and Chita provinces as quasi-chieftain of a band of bloodthirsty Cossacks, Mongols, and Serbian prisoners-of-war until 1920. The issue at stake was which of the anti-Bolshevik groups could survive? Should it consist of Derber's SRs? Horvath's conservative monarchists? Or Semenov's cruel opportunists? After the example set by Kerenskiy's Provisional Government, a coalition was out of the question. The leadership quandary was further complicated by the presence of erstwhile tsarist and Provisional Government officials, together with mercenary allied elements from Japan, Britain, and France. Moreover, in early spring 1918, another ingredient was injected into the brew: Admiral Kolchak.[6] The son of an army officer, Kolchak (1873–1920) was in his own right a highly respected career naval officer. In the service of the Russian Provisional Government, he was on his way back from a mission to the United States via Japan when the Bolsheviks took power.

During the Bolshevik Revolution, the infamous Czech Legion was still operating in Ukraine. The Czechs declared themselves neutral, their enemies being the Axis powers, not the Bolsheviks. After Brest-Litovsk, two divisions of the "autonomous Czechoslovak army" found themselves awkwardly positioned in a country that had made peace with their sworn enemies. To be reunited with the Allied powers, they would have to cross Siberia on the Trans-Siberian Railroad, for which they obtained the reluctant permission of the Bolsheviks. Along the way, they experienced an untoward incident in Chelyabinsk, which provoked the Bolsheviks to arrest some of their compatriots. The Czechs rose in revolt, seized the local arsenal, and freed the prisoners. By May, the Czech Legion "owned" the Trans-Siberian Railroad between Penza and Irkutsk. Omsk, Tomsk, and virtually every city and town between the Volga and Vladivostok fell into anti-Bolshevik hands.

Regionalism: The Last Gasp

Two very different trends in government emerged in the Siberia of 1918: The Regional Duma, based in Tomsk, was composed of leftists and SRs; the Siberian Provisional Government, based in Omsk, was more moderate and essentially nonpartisan. Paralleling the two governmental groups, two different types of regionalism began to evolve: one increasingly associated with the ambitions of the national SR Party, and one favoring Siberian autonomy for anti-Bolshevik purposes.

Such a divided house could not stand for long. A magnet for White Russians, in its first official act, the Omsk government declared itself independent of Russia. The Tomsk government, meanwhile, focused on the selection of delegates to Chelyabinsk for a series of negotiations over the creation of a united anti-Bolshevik government that would stretch from the Volga to the Pacific. As always, the duma was conspicuous for the prolixity of its speeches and bitter disputes among the SRs and moderates. The hullabaloo alienated Siberians, especially the Omsk government. The governments became further divided over the incipient war with the Bolsheviks. Conservative Whites strongly supported the Omsk government and made Kolchak their minister of war. The Regional Duma, one of the representatives of which was Derber, could rely only on the now much-dispersed members of the Czech Legion, who had no wish to become mired in a Russian civil war.

It appeared that Siberia's house soon would come crashing down, when in September 1918, a coalition government, called the Directory, was formed in the Urals city of Ufa. Under its aegis, the Siberian Provisional Government and the Regional Duma were dissolved, and the Directory was relocated in Omsk. A bastion of conservative jingoism, the Directory itself had been proposed as a temporary institution, pending the convocation of a Constituent Assembly. Its membership clamored for a strong military dictatorship to fight the rapidly approaching Red Army. The Directory had little domestic support, and none at all from the Allies—especially the British, who strongly sanctioned Kolchak. On November 18, 1918, a military coup occurred in Omsk, the Directory was overthrown, and Admiral Kolchak was declared "Supreme Ruler of All the Russias."[7]

Intervention and the Far Eastern Republic

The zenith of Kolchak's career came in summer 1919, when the Allies recognized him as de facto ruler of Russia. The other White Army generals, including Semenov and Horvath, who was now "High Plenipotentiary" in the Russian Far East, officially accepted his authority. His ragtag army had been surprisingly successful, having taken Ufa and Perm' in the Urals and being poised to retake Samara on the Volga River. Lenin was so concerned about this course of events that he seriously contemplated an immediate armistice and the recognition of an independent Siberia.[8]

The éclat was fleeting, however. Between summer and fall, as a result of peasant revolts, broken supply lines, bad equipment, incompetent officers, and betrayals by the Allies, Kolchak's army began to retreat and to disintegrate. The climax came when the peripatetic Czechs renounced all further Siberian action and demanded immediate evacuation. Shortly afterward, Kolchak abrogated his lofty title and left Siberia in the charge of Semenov. As he fled eastward on the Trans-Siberian, Kolchak was stopped by the pariah Czechs and turned over to the Red Guard. Before dawn on February 7, 1920, he was shot by a Bolshevik firing squad outside Irkutsk.

The chaos and treachery associated with the intervention of representatives of fourteen other countries sealed Kolchak's fate. Under the guise of protecting the Czech Legion, the Japanese sent in a contingent of 80,000 troops to gain exclusive control not only of Eastern Siberia but also of northern Manchuria. Originally, the destiny of the 50,000 Czechs—15,000 of whom eventually fled Siberia through Vladivostok—was the primary reason for the presence of all the interventionists. Britain and France had deployed 30,000 to 40,000 troops in Russia, mostly in the European part. Those in Greater Siberia were supposed to aid and advise Kolchak. The United States had dispatched an expeditionary force of more than 10,000 to protect the Trans-Siberian Railroad between Lake Baykal and Vladivostok. Nine other countries also sent token contingents that spent the bulk of their tour milling around in the vodka and flesh parlors of Vladivostok and Harbin: Vladivostok was a major arsenal, and the Allies did not want it to fall into German or Bolshevik hands. Harbin, a strategic railway locomotive depot and the headquarters of the CER, was also home to a growing population of 35,000 Russian expatriates.[9] However, by summer 1920, only the Japanese remained to face the Bolsheviks in Greater Siberia. Neither side wanted a confrontation. Poland was menacing Lenin in the west, and the last thing he wanted was a second front. The Tokyo government became divided on the issue of continued occupation of the Russian Far East.

The notion of a buffer state between Japan and Russia, which arose around this time, may have originated with a Siberian Bolshevik named A. M. Krasnoshchekov. Of Ukrainian Jewish heritage, Krasnoshchekov was a veteran revolutionary who had served with Trotsky and Martov and had spent sixteen years in North America, working with the labor movement (1901–1917). In the United States, he befriended among others Emma Goldman, "Big Bill" Haywood, and Vladimir ("Bill") Shatov.[10]

Upon his return to Russia in 1917, Krasnoshchekov spent the next two years serving alternately in different temporary governments, in hiding, and in jail. In the city of Ulan-Ude, on April 6, 1920, he organized a constituent assembly, comprising the likes of Shatov, who also had returned to his native Russia. Krasnoshchekov declared himself both prime minister and foreign minister of the Far Eastern Republic (FER). With Trotsky's and Lenin's blessings, the Bolshevik government officially recognized "the halfway house between Bolshevism and the bourgeois world" on May 14.

The Japanese were less than enchanted with the new government. The FER consisted of modern Buryatia, Chita province, Amuria, southernmost Khabarovsk kray, Primor'ye, and Sakhalin—a region three times larger than France. It had a population of two million people, comprising more than one million Russians, 500,000 Ukrainians in Amuria and Primor'ye, 60,000 Koreans, and the Japanese expeditionary force, which remained on the mainland until October 1922 as a result of hostilities in Nikolayevsk. Because of the bloody "Nikolayevsk Incident," in which hundreds of Japanese were killed, Japanese troops in Karafuto (southern Sakhalin) were ordered to occupy Russian (northern) Sakhalin, where they stayed until 1925.[11]

The buffer republic was needed only as long as Japanese soldiers were on mainland soil. On October 25, 1922, as the last of the Japanese interventionists boarded ships bound for Yokohama at one end of Vladivostok, several units of the People's Revolutionary Army and Primorskiy partisans marched into the city at the other end. Three weeks later, on November 15, the whilom republic was eradicated and assimilated into the RSFSR.

Despite its brief duration, the FER did set a "symbolic" precedent. It had a mixed economy and a superficially democratic political framework. It was autonomous: Day-to-day decisions were made locally.[12] This was ironic, because the republican leaders were Bolsheviks or members of the Peasant Majority Party. In 1920, spokesmen for the leadership assured outsiders that the FER would never embrace communism because all but a few of its people were private landowners who opposed the fundamental tenets of Marxism-Leninism. They were heard to say, "We want Bolshevism, but not communism. It may be all right for *Russia* but we don't want it here." Within a decade, however, communism is exactly what the Siberian farmers would be forced to accept.[13]

THE NEP AND GREATER SIBERIA

In the wake of the annulment of the FER, the Bolsheviks tried to erase all traces of regionalism from Greater Siberia. While Lenin was still alive, in 1923–1924, his henchmen held show trials of Siberian autonomists in Chita, the erstwhile capital of the FER. These and other actions dismayed the majority of Siberian peasants, many of whom previously had admired the Bolsheviks.

Mercifully, Potanin died in 1920, before such indignities could be foisted upon him.[14] His legacy outlived him, however, in the form of the individualism and self-reliance of Siberian peasants. In contrast, resigned submissiveness was the cachet of their relatives in European Russia. With the insulation of distance and poor communications between them and the core, Russian Siberians, like the English migrants to North America, quickly shed their European roots and developed a quasi-bourgeois ethos.

But even self-reliant individualists needed leaders, and civil war and intervention had taken their toll on such persons. Kolchak's White Army had executed half of the leading Bolsheviks. In January 1921, an uprising of up to 60,000 peasants in Western Siberia, including the cities of To-bol'sk and the "Siberian Kronstadt," Krasnoyarsk, also decimated communist ranks. When after three months the smoke finally cleared, more than 5,000 Siberian Bolsheviks and provincial leaders lay dead.[15]

Between 1920 and 1922, Greater Siberia was not immune from the chaos that ill-advised, compulsory requisitioning of produce wreaked in Russia. Quite the contrary, because average Siberian settlers had "more than tripled" their worth in a single decade and were clearly better off than their cousins in European Russia, they had to endure the brunt of the forced procurement of grain. According to James Hughes, between 1920 and 1922, the Bolsheviks procured at least one-fourth of their grain in Western Siberia alone, which had a mere 6 percent of Russia's popula-tion.[16] Despite the ostensible necessity of such actions—rural famine in European Russia and widespread starvation in the cities—they placed a terrible burden on Siberian peasants and provided yet another example of central Russia's resented colonial policy. Moreover, in the aftermath of forced procurement, Siberians suffered their own famine in 1922 and 1923, which caused a temporary *westward* migration.

Ironically, the Siberian famine corresponded with the first year of Lenin's New Economic Policy (NEP), 1922, during which capitalism was permitted to return to the countryside to stimulate more food for the cities. During the NEP, the Central Committee appointed experienced Bolsheviks of non-Siberian origin to carry out the policies of the core in its trans-Uralian periphery.

The NEP was slow to take root in Siberia. Between 1921 and 1925, the peasants in the region practiced subsistence farming. Authorities accused them of hoarding grain, but the farmers were merely responding to mar-ket indicators. Grain prices remained low, and purchasable manufactures were so scant that richer peasants (whom the Bolsheviks dubbed *kulak*s) chose to feed their surplus grain to their livestock instead of selling the produce at or below cost. The long-standing distrust that Siberian peas-ants had for authority also nurtured their antipathy toward the NEP. This was not helped by the Bolsheviks' callous disregard for the needs of Siberians. Thus, as Communist Party (CPSU) membership tripled in Rus-sia as a whole between 1924 and 1928, it merely doubled in Greater Sibe-ria.[17] Siberian Communists were young, rural, poorly educated males, who were easily bribed by the kulaks.

Greater Siberian kulaks were indomitable in spirit and action. In the 1925 election campaign, they stubbornly resisted the Bolsheviks by fo-menting unrest among their poorer peers, and called for "soviets [local councils] without communists." They controlled turnout and even rigged several of the elections in their favor: In the Altay, they won 10 percent of seats in the local councils.[18] The Party's only recourse was to disenfranchise the kulaks. This it did in the 1927 elections, which amounted to a Communist Party sweep.

The NEP's purpose was to increase the marketing of "dry gold" (see Chapter 4), which in 1925 was both the staple food and the main earner of hard currency for industrialization. In the mid-1920s, the Bolshevik boss of Siberian kray (Sibkray)[19] was an ultra-NEPist Ukrainian named S. I. Syrtsov. Syrtsov believed that grain acquisitions could be increased by lowering taxes, hiring surplus farm labor, liberally leasing land, and raising procurement prices. At the time, Sibkray's economic base was 81 percent agricultural and 19 percent industrial, one-third of the latter being food processing. Syrtsov urged the inchoate manufacturing base to increase its output of farm machinery, half of which was then imported from European Russia. A Bukharinite supporter of Stalin, Syrtsov was convinced that Siberian industry should serve the purposes of Siberian agriculture. At the NEP's peak, he exhorted the Siberian peasantry to "accumulate" and get rich, concepts much admired by Siberians but disdained by future leader Joseph Stalin.

In 1926, the NEP finally gained success in Siberia, and grain flooded the USSR. Sibkray's collections were 54 percent greater than those of 1925. Procurements were aided by the fact that the weather was good, the dirt roads were dry, taxes were low, and the grain that had been stored the year before was finally marketed.

The happy coincidences of 1926 would not be duplicated in 1927. By January 1928, Soviet grain collections were only 71 percent of the previous January. In Siberia, they were down by half. Because procurements were lower, hard-currency-earning grain exports also were deficient. Everyone and everything was to blame, but Stalin was convinced that the kulaks were the most guilty. Despite evidence to the contrary, he was adamant that the richer peasants had orchestrated a mass conspiracy against Moscow's central authority—and Sibkray had the richest and most defiant peasants of all. Between 1925 and 1927, Siberia's kulaks became ever more politically hostile to the Soviet regime. Although Sibkray accounted for only 5.9 percent of the population, in that three-year span, it contributed 29 percent of all terrorist acts against Party and local council officials, including murder, assault, arson, and other crimes. Making matters worse, rumors flew that the Chinese, with whom the Bolsheviks were on poor terms, had taken the Kuznetsk Basin. Conventional peasant logic posits that in times of instability (war, famine, political crisis, and so on), it is wise to hoard as much of your grain as possible.

Although they indicted the richer peasantry for inciting the unrest that stimulated the hoarding, Sibkray authorities, including Syrtsov, did not contemplate "liquidation of the kulaks." This was true, even though throughout 1927 a continuous stream of orders from Moscow adjured them to "get tough" with the accused offenders. Few of them took the ukases seriously, because Stalin still had rivals in Moscow, and he had not yet revealed his truly nefarious side. Moreover, there were few indications that the NEP, which had been so successful, was about to be reversed.

The End of the NEP: Stalin Visits Sibkray

On January 6, 1928, Stalin ordered the provincial governments to exercise "all means" necessary to procure grain surpluses believed to be in rural areas. Local authorities would be held personally responsible for the success or failure of the mission. With their jobs and ultimately their lives on the line, most officials used excessive force to comply with the order. Nine days after the edict, during the time that members of the Left Opposition (Radek, Trotsky, and others) were being forced into exile, Stalin decided to go on a fortnight's tour of Siberia. It would be the first and last time that he would ever visit a peasant village.[20]

What Stalin saw stunned him. First, although Syrtsov was a loyal servant and protégé, not all Siberian NEPmen were so dedicated. The leader, after all, had not yet turned against the Bukharinite Right Opposition and was still in the process of consolidating his power. Having not yet learned to fear Stalin, many NEP supporters displayed open hostility to the new procurement policies and voiced these opinions. Stalin interpreted this as insubordination, and this added fuel to the fires of his later purge of Siberian Party members. Second, Stalin was enraged by the sight of what he claimed were huge piles of marketable grain in open-air shelters on kulak farms. When his Siberian hosts informed him that kulaks would sell their surpluses when and if the regime raised the procurement price, Stalin characterized such behavior by the kulaks as "unbridled speculation." (Later, Stalin would recall local leaders' questioning of his orders as a sign that they supported the kulaks.) To Stalin, the kulak was the bogeyman, and since the NEP had strengthened the kulaks, the leader continuously and blatantly informed his Siberian hosts that the policy had run its course.

Syrtsov and the other Siberian Bukharinites were horrified. This was a new Stalin, a Stalin whose decisions crystallized because of what he saw in Sibkray in January 1928. He would end the NEP, resort to mass collectivization, and liquidate the kulak. Thereafter, Sibkray and the Soviet Far East (SFE) would suffer the gravest of indignities.

The Wake. Stalin apparently never forgot what he saw in Sibkray. He concluded his sojourn "with shouts of opposition to his instructions from local officials and peasants" ringing in his ears. To him, Siberians, especially the Siberian Party, were "degenerates": The kulaks had corrupted all of them. Shortly after his Siberian tour, Stalin purged one out of every four rural Siberian members of the CPSU for alleged collaboration with the kulaks. By February 1929, the purge had ruined the careers of more than half the members and candidates of Sibkray's central committee.[21]

Syrtsov himself was granted a temporary reprieve; but in late 1930, he criticized the government's handling of collectivization and industrialization and spoke of limiting Stalin's authoritarian powers. On December 1, 1930, after fewer than two years in Moscow, he was expelled from both the Politburo and the Central Committee. According to Robert Conquest, Syrtsov died in prison in 1938. As early as 1962, Khrushchev restored him to favor within the Party. In 1988, Gorbachev rejuvenated Bukharin to "good odor," an action that no doubt enhanced the images of Syrtsov and many other NEPists.[22]

The Special Case of the Soviet Far East. Reliable control of the SFE evaded the grasp of the central Party apparatus until the 1930s. Stalin never had any intentions of giving the region autonomy. Because he had to fight opponents on the Party's right and on the left, however, he had to ignore the question of the SFE for the time being. This was evidenced by the lack of enforcement of central policy decisions in the region: For example, the NEP did not end in the SFE until 1931.[23] Moreover, between 1922 and 1938, it seemed that the core had little idea about what to do with its "periphery on the periphery," changing its designation no fewer than three times (to guberniya, oblast, and kray). Accordingly, until 1938, the SFE was the fief of a small cohort of Party activists and military officers, several of whom had become self-reliant, free thinkers as a result of their common experiences in the civil war, the intervention, the FER, and so on.

Under these individuals, the SFE enjoyed almost total economic independence. All manner of entrepreneurial activity was permitted. Chinese merchants controlled retailing in Vladivostok; the British and Americans developed the regional resource base; and the Japanese held mastery over the fisheries. As a maritime region with outlets to the Pacific Basin, the hinterland of the SFE was the whole of the developed world.[24]

The SFE of the 1920s and 1930s was truly the "Wild East." First, as a consequence of the local administration's live-and-let-live philosophy, the region attracted an indiscriminate assortment of political dissidents, outlaws, and Stalin's bureaucratic rejects. Second, while political purges raged west of Lake Baykal, until 1937, the turnover of personnel in the SFE was virtually nil. Third, until then, the fiefs usually made unilateral decisions that were often at odds with the policies of Moscow: They not only exempted far eastern peasants from the draft in 1929 but also delayed collectivization until the 1930s. Fourth, they could carry out these renegade acts because the Special Far Eastern Army ranked among the best trained and equipped fighting forces in the USSR.[25]

GREATER SIBERIA UNDER STALIN

Given Stalin's disaffinity for what he saw in Sibkray in 1928, it is not surprising that Siberians suffered during the quarter century of his rule. He used a three-pronged strategy. First, more than ever before, Greater Siberia became a "resource colony." Second, the region became a "net" that was far "deeper" than ever before: a terrible, macabre place where exiles languished, putrefied, and experienced painful, anonymous deaths. Third, Stalin further dismembered Siberia's past half-dozen provinces into more than twenty political-administrative units.

Industrialization

Stalin's principal economic goal was to convert the USSR from an agrarian economy to an industrial one as quickly as possible. Toward that end he instituted a series of five-year plans (FYP), in which underdeveloped Greater Siberia would play a key role. The primary target of the first FYP, for example, was a second metallurgical combine that would provide backup for the fifty-year-old Donbas in eastern Ukraine. The Urals-Kuznetsk Combine (UKK), stripped of its details, involved the construction of two integrated iron-and-steel centers: one at Magnitogorsk, in the Urals, and another at Stalinsk (Novokuznetsk after 1961), in the Kuzbas. Each mill was dependent on a costly, 2,250-kilometer (1,400-mi) exchange of Urals iron ore and Kuzbas coking coal. The Stalinsk plant alone consumed 44 percent of Western Siberian industrial investment in the first FYP and 25 percent of the same in the second.[26] Surviving in tents, exiled kulaks and idealistic Soviet and foreign volunteers built the two steel mills in just over three years. By 1938, they were the country's leading iron and steel producers, yielding a cumulative output of 20 percent of all Soviet steel.

Metallurgy spawned related industrial activities. Relying on coking coal for fuel, the steel mills ignited an explosion of Siberian coal production, which jumped 270 percent between 1928 and 1932, and another 250 percent during the next lustrum. The Kuzbas became the second leading coal producer after the Donbas, as its coking coal output rose from 10 percent to 26 percent of local output by 1940. Coking coal also served as raw material for Kemerovo's coke-chemical industry, which with the help of shock teams from the United States, yielded sulfuric acid, fertilizers, dyes, and plastics. New coal-fired electrical power plants in Greater Siberia lifted electrical production more than 1,000 percent between 1928 and 1937.

Although these novelties expanded the influence of Greater Siberia's manufacturing sector, the region continued to be a resource frontier. Raw material development focused on valuable metals (gold, tin, tungsten, and molybdenum) and nonmetals (mica and fluorspar), which were not found in Soviet Europe.[27] Accordingly, the core, not the periphery, demanded these minerals. By 1940, Greater Siberia was contributing the lion's share of the USSR's gold, 95 percent of its tin, 80 percent of its tungsten, 70 percent of its molybdenum, and almost all of its fluorspar and mica.

As an enterprise, the UKK was the biggest single prewar investment in Greater Siberia; but as a region, the SFE attracted the greatest share of money. Enthusiastic Young Communists (*Komsomol'tsy*) built a new industrial center on the Amur, aptly named Komsomol'sk, which had, among other factories, an unintegrated steel mill. Both Komsomol'sk and the upstream city of Khabarovsk acquired refineries, in which they processed crude oil piped in from northern Sakhalin. (Until the 1970s, the refineries and the steel mill satisfied 25 percent of the SFE's consumption of both steel and petroleum.) Defense-related industries, such as aircraft assembly and shipbuilding, were also developed in the prewar period.

Through the present day, Greater Siberia has lagged in machine building and metalwork. At the end of the second FYP, as a share of the region's gross industrial product, machine building and metalwork amounted to only 17 percent, compared to a 30 percent average for the USSR as a whole.[28] Machine tools, a crucial indicator of metal fabrication, was only 2 percent of the SFE's industrial product at the time.

This was not true of other industries. Stimulated by the need for new construction, cement output alone expanded elevenfold, to 8.8 percent of the Soviet total. Railways, too, experienced a miniboom because of the completion of interregional lines, such as the Turksib between Barnaul and Tashkent. The Turksib carried roundwood to treeless Central Asia in exchange for cotton. The original "Little BAM" railway was laid perpendicular to the Trans-Siberian between the Amur River and the little town of Tyndinskiy (Tynda), pointing toward its projected destination, Yakutsk. Finally, a short feeder was built between the Yenisey River port of Dudinka and the new town of Noril'sk (see Chapter 2). The need for building materials and railway ties spurred logging and wood processing, which even today are important Siberian industries.

The authors of the third FYP (1938–1942) acknowledged the growing militarism of Japan in the east and of Germany in the west: They recognized the weakness of their position in the Far East and the vulnerability of key industries in Soviet Europe. Between 1938 and 1941, when the German invasion truncated the third FYP, the share of investment in the SFE equaled the total investment in Eastern and Western Siberia combined.

PHOTO 5.1 *Novosibirsk Railway Station, on the Trans-Siberian Railroad.* SOURCE: *ITAR-TASS.*

Between 1937 and 1940, the SFE doubled its industrial output, while Eastern and Western Siberia witnessed gains of 30 and 50 percent, respectively. As a result of the efforts of the slave labor force (see below), the SFE became the USSR's leader in gold production, a position it would hold until 1991. The goal was to ensure that the SFE was strong enough to withstand a Japanese assault; the purpose was obviated in 1941, when Japan and the USSR cosigned a neutrality pact, which remained in effect until August 1945.

In the west, the goal was to disperse Soviet industry deeper into the interior, including Siberia. This was a timely decision. Nazi troops ultimately occupied one-fourth of Soviet Europe, comprising 45 percent of the USSR's prewar population and one-third of its total industrial capacity. The eastward evacuation of whole factories and their employees, which had begun in 1938, only accelerated with the outbreak of hostilities. Between July and November 1941, more than 1,500 factories were moved to the Urals, Turkestan, and Siberia: 244 to Western Siberia and 78 to Eastern Siberia.[29] The dismantlements occurred often at a moment's notice, just ahead of the advancing Germans. In Siberia, the primary recipients of the enterprises, Omsk and Novosibirsk, became boomtowns (Photo 5.1).

Although the UKK was a white elephant in the 1930s, it paid off during the war. With the Donbas occupied, the Kuzbas became the leading coal producer, including almost half of the metallurgical variety. With Soviet Europe's steel mills in enemy hands, the Kuznetsk steel mill churned out one-third of the country's pig iron and one-fourth of its steel. The region also produced aluminum and ferroalloys from plants that had once been in Russia and Ukraine. As a recipient of the Monchegorsk nickel smelter during the war, Noril'sk eventually would become world-famous for its production of that strategic metal. The manufacture of agricultural machinery also shifted eastward, the principal beneficiaries being Rubtsovsk in Altay kray and Krasnoyarsk. Until 1991, the former produced one-third of the USSR's tractor-drawn plows, and the latter, one-fourth of the grain harvesters. During the war, they produced military equipment.

Not all the evacuation occurred from west to east. In 1942, during the height of Nazi occupation, the existing Little BAM railway was pulled up, evacuated westward, and relaid between Saratov and the besieged city of Stalingrad (Volgograd).

The war's influence on Soviet industrial patterns was dramatic. Compared to 1940, Soviet Europe's industrial product fell by at least 25 percent (80 percent in Belarus). In contrast, Western Siberia's industrial production tripled, just as it doubled in the rest of Siberia.[30] Growth of the machine-building and metalwork sector was especially dramatic, expanding elevenfold between 1940 and 1943, with the output of defense plants soaring by a factor of 34. By 1945, one of every four warplanes was assembled in Western Siberia.

The glory was short-lived, however. Between 1946 and 1950, for example, Siberia's share of Soviet capital investment reached a nadir of 9.6 percent. Helping to precipitate the decline was the exigency of rebuilding Soviet Europe. Some of the wartime industries and their attendant labor forces returned to their original locations after the war; consequently, the boomtowns of Omsk and Novosibirsk witnessed a decline of four to five percent of their industrial output by 1950. Only the nonferrous metals and forest products sectors experienced growth rates that exceeded the national average.

The Gulag

Despite the slowdown in the wake of the war, the industrialization of Greater Siberia was an unbridled success. All over the region, men and women responded to the challenges of "socialist competition." Numerous small-scale enterprises aspired to mimic larger vanguard industries. Grassroots heroes like Donbas coal miner Aleksey Stakhanov sprang from nowhere to everlasting fame. Soon Siberian "Stakhanovites" routinely broke production records by 400, 500, and sometimes 1,000 percent. The Stalinist press praised tyro blue-collar icons in much the same way as modern media treat sports heroes.

Many of the heroes, however, were unsung and are essentially lost to history. Under Stalin, Greater Siberia's reputation as the world's largest outdoor prison camp and execution chamber reached its pinnacle. No one knows their precise number, of course, but Alexander Solzhenitsyn inventoried approximately 225 camp regions, of which 120 were Siberian—50 in Western Siberia and 70 farther east.[31] Each region may have contained dozens of full-scale operations. At its peak in the 1940s, the Kolyma Basin in Magadan oblast, for example, comprised 120 forced labor camps.[32] The massive camp system, which Solzhenitsyn dubbed the Gulag archipelago, "housed" an estimated 40 million persons at one time or another. Greater Siberian locations hosted 17 million, including 4 to 6 million in the Kolyma camps alone.[33] Given Kolyma's peak capacity of 500,000, the Gulag might well have held a total population of between 3 and 4 million at any given moment.

The prisoners worked as builders, farmers, fishermen, loggers, track-layers, tunnelers, and miners. As in tsarist times, they were criminals and politicals from every corner of the realm. Accused of consorting with the Nazis during the war, entire nations were deported to Asiatic Russia. They comprised Crimean Tatars, Volga Germans, Chechens, Ingush, Karachays, Moldovans, Jews, and many other groups. During the war, POWs from Germany, Poland, Hungary, Italy, Romania, and Japan replenished the millions of domestic exiles who died in the camps.

And die they did, like the flies that fertilized the suppurating boils on their skin. Elizabeth Pond wrote that only one in fifty, or possibly one in a hundred, survived in Kolyma. From 1937 until Stalin's death, the main aim of the camps was less to mine gold "than to kill off prisoners." To end an inmate's life, it usually took only 20 to 30 days, working 12 to 16 hours a day on starvation rations. At Elgen, which in Sakha (Yakut) means "dead," the typical harvest of such intensive labor was a single kilogram of gold per prison laborer. Elgen was just one of 80 gold mines in the Kolyma system. The average number of miners at peak capacity was 5,000, although the number varied between 2,000 and 10,000 per mine. They dug for gold in the open air with only the most primitive of tools, and more often than not, with their bare hands. After twenty years of operation, Kolyma's death toll was 2–3 million.

Many died on the way to the camps.[34] Prisoners were forced to stand silently, inadequately clothed in poorly ventilated boxcars or open gondolas. If they were bound for Vladivostok, they suffered this way for 20 days or more. With 80 prisoners per car, it was almost impossible to reach the two-inch holes that served as latrines. Their diet, when food was available, consisted of salted cabbage soup or herring and soggy black bread—a combination that left them with gum disease, skin lesions, and conjunctivitis. In Vladivostok, the future inmates of Kolyma were herded on board prison ships, including the U.S.-built *Dallas* and *Puget Sound*. At sea, guards gleefully threw prisoners to the sharks. They boiled a few alive. Other prisoners were hosed with seawater and allowed to freeze. In Kolyma, the rags they wore were often stolen, encouraging omnipresent frostbite. The food was so bad in the camps that many resorted to eating vehicular grease and moss.

Although it ranks among the most environmentally harsh regions on earth, Kolyma is hardly unhealthy to people who are well fed and decently clothed. Between 1932 and 1937, an unconventionally humane camp commander, E. P. Berzin, recognized these basic truths and chose not to overwork the inmates. Instead they were well paid, permitted to send money to their families, and given shorter terms for good work and behavior. But a week before Christmas 1937, Berzin was arrested as a "Japanese spy," and such humane treatment was abruptly curtailed.

Expunging Far Eastern Regionalism. On the eve of World War II, the far eastern branch of the Red Army came under the direct control of Moscow for the first time since the 1920s. Precipitating the maneuver was the growing Soviet fear of the Japanese, with whom the Red Army engaged in two little-known battles, near Lake Khasan in 1938 and at Nomohon in 1939. The action at Lake Khasan ended in failure and embarrassment for Marshal V. K. Blyukher, one of the most respected military commanders in the Red Army and a longtime regional spokesman for the Far Eastern Territory (later Khabarovsk kray and Primor'ye). A short time after the defeat at Lake Khasan, Blyukher was falsely accused of being involved in the "military plot" against Stalin. In October, he was arrested and, one month later, he was beaten to death. Other prominent Red Army military commanders would meet the same fate.

A year later, an unknown colonel, Georgiy Zhukov, would gain his first major combat experience as commander of the SFE's First Army Group against the Japanese at Nomohon, along the Soviet-Mongolian border. Zhukov's inexperienced but brilliantly led troops routed the enemy, an occurrence that may have played a role in the Japanese High Command's decision to accept the terms of the Neutrality Pact two years later.[35] After the military purge, Zhukov, who had been promoted to general because of the Nomohon affair, was one of the few experienced field commanders in Stalin's much-depleted officer corps.

Blyukher's ouster from the SFE was only the tip of the iceberg. John Stephan intoned that "death stalked party secretaries, chairmen of city and rural soviets, [Army and Navy] officers, chekists, railway officials, factory managers, collective farm chairmen, engineers, journalists, agronomists, scientists, writers, and teachers."[36] Before the purge, 35,000 Chinese lived in the SFE. By 1939, most had been arrested and deported, or forcibly relocated. SFE Koreans, who numbered 200,000 in 1937, were given six days to pack up and leave. Given the choice of deportation to

Manchukuo or Central Asia, up to 180,000 chose the latter. Among them were Kim Il-sung and his wife, who in 1942 gave birth to Kim Jong-il on Soviet soil.[37]

Stalin's memories of Sibkray and knowledge of the upstart SFE persuaded him to expunge all traces of regionalism. Between 1936 and 1938, the Great Terror viciously took its toll on Siberian politicos. Orchestrated by Stalin's police chief, Nikolay Yezhov, a man low both in stature (he was described as a "bloodthirsty dwarf") and in intelligence, the "enemies of the people" were purged irrespective of fact or fiction. More than half of the 2,000 voting delegates to the Seventeenth Party Congress (1934) were arrested. None of the 32 delegates from the SFE, and virtually all of those representing the rest of Siberia, returned to the Eighteenth Party Congress in 1939. By that year, almost 71 percent of the full and candidate members of the Central Committee of the CPSU had been shot or "had committed suicide," including *all* of the members from the SFE. Citing a Japanese source, Stephan has reported that more than one-fourth of the Communists in the SFE were purged in 1936–1938: "No [SFE] first secretary between 1923 and 1938 escaped the juggernaut. Virtually all . . . were liquidated [before World War II]." Ultimately, 250,000 people were repressed in the SFE—many sent to Kolyma. Of these, up to 50,000 were simply shot. This rate of repression was four to five times higher than the rate for the USSR.[38]

Stalin's Last Hurrahs: "The Road to Nowhere" and "The Mortal Road." Stephan has written that after the war (1945–1953) no other Soviet region had a higher concentration of prison laborers than the SFE. Labor always has been in short supply in the SFE, and prisoners, together with Red Army personnel (also in disproportion to other Soviet regions), filled the significant void created by the lack of voluntary workers. In Stephan's words, "Camps ringed Vladivostok, Khabarovsk, Vanino, Nakhodka, Blagoveshchensk, and Nikolayevsk." Postwar camps in the SFE burgeoned with "Vlasovites"—the name the locals gave indiscriminately to inmates—and with Japanese POWs, most of whom were repatriated between 1947 and 1949 but a few of whom were incarcerated until 1958.[39] SFE penal laborers mined coal, cut forests, designed and built new housing for free settlers, constructed ports and railways, and tried to dig a tunnel under the Nevel'skoy Strait between the mainland and Sakhalin Island.

The 7-kilometer (4-mi) Nevel'skoy Strait is the narrowest breach between mainland Khabarovsk kray and Sakhalin. It is only because of the strait that Sakhalin is an island. With maps in hand, Stalinists surely must have mused about the possibility of spanning this gap and linking Sakhalin with the Trans-Siberian Railroad, the center, and the rest of Soviet civilization. Why not dig a tunnel beneath the strait? However, the strait's looks were deceiving. Northern Sakhalin is the former delta of the Amur River, and deep, shifting sands fill the shallow Nevel'skoy Strait. As a former tunneler described the situation in 1989: "Placed before us was the daunting task of building as expeditiously as possible a tunnel so that Stalin himself could ride by rail between Moscow and Sakhalin. The project was totally useless."[40] Nevertheless, throughout the winter of 1952–1953, preparations were made to dig the tunnel, using prison labor. A barrage was raised to protect the workforce, and all the equipment was in place, when Stalin died suddenly of a stroke in March 1953. Concomitantly, all work ceased. During the spring, as always happens, the sea ice broke up. The dam, several pieces of equipment, and virtually all traces of the Sakhalin Tunnel were swept away. So far as anyone knows, no lives were lost on the "Road to Nowhere." However, that was not the case with the "Mortal Road."

In the late 1940s, railway building was restricted to the South Siberian trunk line and lesser lines associated with resource development. Terror and deportations had stymied construction of the BAM railway between Tayshet and Sovetskaya Gavan', which would not receive further attention until the 1970s. Another railway project, however, was a product of Stalin's megalomania.

On Lenin's birthday (April 22, 1947), the CPSU approved the construction of the Trans-Polar Railway (TPR), the first stage of which would stretch from the Pechora Basin to Igarka, south of Noril'sk, on the Yenisey River. Eventually, the already grandiose project, part of Stalin's "Great Plan for the Transformation of Nature," was to extend to the Chukchi Peninsula. Only three-fifths of the Pechora-Igarka segment had been finished, by the blood, sweat, and lives of slave laborers, when the Great Leader himself died. Although it is the least known of Stalin's pet projects, the TPR was probably as deadly as Kolyma. For each of its 911 kilometers (570 mi) of rails laid, 1,000 to 1,400 prisoners were needed.[41] Every five to ten kilometers (3–6 mi), there was a labor camp. Water was everywhere, but there was not a drop to drink. The food was so foul that pellagra was epidemic. The slaves dropped dead as they worked.

Today, evidence of the "Mortal Road" still may be seen in the Lower Ob' Basin (Map 5.1). The project was abandoned in such haste that the rusting, buckled tracks still bear the weight of eleven steam locomotives and dozens of rail cars. Many of the wooden labor camps yet stand, albeit awkwardly, on the trembling permafrost. Festooned across the gateway of the occasional "ghost camp" hangs a faded banner inscribed with such sayings as "Glory to the Great Stalin, Camp Leader of the World."[42] All too often, the bleached bones of an unknown inmate jut from the muskeg. To this day, nobody knows the total number of those who reaped immortality on the "Mortal Road."

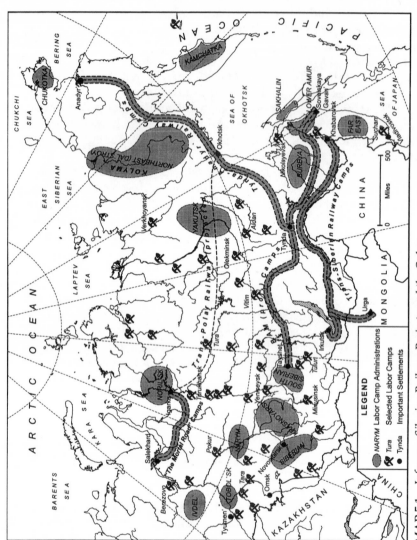

MAP 5.1 *Infamous Siberian Railway Projects and the Gulag*
SOURCES: AFL, Free Trade Union Committee, *"Gulag"—Slavery, Inc.: The Documented Map of Forced Labor Camps in Soviet Russia* (New York: AFL, 1951); David Miller, National Geographic Society; and *Gudok*, March 12 and April 28–29, 1988.

STALINISM AND THE NATIVE QUESTION

In November 1917, the Bolsheviks proclaimed a constitutional policy of self-determination, equality, and sovereignty for all nationalities. Although they truly intended to abrogate nomadism, clan hierarchies, shamanism, and all other "primitive" aspects of Greater Siberia's indigenous life, the Bolsheviks used altruism and paternalism to bring the natives into the twentieth century. To show their affection for the native peoples, the Bolsheviks abolished the fur tribute for the first time since 1822; canceled their debts; prohibited the sale of alcohol; and created departments of "northern studies" in institutions of higher learning. Consequently, life among the natives of Siberia actually improved between 1917 and 1929, unless they had been in hostile territory during the civil war. According to Fondahl, "Many native people still accept the 1920s and early 1930s as a period of great cultural development [supported by] the new Soviet state."[43] Nomadism was practiced by more than half of the indigenous population; clan structure survived; and mutual aid and care for the aged endured. Shamanism was abolished by decree in the 1920s but was permitted to continue through the 1930s. Natives who had no written alphabet—such as the Nentsy, Evenks, Chukchi, and Nanays—obtained one, usually in Latin, not Cyrillic, script. Finally, the Bolsheviks established an organized system of trading posts where indigenes could trade their furs for commercial goods instead of trinkets and alcohol.

Dozens of new national districts were created to lend credence to the idea of sovereignty. To gain the status of a nationality under the Bolshevik ethnic policy, a group had to have a homeland. In the 1920s, Soviet Jews had no homeland except Palestine. To guarantee their status as a nationality and to discourage Zionist thoughts, the Bolsheviks established a Jewish homeland just west of Khabarovsk, in the SFE—about as far from Moscow and Kiev (not to mention Jerusalem) as a person could get. Naturally, few Jews were ever attracted to the spot, and the population of the "homeland" peaked at 9,000 migrants in 1932. By 1939, Jews accounted for only 18 percent of "their" province's population of 108,000. That share was about as high as it ever would be.[44]

In the 1930s, Stalin's nationalities policies shifted from self-serving philanthropy to pragmatic authoritarianism: What was good for the Russians was good for the natives, too. The CPSU forced collectivization on Greater Siberian natives, just as it did on everybody else. By 1937, all prosperous members of the indigenous communities had been liquidated, and collectivization among native groups ranged from 70 percent in Yakutia to more than 90 percent in Khakassia and Buryatia. Throughout the 1930s, the Yakuts and Buryats stubbornly resisted collectivization, resorting to arson, sabotage, and slaughter of their livestock. Although 92 percent of the

Buryat nation lived in Russian-style villages by 1937, the population of their herds had fallen by more than 60 percent. The population of the Buryats themselves declined by almost 13,000 between 1926 and 1939.[45] By the early 1950s, very few groups could claim to have members who were truly nomadic. The Bolsheviks' antireligious fervor also took its toll on shamanism and Buddhism. The former Roman alphabets were converted to Cyrillic, and all peoples were exposed to Russian language training.

Industrialization in such places as Novosibirsk, Noril'sk, Komsomol'sk, and the camps in the Kolyma Basin disrupted the lives of the natives. When their bear-hunting and stone-pine-nut gathering grounds were despoiled by the Russians, the Sel'kups who lived near Novosibirsk and Tomsk were compelled to move northward, into the valleys of the Ket' and Tym rivers. The smelters at Noril'sk destroyed the summer pastures of reindeer-herding Nganasans and Entsy. Komsomol'sk was built in the middle of the ancient homeland of the Nanays, who were forced to sedentarize as a result. Some even joined the construction effort. The activities in Kolyma forever altered the lives of some of the more remote Yakuts and Evens. In her Ph.D. dissertation, Fondahl described the fate of the Vitimo-Olekma (Evenk) and the Okhotsk-Even national okrugs, the latter of which was abolished ostensibly because the "capital," Nagayevo, became the chief transit point for Kolyma-bound prisoners.[46] After Soviet troops invaded eastern Poland in 1939, Soviet authorities delighted in the deportation of hundreds of thousands of Polish soldiers and civilians to Yakutia and the Kolyma, where they cleared forests and mined gold until they died. When the supply of Poles dwindled, these regions became "havens" for German POWs.[47]

The lives of the natives were further changed by the war effort. A policy of universal conscription touched the life of every Soviet family, including those of native Siberians. To gauge the direct and indirect effects of the war on Greater Siberia's ethnic minorities, one need only examine the censuses of 1939 and 1959, between which only three groups (Buryats, Khakass, and Khants) increased their numbers. All others suffered declines of 2.2 percent or more, reaching an extreme of 17 percent among the Evenks. In a single district of Yakutia, 22 out of 40 Evenks conscripted were killed in the war.[48]

CONCLUSION

The independent spirit of Siberians was a factor to be reckoned with in the 1920s and 1930s. Although regionalism was largely erased in Western and Eastern Siberia (Sibkray) by 1924, its inspiration endured in the minds of Siberian peasants under the New Economic Policy (NEP). Siberian kulaks were ideally suited to conduct the kind of free enterprise that the NEP encouraged. Servitude was anathema to them, and European Russia's toadying minions were offensive. This free-spiritedness, which stemmed from the Siberian kulaks' nineteenth-century origins (see Chapter 4), was even more endemic in the SFE, which was so far away from the core that Stalin chose to ignore it until the late 1930s.

What Stalin saw in Sibkray in early 1928 sickened him. His Siberian sojourn, as historian James Hughes has suggested, may very well have been the proverbial last straw. From then on, Stalin aggressively pursued a harsh policy of forced collectivization combined with kulak liquidation. While we cannot know whether Stalin's mind was permanently set against Siberia and the Siberians, it is clear that by 1940, any Greater Siberian authority who had shown the slightest inclination in the 1920s or 1930s toward free thinking was dead.

Under Stalin, the rape of Greater Siberia was complete. Not only was the region a massive pantry to be opened and closed at the whim of the core but it also had become a "Nesselrodian net" that was far, far deeper than any ever before encountered. Never before in human history had a geographic region been used so effectively as an instrument of oppression and execution. By 1953, the periphery and its residents, including its native minorities, were absolutely subordinate to Moscow.

NOTES

1. Anthony P. Allison, "Siberian Regionalism in Revolution and Civil War, 1917–1920," *Sibirica*, Vol. 1, No. 1 (Summer 1990), p. 80.

2. F. A. Kudryavtsev, ed., *Sibir' v epokhu kapitalizm* Vol. 3 of *Istoriya Sibiri*, ed. A. P. Okladnikov (5 vols.; Leningrad: Nauka, 1968), p. 286; and Paul Goble's commentary in "Panel on Siberia: Economic and Territorial Issues," *Soviet Geography*, Vol. 32, No. 6 (June 1991), p. 369.

3. Allison, "Siberian Regionalism," pp. 80–84, 94–95. Shortly after this, Potanin's health began to deteriorate, and in summer 1920, at age 85, he died in Tomsk. During the 1930s, the cemetery in which he was buried was leveled. His remains, together with all the others interred at the site, were lost, only to be found again twenty years later. Today, a bust bearing his visage stands next to a more appropriate gravesite, on the campus of Tomsk University. The grave of his wife was similarly desecrated when a stadium was built over her cemetery in Kyakhta. Like those of her husband, her remains were disinterred many years later and transferred to a high tumulus overlooking the main road into Kyakhta. Her new resting place is also marked by a bronze bust in her image (Valentin Rasputin, *Sibir', Sibir'* . . . , [Moscow: Molodaya gvardiya, 1991], pp. 197–198).

4. George F. Kennan, *The Decision to Intervene*, Vol. 2: *Soviet-American Relations, 1917–1920* (2 vols.; New York: W. W. Norton, 1956), p. 59.

5. I. V. Vlasova, "Poseleniye Zabaykal'ya," in *Byt i iskusstvo russkogo naseleniya Vostochnoy Sibiri*, eds. I. V. Makovetskiy and G. S. Maslova (Novosibirsk: Nauka, 1975), p. 26.

6. Kennan, *The Decision to Intervene*, pp. 62–63, 65–71, and 132–133; William S. Graves, *America's Siberian Adventure, 1918–1920* (New York: Peter Smith, 1941), p. 108; and Richard Luckett, *The White Generals* (London: Longman Group, 1971), p. 391. Graves observed that Semenov and another notorious Cossack, I. P. Kalmykov, roamed the country like animals, killing and robbing at will, and that "the anti-Bolsheviks killed 100 people in Eastern Siberia to every 1 killed by the Bolsheviks." Luckett notes that between 1920 and 1945, Semenov was employed as a mercenary by the Japanese in Manchuria (Manchukuo), where "through some unaccountable lack of vigilance," he was caught and hanged by the Soviet Army. Ironically, in 1993, his Cossack descendants paid him tribute in Chita (*Sibirskaya gazeta*, September 9, 1993).

7. Allison, "Siberian Regionalism," pp. 85–90; Luckett, *The White Generals*, pp. 216–222; and N.G.O. Pereira, "Regional Consciousness in Siberia Before and After October 1917," *Canadian Slavonic Papers*, Vol. 30, No. 1 (March 1988), pp. 120–133. Derber (1888–1929) ceased his political activities after the dissolution of the Siberian Duma and worked as a writer and foreign affairs analyst until his death. Toward the end of his life, he supported the economic integration of the SFE into the Pacific Region. Horvath (1858–1937), who served as Director of the CER until 1920, briefly became "Temporary Ruler" of Russia in July 1918, before serving as Kolchak's "High Plenipotentiary" in the Far East, a position he held through 1920. He retired to Beijing in 1924 (John J. Stephan, *The Russian Far East: A History* [Stanford: Stanford University Press, 1994], pp. 315–316 and 319).

8. Luckett, *The White Generals*, p. 245. The British offered to meet the Bolsheviks on the island of Prinkipo in the Sea of Marmara to discuss the details of a truce, one of their demands being Siberian independence. Although Lenin appeared to take the Prinkipo proposals seriously, the Japanese and Whites rejected them outright. For a colorful account of what may have happened, see Ric Hardman, *Fifteen Flags* (Boston: Little, Brown & Company, 1968), p. 153.

9. E. H. Carr, *The Bolshevik Revolution, 1917–1923*, Vol. 1: *A History of Soviet Russia* (New York: W. W. Norton & Co., 1985), pp. 352–355; Olga Bakich, "A Russian City in China: Harbin Before 1917," *Canadian Slavonic Papers*, Vol. 28, No. 2 (June 1986), pp. 129–148; Simon Karlinsky, "Memoirs of Harbin," *Slavic Review*, Vol. 48, No. 2 (Summer 1989), pp. 284–289; and David Wolff, "Russia Finds Its Limits," in *Rediscovering Russia in Asia: Siberia and the Russian Far East*, eds. Stephen Kotkin and David Wolff (Armonk, N.Y.: M. E. Sharpe, 1995), p. 46. In 1913, half the population of Harbin was Russian, 5,000 of whom were Jews, representing the second largest Jewish population in Eastern Siberia (after that of Irkutsk). Even today, all the railway stations along the CER are of turn-of-the-century Russian design.

10. Henry Kittredge Norton, *The Far Eastern Republic of Siberia* (reprint; Westport, Conn.: Hyperion, 1981), p. 130; Ye. Krivosheyeva, *Bol'shoy Bill v Kuzbasse* (Kemerovo: Kemerovskoye knizhnoye izdatel'stvo, 1990), pp. 49–58; and Carr, *The Bolshevik Revolution*, p. 355.

11. The bizarre "Nikolayevsk Incident" resulted in the massacre of close to 700 Japanese civilians and soldiers (John Stephan, *Sakhalin: A History* [Oxford: Clarendon Press, 1971], p. 98). Further insight into the episode and the subsequent occupation of northern Sakhalin, where the Japanese committed themselves to the exploration and development of Sakhalin oil, is in Hara Teruyuki, "Japan Moves

North," in *Rediscovering Russia in Asia: Siberia and the Russian Far East*, eds. Stephen Kotkin and David Wolff (Armonk, N.Y.: M. E. Sharpe, 1995), pp. 55–67.

12. See Paul Goble's comments in "Panel on Siberia," p. 370.

13. Norton, *The Far Eastern Republic*, p. 370. Krasnoshchekov and Shatov were recalled to Moscow in summer 1921, never to return to the Russian Far East. Although both would serve the regime in rather high posts—Shatov directed the construction of the Turksib Railroad from 1927 to 1930—they were arrested and shot in 1937 (Stephan, *The Russian Far East*, pp. 322 and 333).

14. See footnote 3, this chapter.

15. N. Ya. Gushchin and V. A. Il'nykh, eds., *Klassovaya bor'ba v sibirskoy derevne, 1920-ye-seredina 1930-kh gg.* (Novosibirsk: Nauka, 1987), pp. 63–66.

16. James Hughes, *Stalin, Siberia and the Crisis of the New Economic Policy* (Cambridge: Cambridge University Press, 1991), pp. 7 and 18–22; and Frank Lorimer, *The Population of the Soviet Union: History and Prospects* (Geneva: League of Nations, 1946), pp. 67–69.

17. Hughes, *Stalin, Siberia and the Crisis*, p. 38.

18. *Ibid.*, pp. 30, 38, 45, and 57–62.

19. The approximate boundaries of Sibkray encompassed modern Western Siberia, Krasnoyarsk kray, and Irkutsk oblast.

20. I. M. Razgon, ed., *Sibir' v periode stroitel'stva sotsializma*, Vol. 4 of *Istoriya Sibiri*, ed. A. P. Okladnikov (5 vols.; Leningrad: Nauka, 1968), p. 235; Hughes, *Stalin, Siberia and the Crisis*, pp. 123–148. I am deeply indebted to the work of James Hughes for the following summary of Stalin's sojourn.

21. *Ibid.*, pp. 197–200.

22. Robert Conquest, *The Great Terror* (London: Macmillan, 1968), p. 539; Robert Conquest, *The Great Terror: A Reassessment* (New York: Oxford University Press, 1990), p. 480; and *Izvestiya*, April 3, 1988.

23. John J. Stephan, "Far Eastern Conspiracies? Russian Separatism on the Pacific," *Australian Slavonic and East European Studies*, Vol. 4, No. 1/2 (1990), p. 143; Stephan, *The Russian Far East*, pp. 160–224. Until 1938, Moscow had no telecommunications link to the Russian Far East (p. 201).

24. Stephan, "Far Eastern Conspiracies," pp. 142–143.

25. *Ibid.*, pp. 144–145; Allan Rodgers, ed., *The Soviet Far East: Geographical Perspectives on Development* (London and New York: Routledge, 1990), p. 23; and Walter Kolarz, *The Peoples of the Soviet Far East* (New York: Praeger, 1954), pp. 4–10.

26. Theodore Shabad and Victor L. Mote, *Gateway to Siberian Resources (the BAM)* (Washington, D.C.: Scripta, 1977), p. 7.

27. Razgon, *Sibir' v periode*, pp. 321, 325, and 370.

28. Shabad and Mote, *Gateway to Siberian Resources*, pp. 9 and 11–12.

29. Alexander Werth, *Russia at War, 1941–1945* (London: Barrie and Rockcliff, 1964), p. 216; and Robert C. Kingsbury and Robert N. Taaffe, *An Atlas of Soviet Affairs* (New York: Praeger, 1965), p. 55.

30. Glavnoye upravleniye geodezii i kartografii pri Sovete Ministrov SSSR, *Atlas obrazovaniya i razvitiya Soyuza SSR* (Moscow: Akademiya nauk SSSR, Institut istorii SSSR, 1972), pp. 23–30.

31. Alexander Solzhenitsyn, *The Gulag Archipelago*, Vol. 3/4 (New York: Harper and Row, 1974), pp. 2–5. (Gulag is an acronym for *Glavnoye upravleniye is-*

pravitel'no-trudovykh lagerei [the Central Administration of Corrective Labor Camps].)

32. Robert Conquest, *Kolyma* (London: Macmillan, 1978), pp. 215–216.

33. Conquest, *The Great Terror: A Reassessment*, p. 486; Conquest, *Kolyma*, pp. 227–228; Nikolay Shmelev, "Avansy i dolgi," *Novyy mir*, No. 6 (1987), pp. 142–158; and V. N. Komissarov, "Stalinskiye lagerya Zapadnoy Sibiri," *EKO*, No. 1 (1990), pp. 58–59 and 193.

34. Elizabeth Pond, *From the Yaroslavskiy Station: Russia Perceived* (rev. ed.; New York: Universe Books, 1984), p. 261. The commentary on transportation to the Gulag comes from the horrific eyewitness account of Michael Solomon, *Magadan* (Princeton, N.J.: Vertex, 1971), pp. 47, 71–72, and many other entries.

35. Alan Wood, ed., *Siberia: Problems and Prospects for Regional Development* (London: Croom Helm, 1987), pp. 178–179; F. M. Borodkin et al., *Goroda Sibiri i Dal'nego Vostoka: Kratkiy ekonomiko-geograficheskiy spravochnik* (Moscow: Progress, 1990), pp. 407 and 465; Conquest, *The Great Terror: A Reassessment*, pp. 430–431; and Alvin D. Coox, *Nomohon: Japan Against Russia, 1939* (2 vols.: Stanford: Stanford University Press, 1985).

36. John J. Stephan, "'Cleansing' the Soviet Far East, 1937–1938," *Acta Slavica Iaponica*, Vol. 10 (1932), p. 52.

37. *Ibid.*, p. 47; Dae-Sook Suh, *Koreans in the Soviet Union* (Honolulu, Hawaii: Center for Korean Studies/Center for SUPAR, 1987), pp. 51 and 89; and Kim Hakjoon, "The Emergence of Siberia and the Russian Far East as a 'New Frontier' for Koreans," in *Rediscovering Russia in Asia: Siberia and the Russian Far East*, eds. Stephen Kotkin and David Wolff (Armonk, N.Y.: M. E. Sharpe, 1995), p. 305.

38. Stephan, "'Cleansing' the Soviet Far East," pp. 51–52. The minimum estimate of SFE incarcerations—200,000—is greater than the maximum number of inmates held in tsarist prisons of all types (183,949 in 1912), according to Robert Conquest (*Kolyma*, p. 229).

39. Stephan, *The Russian Far East*, pp. 245–248.

40. *Gudok*, August 24, 1989, p. 4, and December 5, 1989, p. 4. The second of these articles was entitled "The Road to Nowhere."

41. Rumor had it that Stalin personally designed the route of the TPR, basing his decisions on the prognostications of geologist-academician I. M. Gubkin, who in the 1930s predicted the existence of oil and gas in the Ob' Basin. Gubkin's ideas would be borne out by events in 1959 (*Gudok*, March 12, 1988, p. 2, and April 28, 1988, p. 2).

42. *Gudok*, April 29, 1988, p. 2.

43. Gail Fondahl, "Siberia: Native Peoples and Newcomers in Collision," in *Nations and Politics in the Soviet Successor States*, eds. Ian Bremmer and Ray Taras (London: Cambridge University Press, 1993), p. 484.

44. James Forsyth, *A History of the Peoples of Siberia* (Cambridge: Cambridge University Press, 1992), p. 326. I am indebted to Dr. Forsyth's work for most of this section (pp. 340–361).

45. *Ibid.*, p. 334.

46. Fondahl, "Siberia: Native Peoples," p. 505.

47. Nikolay Ushakov, "Prisoner Pioneers," in *Yakutia: Frozen Gem of the USSR*, 1978. Available on-line at <http://www.maximov.com/Russia/Sakha/yakutia_past.html#origins> (28 September 1997).

48. Forsyth, *A History of the Peoples of Siberia*, pp. 348 and 351–352.

▪ SIX ▪

Salad Days:
The East-West Debate
and Greater Siberia

I am a Siberian. [Siberia] is my home. I was born there. I grew up there, and my years there were my best years. I am a Communist, but not a Stalinist. There were executions in my family. There were persons who were repressed and arrested. I learned about Stalinism by the skin of my own neck.

—Yegor Kuz'mich Ligachev

INTRODUCTION

Imagine yourself the potentate of a rich and expansive land. One part of the land, the part in which you live, is well developed and relatively sophisticated. The other part is rich in potential but undeveloped and wild. You have limited investment funds. How do you allocate them? This was essentially the problem that Soviet leaders faced after 1953.

While Stalin lived, bureaucrats, managers, and ordinary people followed orders because they feared for their lives. Provincial leaders, after the 1930s, rarely made a decision without consulting their Moscow overlords. Regional development was not up for grabs. In the wake of Stalin's death, however, the reins were loosened. Soviet authorities in the post-Stalin period reorganized themselves, looked at the map, and had to decide what to do. Some wanted to continue to invest in the core; others wanted to increase allocations to the periphery. The east-west debate was subdued. Some question whether any debate took place. Nevertheless, the dichotomy represented one of the crucial controversies in the USSR after Stalin.

LABOR, RESEARCH, AND DEVELOPMENT AFTER STALIN

PHOTO 6.1   *Yegor Kuz'mich Ligachev*
SOURCE: *Embassy of the USSR, Washington, D.C., 1989.*

Just as no family in Greater Siberia avoided the juggernaut of World War II, none, even that of an *apparatchik* like Yegor Ligachev (see epigraph above), eluded Stalin's megalomania. During the 1930s, the massive use of forced labor was justified on economic grounds: The region was virgin territory, and there was a labor shortage; the new projects were labor intensive; and there was a deficit of machinery. Moreover, capitalism's "spontaneous order" was lacking; and penal labor could be deployed at will.

Siberians grew up in the shadow of labor camps, and many had direct experience or a family history in the camps: After their release, the *zeks* (inmates) sometimes made Siberia their home. As Wheatcroft has observed, "By the mid-1950s, leaving aside the important question of morality, there was no longer an economic rationale [for keeping hundreds of] thousands of people incarcerated in labor camps."[1] After the war, excavator/bulldozer-turned-weapons plants renewed the manufacture of excavators and bulldozers. Given the availability of earthmovers, the mining industry mechanized quickly. The same was true of other equipment. The new economics demanded the mechanization of what until then had been very labor-intensive operations. By 1955, Nikita Khrushchev had decided to abolish the costly "roofless prison" and to rehabilitate the inmates.

Although it did not evaporate with Stalin's demise, the labor camp population gradually diminished after Khrushchev's speech to the Twentieth Party Congress in 1956. Celebrity-survivors such as Molotov's wife, the doctors from the "Doctors' Plot," Yevgeniya Ginzburg and her son (Vasiliy Aksenov), and Varlam Shalamov returned to the core after enduring incredible hardships in the periphery. In contrast, Tomsk-born writer Georgiy Shelest, an "alumnus" of Kolyma, spent his final days in Chita. Ethnographer-chekist Albert Lipskiy, who had spent the war in a Central Asian labor camp, worked in an Abakan Museum until his death in 1973.

Hundreds of thousands of ailing, unsung zeks took menial jobs in Greater Siberia, where they toiled largely in silence to the end of their lives. In the old days, they might have become beggars, looters, and debauchers of Siberia's scarce womenfolk. In truth, some of the criminal elements were recidivists, who never did adjust to life "on the outside."

Although Greater Siberia should have had plenty of unskilled labor in 1956, it lacked the numbers and specialists to implement ambitious future targets such as the hydroelectric cascades and their attendant energy-intensive industries (aluminum, pulp and paper, and so forth); the oil and gas development of the Ob' Basin; and the BAM railway. To attract the specialized labor forces required for these enormous projects, planners used economic incentives. To train the scientists and engineers needed to guide overall planning and implementation of Greater Siberian development, the regime founded the "science city" of Akademgorodok.

Labor Incentives

The idea of using rights and privileges to entice the migration of workers to out-of-the-way places had been around since May 1932, but the abundance of slave labor during the prewar and war years rendered the concept almost unnecessary. The Young Communists who built Komsomol'sk-na-Amure, for example, received a "northern increment" that included higher base wages that increased over a five-year period, longer annual vacations, better pension plans, and priority housing privileges. In August 1945, planners enhanced the northern increment with wage coefficients that increased in a northerly and easterly direction. Thus, a worker on the Chukchi Peninsula theoretically obtained the highest salary in the realm. To attract workers who had special skills (excavator operators, mechanics, and so on), the regime created wage differentials appropriate to the need. A good mechanic, for instance, could earn up to six times the average Soviet salary *in addition to* the perquisites of the northern increment.[2]

These incentives obviously added substantial costs to Siberian development, stimulating a reevaluation of old dogmas. Was it really necessary to strive for "industry in depth" in a world of intercontinental ballistic missiles? Was the socialist concept of planned proportional development (PPD) of all regions of the country—even environmentally harsh ones—really practical?[3] Without affirmation of these ideals, Greater Siberia would be left out in the cold. Whether to invest in Europe or Asia was a question that would vex Soviet planners through the 1980s.

Under Khrushchev, planners rarely concerned themselves with the comprehensive, integrated approach of PPD; rather, they came to regard Greater Siberia merely as a storehouse of raw materials that served the interests of the core. Of course, the periphery continued to attract the attention of Soviet military advisers, who considered the Soviet Far East (SFE) an especially vital strategic interface with the powers of the Pacific Basin. In the words of Alan Wood, the SFE to them "embodied both an outpost and a bastion, exemplifying both vulnerability and security." The vulnerability required constant vigilance and a comparatively large military presence; such a presence would guarantee the security of the core's eastern flank. At their near-constant urging, by the end of the 1980s, the Pacific Fleet had become the largest of the four Soviet fleet commands and the defense industry had become proportionally the SFE's largest employer.[4]

The new, pragmatic approach toward the region was epitomized by the actions of Nikita Khrushchev, who in 1960 downgraded the value of the northern increment, weakened its incremental buildup, and reduced the number of perquisites for otherwise deserving recipients. Khrushchev felt that improved living conditions alone would suffice to attract permanent settlers to Greater Siberia.

Akademgorodok: Siberia's Science City

During Khrushchev's tenure as undisputed Premier (1958–1964), Soviet science made remarkable progress. Khrushchev believed that science married to socialism would accelerate the achievement of communism. "Convinced that cities of science already existed in America, he supported the construction of scientific cities around Moscow" and placed his "personal stamp of approval" on construction of Siberia's Akademgorodok.[5]

The "father of Akademgorodok" was mathematician M. A. Lavrent'yev, who engendered the notion of building a city for scientists while Stalin still lived. Lavrent'yev would not be able to realize his dream, however, until Khrushchev de-Stalinized the Communist Party, after 1956. The mathematician and his colleagues envisioned a world-class scientific community free of the pressures of Soviet politics and the economy. He had little trouble persuading the ebullient Khrushchev, who was so enamored of the project that he visited the construction site twice.

Although problems abounded during the construction of the city and its institutes, the end result was superior to most Soviet architectural and urban designs. The setting helped: a beautiful wooded valley located along the banks of the Sea of Ob', a reservoir created by the recently built Novosibirsk dam (1950–1959). The builders did in fact "design with nature." In any season, Akademgorodok superficially reminded one of a rustic village in Vermont or Sussex, perfectly integrated into the environment. The scholars lived in Western-style detached cottages set back from the roads, in the woods. When I visited the town in 1985, I got the "house tour": Academician so-and-so lives there; that's Aganbegyan's place; over there is so-and-so the chemist's cottage. . . . And just down the road was the reservoir for summer watersports and winter ice fishing. These amenities easily lured some of the best Soviet minds away from the numbing milieus of European Russia.

The first scientists were young, so-called children of the Twentieth Party Congress. Far from Moscow, Akademgorodok's own Party *apparatchiki* were more flexible than their peers in the core. In Siberia's science city, youthful scientists such as physicist Gersh Budker, sociologist Tat'yana Zaslavskaya, and economist A. G. Aganbegyan exercised academic freedom to expand the limits of fundamental research. One of Lavrent'yev's priorities in Akademgorodok was to establish an atmosphere of science without walls, an interdisciplinary scholarly community in which people could speak and socialize freely, without the impedimenta of "Party discipline."[6]

Until 1968, Lavrent'yev succeeded in bringing free thinking to his new town, but by Soviet standards, the community was far too informal: "At social clubs, the scientists played cards, drank, and sang into the wee hours. There were rumors of prostitutes."[7] Such ribaldry could not long last in the USSR of the late 1960s. In fact, the freedom did end when the Siberian scholars rose up in protest against the trial of the writers Sinyavskiy and Daniel'; when in song they satirized the Communist Party; and when they took a stand against the invasion of Czechoslovakia. Thereafter, not only were the scientists and students of Akademgorodok more closely watched but "the 'bulldozer' science of river diversion, schemes for development around Lake Baykal, and the BAM were seen as more important than fundamental research."[8] Fundamental researchers, such as Aganbegyan and Zaslavskaya, went into the business of pragmatic regional planning and development.

THE SIBERIAN ECONOMY, 1950–1985

During the 1950s, the periphery once again became a resource frontier. The output of Greater Siberia's extractive industries, including nonferrous metals, agriculture, and forestry, exceeded Soviet averages. Mechanization enabled a shift from the small-scale manual digging and panning of placer deposits to larger-scale, machine-run hydraulic and lode mining of precious and rare metals. The environment suffered, but production soared.

Khrushchev's Virgin Lands Program resulted in the conversion of long-term fallow or virgin soil into cropland in the Altay foreland. Although yields were relatively low, sowings of spring wheat were so extensive that harvests were abundant in good years. Even though most of the new sowings were in northern Kazakhstan, those of the Altay contributed more than 40 percent of the annual harvest.[9] In agriculture, Akademgorodok soon proved its mettle. From the 1960s onward, agronomists at VASKhNIL, a branch institute of the science city, provided technical advice and guidance to the managers of collective and state farms in the Virgin Lands. The increased output of grain soon competed with coal for space on the Trans-Siberian and South Siberian trunk lines, necessitating the construction of the Central Siberian railway between Barnaul and Chelyabinsk.

During the war, Greater Siberia's forest products industry declined, but in the 1950s, it rallied, particularly with the addition of the western terminus of the projected BAM railway. Doubling as a lifeline for the dam builders in the new town of Bratsk on the Lena River and as a conduit for the raw materials of the Lena watershed, the Tayshet–Ust'-Kut branch supplied iron ore to the Kuzbas steel mills and timber to the burgeoning forest products operations around Bratsk. Other railway spurs—to Sergino on the Ob', to Bol'shaya Ket' in the Yenisey Basin, to Reshoty in the Angara Basin, and between Khabarovsk and Postyshevo in the SFE (the eastern terminus of the BAM)—opened up rich new logging areas.[10]

Development of the Greater Siberian economy was impossible without electricity, and Khrushchev was the greatest advocate of hydroelectric power in Soviet history. Under his watch, no fewer than nine Siberian dams were approved, under construction, or actually built. These included the already mentioned 400-megawatt (MW) Novosibirsk and 4,050-MW Bratsk dams; the 662-MW Irkutsk dam; the 6,000-MW Krasnoyarsk dam; the 6,400-MW Sayanogorsk dam; the 4,320-MW Ust'-Ilimsk dam; the 308-MW Vilyuy dam; the 441-MW Khantayka dam; and the 1,290-MW Zeya dam. The enormous multipurpose stations provided energy to satisfy the peak demand at Novosibirsk; the needs of new aluminum refineries near Irkutsk, Bratsk, Krasnoyarsk, and Sayanogorsk; the consumption of the Noril'sk nonferrous metallurgical combine; and the requirements of the wood-processing industry (especially pulp and paper mills) of Bratsk and Ust'-Ilimsk. They also improved navigation, diversified recreation, and controlled floods. They had the unfortunate side effects of inundating the often massive floodplains, swamping uncut timber reserves, and forcing the removal of households and villages. The Vilyuy and Khantayka dams, built to supply energy to the Mirnyy diamond mines and the Noril'sk facilities, respectively, were the first dams ever raised on permafrost. Zeya was to be the energy source for the eastern BAM service area.[11]

As an indicator of the growth inherent in hydroelectricity-based industries, neither Bratsk nor Ust'-Ilimsk registered more than a few thousand residents in 1955, many of them former zeks. By 1990, their populations were 258,000 and 111,000 persons, respectively. Most of the working people of Bratsk were employed in either the USSR's largest aluminum refinery or its greatest forest products complex, where each year 6 million cubic meters of roundwood were consumed to produce up to 1 million tons of wood pulp, paperboard, lumber, and plywood. Ust'-Ilimsk's facilities added another 500,000 tons of pulp. Unfortunately, the operations polluted vast tracts of otherwise pristine wilderness.

West Siberian Oil and Gas

Khrushchev's stress on large-scale hydroelectric projects in Soviet Asia resulted in a slight increase in capital investment in the periphery. Between 1960 and 1965, Greater Siberia attracted 12.1 percent of the funding versus 11.3 percent in the 1950s.[12] The increased outlay was not entirely created by dam and railway building, however. Oil and gas development in the Ob' River Basin, accompanied by pipeline construction, also required fresh infusions of financial aid.

Support for the development of the periphery expanded after Leonid Brezhnev took power in 1964. During the eighth FYP (1966–1970), capital investment in Greater Siberia jumped from 12.1 percent to 15.2 percent, a proportion that had not been matched since the 1920s. The explanation for this sudden outpouring of generosity was the development of West Siberia's oil and gas fields.

Middle Ob' Petroleum. As Academician Gubkin predicted in the 1930s,[13] commercial oil deposits were discovered in the marshland forests near the junction of the Ob' and Irtysh rivers. The first gusher "came in" in 1959, in the Shaim field on the upper Konda River, a left-bank tributary of the Irtysh. Initially, without a pipeline, Shaim crude was transported by barge down the Konda to the Irtysh and conveyed upriver to the Omsk Refinery, which soon became the USSR's largest petroleum processor. In 1960, a 400-kilometer (250-mi) pipeline linked the field with Tyumen', whence rail tank cars carried the fuel either to Urals power plants or to Omsk.

The Shaim discovery was followed in 1961 by other gushers, in the Megion and Ust'-Balyk regions of the Middle Ob'. In the midst of the wildcatting in Ust'-Balyk was Nefteyugansk, which was a mere village in 1964 but had burgeoned to a city of almost 100,000 by 1992.[14] The Ust'-Balyk and Megion fields turned out to be "giants," meaning they each contained 100 to 500 million metric tons (Mmt) of petroleum reserves. Together with the West Surgut and Pravdinsk fields, these fields were connected to the Omsk Refinery by pipeline in 1967. That same year, the Tyumen'-Tobol'sk railway provided another means of transportation for the oil. An extension of this railway reached Surgut in 1974.

The importance of the Surgut region was enhanced further by the 1966 discovery of the supergiant oil pool at Lake Samotlor, located 250 kilometers (130 mi) to the east. Described as a "floating bog" beneath 1 to 2 meters of water and 15 to 20 meters of "quaking, decomposed peat," Samotlor was one of the world's most troublesome but greatest oil fields. In its original state it held 1.5 billion metric tons of crude oil, or more than five times the volume of Ust'-Balyk. Before it began to decline in output in 1984, Samotlor alone produced one-third of the USSR's annual production of petroleum.[15]

Attracting labor to one of the world's nastiest environments was not an easy task. In winter, the subfreezing temperatures were legendary. In spring, floods converted the oil fields to islands. In summer, the humidity and insect swarms were unbearable. The original "roughnecks" were a motley contingent of students from Moscow, Leningrad, and Kiev, one-third of whom usually departed before one year was out. Many of them had to live in automobile cabins, dugouts, and even tents, with no amenities, in freezing temperatures. *Uslovniki*, or trusties on parole for crimes that ranged from murder to theft, were rushed in to offset the turnover of "free labor." If they did an honest day's work, the trusties got an honest day's pay. Sufficient "honest" days, and a parolee could take a wife, or if already married, could have his family with him in the oil fields (lucky family!). A year in the oil fields equaled a year's imprisonment, and at the expiration of his sentence, the former *uslovnik* obtained a new passport and all the rights of a Soviet citizen.[16]

Between 1961 and 1969, almost 60 oil fields were identified in the Middle Ob'. Eighteen, including supergiant Samotlor, were very large fields, each with more than 50 Mmt of petroleum reserves. At the time, it seemed that Western Siberia might contain a "limitless" supply of oil; however, there was but one Samotlor. After that, only one other supergiant (>500 Mmt), the Fedorovo field north of Surgut, was uncovered, and it gushed in 1971.

Lower Ob' Natural Gas. Exploitation of West Siberian natural gas began in 1953, near the town of Berezovo, on the left bank of the lower Ob' River. Because of environmental harshness and relative inaccessibility, gas field development progressed slowly. Finally, in 1966, a 100-centimeter (40-in) pipeline connected the main gas field at Punga with cities in the northern Urals.

The Berezovo strike was modest compared to the discoveries made between 1965 and 1974. In that decade, roughnecks tapped no fewer than six supergiant gas fields (reservoirs containing more than 283 billion m³, or 10 trillion ft³). The mightiest of these, including Urengoy, Yamburg, Zapolyarnoye, and Medvezh'ye, totaled 10 trillion cubic meters of reserves,

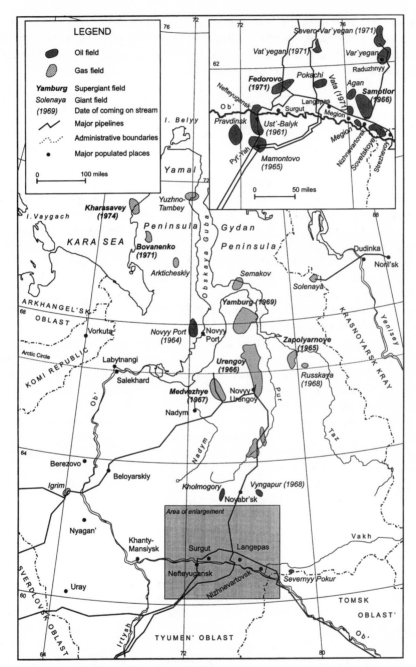

MAP 6.1   *Ob' Basin Oil and Gas Fields*
SOURCE: Joseph P. Riva, Jr., *Petroleum Exploration Opportunities in the Former Soviet Union* (Tulsa, Okla.: PenWell Books, 1994), p. 153.

or 40 percent of the USSR's supply of gas and 13 percent of the world's reserves.[17] By the time Gorbachev took office in 1985, more than 100 natural gas fields had been discovered in Western Siberia, containing one-third of the identified reserves on the planet.

SIBERIAN POLITICIANS AFTER THE STIGMA

The fortuitous events of the 1960s enhanced the careers of Siberian politicians. Stigmatized by Stalin, they had lain low for decades. Since 1937, few Siberian-born or -based Party leaders had served on the Politburo (known as the Presidium between 1953 and 1966). Astrakhan'-born A. B. Aristov (1903–?) had served in Krasnoyarsk, Chelyabinsk, and Khabarovsk from 1944 to 1955 before being appointed to Khrushchev's Presidium. There he remained until 1961, when Khrushchev, reputedly questioning Aristov's loyalty, made him Soviet Consul to Poland. In 1966, Tver'-born G. I. Voronov (1910–?), who since 1936 had spent his formative years as a ranking Party official in Tomsk, Kemerovo, Chita, and Orenburg provinces, ended up serving a dozen years first as candidate, then full member of the Presidium/Politburo. By 1973, he fell out of favor with Brezhnev over the latter's rivalry with Aleksey Kosygin.[18]

This was not the case with Konstantin Chernenko, who became one of Brezhnev's protégés while the two men were serving together in Moldova (then Moldavia). Born in 1911, in the village of Bol'shoy Tes (then in Achinsk okrug, in today's Krasnoyarsk kray), Chernenko was a true Siberian but might as well have been born a Muscovite. Throughout his life, he was a staunch Party loyalist. He did anything the Party asked him to do, whether it was the forced requisitioning of grain; the Russification of Nganasans, Evenks, and Khakass; the mass reeducation of Moldavians; or the purging of Jews. In Moldavia, where he became one of Brezhnev's favorites, for instance, Chernenko received the Labor Order of the Red Banner for his achievements, including his success in cleansing his agitprop department of Jews.

The Brezhnev-Chernenko alliance proved mutually beneficial, with Brezhnev nurturing Chernenko's careerism and Chernenko massaging Brezhnev's massive ego. Later, when both were in Moscow, Brezhnev was Head of the Party and Kosygin was Head of State. One of Chernenko's tasks was to manipulate the Politburo agenda so as to favor Brezhnev's interests at the expense of his chief rivals, Kosygin and Nikolay Podgornyy.

Chernenko was not a complete lickspittle, however. He was the first Party official to computerize his Moscow offices. He wrote prodigiously, albeit perfunctorily, and he rewrote the country's constitution. For his role in devising the 1977 Soviet Constitution—which later would become the bane of Boris Yeltsin's existence—Chernenko was made candidate member of the Politburo. A year later, he became a full member, and still later, general secretary of the CPSU (1984–1985).

It is doubtful that Chernenko was the source of Brezhnev's well-known admiration for Siberia. He was a true Bolshevik who owed everything to the Party. Reading Chernenko's biography,[19] one finds no hint of regionalism or regional loyalty. We also cannot measure the strength of Chernenko's relationship with another Siberian who rose to the top, Vladimir Dolgikh.

Dolgikh also came from Krasnoyarsk kray, where he was born in the village of Ilanskiy in 1924. While still a teenager, he allegedly met Chernenko just before the latter left the Krasnoyarsk organization. Unlike Chernenko, Dolgikh became a decorated war hero. After the war, the hero, now a Party member and barely 21, returned to his native Siberia to study engineering. While Chernenko honed his agitprop skills in Moldavia, Dolgikh became the principal engineer of a large Krasnoyarsk factory.[20] Patient and persevering—according to Yeltsin, Dolgikh never did anything "half-cocked"[21]—he eventually became director of the Noril'sk Metallurgical Combine, where he won five Orders of Lenin.

Although very different in intellect, Dolgikh is said to have maintained contact with Chernenko, who as a friend of Brezhnev might have played a role in Dolgikh's ultimate rise to full membership in the Central Committee (1971). In that position Dolgikh met Boris Yeltsin. Yeltsin admired the forthright honesty and "sober judgment" of Dolgikh, who, he opined, "was the most professional and efficient secretary on the Central Committee." Later, while serving as the person in charge of heavy industry and energy development on the Secretariat, Dolgikh was promoted to candidate member of the Politburo. He would hold the post until he was pensioned off in 1988. According to Yeltsin, Dolgikh was the "most useful" Politburo member, even though as a mere candidate he was outranked by full members like fellow Siberian Yegor Ligachev.[22]

Ligachev was born in the tiny village of Dubinkino in Siberia, in 1920. Until 1938, his experiences were exclusively Siberian. There he bore witness to Stalinist terror (see the epigraph to this chapter).[23] After a five-year interval of study in Moscow, Ligachev became an engineer in a Novosibirsk aircraft plant, where in 1944 he joined the Party. Until 1961, Ligachev spent most of his time working his way up through the ranks of the Novosibirsk Party apparatus, when suddenly he became deputy chief of the Russian Republic's agitprop department in Moscow. Four years later, at the age of 45, he was back in Siberia.

For the next eighteen years, a now-toughened Ligachev served as first secretary of Tomsk oblast. Having been to Moscow and back, it might have been easy for him to rest on his laurels. Instead, he built one of the most powerful political machines in Russia and became a major spokesman for the economic development of his province in particular and Western Siberia in general. Perhaps his "exile" was a blessing in disguise: His highly disciplined leadership style contrasted sharply with the looseness of the Brezhnev era. Moreover, Ligachev's penchant for discipline placed him in good odor with his eventual benefactor, Yuriy Andropov, who ensconced him in the Secretariat in 1983. From that vantage point, as cadre secretary, the Siberian would climb to the post of second secretary, behind Mikhail Gorbachev, and full member of the Politburo (1985).

Group Politics? West Siberian Energy and the BAM

During the 1960s, Siberian Party leaders like Ligachev, Dolgikh, and others contented themselves with building patron-client relationships in Greater Siberia, an activity Brezhnev condoned. The satraps built their confidence and staying power with cadres of loyal friends and associates. No longer did they live in terror of the midnight knock on their doors. The core accepted the prefectural fiefdoms as a means of maintaining their fealty. As long as provincial leaders could guarantee their economic quotas, they were free to handle local affairs pretty much as they saw fit within their own prefectures. In general, the farther away a provincial Party head was from Moscow, the more freely he could wield his considerable power. Proximity to Japan and the Pacific Basin also enabled Party prefects in Primor'ye and on Sakhalin to negotiate directly (and independently) with capitalist companies as early as the 1970s.[24]

Bidding for investment by regional Party bosses probably always existed in the Soviet Union, albeit informally and "behind closed doors." Throughout the Soviet period, there were officials who favored the concentration of industrial production and those who favored its dispersal. The struggle emerged openly in 1959 at the time of the Twenty-First Party Congress and continued for the next twenty years. From the 1960s onward, Siberian leaders steadily and deliberately demanded and received more attention from the core. Two major successes reflect positively on their abilities to match wits with Moscow policymakers: West Siberian oil and gas development and the construction of the BAM.

The West Siberian Energy Coalition. Akademgorodok served not only as a fount of scientific research but also as a sounding board for advocates of Siberian development. One of Siberia's champions was none other than Lavrent'yev himself, who teamed up in the 1960s with economist G. A. Prudenskiy to support the exploration and development of West Siberian hydrocarbons.[25] The two men were joined by another colleague, Academician A. A. Trofimuk, one of Lavrent'yev's deputy directors at the science city. A geologist, Trofimuk earlier had gained fame in the Volga-Urals oil fields (the "Second Baku").[26] He was convinced that the USSR, and Western Siberia, especially, possessed infinite reserves of oil and gas. By 1970, Second Baku oil and gas production would peak. Trofimuk used this to argue the case for more investment in the future of Western Siberia. Rallying to his cause were his colleagues at Akademgorodok, comprising geologists, Siberian politicians, enterprise managers, and fellow academicians.

One of his supporters was Aganbegyan, who was not yet 40. Abel Gezevich was Prudenskiy's second in command at the Institute of Economics and Organization of Industrial Production (EKO), and a key proponent of the Liberman economic reforms. Together with Zaslavskaya, Aganbegyan would champion Siberian causes for the next twenty years. (The duo also advocated economic restructuring—perestroyka—as early as 1965.) Not immune to politics, Aganbegyan probably met Ligachev in 1961, when both men lived in Novosibirsk. Four years later, far away in Stavropol' kray, a young Gorbachev became familiar with the ideas of Aganbegyan and Zaslavskaya. He would meet neither of them until 1979, but he would not forget them.[27]

The "academic lobby" no doubt encouraged Tyumen' oblast Party bosses A. K. Protozanov and B. Ye. Shcherbina to strongly endorse the development of the hydrocarbons of their region in order to offset the incipient decline of Second Baku production. They also called for the rapid, comprehensive, and long-term development of Tyumen' oblast to accommodate the new industry.

The new Party boss of neighboring Tomsk province, Ligachev, also jumped on the bandwagon. At scientific conferences between 1966 and 1968, he challenged the Moscow regime to invest in Tomsk hydrocarbons, which after all were closer than Tyumen' resources to the big industrial centers of Novosibirsk and the Kuzbas.

Such bluster emanating from the periphery had not been heard in forty years. It could not fail to gain the attention of senior officials at the State Planning Agency (Gosplan). At Brezhnev's urging, M. G. Pervukhin ordered Gosplan's Council for the Study of Productive Forces (SOPS) to derive a comprehensive plan for the development of West Siberian energy by the end of 1968. Also exhorting him were Trofimuk and his fellow geologist G. P. Bogomyakov, who would succeed Shcherbina as Tyumen' Party boss in 1973 and serve until the end of the 1980s. They vigorously lobbied for a long-term, comprehensive plan for Western Siberia. Aganbegyan joined them, pushing for the development of a major petrochemical industry along with petroleum extraction and refining.[28]

By 1966, new development projects in Greater Siberia had depleted the supply of ex-zeks, creating a labor shortage. Accordingly, the Supreme Soviet restored the northern increment and wage incentives to their 1960 levels, and in some cases, upgraded them. These were the incentives that attracted the students and trusties mentioned earlier to the oil fields.

The labor crisis was overcome, but at no small expense. Greater Siberia's share of Soviet capital investment in 1961 to 1965 had been 12.1 percent. During the next five years, it sprang to 15.2 percent.[29] According to Leslie Dienes, the monthly wages of a worker in Western Siberia now averaged 111 percent of the Soviet mean; in Eastern Siberia, 126 percent; and in the SFE, 158 percent. Given unweighted returns in the form of labor productivity of 101, 83, and 94 percent, respectively, authorities both inside and outside the USSR were justified in questioning the wisdom of such unrequited largesse.[30]

The realities of exchange theory rarely played a role in Soviet decision-making. On December 11, 1969, the Party and government jointly approved a SOPS plan that would comprehensively develop Tyumen' and Tomsk provinces. The plan designated more than one dozen ministries, state committees, state planning agencies, and other institutions to increase oil and gas output, to lay pipelines, to build railways, to string electric power transmission lines, and to create a vast infrastructure. Oil production was slated to reach 30 Mmt in 1970, 120 Mmt in 1975, and 230–260 Mmt by 1980. All of these targets were exceeded.[31]

During the next decade (1970–1980), the Kremlin power struggle peaked. Until 1970, Premier Kosygin had been as prominent as Brezhnev in international and domestic politics. The two men were as different as night and day. Brezhnev was pro-rural and emphasized agriculture. Kosygin was pro-city and emphasized industry. Brezhnev was extroverted and rumbustious. Kosygin was introverted and reserved. Brezhnev increasingly sided with the Siberian pressure groups; nevertheless, until 1978, he preferred to leave questions of energy policy in the hands of Kosygin, who tended to support the intensification of existing industry in the core and a balanced energy policy for the country as a whole.

Between 1970 and 1975, the East-West debate tested political careers. By then, Brezhnev had become the strongest Soviet political leader. Erstwhile "Siberian" Gennadiy Voronov fell from grace because he sided with Kosygin. The Ukrainian Party boss, Petro Shelest, lost his place on the Politburo because he opposed the diversion of investments away from Donbas coal mines into the development of West Siberian hydrocarbons.[32] But Kosygin could claim an occasional victory also. This was borne out during his speech at the Party Congress in March 1976, when he declared, "Future growth of our energy potential will come *primarily* from hydroelectricity, nuclear energy, and cheap coal."[33] To Siberians, who had striven to obtain greater investment in oil and gas, Kosygin's ideas were a slap in the face. Bogomyakov angrily criticized a plan to extract and transport cheap Siberian coal (from the Kansk-Achinsk Basin) to Soviet Europe because it drew away scarce capital from the development of cleaner, more economical natural gas. He contended that if new oil deposits were not opened up, there would be a collapse of West Siberian oil production. Shortly afterward, the U.S. CIA confirmed his contention.[34] None of this dissuaded the 1976 Party Congress delegates from rubber-stamping Kosygin's ideas. The West Siberian energy coalition had to regroup.

For Brezhnev, the turning point in the debate came in 1977. Throughout that year, the Siberians conducted a media blitz against the central agencies that were alleged to have repudiated further investment in the West Siberian energy complex. The loudest criticism emanated from junior regional politicians and lesser members of EKO. They were joined by the powerful Trofimuk and Shcherbina, who called for an expansion of the role of oil and gas in the country's energy balance. The climax came at the Party's December 1977 plenum, where the Siberian "lobby" (Bogomyakov, Ligachev, Trofimuk, Aganbegyan, and a host of others) mounted its final offensive. The Siberians obviously impressed Brezhnev, who immediately urged the initiation of a crash oil and gas development program for Western Siberia.[35] Four months later, the general secretary took a whirlwind tour of Greater Siberia, during which he made several pro-Siberian speeches. Upon his return, as he had in the past, he challenged Soviet youth to go east to develop Siberia's vast resources.[36]

Political jockeying over the issue of Siberian oil and gas persisted until Kosygin's death in 1980. Political scientist Gordon Smith contended that the pro-Siberian faction on the Politburo consisted of 9 of the 20 full and candidate members. Curiously, Chernenko was not listed among the supporters, although Dolgikh was. Smith also determined that 77 members of the Central Committee were behind the project, exclusive of legions of unified backers in Western Siberia. Kosygin had a maximum of 5 supporters on the Politburo, including the Premier himself, and a few dozen advocates on the Central Committee. Representing different parts of the country, Kosygin loyalists were less unified and more vulnerable than the highly organized Western Siberians.[37]

Eastern Siberia's On-Again, Off-Again Railway: The BAM. Lobbying for Siberian projects did not start and end with West Siberian oil and gas. For nearly a century, visionaries dreamed of building a railway north of Lake Baykal to the Pacific Ocean. Because it avoided the sinuous Amur bend, the route was 400 to 500 kilometers (250 to 300 mi) shorter than that of the Trans-Siberian Railroad. Because it was a similar distance inland from Manchuria, it was also more secure from Yellow Peril than was the Trans-Siberian.

Before 1960, however, engineers could not overcome the environmental obstacles that plagued the Baykal-Amur Main Line (BAM) for each of its

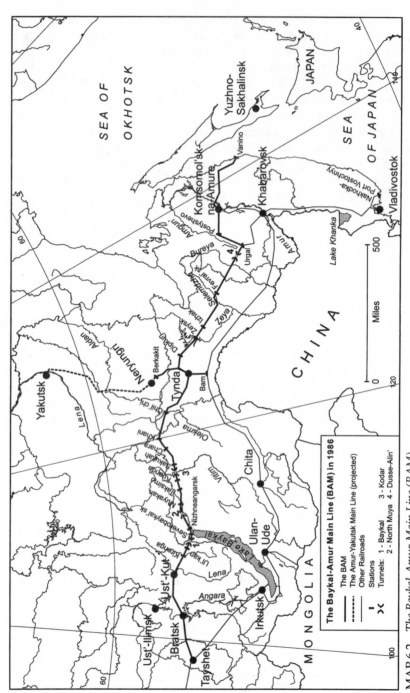

MAP 6.2   *The Baykal-Amur Main Line (BAM)*
SOURCE: Swearingen 1987, *Siberia and the Soviet Far East*, p. 48.

4,434 kilometers (2,754 mi). Between Tayshet on the Trans-Siberian Railroad and Sovetskaya Gavan' on the Tatar Strait, the BAM would negotiate virgin taiga, mountains, rivers, and bogs perched atop gelatinous permafrost for more than two-thirds of the distance. Engineers would have to bore more than 30 kilometers (19 mi) of tunnels through earthquake-prone rock. Accordingly, the actual laying of track in this hazardous region proceeded at a snail's pace. Serious efforts began only after the 1920s, with the first construction of the "Little BAM," which lay approximately midway across the main east-west axis, and the work was interrupted by the war. Between 1941 and 1957, the BAM terminuses were completed to Ust'-Kut in the west and to Postyshevo in the east, leaving 3,115 kilometers (1,934 mi) undone.[38]

The BAM represented a departure from the core's usual treatment of the periphery. Given its constraints, the railway, from the beginning, held little promise for immediate returns. Criticized as a "frozen asset" and *avantyurizm* (adventurism), the BAM would be more costly than beneficial for many years to come. Kosygin's forces must have been as bewildered by the resolution to build the BAM as they were upset with the regime's favoritism of West Siberian oil and gas.

But the railway obtained powerful advocates. Sino-Soviet relations reached their lowest ebb during the 1960s. The Chinese were threatening to retake the controversial borderlands that had been made Russian by the Aigun' and Peking treaties (see Chapter 3).[39] Thus, planning for the BAM took on a strategic aspect. For a while, the ministry of defense was the railway's most dedicated pressure group.[40]

Compared to the brouhaha surrounding West Siberian hydrocarbons, the BAM issue at first attracted only subtle pressure from Siberian leaders. Perhaps because of its strategic sensitivity in the early stages, the acronym "BAM" did not appear in the Soviet press until 1970.[41] Even then, it was subsumed under the general blueprint of the North Siberian Railway (NSR). Yakutian first secretary, G. I. Chiryayev, argued for an extension of the NSR from Nizhnevartovsk near Samotlor across the Central Siberian Upland to his homeland, where supplies occasionally required a year or more to reach remote destinations. Otherwise, Siberian scholars boosted the development of Udokan copper and South Yakutian coal, iron ore, and phosphates without mentioning the BAM or its potential role.[42]

Before the 1971 Party Congress, the BAM gained the support of a truly powerful Communist, V. P. Lomakin, the first secretary of Primor'ye. As head of the so-called Vladivostok Group, the patron-client tentacles of which reached Party leaders throughout the SFE, Lomakin wielded massive influence. Lomakin argued energetically for improvements in SFE transportation, which included not only the BAM but also a 4,000-kilometer (2,500-mi) oil pipeline from Angarsk, near Irkutsk, to the Pacific Coast.

Pro-BAM forces in Moscow already had rejected the pipeline as insufficiently versatile. They boasted that the railway would outperform the pipeline, as a "super main line" that would spirit eight-axle rail tankers from the Ob' oil fields to the Pacific at high speeds. Two years later, at the time of the Arab oil embargo, this became one of the cogent arguments in the BAM's favor: As much as 70 percent of all BAM deliveries [were to be] West Siberian oil, all of which would be destined for export.[43]

With the Party's blessing, BAM enthusiasts went public. The railway ministry's newspaper, *Gudok*, promulgated a spate of articles by railway engineers and authorities who backed the idea of a second trunk line. Chiryayev continued to be the most conspicuous BAM supporter among local Party officials. (His protégés would lobby for better transportation well into the 1980s.[44]) The Yakuts depended on unreliable Lena River transport for three-fifths of their supplies and consistently argued for a rail link as a way to overcome the bottlenecks.

The majority of the propaganda ceased, however, when the delegates to the 1971 Party Congress endorsed only the construction of the port of Vostochnyy, east of Nakhodka, and the re-laying of the Little BAM to Tynda. The latter appeased the Yakut delegation, since it was headed in the direction of Yakutsk. For the next two years, little was said about the main, east-west axis. Even in early 1974, shortly "before the announcement of BAM construction, there were no promotional arguments for the railway."[45]

Meanwhile, a series of compensation agreements with Japan, enhancing Soviet trade with that country and expanding Siberian resource development projects, must have piqued enthusiasm for the BAM both at the local and national levels. In addition, the 1973 Arab oil embargo, with all its implications for higher raw material prices, surely impressed Brezhnev. In the end, however, without strong grassroots organizing for the BAM, Brezhnev alone may have been responsible for the decision.[46] He certainly stood alone on March 15, 1974, when he announced that the east-west axis of the BAM would be "the construction project of the century."[47]

Throughout the decade of construction (1974–1984), Soviet citizens were led to believe that the BAM was part pyramid and part colossus of Rhodes. Hardly a day went by without considerable media attention being devoted to the railway and its construction workers. A whole new geography could be grasped from the news reports alone.

During tracklaying, one figure in particular, apart from Brezhnev, was identified with the BAM. It was not Dolgikh, who characteristically maintained a low profile even when giving an occasional speech to BAM workers. Nor was it Ligachev, who, until Andropov brought him to Moscow again, contented himself with solidifying his Tomsk power base.

It was hardly Chernenko, who had long since shed his Siberian roots. It was Academician Aganbegyan, who together with his colleagues in Akademgorodok, Irkutsk, and Khabarovsk, was charged with comprehensively planning the BAM and the would-be industries of its service area. Between 1975 and 1983, almost 10,000 articles, books, and analyses were completed pertaining to the BAM and its economy.[48] Aganbegyan himself was responsible for several dozen authored or multiauthored pieces, and he was quoted endlessly in the press. His most important role, however, was to serve as the director of the Scientific Council on BAM Development, through which he consulted directly with SOPS.

With the end of tracklaying, the BAM fanfare died. Brezhnev and Andropov were dead. Chernenko was nearly dead, and an entirely new philosophy of leadership was nigh. One of the first acts of the new leadership was to summon Aganbegyan from Novosibirsk to Moscow. The BAM had seen its heyday.

GREATER SIBERIAN INDIGENES, 1953–1985

Compared to their predecessors in 1953, Siberian minorities in 1985 were more numerous, more modern, more urban, and better fed. They were also less religious, less likely to live in clans, less nomadic, and more likely to speak Russian with some fluency. Increasing numbers had forgotten their native language but not their native culture. Much of the "progress" described in this chapter was associated with the intrusion of Russians into autochthonous Siberian regions and proved devastating to the native homelands. Deforestation and pollution often had wide-ranging physical and human consequences. Although the BAM, and the urbanization associated with the new energy complex, had citified a few individuals, the bulk of the most-affected groups (Khants, Mansi, Sel'kups, and Evenks) simply moved deeper into their homelands.[49] One group, the Komi, whose traditional territories are west of the Urals, fled from the Russian advance in such numbers that they soon equaled the Nentsy population of Yamalo-Nenetsia.[50] In every case, the changes eroded traditional ways of life and personal dignity, which stimulated alcoholism and suicide. Especially hard hit were the peoples of the southwest (Khakass, Altays, and Tatars) and those of the northeast (Chukchis, Eskimos, Itel'men, and Koryaks). The peoples of Amuria and Sakhalin were increasingly urbanized and Russianized. By 1985, all of the groups were heavily collectivized, although some— such as the Khants, Mansi, and Sel'kups—carried on seminomadic fishing along the Ob'. A few of the remotest Even clans still maintained a nomadic lifestyle, herding reindeer in the wilds of Yakutia.[51]

Essentially a Russian fief for dozens of years, Tuva (now Tyva) was an independent state between 1921 and 1944, when it became the Tannu-

Tuva autonomous republic. Until then, 85 percent of the Turkicized Mongol Tuvans were pastoral nomads who raised cattle, horses, sheep, and reindeer. Virtually none lived in cities. Soon thousands of Russians and Ukrainians flooded the region and created the first cities. Kyzyl, their capital, was an artificial Soviet creation devised as an outpost for forced collectivization, procurement, and industrialization. The Tuvan reaction to collectivization was the same as that of the other Turkic and Mongol tribes: They slaughtered their livestock to avoid selling them. By the time collectivization was complete there, in 1955, Tuvan herds had plummeted from 1.5 million animals in 1944 to 600,000. The understandable hatred of Tuvans for Russians would persist.[52]

While the Russians assimilated the Tuvans in the south, they drilled diamond mines and raised hydroelectric dams in Yakutia. The invasion of Russian workers was so impressive that even though Yakuts increased their numbers by 62 percent, they watched their share of the republic's population fall from 46 percent in 1959 to 33 percent in 1989. Always adaptable, the Yakuts reasserted their national spirit in a way that was not so much anti-Russian as pro-Yakut.[53] The reaction was also linked to the vivid memories of Stalinist repression in the 1920s and 1930s. Yakuticization included the repudiation of their well-known habit of christening their children with Russian names and patronymics. Instead, they began to use appellations that were purely Yakut. Before long, where they lived together, Yakuts and Russians were at loggerheads. In the words of James Forsyth, "Yakut resentment against Russians was matched by a Russian tendency to brand Yakuts as primitive." Riots erupted in Yakutsk in 1979. They were reportedly so serious that Uniate convict Vyacheslav Chornovil, who was an eyewitness, beseeched Soviet authorities to change his place of exile.[54] The antagonism continued into the 1980s.

CONCLUSION

In the wake of Stalinist repression, the stigma that had been responsible for the purges of Greater Siberian leaders finally evaporated under Khrushchev. The prejudice had been formidable: Between 1938 and 1955, no Siberian-born or -based Party member was appointed to the country's highest offices, the Politburo and Secretariat. Thereafter, however, Siberians became increasingly evident among the nomenklatura; and by the mid-1960s, they had regained the confidence that they had lost in the 1930s. From 1960 to 1985, all over Greater Siberia, provincial Party leaders, academics, students, and writers persistently beseeched the core to invest in their much-neglected region.

This constant pressure from the Siberian provinces, together with Leonid Brezhnev's invaluable personal bias, won funding for the expensive West Siberian energy complex and the BAM. According to geographer Ronald Liebowitz, of the total investments in the Russian Republic, Siberia attracted 25.8 percent of the money in 1970, 31.4 percent in 1980, and a whopping 37.2 percent by 1990.[55] With a mere 22 percent of the Russian population in 1990, Siberians acquired 1.7 rubles of investment for every one invested elsewhere in the republic. One of every five rubles invested in Russia went to the West Siberian Energy Complex alone (Tomsk and Tyumen' provinces, including Yamalia and Khantia-Mansia). Between 1970 and 1990, the Politburo approved the allocation of an additional 80 billion rubles (Br) for new investments (41 Br to 120 Br). Of this, 16 billion went to Tyumen' province and 19 billion went to the BAM. According to Dienes, the lobbying effort had been so effective that Tyumen' and the BAM absorbed more than one-half of the Russian increment between 1975 and 1985.[56] By that year, exports of West Siberian oil and gas were the country's leading source of hard currency; the BAM was poised to go into full operation; and construction of the Amur-Yakutsk Main Line (AYAM), comprising the Little BAM and its extension to Yakutsk, had been launched.

All of this had given a great boost to the Russian Siberian ego, but it had dearly cost the Siberian environment and its native populations. By 1985, Siberian indigenes had the lowest longevities, the lowest confidence levels, the highest rates of alcoholism and suicide, and the least respect for their Russian masters of any groups in the Soviet Union.[57] The salad days of Siberian economic development were overripe, however, if not bletted. The dog days lay just around the corner.

NOTES

1. Stephen G. Wheatcroft, "Glasnost' and Rehabilitations," in *Facing Up to the Past*, ed. Takayuki Ito (Sapporo, Japan: Hokkaido University, Slavic Research Center, 1989), pp. 200–201.

2. John Sallnow, *Reform in the Soviet Union: Glasnost' & the Future* (London: Pinter, 1989), pp. 48–49.

3. As late as 1987, planned proportional development was still recognized as "the first principle of socialist distribution of production" by none other than A. G. Aganbegyan, Gorbachev's chief economic adviser and the "father of perestroika" (A. G. Aganbegyan and D. D. Moskvin, *Chto, Gde, Pochemu?* [Moscow: Prosveshcheniye, 1987], p. 9).

4. Alan Wood, ed., *Siberia: Problems and Prospects for Regional Development* (London: Croom Helm, 1987), p. 171.

5. Paul R. Josephson, "New Atlantis Revisited," in *Rediscovering Russia in Asia: Siberia and the Russian Far East*, eds. Stephen Kotkin and David Wolff (Armonk, N.Y.: M. E. Sharpe, 1995), pp. 93–94.

6. *Ibid.*, p. 90.

7. *Ibid.*, p. 101.

8. *Ibid.*

9. United States, Central Intelligence Agency, *USSR Agricultural Atlas* (Washington, D.C.: CIA, 1974), p. 47.

10. The South Siberian was extended to Tayshet, linking the new West Siberian Steel Mill in the Kuzbas with the iron ore fields around Zheleznogorsk, in the Lena Basin. The South Siberian also funneled Virgin Lands wheat to grain-deficient Eastern Siberia and the SFE. Traffic was expected to be so intensive that the South Siberian was the first Soviet railway to be electrified "as it was laid" (*Gudok*, December 18, 1985, p. 2). For the other railways, see B. I. Shafirkin, ed., *Ekonomicheskiy spravochnik zheleznodorozhnika* (Moscow: Transport, 1978), p. 267; A. G. Aganbegyan and A. A. Kin, eds., *BAM: pervoye desyatiletiye* (Novosibirsk: Nauka, 1984), p. 172; A. Zlobin, "Na Sibirskoy magistrali," *Novyy mir*, January 1959, p. 126; and *Razvitiye yedinoy transportnoy seti SSSR* (Moscow: Transport, 1963), p. 28.

11. Farley Mowat, *The Siberians* (Toronto: Bantam Books, 1970), p. 138; Theodore Shabad and Victor L. Mote, *Gateway to Siberian Resources: The BAM* (Washington, D.C.: Scripta, 1977), pp. 27–33; and Robert G. Jensen, Theodore Shabad, and Arthur W. Wright, eds., *Soviet Natural Resources in the World Economy* (Chicago: University of Chicago Press, 1983), p. 38.

12. Alan B. Smith, "Soviet Dependence on Siberian Resource Development," in *Soviet Economy in a New Perspective*, for U.S. Congress, Joint Economic Committee (Washington, D.C.: Government Printing Office, 1976), p. 483.

13. *Gudok*, March 12, 1988, p. 2.

14. Estimated on the basis of *Demograficheskiy yezhegodnik SSSR, 1990* (Moscow: Finansy i statistika, 1990), p. 21.

15. Matthew J. Sagers, "News Notes," *Soviet Geography*, Vol. 32, No. 4 (April 1991), pp. 253 and 257.

16. Violet Connoly, *Beyond the Urals* (London: Oxford University Press, 1967), p. 261.

17. Leslie Dienes and Theodore Shabad, *The Soviet Energy System* (Washington, D.C.: Victor H. Winston & Sons, 1979), p. 87.

18. Jerry F. Hough and Merle Fainsod, *How the Soviet Union Is Governed* (Cambridge, Mass.: Harvard University Press, 1979), pp. 219–220, 230, 231, 238–239, 248, 269, 271, 272, 411, and 426. The biographies of Aristov and Voronov may be found in *Bol'shaya Sovetskaya entsiklopediya* (1970), Vol. 2, p. 194, and Vol. 5, p. 368.

19. Ilya Zemtsov, *Chernenko: The Last Bolshevik* (New Brunswick, N.J.: Transaction, 1989), p. 3.

20. Alexander Rahr, *A Biographic Directory of 100 Leading Soviet Officials* (3d ed.; Munich: Radio Liberty Research, 1986), p. 63.

21. Boris Yeltsin, *Against the Grain* (New York: Summit Books, 1990), pp. 149–150.

22. Rahr, *A Biographic Directory*, p. 63; and Yeltsin, *Against the Grain*, p. 150.

23. Ye. K. Ligachev, "My View of *Perestroyka*: Gains and Losses," a public seminar presented at the Kennan Institute, Washington, D.C., November 15, 1991; Alexander G. Rahr, *A Biographic Directory of 100 Leading Soviet Officials* (4th ed.; Munich: Radio Liberty Research, 1989), pp. 99–101.

24. Brezhnev not only condoned the creation of patron-client relations, he encouraged them. Yeltsin climbed the ladder of success through the "Sverdlovsk

Group"; Ligachev, through the "Tomsk Group"; and Gorbachev, through the "Stavropol' Group." See Joel C. Moses, *Regional Party Leadership and Policy-Making in the USSR* (New York: Praeger, 1974) and other similar works by the same author; Gavin Helf, *A Biographic Directory of Soviet Regional Leaders, Parts 1 and 2* (2d and 3d eds.; Munich: Radio Liberty Research, 1988 and 1990); T. H. Rigby and Bohdan Harasymiw, eds., *Leadership Selection and Patron-Client Relations in the USSR and Yugoslavia* (London: George Allen & Unwin, 1983); and Rigby's other works. Sakhalin officials contacted Western oil firms as early as the 1960s, apparently without notifying Moscow (private conversation with a Marathon Oil executive, August 19, 1997).

25. Han-ku Chung, *Interest Representation in Soviet Policymaking: A Case Study of a West Siberian Energy Coalition* (Boulder: Westview, 1987), p. 85.

26. *Bol'shaya Sovetskaya entsiklopediya* (1977), Vol. 26, p. 250; Chung Han-kuk, "Politics of Soviet Development Policy: Comparison of Two Siberian Lobbies," *American and Soviet Studies Annual* (1986), pp. 45–47; Gordon B. Smith, *Soviet Politics: Continuity and Contradiction* (1st ed.; New York: St. Martin's, 1988), p. 123.

27. Anders Aslund, "Gorbachev's Economic Advisors," *Soviet Economy*, Vol. 3, No. 3 (1987), p. 259; Rahr, *A Biographic Directory*, 4th ed., p. 8. The Liberman reforms involved a slight liberalization of the command economy and a greater emphasis on the needs of consumers.

28. Chung, *Interest Representation*, pp. 73 and 91.

29. Smith, "Soviet Dependence," p. 483.

30. Leslie Dienes, "Investment Priorities in Soviet Regions," *Annals of the Association of American Geographers*, Vol. 62, No. 3 (September 1972), p. 444.

31. Chung, *Interest Representation*, p. 34.

32. On Voronov, see Zemtsov, *Chernenko: The Last Bolshevik*, p. 104. On Shelest, see Richard Bridge, "The Northern Economy in the 1970s and 1980s: Some Factors, Some Results," *Sibirica: Report of the British Universities Siberian Studies Seminar*, Vol. 2 (1986), pp. 18–19.

33. SSSR, KPSS, *Materialy XXV s"yezda KPSS* (Moscow: Politizdat, 1976), p. 140.

34. CIA, *The International Energy Situation: Outlook to 1985* (Washington, D.C.: Government Printing Office, 1977); and G. Segal, "CIA's Dire Forecast for USSR Oil Looks Accurate as Output Slumps," *Petroleum Review*, January 1979, pp. 17–18.

35. Smith, *Soviet Politics*, p. 123.

36. *Pravda*, April 26, 1978. In 1974, he exhorted *komsomol'tsy* to migrate to the BAM service area.

37. Smith, *Soviet Politics*, p. 126. Chung argued that no high-ranking Party figure "except Brezhnev" ever publicly committed himself to the project. He also noted that even though he was more involved in energy affairs than anyone else in the Secretariat, Dolgikh did not take a strong stand on oil, favoring drilling in both Western Siberia and the Volga-Urals, and felt gas was better used as a chemical feedstock than as a fuel. Chung, *Interest Representation*, p. 155.

38. Aganbegyan and Kin, eds., *BAM: Pervoye stoletiye*, p. 5; *Pravda*, July 16, 1977; and *Gudok*, December 26, 1980.

39. W. A. Douglas Jackson, *Russo-Chinese Borderlands* (2d ed.; Princeton, N.J.: Van Nostrand, 1968).

40. For a while, Westerners debated whether the BAM was built to serve the military or to serve the Siberian economy. My contention is that any railway, re-

plete with its implications for supply and delivery, potentially serves a military purpose. Émigrés who worked on the planning of the BAM project in the 1960s and early 1970s stated flatly that the only motivating factor at that time was a military-strategic one. Later on, economic considerations became paramount. See Jensen, Shabad, and Wright, *Soviet Natural Resources*, p. 239; and Allen S. Whiting, *Siberian Development and East Asia: Threat or Promise* (Stanford: Stanford University Press, 1981), pp. 81, 93–94, 99–107, and 212.

41. *Gudok,* July 2, 4, and 6, 1970, as cited in Chung Han-ku, *Politics of Soviet Development*, p. 59.

42. *Pravda,* March 16, 1974.

43. F. D'yakonov, "Dal'niy Vostok: Problemy i perspektivy," *Ekonomicheskaya gazeta,* No. 5 (January 1975), p. 13; Victor Biryukov, "The Baykal-Amur Mainline: A Major National Construction Project," *Soviet Geography: Review and Translation,* Vol. 16, No. 4 (April 1975), pp. 225–227; Lomakin's commentary is found in *Sovetskaya Rossiya,* March 19, 1971.

44. Chiryayev wrote a series of pro-BAM articles, beginning in 1971. See, for example, G. I. Chiryayev, "Problemy osvoyeniya Severa," *Ekonomicheskaya gazeta,* No. 12 (March 1971), p. 7; "BAM i Yakutiya," *Ekonomicheskaya gazeta,* No. 32 (August 1974), p. 5; and *Sovetskaya Rossiya,* June 4, 1975. Chiryayev's successor, Yu. N. Prokop'yev, would later champion the need for AYAM, the extension of Little BAM north to Yakutsk (see *Gudok,* September 26, 1984, and his remarks at the 27th Party Congress, *Pravda,* March 5, 1986).

45. Chung Han-ku, "Politics of Soviet Development," p. 61.

46. Robert N. North, "The Soviet Far East: New Centre of Attention in the USSR," *Pacific Affairs,* Vol. 51, No. 2 (Summer 1978), p. 207; and Marius J. Broekmeyer, "Some Questions Concerning the Construction of the BAM," in *Sibirie I: Siberian Questions,* ed. Boris Chichlo (Paris: Institut d'études slaves, 1985), p. 319. Broekmeyer implies that Brezhnev "wanted to glorify himself with a grandiose trunk line. Why else did he choose the 20th anniversary of the Virgin Lands as an opportunity to mention the BAM for the first time . . . ?"

47. *Izvestiya,* April 5, 1969.

48. Akademiya Nauk SSSR, Sibirskoye otdeleniye, *Problemy BAM* (Novosibirsk: Gosudarstvennaya publichnaya nauchno-tekhnicheskaya biblioteka, 1975–1983 [annual volumes]). I am grateful to Pat Polansky of the University of Hawaii for permitting me to photocopy all nine volumes of this rare bibliographic reference.

49. John Massey Stewart, "The Khanty: Oil, Gas, and the Environment," *Sibirica: The Journal of Siberian Studies,* Vol. 1, No. 2 (1994/1995), pp. 25–34.

50. James Forsyth, *A History of the Peoples of Siberia* (Cambridge: Cambridge University Press, 1992), p. 385. Oil and gas development in the Timan-Pechora region laid waste to much of the Komi homeland.

51. Piers Vitebsky, "Perestroika and Cultural Change Among the Reindeer Herders of Siberia: A Field Report" (paper presented at the conference on "Siberia in the Twentieth Century," Glasgow, Scotland, September 1989).

52. Gail Fondahl, "Siberia: Native Peoples and Newcomers in Collision," in *Nations and Politics in the Soviet Successor States,* eds. Ian Bremmer and Ray Taras (London: Cambridge University Press, 1993), pp. 499–503.

53. Forsyth, *A History of the Peoples of Siberia,* p. 380.

54. Piers Vitebsky, "Yakut," in *The Nationalities Question in the Soviet Union*, ed. Graham Smith (London: Longman, 1992), p. 309.

55. See Ronald Liebowitz's commentary in "Panel on Siberia: Economic and Territorial Issues," *Soviet Geography*, Vol. 32, No. 6 (June 1991), p. 382.

56. Leslie Dienes, "Perestroyka and the Slavic Regions," *Soviet Economy*, Vol. 5, No. 3 (July–September 1989), pp. 255–256.

57. Aleksandr I. Pika and Boris Prokhorov, "Soviet Union: The Big Problems of Small Ethnic Groups," *Russia: Khanty-Mansi Autonomous Area*, available on-line at <http://www.lib.uconn.edu/ArcticCircle/SEEJ/Yamal/pika1.html> (21 September 1997), p. 5. Pika and Prokhorov note that in the late 1980s, murders and suicides among indigenous peoples were 3 to 4 times higher than the Soviet average, and male and female life expectancies were 45 and 55, respectively, or 18 years inferior to the USSR norms. For reports on the state of the environment of Greater Siberia, see Eugene Linden, "The Tortured Land," *Time*, September 4, 1995, pp. 42–53; and *Sibirica: The Journal of Siberian Studies*, Vol. 1, No. 2 (1994/95), pp. 7–49.

SEVEN

Dog Days and the Rise of the Little Siberians, 1985–1993

The government will not withhold funds from Siberian development, but it is justified in demanding that those funds yield a return and not be frozen.
—**Mikhail Gorbachev, June 12, 1985**

We will never stop our strike because Gorbachev tells us to. What he says doesn't go any farther than Red Square. We live far away in Siberia. This is the land of the gulags, the place where prisoners have been sent since tsarist times. We have rebel blood.
—**Alexander Smirnov,**
Novokuznetsk Miners' Strike Committee (April 1991)

INTRODUCTION

Greater Siberia again fell on hard times. Whereas Brezhnev probably lavished too much attention on Siberian projects, Gorbachev vowed to economize. From the beginning, Mikhail Sergeyevich had to face at least two difficult economic facts: (1) His country was increasingly short of investment capital, and (2) declines in productivity were inexorable and commonplace. The highest rates of return on investment were obtained in Soviet Europe, not in Greater Siberia, which in fact was being subsidized at an annual rate of 2 percent of the country's net material product. As early as 1985, the handwriting was on the wall: Using words like "intensification," "scientific and technological progress," "modernization," and "resource-saving policies," Gorbachev obviously favored the core at the expense of the periphery. Although like the core the periphery had factories and mines in need of renovation, the periphery was underdeveloped and required many more "greenfield" projects. BAM, for example, fell into disrepair almost as soon as the trains began to roll. Hundreds of West Siberian oil fields became idle for want of appropriate equipment. Meanwhile, Gorbachev salved Siberian wounds by promising much, but he delivered little.[1]

After 1986, Gorbachev's policies of *perestroyka*, *glasnost'*, and *demokratizatsiya* permitted Siberians to air their grievances against Moscow for the first time since the NEP (see Chapter 5). These policies also unleashed unprecedented labor protests and "waves of nationalism" among Soviet minorities.[2] In the process, Gorbachev purposefully set about destroying the vestiges of Brezhnev's patronage system, which for all its faults, had attracted investments to Siberia. These occurrences marked the beginning of the end of the Soviet Union.

KUZBAS GOES ON STRIKE

Despite the good intentions behind them, Gorbachev's reforms wreaked political and economic havoc throughout the USSR. Gorbachev wanted to establish the preconditions for the formation of a civil society within the purview of a fundamentally changed Communist Party: one in which "rights are effectively secured and in which interest groups can assert themselves."[3] *Perestroyka* and *glasnost'* gave vent to long-suppressed freedoms of speech and press and a plethora of diverse social interests, including those of the working class. The State Enterprise Law of 1987, which was to be implemented by January 1, 1990, was designed to shift control over industrial activities from the central ministries to the individual enterprises, and in the process, to guarantee the workers some authority over the same enterprises and plant managers. By making economic enterprises responsible for their own fates through *khozraschet* (cost-accounting), Gorbachev sought to create an economy that would be more responsive to the needs of the people. However, so much redundancy and waste were built into the Soviet economy that Gorbachev's policies actually laid the foundations for the future bankruptcy of major employers. By raising the level of efficiency in such an economy, there would be less, not more, to do. Fewer workers would be needed, and the economic system might even collapse.

The irony of state corporate socialism was that the working class remained alienated from the power structure that claimed to be its vanguard: The proletariat and the CPSU were never really integrated. In provinces such as Kemerovo oblast, miners lived in squalor. As demand for Kuzbas coal withered under the new economic stimuli, conditions worsened. "Working class resistance increased against attempts to solve the economic crisis at the expense of living standards and social welfare."[4]

Until 1989, Soviet workers rarely if ever vented their grievances publicly. Ordinarily, they turned to their trade union representatives, who would forward their complaints to the Central Committee of Soviet Trade Unions. That was precisely the channel that the miners in Kiselevsk, a city of 128,000 people in the Kuzbas, decided to use in December 1988. Their principal spokesman was 58-year-old Teimuraz Avalyani, the town's first secretary. Avalyani was a seasoned veteran in the struggle against injustice, having been harassed by police in the 1970s for criticizing Brezhnev. He would later run against Gorbachev in the first open election for CPSU general secretary in seventy years. If anyone could communicate their grievances to the appropriate authorities, Avalyani was the perfect choice—or so the miners thought.

Between 1987 and 1989, decentralization and self-management had destabilized the coal industry. The miners began to vent their frustrations over disorganized work schedules, the lack of modern equipment, the indifference displayed by mine directors over the daily needs of the miners, and crowding in the mine shafts. Their mine directors had failed them. "They" (the miners) could do a better job. It was time to implement the terms of the enterprise law. They wanted economic independence and more control over mine activities. The Moscow trade unionists returned their complaints to their mine director without comment.[5]

Storm clouds gathered. Kuzbas miners expressed their dismay by voting against incumbent Communists in the city of Kemerovo, candidates for the regional executive committee, and the directors of the Kemerovo coal and railway administrations. Kemerovo's delegation to the Congress of People's Deputies tried to warn congressional leaders of the serious crisis in the Kuzbas, but "national" problems took precedence.[6]

Exasperated by the rebuff and apathy in the core, 344 Kuzbas miners initiated a strike in Mezhdurechensk on July 10, 1989.[7] The following day, 15,550 miners from ten other Kuzbas operations joined them. They now expressed their grievances in terms that anyone could understand. They wanted more control over the mines, guaranteed safety in the workplace, higher pay, better food, cleaner water, soap, pollution control, and a national debate on the Soviet Constitution (see Photo 7.1).

Gorbachev interpreted the protests as an affirmation of his reforms, and in turn, supported the miners. He dispatched his much-maligned Coal Minister, M. I. Shchadov, whose views were quite different, to Kemerovo. By then, miners throughout the USSR made no secret of their desire to force the unaccommodating Shchadov into retirement. His ministry had always treated them as a "colonial work force."[8] Long accustomed to rubber-stamp treatment and perfunctory applause, Shchadov was met with catcalls and whistles by the discontented thousands who had gathered in the town square of Mezhdurechensk. In sweltering, ninety-five-degree heat, the min-

PHOTO 7.1 *Miner on strike in the Kuzbas (1989).* SOURCE: *Dmitriy Korobeynikov, Novosti Press Agency (Kemerovo Bureau).*

ers, helmeted and in the same clothes they wore into the pits, initially sat stoically on the scorching pavement, only occasionally drinking water out of nearby fireplugs. They listened as Shchadov pleaded with them to return to work and promised that he would take their demands into consideration. The operations at Mezhdurechensk were undoubtedly significant. They produced one-fifth of all Kuzbas coal, the majority of the region's coking variety, and 2.5 percent of Soviet coal output. The loss of Mezhdurechensk production for any length of time could prove disastrous.

The miners knew this. It was their trump card. They were tired of waiting and hearing the same jaded promises and formulas. Yes, they earned decent salaries (up to ten times the Soviet average), but what could they buy? The strikers' assessment of their plight was "you have to work hard to live worse." When they did work hard, the railways could not accommodate the excess coal. At any given time, twelve million tons of the fuel languished in bins awaiting shipment over the South Siberian Railway. Even worse, the underground mines were dangerous because of a chronic shortage of mine props—and this in a region (Siberia) with the greatest forests on earth.

Their pollution protests were well taken. The Kuznetsk Basin is a narrow hollow, for the most part only about 100 kilometers (60 mi) wide. It is drained by the Tom' River and its tributaries. The air in the basin often stagnates because of the nightly drainage of cold air from the Salair and Kuznetsk ranges and the periodic elevated temperature inversions. The latter are most prevalent in the cold winters. In 1989, the heavy industry in the basin—comprising coal-burning power plants, coke ovens, iron and steel mills, nonferrous metallurgical smelters, and a variety of chemical enterprises—belched out more than one million metric tons of atmo-

PHOTO 7.2   *Severe air pollution at the West Siberian Steel Mill, near Novokuznetsk (1990).* SOURCE: *TASS.*

spheric emissions annually, half of which was sulfur dioxide. The steel-producing town of Novokuznetsk ranked third among Russia's most polluted cities (Photo 7.2). Kemerovo and Prokop'yevsk also ranked in the top 25. In Greater Siberia, only Noril'sk was more notorious.[9]

Even in Kemerovo, which was much less noxious than Novokuznetsk, air pollution exceeded Soviet standards not by dozens but by hundreds of times. Area coal miners died at age 48, having achieved only three-fourths of the average Soviet life span. Chronic childhood sicknesses were 188 percent of the norm. The rate of illness among persons 15 to 19 years of age was twice the average. Half of the pregnant women of the region suffered chronic illness. Still-births numbered 20 per 1,000 live infants. Among coal miners and their families, these averages were the highest in the USSR.[10]

Among the miners' grievances, none was more critical than the need for clean water. The Tom', the water of which had been "as pure as well water" in 1946, was by 1989 a "sewer" that contained compounds of lead, zinc, sulfur, phenol, and cyanide. Seventy percent of the morbidity in the region was directly attributable to bad water. The primary cause was acid leachate from Kuzbas strip mines. The region's strip mines scar thousands of acres of fertile Kuzbas earth. The open pits occasionally reach depths of 300 meters (900 ft), and they have disrupted the courses and purity of hundreds of creeks, streams, and rivulets that feed the Tom'. A single strip mine affects the water balance within 25 kilometers (15 mi) of the center of the depression. By 1989, the sum of all the dozens of Kuzbas strip mines accounted for one-fifth of the entire basin, or an area the size of the U.S. state of New Jersey. In parts of the Kuzbas, the water table was beyond repair, leaving some localities high and dry. Lower water tables had led to subsidence, which was augmented by earth temblors induced by the use of explosives in the mines. Despite the hazards, only 3 to 6 percent of the strip mines had been reclaimed. Ignorant of, or choosing to ignore, these nightmarish statistics, Shchadov from his vantage point in Moscow adjured that Kuzbas coal output be increased from 160 Mmt in 1989 to 220 Mmt in 1999, the majority coming from further use of strip mines.[11]

The coal miners' strike mushroomed within and beyond the borders of the Kuzbas. By July 12, it had expanded to include 10,000 more miners, from Osinniki and Prokop'yevsk. Within 48 hours, mines in Novokuznetsk, Leninsk-Kuznetskiy, Belovo, Kemerovo, and Berezovskiy shut down, affecting 134 operations and 111,125 mine workers. By the end of the week (July 17), the work stoppage had peaked at 158 enterprises and 177,682 strikers. By then, the firestorm had spread from the Kuzbas to Karaganda, Pechora, L'vov, Rostov, and the Donbas.[12]

To orchestrate their efforts, the miners established strike committees in every mining town. The Association of Kuzbas Laborers, based in Kemerovo, coordinated the committees regionally. The immediate purpose of the units was to oversee implementation of the contract to end the strike, which came to fruition in the latter half of 1989.[13] As time went on, however, they superseded the discredited local officials, who had failed to provide basic services not only to the miners but also to other local residents. Initially, the committees worked around the clock, fielding grievances from all comers. Mezhdurechensk, for instance, a city of 107,000, had only two movie theaters and two bathhouses. The principal concerns of the non-miners were medical care, home improvements, and financial aid. In the eyes of the public, the miners were heroes who could accomplish miracles. In the words of William Mandel: "[Strike committees found themselves] besieged by citizens who assumed that at last they had an institution to help them. Petitioners lined up all day for a stamp and signature to enable them to get a bank loan, advice as to what to do when the person renting them a room wanted to terminate the lease, and a host of other daily cares."[14]

Members of the strike committees soon realized that such matters lay well beyond their purview. In the words of one committee member: "We're not asking for sausage. There's no place to turn for it, and none to be had."[15] What the strike committees wanted was the opportunity to fulfill their own self-interest and their own destiny. They were concerned by the fact that in 1990, the Kuzbas yielded 15 billion rubles of regional product, but the core took all but 17 percent of the profit out of the region: "We have been used as a colony for centuries. What we produced was taken away from here, and we were given virtually nothing in exchange."[16] They were left with cold showers, dirty clothes, environmental disruption, and little real power to better their circumstances. In moments of fervent discussion, strike committee members sounded like Yadrintsev, Potanin, or the Siberian kulaks: "We're seeking separation. Why? We must split off in order to break that rigid, [stupid] centralization. And only after we have broken [with it], when we have local budgets and our own funds, will we possess real power, because money is power!"[17]

In an electoral system, real power is also political power. Another Gorbachev reform was to democratize the Soviet political system. One of the aspects of the process was multicandidate elections. After the strike in the Kuzbas, incumbent Party and government officials and the would-be power brokers on the strike committees stood at daggers drawn. The January 1, 1990, deadline for implementing decentralization and self-management came and went. For various reasons, the core failed to act, and the confrontation in the Kuzbas deteriorated. The questions of self-financing and control of the coal mines became key issues in the ensuing provincial elections in March. In Kemerovo oblast, the strike committees put forward their own slates, and in most cases their candidates did quite well, winning two out of five elections. A few months later, shortly after he had assumed his duties as chairman of Russia's Supreme Soviet, Boris Yeltsin met representatives of the Kuzbas strike committees to discuss the impasse on decentralization. Yeltsin, who himself sought independence for the Russian Republic from Gorbachev's USSR, was delighted to give his support to the miners. The Kuzbas-USSR crisis over who had authority over coal in Kemerovo oblast thus became part of the imbroglio between republics and the Soviet Union, "and most particularly between Gorbachev and Yeltsin."[18]

NATIONALITIES POLICIES

The bid for economic sovereignty was not the exclusive realm of Kuzbas coal miners, the vast majority of whom were nonnatives. As Peter Duncan presciently observed in 1994, since 1986, one of the most urgent tasks of the central authority, whether Soviet or Russian, has been "to find a mechanism to balance the rights of [Siberia's] indigenous peoples with [those] of the ethnic Russian majority."[19] Before the Revolution, the myriad Siberian groups had no self-government. The Bolsheviks designed their nationalities policy to co-opt ethnic groups by creating "nationalities" with "homelands." Overnight, clans such as the Kachas, Sagays, Beltirs, Kyzyls, and Koybals woke up to find themselves united as the "Khakass nation," in their own national *uyezd*.[20] Similarly, in the mountains west of what would become Khakassia, the Tubulars, Chelkans, Ku-

PHOTO 7.3 *Shor hunter with dog.* SOURCE: *Dmitriy Korobeynikov, Novosti Press Agency (Kemerovo Bureau).*

mandas, Telengits, Telesy, Altays, and Teleuts discovered that they were all now Oirots (Altays), living in an Oirot autonomous oblast (today's Altay Republic).[21] In the decade between 1929 and 1939, the neighboring Shors had their own national okrug, which the commissars disbanded ostensibly because they thought it might impede the development of the coal and iron resources of the Kuzbas (Photo 7.3).[22] At least one of the amalgamated groups has never accepted the common national status (Teleuts have always considered themselves distinctive among the Altays).

The creation of ethnic homelands left the impression that the Bolsheviks were democratizing their society, when in fact the goal was not the dispersal but the further concentration of authority by means of the tentacles of the CPSU. Before 1929 and after 1953, CPSU leaders implemented a policy similar to the United States' affirmative action, whereby native Communists usually occupied the highest-ranking posts within their homelands.[23] Quoting Duncan, "Quota systems intended to mobilize the non-Russian population in the service of the Moscow regime gave over-representation to the members of the local nationality [in important positions]."[24] This created a political paradox between an increasingly Russian central leadership and staunchly indigenous nomenklaturas in the provinces. The dichotomy continued to exist even as the proportion of ethnic Russians expanded with the influx of workers bound for the new development projects. In exchange for their loyalty to Moscow, the native leaders gradually acquired perquisites that enabled them to disregard their minority status and discreetly to pursue their economic and social interests and those of their homelands. Thus, as Gorbachev's democratization policies weakened the position of the CPSU, they also undermined the position of the overrepresented native minorities and strengthened the hand of the underrepresented ethnic Russian majorities in the indigenous homelands.

Glasnost' and the Little Siberians

The history of the twentieth century is one of perpetual collision between members of the expanding, technologically developed world and the innocent bystanders on the margins, who represent traditional societies. This truly was the case within the Soviet Union, which aspired to military-industrial superiority throughout its seventy-four-year lifetime. The speed of its transmogrification from an overwhelmingly rural, agricultural society to an urban-industrial one is nonpareil in human history. Yet, as it sped toward its goals, the USSR trampled on anything and anyone in its way.

The implications of *glasnost'* for ethnic groups in the USSR finally hit home after Gorbachev's "Murmansk Initiatives" speech on October 1, 1987, in which the general secretary declared, "Problems of the North's indigenous population require special attention." Until then, the Soviet propaganda machine had masked the truth about the nature of life among the minorities, preferring to vaunt the successes of industrialization over the needs of Russians and non-Russians alike. From 1988 onward, however, the liberated press promulgated remarkably frank articles and broadcasts regarding the plight of Soviet ethnic groups, particularly the peoples of the European North and Greater Siberia. As the press revealed, in the face of Soviet technological progress, the needs and opinions of these peoples "carried little weight."[25]

Unlike technology-based societies, which create artificial milieus to overcome quotidian demands, traditional societies and their environments possess intimate, mutually beneficial relationships, in which the disruption of one cannot fail to disrupt the other. Piers Vitebsky, who lived among Siberian natives, has remarked that "competence in [reindeer] herding," for example, "depends on intimate knowledge of one's animals and of their interaction with the landscape across which they move; it uses special vocabulary and imagery of reindeer behavior and moods; and requires unceasing teamwork from before dawn till after dark."[26] Thus, Soviet megaprojects like West Siberian oil and gas development and the BAM could not fail to ravage the simple lifestyles of the "little Siberians." In Khantia-Mansia and Yamalo-Nenetsia alone, ecologists estimated that Soviet "progress" had damaged or destroyed 11 million hectares (27 million acres) of reindeer grazing area and 28 rivers with commercial fisheries, including 18,000 hectares (44,000 acres) of spawning and feeding grounds. The despoliation came from air pollution created by the widespread flaring of wellhead gas into the cold, stable air of Western Siberia and the 3,000 to 4,000 accidents that occurred in the oil and gas fields each year.[27] The high rate of accidents such as leaks, spills, blowouts, wildfires, and so on could be explained in part by the attitudes

PHOTO 7.4   *Khant man with reindeer.* SOURCE: *Dmitriy Korobeynikov, Novosti Press Agency (Kemerovo Bureau).*

of the Siberian roughnecks, who were basically transient workers, on the job for only three to four weeks at a time.[28] The oil and gas field workers could not have cared less for the wilderness swamps and woodlands on which the natives depended for their livelihoods. Fondahl tells of such workers stealing Khant "sleds and winter clothing, poaching reindeer, and desecrating native burial grounds." The behavior enraged one Khant to such a degree that he proclaimed he would shoot any oilman who ventured into his hunting range (Photo 7.4).[29] Despite suffering the abuse of progress, the Khants, Mansi, and Nentsy saw nothing of the huge profits made from the extraction of hydrocarbons in their homelands. In fact, they were not even invited to take part in the planning process.[30]

With the advent of *glasnost'*, a few Siberian indigenes made it clear that they wanted to live separately from nonnatives. Several Evenks residing in the BAM region of Irkutsk oblast chose to leave the state farms for life in the taiga. They drove their reindeer into the forests and became state hunters, a lifestyle that markedly improved their health and living standard.[31] Between 1962 and 1986, programs of rural consolidation and resettlement reduced the number of native communities on Sakhalin Island by at least two-thirds. The number of Nivkh settlements alone, on the island's northwest shore, fell from 82 to 13. In 1989, Nivkh and Orok reindeer herders sought permission to return to the sites of their former villages and hunting grounds. Although the total number of Sakhalin indigenes in 1989 was only about 2,500, their spokesman, veteran writer and Communist Vladimir Sangi, championed their cause.[32] Testing the limits of *glasnost'*, the Chukchi proposed a program designed to resettle the *prishliye* rather than themselves, encouraging the latter to emigrate elsewhere in the USSR. And the Ugrian popular front, Spaseniye Yugri, urged the government to relocate the Khants and Mansi to settlements of no more than 150 persons, ringed by protected natural buffers. The concept of exclusive native zones (reservations, national parks, and so on) obtained a measure of popularity among Greater Siberian autochthonous groups during the Gorbachev years.[33] Accordingly, by the time Gorbachev was ousted by Yeltsin, the indigenous groups of Greater Siberia were primed for true sovereignty, including the commercial exchange of their resources.

The Parade of Sovereignties

The Kuzbas strike committees were symbolic of what was happening on a quieter scale elsewhere in Greater Siberia. By spring 1990, with Gorbachev's democratization plans in full swing, indigenous leaders in the autonomous regions feared that they would lose their positions and privileges unless they declared their regions sovereign states. At the last moment, they obtained indirect help from the Yeltsin-led RSFSR Congress of People's Deputies, which approved the Declaration of State Sovereignty of the Russian Republic. Under this act, USSR laws were invalid if they conflicted with those of the RSFSR. Because it eroded central authority, this act gave Yeltsin the upper hand in his power struggle with Gorbachev. In desperation, Gorbachev's forces exhorted indigenous leaders in Russia to declare their homelands sovereign states. This Tatarstan was prepared to do, but before it could become a full Union republic within the USSR, Yeltsin co-opted the "'parade of sovereignties,' telling the republics to 'Take as much sovereignty as you can swallow.'"[34]

In the months that followed, Siberian ethnic groups, led by their respective popular fronts, took Yeltsin at his word and demanded greater sovereignty over their resources, less environmental degradation, and greater influence over the Russian majority within their homelands. The Yakuts led all others, declaring their Yakut-Sakha Republic sovereign on September 27, 1990. Two days later, the Chukchi pronounced their region a sovereign autonomous okrug separate from Magadan oblast, under whose jurisdiction they had been since 1953. On October 8, 1990, the Buryats formalized their sovereignty, and like the Yakut-Sakhans, upgraded their homeland status from ASSR to SSR. One day later, the Koryaks declared not only their sovereignty but also their intention to secede from Kamchatka oblast. (The latter announcement proved premature: As of 1998, Koryakia remained subordinate to Kamchatka.)

PHOTO 7.5   *Ninety-two-year-old Nanay woman with pipe.* SOURCE: *Dmitriy Korobey-nikov, Novosti Press Agency (Kemerovo Bureau).*

On October 18, 1990, the Yamalo-Nentsy not only pronounced themselves a sovereign republic but also claimed rights to the monumental gas and oil fields found within the boundaries of their homeland. A week later, titular leaders of Gorno-Altay raised the status of their homeland to a sovereign ASSR and declared themselves the exclusive owners of all its resources. Still later in the year, Khakassia, Tyva (formerly Tuva), and Khantia-Mansia pronounced themselves sovereign.[35]

In the RFE, leaders of the Jewish Autonomous Oblast (JAR) declared their province autonomous of Khabarovsk kray and expressed a desire to make Birobidzhan truly Jewish. Elsewhere in the region, Murav'yev-Amurskiy, Admiral Kolchak, and Ataman Semenov (see Chapters 4 and 5) were given special homage. Ethnic Koreans expressed their desire for an autonomous homeland southwest of Vladivostok, around the Gulf of Pos'yet. Descendants of the Amur and Ussuri Cossack Hosts staked claims to sections of the Amur, Ussuri, and Tumen (also Tuman) rivers (Photo 7.5).[36]

Most of the declarations took place peacefully; but in the year preceding its "independence," the Tyva Republic was fraught with tension. In early 1990, the Tuvan (soon to be Tyvan) Popular Front was born, and before long, street fighting between the titular Tuvans and the hated Russians had resulted in at least 88 deaths and in the mass departure of more than 3,000 Russians.[37]

REGIONALISM AND FEDERALISM

The phenomenon of regionalism in Russia has little to do with democracy and much to do with local control over raw material wealth. By early 1991, Kuzbas miners and Siberian minorities were solidly in the Yeltsin camp on the question of sovereignty but were not yet sure of his position on the sharing of economic power. The strike committees and ethnic minorities increasingly saw the Gorbachev regime as an adversary that was interested only in maintaining the core at the expense of the periphery. As the confrontation between Gorbachev and Yeltsin intensified, Kuzbas miners further sided with Yeltsin. When it became clear that the Gorbachev regime was incapable of redressing their grievances, they again ceased to work.

The coal miners' strike of 1991, which persisted for more than two months, was worse than its predecessor. In the Kuzbas, as a result of both work stoppages, the gross output of coal had imploded from a peak of 159 Mmt in 1988 to 109 Mmt in 1992—a 31 percent collapse in only three years.[38] Coal shortages were experienced throughout the USSR. Kuzbas strike committees boldly demanded the resignation of Gorbachev and his government, and were beginning to distrust Yeltsin, who now found himself in the middle of the fray. To break the impasse, Yeltsin flew to Kemerovo on May Day 1991. He urged the miners to consider terminating the strike if he could persuade Gorbachev to transfer jurisdiction over Russia's coal mines from the ministry of coal to the RSFSR. This was accomplished by May 6, and four days later, the strike ended. In the words of Paul Christensen, "Attention focused on the miners' demands that Gorbachev resign, but [they] accepted the compromise *only because Yeltsin promised to cede greater control over the coal industry to the localities.*"[39]

Christensen furthermore characterized the victory of the Kuzbas miners as, inter alia, a "triumph of regionalism over centralism," which in many respects set the tone for Greater Siberian politics in the 1990s.[40] The victory could not have been won, however, without the schism in the core between Gorbachev's "empire savers" and Yeltsin's "nation builders."[41] Shortly after the August coup attempt, in fall 1991, the North Caucasian republic of Chechnya declared its independence. The ultimate debacle of the USSR followed in December, with Gorbachev's resignation. Given its problems with ethnic sovereignty and brewing regionalism, Russia, it seemed, was also on the brink of collapse.

Westerners wonder why Yeltsin, at the peak of his popularity, did not thoroughly expunge the Communists and their old, patchwork constitution, paving the way for radical reform on a tabula rasa. The view represents a total lack of understanding of Russian history and culture, and such an act probably would have led to civil war. Yeltsin thus avoided the disaster by mixing the past with the present: He destroyed the nomenklatura system but not the men in office. As Jeffrey Taylor wrote in 1997, "In the provinces those who had effectively presided over the ruin of the country were left to direct its 'reformation,' with predictable results."[42] Yeltsin also chose to reform the country within the framework of the old

Soviet constitution because, for the moment, he had no alternative, again with predictable results. By leaving the "Red Directors" in power in the periphery and the majority of old guard Communist parliamentarians in the core, he squelched the threat of civil war as he consolidated his own authoritarian power base.

In Yeltsin's opinion, federalism mixed with authoritarianism was the only means to countervail the nascent ethnic secessionists and regionalists. To prevent Russia's disintegration, he initially granted substantial powers to provincial leaders, which they could effectuate within their regions. In this way he temporarily emasculated thoughts of secession and deflected attention away from the hated core. His notion of federalism was embodied in the Federation Treaty of March 31, 1992, which was signed immediately by all but four of the twenty-one constituent republics.[43] One of the dissenting republics was Yakut-Sakha (now Sakha [Yakutia]), the leaders of which wanted a greater share of the profits made from their homeland's lucrative diamond and gold trade. Meanwhile, regional leaders elsewhere in Greater Siberia concentrated on ways to attract foreign capital.

Joint Ventures and Free Economic Zones

The joint venture (JV) was to be crucial to the success of *perestroyka,* particularly in Greater Siberia, where development costs were often higher than the core could afford. During the 1970s, Brezhnev had authorized mutual compensation agreements (MCAs) in the periphery whereby foreign firms from, say, Japan and the United States would supply technology and know-how to develop a Soviet project in exchange for a share of the project's future output. The difference between JVs and MCAs was that foreigners, under *perestroyka,* could share up to 49 percent of project ownership. The Politburo later amended the program to permit the outside investor to be the majority "shareholder."

JVs became legal in 1988 but were slow to take off because of the lack of legal safeguards. In June 1989, only 520 JVs were registered in the entire USSR, the vast majority of which were found in the manufacturing regions of the core. Greater Siberia attracted few investors. As late as January 1, 1991, the region claimed only 102 JVs, few of which were engaged in manufacturing, which was needed most.[44]

With the collapse of the USSR, international entrepreneurs flocked to the successor states. Whereas 3,000 JVs were registered in the USSR at the end of 1990, their number had reached 5,000 by the spring of 1992 and 6,000 a year later. More than half were located in Russia, almost three in ten of which were in Greater Siberia. Approximately 450 JVs functioned or awaited approval in the Russian Far East (RFE) alone. Indicative of gradual federalism, 22 percent of Greater Siberia's JVs were documented in Novosibirsk and 6 percent were registered in Khabarovsk, Vladivostok, and Magadan. The balance of the registrations were filed in Moscow.[45]

Because of their proximity to the Pacific Rim, representatives of the RFE were especially active in wooing JV candidates. In exchange for their participation in the region, foreign investors were given a tax holiday of three years instead of two, which was the Russian standard. Khabarovsk kray and Sakhalin oblast offered their own incentive plans. Consequently, by the end of 1993, there were over 1,000 JVs with Chinese, Japanese, Korean, North American, European, and Australian partners. They owned restaurants, department stores, hotels, boutiques, computer shops, sturgeon hatcheries, rendering plants, and Dutch windmills. By the beginning of 1994, more than 3,000 JVs were registered in Greater Siberia, split evenly between Siberia proper and the RFE.[46]

JVs were not the only incentive used to attract foreign investment to the USSR and its successor states. As early as 1987, the Gorbachev regime created ad hoc committees to investigate the possibilities of establishing duty-free economic zones modeled after those previously established in China.[47] The Soviet version of the free, or special, economic zone (FEZ, or SEZ) was designed not only to lure foreign investment but also to comprehensively develop the regional economy and to integrate it into the Soviet and global economies. From the standpoint of an investor, FEZs had the following advantages: (1) easier registration procedures; (2) tax privileges; (3) reduced rent, including leasing for up to 70 years and the right to sublet; (4) lower customs tariffs on imports and exports; and (5) simple entry and departure privileges. As in other countries, FEZ status heralded greater economic autonomy for the favored region, something that ran counter to Soviet praxis, with its ham-handed, Moscow-centered approach. Conservatives in the core therefore opposed the FEZ concept, preferring instead the idea of the SEZ, with special privileges but less autonomy.[48] Their opposition considerably slowed the deliberation process.

The first regulations governing FEZs emerged in December 1988,[49] but the RSFSR Supreme Soviet did not rule on the plans until July 1990. FEZs recommended for Greater Siberia comprised Primorskiy kray (chiefly Nakhodka), Chita oblast (Dauria), the JAR, Altay kray, and Kemerovo oblast (the Kuzbas), the last recommendation obviously bowing to the wishes of the coal miners. In May 1991, owing to the charismatic leadership of Valentin Fedorov, Sakhalin Island also joined the fold.[50] As the USSR collapsed, other regions considered for FEZ status included Blagoveshchensk; Magadan; Greater Vladivostok (a region stretching from the Tumen River to Nakhodka); the Kurile Islands (separate from Sakhalin oblast); and the Tumen River region, which would be an international FEZ incorporating parts of Russia, North Korea, and China. The Tumen FEZ also had the support of the Japanese, the South Koreans, and the Mongolians.[51] The ingenuous provincial Russian governments eventually made a mockery of the notion of "special economic status": Before the end of 1991, more than 60 of the 77 Russian provinces then in existence had applied for FEZ status.[52]

By 1993, only three or four of the proposed FEZs in Greater Siberia had any realistic chance of succeeding. All of them were in the RFE. For all its previous bluster, landlocked Kemerovo was unlikely ever to attract sufficient foreign capital to merit such a designation. The world, after all, was shifting to clean fuels, not coal, which was the primary bargaining chip of the Kuzbas.[53] The FEZs of Dauriya, Altay, Blagoveshchensk, and the JAR would no doubt suffer the same fate, although their proximity to China has aided them. The economies of Magadan and the Kurile Islands were simply too weak to support the status. Only Nakhodka, Vladivostok, Sakhalin, and Tumen were promising.

"Independence" and "Autonomy"

Within a year after the collapse of the Soviet Union, a few Siberians dared broach the subject of independence. Others stressed economic autonomy. Huge numbers refused to pay their taxes, and innumerable eighteen-year-old Siberians repudiated registration for the draft. Similar events occurred in the nineteenth and early twentieth centuries. What was remarkable about these latter-day episodes was that the core was virtually powerless to do anything about them. Between spring 1992 and fall 1993, a constitutional crisis raged, pitting "progressives" in the executive branch against the conservative majority in the legislative branch of the Russian government.

The debacle of the Soviet Union destroyed the iniquitous departmentalization (the vertical administrative-bureaucratic hierarchy of ministries) of socialist industry, which Stalin had encouraged, Khrushchev had discredited, and Brezhnev had reinstated. The ministries were vertical fiefs, jealously guarded and sharing little information between and among themselves. This led to overlapping jurisdictions, to duplication, and to the cross-hauling of raw materials and goods between regions. As senseless as the system was, however, it did to a large degree guarantee control over the periphery. Departmentalization was typically indifferent to *all* regional demands; hence, during its post-Stalinist heyday, Siberians were not much worse off than their Moscow or Leningrad comrades.

As departmentalization and other factors finally crushed the government of the USSR, they left a gaping wound. To fill the void, Yeltsin and the parliament rushed in to mobilize the provincial elites. In Duncan's words, "The President sought to win over the republics within the Federation and, in particular, their presidents by promising them greater powers,"[54] stimulating regional revolts over economic autonomy in Sverdlovsk and Vologda oblasts and Primorskiy kray. Yeltsin invoked classic Stalinist tactics, playing off one territory against the other, weakening regional affinities, and stultifying economic redevelopment. He used "imperial visits" to placate his disillusioned subjects in the periphery, leaving behind empty promises and hardened cynics such as Aman Tuleyev of the Kuzbas.[55]

In April 1993, Boris Yeltsin returned to the Kuzbas. The president had been popular there ever since he gave an impromptu speech in the Mezhdurechensk public square, during the 1989 coal miners' strike. In that speech, as president manqué, he vowed to support Kemerovo oblast as a free enterprise zone.[56] Yeltsin—whom the Western press referred to as a "Siberian"[57]—had defied the ministries, called for economic and ethnic autonomy, and appeared to stand for the periphery against the core. By 1993, while those goals were at best only partly fulfilled, the Russian parliament and not Yeltsin was blamed for problems in the regions. In typical Siberian fashion, Kuzbas residents felt certain that Yeltsin eventually would respond positively to their grievances. Thus, when Yeltsin announced his intention to rule by decree in March 1993, the Kuzbas strike committees were the first to rally to his side. During the campaign for the national referendum a month later, Yeltsin's most enthusiastic support came from the Kuzbas.

In April 1993, it was a cautious Yeltsin who met the miners. Whether still grieving the recent death of his mother, fatigued by his battles with the parliament, or belabored by his bad heart, the president was decidedly cool to his jubilant Kuzbas backers. Usually comfortable with crowds, Yeltsin snubbed his fans with a terse "I have a tight schedule," and, reminiscent of the caucuses of the old CPSU, locked himself into meetings with top local executives, handpicked officials, and labor activists (Photo 7.6). Emerging from the meetings, Tuleyev, a former sympathizer with the August coup and one of Yeltsin's leading critics both nationally and locally, observed, "He came here before but none of his promises have materialized. When the tsar visits his subjects he at least should make certain his vows are fulfilled."[58]

It was surprising that Yeltsin's popularity in Greater Siberia had endured as long as it had. As bad as the economy had become under Gorbachev, it only worsened under the shock therapy of Yeltsin's Prime Minister, Yegor Gaydar, in 1992. The policies not only resulted in the expected decline of industrial output but also in a disequilibrium of industrial performance between and among regions. Poorer regions paid more into the federal budget per capita than richer regions.[59] Manufacturing was especially hard hit.

PHOTO 7.6 *Left to right: Aman Tuleyev, Boris Yeltsin, and miners' strike leader Gennadiy Golikov in Kemerovo (1991)*. SOURCE: *Dmitriy Korobeynikov, Novosti Press Agency (Kemerovo Bureau)*.

Fossil fuel extraction fared better because of demand and higher prices. In Siberia, Tyumen' and Kemerovo oblasts temporarily did better than neighboring Novosibirsk oblast, which floundered because its high-tech military industry desperately needed to be converted. Like most of Russia, Siberia lacked the stabilizing influence of a strong middle class, which failed to emerge expeditiously during the transition to a "free market" economy. According to Vladimir Zhdanov, "As living standards declined across Russia, Siberian provinces remained among the country's poorest."[60]

By autumn 1993, the regional soviets increasingly took sides with the Russian parliament against Yeltsin. Witnessing the growing strength of the republics and the rising popularity of the parliament in the provinces, the president dissolved the legislative body and revoked the Soviet constitution by decree in September 1993. Shortly afterward, the conflict between the executive and the legislature became bloody, when Yeltsin ordered tanks to fire on the legislative building, resulting in 150 deaths.

The outcry was immediate. On September 21, 1993, after Yeltsin had dissolved parliament, Communist Vitaliy Mukha, then chairman of the Novosibirsk provincial legislature and head of the three-year-old Siberian Agreement, defied Yeltsin's presidential order and threatened to blockade the Trans-Siberian Railroad (see Chapter 8). Backed by hundreds of disenchanted Novosibirsk supporters, each carrying placards with familiar slogans, such as "For Socialist Siberia!" and "All Power to the Soviets!,"

Mukha momentarily came close to Yadrintsev's and Potanin's dream of an independent Siberian Republic—albeit a recrudescent communist one.[61] Simultaneously, in the RFE, Yevgeniy Nazdratenko, governor of Primor'ye, emotionally called for the establishment of a new Far Eastern Republic, invoking the name of Krasnoshchekov (see Chapter 5). Tuleyev, also enraged by Yeltsin's actions, called for "Siberian independence" and a general political strike against the president.[62]

CONCLUSION

Perestroyka, Gorbachev's internationally noteworthy and domestically notorious reform, emphasized existing big industry in the core over new projects in the periphery. The policy discriminated against the economy of Greater Siberia in spades. Under *perestroyka,* the region was doomed to recession and outright depression. Not surprisingly, Kuzbas miners would strike a second time, in 1991.

Risen like the Phoenix was Gorbachev's old nemesis, Boris Yeltsin, who became Russia's first popularly elected president. To consolidate his power at the expense of the now unpopular Gorbachev, Yeltsin supported the coal miners, the movements for ethnic sovereignty, and an end to communism. Once these objectives came to pass, Yeltsin inherited an economy in shambles, a constitution that favored the parliament, and a parliament full of old guard Communists who were uninterested in rapid reform. Meanwhile, the president played politics. He co-opted the ethnic republics by declaring them sovereign and by giving them apparent political power. He made promises to ethnic Russians in Greater Siberia that he knew he could not keep. He urged them to woo foreign investors with joint ventures and duty-free zones. These efforts helped stave off Russia's seemingly imminent disintegration.

Throughout the period between 1985 and 1993, ethnic Russian residents of Greater Siberia began to look nostalgically upon Brezhnev's *period zastoya* (period of stagnation). Yeltsin's promises were also empty. Soon, he, like Gorbachev, became the object of the Russian people's wrath. In contrast, Gorbachev's *glasnost'* policies enabled long-silent Siberian indigenes to stand up and be counted. They established popular fronts and sovereignty movements, and they readily voiced their concerns over their treatment at the mercy of Soviet industrialization. They were poised to become "the mice that roared."[63]

NOTES

1. Leslie Dienes calculated the annual subsidy in *Soviet Asia: Economic Development and National Policy Choices* (Boulder: Westview, 1987), pp. 87–88. For a Soviet

assessment of Siberia's contribution to the national economy at the time, see Rafik Sh. A. Aliyev, "Vneshnyaya politika Sovetskogo Soyuza v Vostochnoy Azii: Kriticheskoy analiz," *Acta Slavica Iaponica*, Vol. 8 (1990), p. 78. For Gorbachev's original ideas, see Defense Intelligence Agency, *Gorbachev's Modernization Program: A Status Report* (Washington, D.C.: DIA, 1987). Aganbegyan, Gorbachev's chief economic adviser at the time, and the chief architect of *perestroyka*, began his book, *Inside Perestroyka*, with the comment that "the years 1985–1987 were spent wholly in formulating a completely new system of administration, together with a program of radical economic reforms" (Abel Aganbegyan, *Inside Perestroyka: The Future of the Soviet Economy* [New York: Harper & Row, 1989], p. 1). For an interpretation of what Gorbachev's buzzwords meant, see Theodore Shabad, "Economic Resources," in *Siberia: Problems and Prospects for Regional Development*, ed. Alan Wood (London: Croom Helm, 1987), pp. 62–65. Gorbachev went to Greater Siberia a minimum of three times, and gave four speeches: in Tyumen' and Krasnoyarsk (1985); in Vladivostok (1986); and in Krasnoyarsk again (1988). In each speech he criticized and promised much (*Literaturnaya gazeta*, No. 24, June 12, 1985; *Pravda*, July 29, 1986; *Pravda*, August 26, 1987). In the end, he could not deliver.

2. Peter J. S. Duncan, "The Politics of Siberia in Russia," *Sibirica: The Journal of Siberian Studies*, Vol. 1, No. 2 (1994/1995), p. 15.

3. Richard Sakwa, *Gorbachev and His Reforms, 1985–1990* (New York: Prentice-Hall, 1991), pp. 200–201.

4. *Ibid.*, p. 211.

5. Thomas Friedgut and Lewis Siegelbaum, "The Soviet Miners' Strike, July 1989," *The Carl Beck Papers*, No. 804 (March 1990), p. 5; and Paul T. Christensen, "Property Free-for-All: Regionalism, 'Democratization,' and the Politics of Economic Control in the Kuzbas, 1989–1993," in *Rediscovering Russia in Asia*, eds. Stephen Kotkin and David Wolff (Armonk, N.Y.: M. E. Sharpe, 1995), p. 213.

6. *Pravda*, March 30, 1989.

7. Viktor Kostyukovskiy, *Kuzbass: Zharkoye leto 89-go* (Moscow: Sovremennik, 1990), p. 6; and T. Gavrilov and N. I. Lavrov, eds., *Zabastovka* (Moscow: Profizdat, 1989), p. 102.

8. Christensen noted that Gorbachev saw the strike as "evidence of grassroots worker support" (Christensen, "Property Free-for-All," p. 212). For more on Shchadov in Kemerovo, see Kostyukovskiy, *Kuzbass*, p. 12.

9. Victor L. Mote, *An Industrial Atlas of the Soviet Successor States* (Houston: Industrial Information Resources, 1994), pp. I-1 and I-4; and Philip R. Pryde's commentary in "Panel on Siberia: Economic and Territorial Issues," *Soviet Geography*, Vol. 32, No. 6 (June 1991), p. 409. Other pollutants included lead, formaldehyde, ammonia, nitrogen oxides, carbon disulfide, particulates, fluoride, and various hydrocarbons.

10. Kostyukovskiy, *Kuzbass*, p. 12.

11. *Ibid.*, pp. 32–33, 49. To place these assessments in a broader perspective: I visited Kemerovo in September 1991, and veteran Berkeley KPFA broadcaster and Soviet observer, William Mandel, had preceded me in Kemerovo, Kiselevsk, and Prokop'yevsk in February 1990. Both of us were prepared for the worst but were impressed with the moderate pollution levels. The Tom', which I drove along for over 20 kilometers to the north, was quite beautiful, and despite the probable pol-

lution, seemed less contaminated than some of the rivers I had seen in the United States and elsewhere. Air pollution was flagrant in Kemerovo's northern, industrial sector but was not as intolerable as I had anticipated. Mandel later observed: "When I was in Kemerovo and Prokop'yevsk, there were no obvious signs of any environmental problems. For example, the buildings showed no smoke discoloration" (William Mandel, "Soviet Miners Speak," *The Station Relay*, Vol. 5, Nos. 1–5 [1988–1991], p. 3).

12. Gavrilov and Lavrov, *Zabastovka*, p. 102; Friedgut and Siegelbaum, "The Soviet Miners' Strike," p. 6.

13. *Ibid.*, pp. 9–10; Kostyukovskiy, *Kuzbass*, p. 43.

14. Mandel, "Soviet Miners Speak," p. 3.

15. *Ibid.*, p. 6.

16. *Ibid.*, p. 7.

17. *Ibid.*

18. Christensen, "Property Free-for-All," pp. 214–215.

19. Duncan, "The Politics of Siberia," p. 13.

20. James Forsyth, *A History of the Peoples of Siberia* (Cambridge: Cambridge University Press, 1992), p. 363. Originally Khakassia was the Khakass *uyezd*. In 1930, it became the Khakass autonomous oblast.

21. Gail Fondahl, "Siberia: Native Peoples and Newcomers in Collision," in *Nations and Politics in the Soviet Successor States*, eds. Ian Bremmer and Ray Taras (London: Cambridge University Press, 1993), p. 491. The Altay Republic is the former Gorno-Altay autonomous oblast, which was subsumed within Altay kray between 1948 and 1990.

22. *Ibid.*, pp. 492–493. Gail Fondahl has observed that "Gornaya Shoriya's existence may have been seen as an impediment of the [Kuzbas] coal deposits as well as the iron deposits of the okrug itself, and the titular population considered small enough (10–15,000) to disenfranchise without consequence to the state." The effects on the Shors were devastating. Their population declined through 1979. Driven off their farms and out of their villages, they were forced to mine coal. Citing a French source, Fondahl concluded that the urban Shors became alcoholics and drug addicts, which raised the suicide and fatal accident rates.

23. Duncan, "The Politics of Siberia," p. 14. During my 1985 sojourn to Yakutia, my KGB companions made certain that I noticed the ethnicities of my Party and government hosts.

24. *Ibid.*

25. For Gorbachev's comments, see *Pravda*, October 2, p. 3. Also see Forsyth, *A History of the Peoples of Siberia*, pp. 393–394.

26. Piers Vitebsky, "Perestroika and Cultural Change Among the Reindeer Herders of Siberia: A Field Report" (paper presented at the conference on "Siberia in the Twentieth Century," Glasgow, Scotland, September 1989).

27. John Massey Stewart, "The Khanty: Oil, Gas, and the Environment," *Sibirica: The Journal of Siberian Studies*, Vol. 1, No. 2 (1994/1995), p. 25. The damaged grazing area was the size of the U.S. state of Tennessee, or twice the area of Wales. The decimated spawning and feeding grounds amounted to an area the size of England *and* Wales together.

28. *Baykalo-Amurskaya magistral'* (Moscow: Mysl', 1977), p. 191.

29. Fondahl, "Siberia: Native Peoples," p. 488.

30. Forsyth, *A History of the Peoples of Siberia*, p. 396; and Stewart, "The Khanty," p. 30.

31. Fondahl, "Siberia: Native Peoples," p. 488: "Alcohol consumption dropped to 12 to 20 percent of the Evenk village population."

32. *Ibid.*; and Bruce Grant, "Indigenism on Sakhalin Island," in *Rediscovering Russia in Asia*, eds. Stephen Kotkin and David Wolff (Armonk, N.Y.: M. E. Sharpe, 1995), p. 167. Sangi, a prominent member of the USSR Writers' Union, has called for the creation of a Nivkh autonomous republic on Sakhalin. At the time of this writing, in 1997, Sangi continued to be their spokesman.

33. Fondahl, "Siberia: Native Peoples," p. 488.

34. Duncan, "The Politics of Siberia," p. 16; and *Literaturnaya gazeta*, August 15, 1990.

35. Ann Sheehy, "Fact Sheet on Declarations of Sovereignty," *Report on the USSR* (Radio Liberty 464/90, October 31, 1990), p. 24. Examples of popular fronts representing smaller ethnic groups are the Yamal-Nenets national front, *Yamal-potomkam* (Yamal Progeny); the Khantia-Mansia national front, *Spaseniye Yugri* (Salvation of the Ugrians); and the Evenk national front, *Arun* (Renewal). Fondahl, "Siberia: Native Peoples," p. 489. The Chukchi national ("autonomous" between 1977 and 1992) okrug was carved out of sections of the Far East kray and the Yakut ASSR in December 1930, and later in that decade, it became part of the notorious gulag of Dal'stroy, which persisted in one form or another until 1957 (John Stephan, *The Russian Far East: A History* [Stanford: Stanford University Press, 1995], p. 256). Khantia-Mansia also declared itself sovereign owner of the oil and gas resources within its borders (*Sibirskaya gazeta*, December 24–30, 1990, p. 2).

36. Stephan, *The Russian Far East*, p. 293. The JAR's delegate to the Supreme Soviet discussed the notion of making Birobidzhan "genuinely Jewish."

37. Fondahl, "Siberia: Native Peoples," p. 502.

38. Matthew J. Sagers, "The Energy Industries of the Former USSR: A Mid-Year Survey," *Post-Soviet Geography*, Vol. 34, No. 6 (June 1993), p. 392. Also, see Mote, *An Industrial Atlas*, p. III-7.

39. Christensen, "Property Free-for-All," p. 216. The italics are present in the original statement.

40. *Ibid.*, p. 217.

41. Graham Smith, "Ethnic Relations in the New States," in *The Post-Soviet Republics: A Systematic Geography*, ed. Denis J. B. Shaw (London: Longman Scientific & Technical, 1995), p. 36.

42. Jeffrey Taylor, "This Side of Ultima Thule," *The Atlantic Monthly*, April 1997, p. 41.

43. The four included Chechnya and Tatarstan, which refused to sign the treaty; Bashkortostan, which signed but delayed ratification; and Yakut-Sakha, which signed only after it obtained special economic concessions. See Andrew R. Bond, Richard M. Levine, and Gordon T. Austin, "Russian Diamond Industry in State of Flux," *Post-Soviet Geography*, Vol. 33, No. 10 (December 1992), pp. 635–644.

44. See Michael Bradshaw's commentary in "Panel on Siberia," p. 400.

45. Fewer than one in four actually operated. See *Russian Far East Update*, June 1993, p. 10; Alexander B. Parkansky, "Current Issues of Foreign Direct Investment

in Russia," *Acta Slavica Iaponica,* Vol. 11 (1993), p. 21; and Pavel A. Minakir and Gregory L. Freeze, eds., *The Russian Far East: An Economic Handbook* (Armonk, N.Y.: M. E. Sharpe, 1994), pp. 187–188.

46. Stephan, "The Russian Far East," p. 298; and Vladimir I. Ivanov, "The Russian Far East: The Political Economy of the Defense Industry Conversion," in *Socio-Economic Dimensions of the Changes in the Slavic Eurasian World,* eds. Shugo Minagawa and Osamu Ieda (Sapporo, Japan: Hokkaido University, Slavic Research Center, 1996), p. 188. Peter Kirkow contradicts Stephan's claim of 1,000 JVs, stating that in early 1994, there were 461 such businesses in operation in the RFE (Peter Kirkow, "Russia's Gateway to Pacific Asia," *Sibirica: The Journal of Siberian Studies,* Vol. 1, No. 2 [1994/1995], p. 53).

47. V. Ivanov and P. Minakir, "O roli vneshneekonomicheskikh svyazey v razvitii tikhookeanskikh rayonov SSSR," *Mirovaya ekonomika i mezhdunarodnyye otnosheniya (MEMO),* No. 5 (1988), p. 62; A. Kovalev, "Svobodnyye ekonomicheskiye zony: Opyt zarubezhnykh stran i perspektivy ikh sozdaniya v SSSR," *Vneshnyaya torgovlya,* No. 11 (1989), pp. 16–19; and Sophie Quinn-Judge, "Partners Preferred," *Far Eastern Economic Review,* February 2, 1989, p. 54.

48. Denis J. B. Shaw and Michael J. Bradshaw, "Free Economic Zones in the Russian Republic," *Post-Soviet Geography,* Vol. 33, No. 6 (June 1992), pp. 409–411.

49. *Izvestiya,* December 10, 1988.

50. *Gudok,* July 31, 1990; Shaw and Bradshaw, "Free Economic Zones," p. 409; and Lexis Nexis reports on the RSFSR Council of Ministers Decree No. 540 (November 23, 1990), on the Nakhodka FEZ; Decree No. 312 (June 7, 1991), on the Jewish AR FEZ; Decree No. 359 (June 26, 1991), on the Sakhalin FEZ; and Decree No. 497 (September 25, 1991), on the Chita FEZ.

51. Stephan, *The Russian Far East,* p. 298. A Japanese businessman-philanthropist first broached the idea for the Tumen FEZ to Aleksey Kosygin in the 1970s. In summer 1990, Strang International, an Australian transportation company, actively courted Soviet officials, trying to convince them that Vladivostok needed to be a FEZ (*Gudok,* July 19, 1990; and *The Japan Times Weekly International,* February 15–21, 1993).

52. Michael J. Bradshaw, "Foreign Trade and Inter-republican Relations," in *The Post-Soviet Republics: A Systematic Geography,* ed. Denis J. B. Shaw (London: Longman Scientific & Technical, 1995), pp. 145–146.

53. For information on the Kemerovo FEZ, see *Gudok,* November 15, 1990, and December 27, 1990; and *Nasha gazeta,* July 19, 1991. The early optimism about trade with China has faded: China is a coal-surplus nation, with monumental air pollution problems. The driving force behind the Kemerovo FEZ was Governor Mikhail Kislyuk, who has since been deposed. Since 1993, the idea has been moribund. See Christensen, "Property Free-for-All," p. 218.

54. Duncan, "The Politics of Siberia," p. 17.

55. Vladimir A. Zhdanov, "Contemporary Siberian Regionalism," in *Rediscovering Russia in Asia,* eds. Stephen Kotkin and David Wolff (Armonk, N.Y.: M. E. Sharpe, 1995), pp. 122–123.

56. *Sibirskaya gazeta,* September 3–9, 1990, pp. 1 and 5. Almost from the moment that he set foot in Kemerovo oblast, Yeltsin was barraged with the slogan of "full

economic independence for the Kuzbas region" (*Kommersant*, No. 33 [August 20–27, 1990], p. 12).

57. Yeltsin was born in 1931, in the central Urals city of Sverdlovsk, now Yekaterinburg. By the historical definition of Siberia as everything east of the crest of the Ural Mountains, this area could be considered part of the Greater Siberian region. This traditional definition probably explains why in the early 1990s, Western reporters often referred to Yeltsin as "the Siberian." Russians, for their part, rarely have made this identification, because for many decades the Urals—including Sverdlovsk, Chelyabinsk, and Kurgan oblasts, among other territories—have formed a separate economic zone. However, in a March 1993 interview, the Governor of Sakhalin, Valentin Fedorov, did allude to Yeltsin as having been "born and raised in Siberia" (*Independent Newspaper* [English ed. of *Nezavisimaya gazeta*], Vol. 3, Issue 20/21 [March 1993], p. 1).

58. Associated Press, April 15, 1993; and *Sibirskaya gazeta*, No. 38 (September 1991), p. 4. A fiery orator, Tuleyev (b. 1944) is a Kazakh by nationality and a member of the Communist Party of Russia (CPRF). Elected a people's deputy of Russia and Kemerovo oblast in 1990, he has served in high-ranking posts in Kemerovo ever since, most recently as interim governor (through October 1997) after the dismissal of Kislyuk (see footnote 53 in this chapter). As a candidate for the Russian presidency in 1991, he ran fourth—behind Yeltsin, Ryzhkov, and Zhirinovskiy—with 7 percent of the overall vote. He campaigned for the same office in 1996, before ceding the CPRF nomination to Gennadiy Zyuganov. He has been an outspoken critic of Yeltsin, whom he views as a dictator.

59. Duncan, "The Politics of Siberia," p. 17.

60. Zhdanov, "Contemporary Siberian Regionalism," p. 122.

61. *Vedomosti*, October 8–14, 1993; Zhdanov, "Contemporary Siberian Regionalism," p. 126.

62. Stephan, *The Russian Far East*, p. 294.

63. This is an allusion to the popular 1950s film, *The Mouse That Roared*, in which a tiny country struggles to compete with some of the world's most powerful nation-states.

EIGHT

Greater Siberia Today: Roaring Mice and Wage Arrears

They shot it out at noon, not long after a hard summer rain had turned the city road to mud. By the time the turf battle for one of Siberia's wildest outposts had ended, two gang members lay dead, six others were on their way to the hospital, and this untamed city—filled with enough gamblers, con men, and thieves to make Dodge City seem like Larchmont—had taken one step closer to anarchy.

—*The New York Times*, **February 16, 1994**

The coal-mining towns all around are bankrupt. It is hard to find anyone on the street who has been paid in the past six months.

—*Los Angeles Times*, **May 26, 1997**

OCTOBER'S AFTERMATH: NATIONAL SUPREMACY VS. ETHNOREGIONAL RIGHTS?

The bloodletting and spleen venting subsided after the parliamentary crisis of October 1993. That December, after 90 days of government by presidential decree, Russia's electorate affirmed not only a new group of parliamentarians but also a new constitution. Whereas the old Soviet Constitution vested the parliament with most of the political power,[1] the new constitution gave the president most of the clout. The March 1992 Federation Treaty had guaranteed certain rights to the republics that the new constitution took away. The status of the republics was reduced. No longer were they referred to as "sovereign" republics. Instead, they were simply *sub"yekty* (constituent parts) of the realm, like all the other regions. They lost the right to secede, which they arguably had had under the 1992 treaty as well as in the previous period, but which they never could have implemented under

Soviet law. The new constitution sanctified the rights of the individual, not the rights of ethnic groups or other collectives. To soften the blow, the document allowed all ethnoregions except autonomous okrugs (that is, eight of the fourteen ethnic administrative units in Greater Siberia) to assign indigenous languages a status within their borders that was equal to that of Russian, and Article 69 made passing reference to other rights of numerically small native peoples. Overall, however, the new constitution dissatisfied many republican and regional leaders because of its vagueness regarding the extent of home rule. In protest, Sakha (Yakutia), along with Chechnya, Tatarstan, and Bashkortostan, adopted its own constitution, "proclaiming the supremacy of [its] laws over Russian federal laws."[2]

On a positive note, with the creation of the Federation Council, all regions, including the republics, were permitted to maintain two seats each in the upper chamber of the Russian parliament. Since 1996, the elected regional or republican governor and the chairman of the provincial duma have occupied these posts. This framework obviously favors sparsely inhabited Siberian ethnoregions, with titular populations ranging from as few as 3,000 people (Evenk autonomous okrug) to 365,000 persons (Sakha/Yakutia).[3]

Smith notes that the controversies over sovereignty in Russia transcend constitutional guarantees. They also comprise the relationship between federalism and democracy, the essence of core-periphery economic relations, and the definition of cultural autonomy. It would be easy to advise that Russia, with its long history of elitist rule and the absence of pluralism, should disperse and share its centralized powers in order to stimulate democracy among its regions. Smith cogently argues that there is no evidence in political theory that smaller units are more accommodating of democratic politics than larger ones. In the Russian provinces, where many local leaders predate the fall of communism, authoritarian trends are readily observable.[4] In fact, the long tradition of Siberian satrapies almost ensures a continuation of authoritarianism in certain localities in the periphery. In multinational states like Russia, greater federalism may invite the acceleration of centrifugal forces and the labefaction, if not the wholesale collapse, of the system.

The sovereignty issue peaks in core-periphery economic relations. Since 1993, the Yeltsin government and the regions have performed a clumsy balancing act in which the regions demand greater local control over their economies and the core requires revenues needed to balance the national budget. The result is a catch-22: The transition from large, centrally controlled, state-owned enterprises to smaller, market-oriented, privately owned activities has meant that the state must continue to collect revenues from local budgets to finance the activities of the residual state industries. Enterprises and citizens, both of which paid no taxes during the Soviet period, to date have stubbornly resisted parting with meager resources that they know could be put to better use personally or locally. The result has been a nationwide shortage of cash in circulation. The core cannot collect enough taxes to pay pensioners and state workers in the regions, while a privileged few become increasingly rich by hoarding undeclared income at home or in foreign bank accounts.

The core suffers from the long history of tyranny to such a degree that even when it is serious about reform, the residents of the periphery suspect it is up to no good. Sakhans, for example, fear that if they stress their own cultural heritage too much, they may upset the federal structure and invite reaction from the core-sympathizing Russian majority within their republic. Deprived by the Russian constitution of the right to secede, they must operate within a federal system that they distrust; moreover, they must reckon with the fact that without Russia, not to mention the Russians within their midst, they are not economically viable at this time. If these statements apply to resource-rich Sakha (Yakutia), then they are equally pertinent to the other ethnoregions of Greater Siberia.[5]

To a certain degree, the struggle between core and periphery is reminiscent of the ongoing battle in the United States between advocates of national supremacy and proponents of states' rights. "In the general reduction of the rights of the republics, [the always political] Yeltsin was responding to ethnic Russian public opinion," which typically favors strong central control.[6] Duncan suggests that the president may have been influenced by proponents of national supremacy, such as reformer Boris Nemtsov and nationalist Vladimir Zhirinovskiy. Then governor of Nizhniy Novgorod, Deputy Prime Minister Nemtsov, and his philosophical near opposite, the virulent Zhirinovskiy, have been conspicuous supporters of returning to the tsarist system of *gubernii* (governorships), in which "ethnicity was irrelevant."[7]

ORGANIZED INTEREST GROUPS

At the same time as *glasnost'* activated the natives of Greater Siberia, it also spurred the creation of "supraethnic" interest groups, originally with the aim of attracting foreign trade and capital that the regional economies so desperately needed. Whereas ethnic popular fronts mobilized the aspirations of indigenous groups, regional trade organizations hoped to orchestrate the economic interests of the various regions and to serve as a clarion for other Siberian causes.

The Association of Siberian Cities

In existence since the early 1980s but founded officially in 1987, the Association of Siberian Cities (ASC) represented the first unified Siberian interest group since the Directory of 1918 (see Chapter 5). Initially emphasizing environmental causes, ASC members urged the CPSU to cancel river reversal schemes in the Ob'-Irtysh Basin, to clean up the mess left in the aftermath of BAM construction, to repudiate several Siberian dam proposals, and to protect the numerically small peoples of the north.

The concept of siphoning water from soggy Western Siberia and conducting it to sere Central Asia dates from tsarist times. A modern version, known as the Davydov Plan, surfaced in the 1960s.[8] The Davydov Plan included the construction of a long, low dam near the mouth of the Ob', which would have created a Portugal-sized reservoir stretching upstream to the mouth of the Irtysh. The Lower Ob' dam was to be the first of a cascade of dams on the Ob'-Irtysh, the reservoirs of which would back up irrigation water via a series of pump stations and canals into the Turanian Basin of Kazakhstan and Uzbekistan. There, the deliveries not only would have enhanced irrigation but also would have supplied water for drinking and industrial purposes and helped to stabilize the levels of the Aral and Caspian seas. A technical feasibility study of the project's first stage was completed and submitted to Gosplan in the early 1980s.[9] After extensive deliberation, Gosplan and the Council of Ministers approved the plan and directed the Ministry of Reclamation and Water Management to draft detailed engineering designs by 1986.

Behind the scenes, vigorous debates took place. Implementation of the Davydov Plan would cost more than 40 billion 1983 U.S. dollars and competed directly with another multibillion-dollar rural development program in the Central Non–Black Earth zone near Moscow. Naturally, Central Asians favored the river-reversal scheme, whereas opposition included not only European Russians but also latter-day members of the West Siberian Energy Coalition, who worried about the loss of oil well sites, and representatives of the military-industrial complex, who feared the loss of potential investment capital.[10] The ASC joined the opposition late, on ecological and humanitarian grounds: ASC members served as a voice for the obviously disenchanted Khants and Mansi, whose grazing areas would be inundated by the reservoirs. Other opponents were scientists, including geographers and climatologists, who warned that the diversions would reduce the flow of fresh water into the Gulf of Ob', raising its salinity and lowering its temperature. The changes, they said, might even lead to negative effects on global weather patterns. Ultimately, the strongest opposition came from Gorbachev, Gromyko, and Aganbegyan, who tabled—essentially, canceled—the project before the Party Congress in 1986.[11]

Gradually, the ASC reserved its erstwhile ecological causes for other environmental groups. In time, it focused on urban land use and resources and the deteriorating social infrastructure of Greater Siberian cities. Before 1991, Moscow-based ministries represented the absentee landowners of Siberian cities and their hinterlands. In the capital, they drafted and approved urban construction projects destined for Greater Siberia, without concern for the local residents. The ASC sought legal protection against the ministries by imposing a kind of home rule. Home rule would allow Siberian city governments to force the ministries to compensate them for the damage they had caused.

The association's membership grew rapidly. By the end of 1988, the ASC represented 43 cities. A year later, it boasted a membership of 67 cities, or 45 percent of all urban areas in Greater Siberia, with a total population of 11.6 million people, or two-thirds of the region's urban population. By 1990, the number of city members had soared to 78.[12] In that year, the ASC was easily the most powerful Siberian political lobby. Since that time, however, it has been superseded by interregional associations such as the Siberian Agreement and the Far East and Baykal Association for Economic Cooperation.

The Siberian Agreement

As an organization focused primarily on urban land use and infrastructure, the ASC ultimately proved too limited in scope to serve the purposes of many, if not most, Greater Siberian residents. On October 2, 1990, provincial leaders from five Siberian oblasts—Omsk, Tyumen', Novosibirsk, Tomsk, and Khakassia—met in Kemerovo to agree to a united front on the economy and politics of Siberia. The group resolved to coordinate Gorbachev's economic reforms at the provincial level, to organize the exploration and utilization of regional resources, and to cushion the negative impact of *perestroyka* and *khozraschet* on Siberian society. Early on, they criticized the Soviet leader for favoring the western zones of the Russian federation over the east (see Chapter 7).[13]

A month later, the group met again in Novosibirsk, where they registered their association as the "Interregional Association 'Siberian Agreement,'" or in Russian shorthand, *Sibirskoye soglasheniye* (Siberian Agreement, or SA). As we have seen, Siberian prefects had challenged the core over resource allocation for at least three decades. According to Zhdanov, "Each provincial leader fought to secure both as much local investment and as much control over local resources as possible, while minimizing taxes."[14] Occasionally, as with the West Siberian Energy Coalition, the BAM, or the Davydov Plan, common causes drew them together. Accordingly, the ASC and the SA were the next steps in that trend.

When the SA met in Ulan-Ude to adopt its charter in July 1992, its membership included nineteen constituent parts, comprising Altay and Krasnoyarsk krays; Chita, Irkutsk, Kemerovo, Novosibirsk, Omsk, Tomsk, and Tyumen' oblasts; and the ethnoregions of Aga-Buryatia,

Buryatia, Evenkia, (Gorno-)Altay, Khakassia, Khantia-Mansia, Taymyria, Tyva, Ust'-Orda Buryatia, and Yamalia.[15] Note that the organization did not include regions of the RFE. The organization represented regions that collectively accounted for 38 percent of Russia's land area and 16 percent of the country's population and that boasted 18 percent of its value-added industrial product. With such a broad basis, the SA was considerably more than a "mouse that roared." By the end of the year, it received the official sanction of Russia's Ministry of Justice; and in Tomsk, in early 1993, Prime Minister Viktor Chernomyrdin signed an agreement of cooperation with the organization. It soon became evident, however, that "cooperation" was not necessarily the SA's primary mission, although members favored a "strong Russian state" to maintain a stable overall economy. This time it was Yeltsin, not Gorbachev, who received the group's criticism for his pro-Western orientation. While they repudiated Siberian separatism and efforts by the ethnic regions in Russia to expand their powers, members seemed determined to defend Siberian interests against those of the core and to keep more of Siberia's wealth within the region.[16]

Observers lauded the SA as the first step toward the reestablishment of a Siberian parliament (see Chapters 4 and 5). Members recognized the necessity of developing mutually beneficial socioeconomic relations and of strengthening their horizontal interregional production and commercial ties independent of the core. Crucial to these goals was the preservation of the existing system of imports and exports and the stabilization of the network of suppliers and consumers, which *perestroyka* had wrecked. SA leaders made no secret of the fact that they intended to expand their association ultimately to include the whole of Greater Siberia, fulfilling the dream of nineteenth-century Siberian regionalists. They were determined from the start to defend Siberia against the rapacious core.

The so-called Greater Council, comprising governors and heads of the local soviets of each of the 19 territorial units, led the SA, convening at least twice per year. The SA's organizational headquarters was in Novosibirsk, although branch agencies were located in other cities, such as Irkutsk (natural resources), Krasnoyarsk (foreign trade), Tyumen' (energy), Omsk (cultural development), and so on.[17] Other agencies, based in other locations, concentrated on defense plant conversion, crime, and regional ecology.

Between the meetings of the Greater Council, the Executive Directorate managed the day-to-day affairs of the SA. These activities comprised the coordination of communications among association members; the implementation of decisions approved by the Greater Council; facilitation of the conversion to a market economy; and overall economic integration of the constituent parts of the SA.

PHOTO 8.1   *Russian Prime Minister Viktor Chernomyrdin and Vitaliy Mukha, governor of Novosibirsk and chairperson of the Siberian Agreement (1993).* SOURCE: *ITAR-TASS, courtesy of Dr. Aleksey Novikov, Moscow State University.*

Then head of the Novosibirsk *malyy sovet* (standing council) and later governor of the province, Vitaliy Mukha was elected chairman of the Greater Council (Photo 8.1). Although publicly opposed to the notion, Mukha initially conspired to use the SA to promote the concept of an independent Siberian republic. Having been a loyal Communist Party *apparatchik* all of his professional life, Mukha disdained the implementation of *perestroyka* and its consequent political liberalization. The debacle of the Soviet Union enraged him. In response, the die-hard Mukha hoped to keep his pro-Soviet/-Communist regime alive in a secessionist, independent Siberia.

With reactionary Mukha at its helm, the SA increasingly opposed Yeltsin's economic reforms, which proved especially damaging to the fragile economies of Greater Siberia. In March 1993, the president attempted to fire both Mukha and the recalcitrant governor of Irkutsk, Yuriy Nozhikov; but when the SA flexed its interregional muscle by voting unanimously to ignore the sackings, Yeltsin retracted his order *with apologies* to the two governors.[18]

This was not the end of the core-periphery confrontation, however. After Yeltsin dissolved the Russian parliament in fall 1993, Mukha organized resistance among his reactionary colleagues and invited the Supreme Soviet to move its headquarters from Moscow to Novosibirsk. It was at this time that he also threatened to blockade the Trans-Siberian Railroad and to establish a Siberian republic (see Chapter 7).[19] Three days before the Russian executive and legislative branches resorted to violence, a still confident Mukha arranged a meeting in Novosibirsk of all the heads of the Siberian standing councils. The group agreed to sign several documents opposing Yeltsin's actions against the Russian parliament, including a call for his impeachment. For his impertinence, Mukha was rewarded with the support of the Communist Party of the Russian Federation (CPRF) as well as Zhirinovskiy's Liberal Democrats (LDP), the Russian Salvation Front, Pamyat', the Democratic Party of Russia, and other groups.[20]

Although it was the most vocal group within the SA, Mukha's faction did not represent the majority sentiment. Yeltsin's show of force in Moscow encouraged the Greater Council to convene a plenary meeting of the SA. There they distanced themselves from Mukha and other firebrands, even though their opposition was mild. They expressed cautious concern for Russia's political situation and professed their dedication to a peaceful resolution of the conflict by means of early parliamentary and presidential elections. Afterward, Yeltsin dissolved the standing councils, superseding them with regional dumas, and replaced some of the governors, including Mukha. Moderate L. K. Polezhayev, the governor of Omsk oblast, became the new chairperson of the SA, and for the time being, the notion of a Siberian republic retreated into dormancy.[21]

Had the Russian government been stronger in the early 1990s, the SA itself might have died aborning. At the time, core authorities dreaded the prospects of interregional associations in general and Siberian interregional associations, reminiscent of past *oblastnichestvo*, in particular. Before December 1992, the individual responsible for Russia's regional policy, Valeriy Makharadze, boasted to SA leaders that he would "never" register their organization while he served in the Russian government.[22] The political shake-up that took place that winter, however, resulted in Makharadze's ouster, clearing the way for that very occurrence. Before he signed the documents sanctioning the SA, Chernomyrdin also had objected to the notion of "strong regions," which in his mind would tear Russia apart. Even as the prime minister signed the cooperation agreements in Tomsk, certain SA members stunned him when they demanded the abrogation of core-established export quotas in Siberian provinces.

This overtly aggressive behavior must have worried Russian leaders in Moscow, who still feared a Siberian separatist movement led by vestigial, old guard Communists such as Mukha. However, their fears probably were groundless, as Siberians themselves showed little support for such a development: A poll taken in Novosibirsk oblast near the time of Mukha's firing revealed that only 6 percent of those polled favored full independence; 27 percent favored economic separation; and 48 percent were against the creation of a Siberian republic. In contrast, in answer to a question about restoring the USSR, the same poll showed that 49 percent favored the idea, 36 percent opposed it, and 13 percent were indifferent. Having 1.2 billion Chinese neighbors along their southern flank has persuaded most Siberians that independence might not be such a good idea after all.[23] It would appear that some things never change: Even though the idea of a Siberian republic seems comatose, the specter of Yellow Peril is apparently alive and well.

With the passage of the new federal constitution in December 1993, fears of Russia's collapse or dismemberment were quieted. The SA gradually retreated from federation politics and became a pragmatic instrument for the benefit of the local provincial economies. SA leaders rejected the idea that they had any aspirations to separate from Russia, blaming ambitious journalists for spreading the rumors. Between 1993 and 1995, the Greater Council spent much of its time trying to dispel gossip. In late 1993, for example, SA General Director Vladimir Ivankov vowed that he would sue anyone who claimed that his organization planned to establish an independent Siberian republic. He proposed, instead, that the association concentrate more on the contingency of an independent SA, complete with a line-item allocation within the national budget.[24]

Since 1993, the SA's primary mission has been to protect the Siberian economy. It engages in politics only when it is necessary to obtain greater administrative control over taxation, transport and energy tariffs, customs duties, and so forth. In each case, it has had to wrest the authority to conduct its affairs away from the Yeltsin government.[25] To do this, "in the battle for scarce resources, what counts is making a lot of noise and having friends in high places, especially friends from your region who will favor it over others."[26]

An example of SA protectionism occurred in 1994: The SA declared that the core's economic reforms had failed to stabilize the Siberian economy. In the opinion of SA members, the only solution to the problem was for the national government to increase monetary transfers to Siberian budgets; to expand Siberian regional shares of the value-added tax (VAT); to reduce national portions of the VAT, the profit tax, and income tax; to create a national reserve fund for regional needs; and to terminate the process of reassessment of local industrial assets. The demands were obviously selfish and unrealistic. Any region of the country could have made such demands, replicating a kind of *McCulloch v. Maryland* conundrum: The regions could literally tax the national government out of business within their territories.[27]

Basically, the SA serves as an interest group with a lobby in Moscow. It voices the key needs of Siberian regions and represents the economic interests of local industrial elites. For example, it advocates an end to re-assessments of industrial assets, which would allow plant managers to privatize their enterprises at lower values. Naturally, many if not most managers of the largest and most profitable Siberian enterprises are members of the SA.

In the past, the SA has done things that favor some of its constituent members at the expense of others. For instance, the SA refused to take part in Russia's unified wholesale market for the supply of electricity. The Greater Council assumed that the added "sale" stage in the process would inevitably raise the cost of electricity.[28] The assumption proved incorrect because within the market for wholesale electricity, the purchase price equals the sales rate; moreover, expanded competition would tend to decrease the market price. In fact, the SA argument seemed motivated less by economic logic than by energy-surplus regions in Siberia that were attempting to maintain their oligopoly over local rates on the sale of electricity. In energy-redundant regions such as Krasnoyarsk, Irkutsk, and Khakassia, rates are typically three to four times lower than in the energy-deficient provinces that neighbor them. For example, Chita oblast and Buryatia often suffer discriminatory rates because they have no supplier other than Irkutsk oblast. The rate prejudice derives from the fragmentation of the market space. Although originally established to eliminate these kinds of contradictions, the SA occasionally becomes the pawn of powerful Siberian industrial lobbies. Critics have suggested that the SA no longer speaks for and protects all of its constituent members.

Between 1995 and 1997, the SA had only moderate success in serving as a "third force" separate from and in opposition to both the CPRF and Yeltsin's reformers. While the CPRF would like to rule Russia through a resurrected Gosplan, the reformers prefer to lead through the big Moscow banks. The SA has tried to persuade the national government to invest in economic sectors other than resource extraction. It has struggled to prevent the collapse of Siberian agriculture and associated markets, both of which are regionally isolated, unprofitable, and uncompetitive on foreign markets. Agriculture continues to be a major employer in regions such as Altay kray, Omsk oblast, and Novosibirsk oblast. Most recently, the SA has championed the causes of its "donor regions" (those regions that give more to the national budget than they receive). Three SA constituent units are donors, including Krasnoyarsk, Khantia-Mansia, and Yamalia.[29]

The success of the SA has been mixed. Although core authorities definitely listen to the SA when it "roars," significant progress has been lacking since 1992. Eighteen of the nineteen constituents of the association recorded negative economic growth in 1996. Only Krasnoyarsk kray, a donor region, registered any sign of life.[30]

The economy had become so bad that residents of Novosibirsk oblast re-elected Vitaliy Mukha in December 1995. Because his candidacy was supported by the CPRF at that time, Mukha was considered sympathetic to the left opposition; but during the 1996 presidential campaign, he remained neutral. This perhaps paved the way for his reelection to a two-year term as chairperson of the SA Greater Council in December 1996.[31] Mukha feels that "third force" regional associations such as the SA, the Far East and Baykal Association for Economic Cooperation, the Greater Volga Association, the Central Russia Association, and other regional associations in the North Caucasus, the Central Black Earth, the Urals, and the Northwest, should merge and mold themselves into a national force. He views both the CPRF and the "democrats" as two branches of the "Moscow Party." Mukha hopes to galvanize and reinspire confidence in the SA. In his view, the SA must approve of any act of parliament that is intended to regulate or affect any Siberian interest; the SA should have the right to block implementation of the Federal Treaty any time it contradicts Siberian concerns; and the SA should play an active role in national economic programs.[32]

Such flagrant forms of regionalism emanating from the periphery have not fallen on deaf ears in the core. In spring 1997, hoping to close loopholes in existing legislation that had allowed the regions to repudiate national laws, the Russian Duma adopted a bill that reasserted the supremacy of the 1993 Constitution and other national laws over provincial legislation, especially where the two levels conflict.[33] The resolution was quickly tested by reactionaries in the RFE.

The Far East and Baykal Association for Economic Cooperation

The framework for the Far East and Baykal Association for Economic Cooperation, or simply the Far East Association (FEA), was established in Khabarovsk in summer 1990. It represented a clone of several far eastern regional organizations that sprouted about the same time. The FEA's primary goal was to create a unified economic community in the RFE. Its secondary missions were to develop Sakhalin's natural gas resources; to complete the Bureya hydroelectric station, which had been under construction since the late 1970s; to further exploit the raw material base in general; to conserve and preserve valued ecosystems; and to develop joint ventures (see Chapter 7).[34]

In 1997, the FEA was composed of the republics of Buryatia and Sakha (Yakutia); Primorskiy and Khabarovsk krays; Amur, Kamchatka, Magadan, Chita, and Sakhalin oblasts; the Jewish Autonomous Region (JAR); and the Koryak and Chukotka autonomous okrugs. It spans approximately one-third of Russian territory, includes 7 percent of the population, and constitutes 7 percent of the value-added industrial product.[35]

Like the SA, the FEA is protectionist in its economic orientation. This springs from living memories of the core's abuse and rapacious exploitation of its most remote periphery. As Stephan has stated, when the FEA was formed, "it became fashionable to fault Moscow for pocketing Far Eastern revenue, for stunting Far Eastern development, and for circumscribing Far Eastern contacts with Asia-Pacific neighbors."[36] Thus, when *glasnost'* liberated public opinion, residents of the RFE likened past core-periphery relations to pure colonialism. They accused Moscow of betraying them and said that they would save themselves, without the cooperation of the core. There were rumors of new separatism; yet, far easterners, like the Siberians in the west, had little affinity for independence. They depended too much on the core for food, fuel, subsidies, and wages. Moreover, regional rivalries threatened their unity.

Remoteness from Russia's main centers of supply and demand has always been the RFE's key problem. Far eastern industry spends billions of dollars per year in order to bridge those distances. Yeltsin's free market reforms and the concomitant dramatic increase in transportation costs have made the lion's share of economic activities in the RFE unprofitable. The public utility sector that supplies far easterners with electricity and hot water, for example, suddenly found itself unable to pay for imports of Kuzbas coal. This, of course, also created problems for the Kuzbas miners, who needed markets for their product.

The RFE's governors face the daunting task of transforming their former military bastion into a modern economic gateway for integration into the Asia-Pacific Region (APR). With 32 major enterprises, the defense sector remains one of the most important employers in the RFE, occupying 13 percent of the overall regional workforce, which includes 20 percent in Primor'ye and 24 percent in Khabarovsk kray.[37] Before the collapse of the Soviet Union, these industries constituted 90 percent of the output of the region's "military-industrial complex" and 67 percent of all regional manufacturing, including 100 percent of the "consumer goods." According to Russian scholar Vladimir Ivanov, RFE defense plants have always produced at least some civilian goods, ranging from refrigerators to baby strollers. This would imply that defense plant conversions might be relatively painless. This has not been the case, however: Between January and September 1994, in Khabarovsk and Primorskiy krays, the conversions precipitated the loss of 250,000 jobs.[38] Because each worker in the defense industry supports at least three others, the multiplier effect on unemployment is quite extreme. High unemployment in the former military towns of Komsomol'sk-na-Amure and Amursk adds significantly to the RFE's inventory of economic woes. Enhancing the effect is the fact that for more than 20 of the 32 defense plants that are in the process of conversion, both the output of military supplies and the production of civilian goods have declined by at least 50 percent since 1994.[39]

Thus, the FEA has had the unenviable task of lowering transportation costs, reducing the costs of electricity, and subsidizing defense plant conversions. Another FEA mission has been to convince officials in the core to allow RFE provinces to reserve 20 percent of federal customs collections for local economic development and foreign trade. In 1994, the maximum allowable retention was 10 percent.[40] Although the request appeared reasonable at the time, its fulfillment was thwarted by the unprecedented actions of the governor of Primorskiy kray.

Nazdratenko: Thorn in Yeltsin's Side. Like Vitaliy Mukha, Yevgeniy Nazdratenko is a rebel who defends Russian national interests even as he aspires to further a personal political agenda that clashes with that of the core (Photo 8.2). He became the governor of Primor'ye after a regional coup d'état in spring 1993. The coup victim, Vladimir Kuznetsov, had served as governor since 1990. Kuznetsov had been a devoted reformer, whose most conspicuous brainstorm was the Greater Vladivostok FEZ. His undoing was that he asked for more regional power over the project than the authorities in the core were willing to grant, including the establishment of an economic development fund to transfer assets from the national coffers to "a regional authority."[41] Kuznetsov proposed Greater Vladivostok as a Russian alternative to the multinational Tumen FEZ, which would involve giving the Chinese free access to the Sea of Japan via an extension of the old Chinese Eastern Railway (see Chapters 3 and 7). As Peter Kirkow has noted, "[This] naturally clashed with Russian geostrategic interests and its desire to become a new key player in the [APR]."[42] Kuznetsov also successfully lobbied Moscow to relinquish hard currency so that he could buy foreign food supplies for his shortage-plagued region in 1992. He was also the person responsible for obtaining the rights to 10 percent of the state customs duties in the RFE. Ultimately, Kuznetsov's liberal philosophy, together with his proclivity for extended trips to Moscow and abroad, left him vulnerable to hard-liners in the *malyy sovet* (standing council), among the spreading mafia membership, and among local industrial managers, who supported the candidacy of Nazdratenko.

According to Kirkow, Nazdratenko is a flagrant example of how Russian industrial monopolies are "poured into executive power in Russian regions."[43] He is the former chief executive of the Vostok Tungsten Mine and Concentrator, located in central Primor'ye. As a people's deputy to the Russian parliament between 1990 and 1993, Nazdratenko represented the RFE's captains of industry. When he assumed the governorship, "he appointed a new team in which a number of deputies were [simultaneously] leading members of the joint-stock company PAKT, [allowing a] combination of tax-evasion, embezzlement, and control of political power, which became famous as 'Primor'ye Watergate.'"[44] When Yeltsin

PHOTO 8.2   *Yevgeniy Nazdratenko (right), governor of Primorskiy kray, meets with Yeltsin's representatives in Vladivostok, June 28, 1995.* SOURCE: *ITAR-TASS, courtesy of Dr. Aleksey Novikov, Moscow State University.*

dissolved the parliament, Nazdratenko, like the SA's Mukha, initially rallied to the cause of Alexander Rutskoy and the other putsch leaders. When it became obvious that Yeltsin would win, however, the governor sided with the more moderate views of his own local legislature.

During summer 1993, far eastern regionalism gathered steam. There is considerable evidence that Nazdratenko urged the *malyy sovet* to declare Primor'ye a sovereign republic, although Nazdratenko himself denied involvement. He might have done so in order to divert attention away from the PAKT scandal. As support for sovereignty grew, some of its advocates lauded the concept of the Far Eastern Republic (FER) and invoked the name of Alexander Krasnoshchekov (see Chapter 5) as "a champion of independence and democracy."[45] To convince core authorities that Primor'yans were serious about this latter-day FER, Nazdratenko's forces gathered the signatures of the thousands who supported regional sovereignty and asked for preferential treatment in fiscal arrangements and in foreign commerce. At the peak of the confrontation in Moscow, Nazdratenko allegedly announced that in the event of a prolonged conflict, Primorskiy kray conceivably might "separate" from the Russian Federation. Nazdratenko also has denied this allegation, claiming that what he really said was that the parliament should have been dissolved in April 1993!

Irrespective of what he claims to have said or done, the opportunistic Nazdratenko often has shown his contempt for the Yeltsin government. When Chernomyrdin visited Primor'ye in August 1993, Nazdratenko served the prime minister with five separate demands, regarding import duties, export tariffs, the consignment of all federal taxes to the region for the next three years, the introduction of special local taxes on transit cargoes, and regional autonomy in matters of yearly export quotas and export licensing on fish and wood products.[46] To temporarily co-opt its rebellious subject, the government responded with a onetime subsidy of $12 million to keep regional electricity rates at 28 cents per kilowatt-hour for industrial users. In part because of Nazdratenko's "unilateral decision" to dispense with privatization of the energy industry, the core also subsidized the far eastern coal mining industry. Finally, in early 1994, the national government allocated another $81 million to the region for the purpose of stabilizing its economy.[47]

Nevertheless, Nazdratenko is hardly a hero. A number of Russian intellectuals call his ruthless, authoritarian administration "a fascist regime" that is rife with corruption.[48] Others refer to him as a racist. An inveterate initiator of policy campaigns with telltale names like "Operation Hemp," "Operation Arsenal," "Operation Foreigner," and others, Nazdratenko zealously attacks issues he deems critical to his region. In "Operation Foreigner," for example, he forcibly evicted more than 200,000 Chinese from Primorskiy kray.

The democratically elected mayor of Vladivostok, Viktor Cherepkov—among others—would assert that Nazdratenko is homophobic. Elected in summer 1993, Cherepkov initially committed some rather unpopular administrative blunders that caused dissension within Primor'ye's executive ranks. Evidently, in response to a televised newsreel that showed him embracing Rutskoy, Nazdratenko blamed Cherepkov for the footage and therefore shut down the local television station; cut the Vladivostok city budget; and covertly sabotaged the city's water, electric, and heating systems. The editor of the newscast was subjected to threats. When these measures failed to intimidate him, police allegedly shot at him "by mistake." Another journalist who was antipathetic to Nazdratenko was seized and beaten by unknown assailants. Cherepkov's office and apartment were illegally ransacked, and his son was arrested on charges of "aggravated assault." In a subsequent televised interview, Nazdratenko characterized Cherepkov as *goluboy* (gay) and spoke at length on the subject. Evidently without having all the facts, Yeltsin fired Cherepkov in March 1994, following baseless allegations that the mayor had taken bribes. According to Kirkow, this came on the heels of the mayor's "brutal ouster from office by armed [Nazdratenko] police." The charges against Cherepkov were later dropped, but two years passed before he was reinstated as mayor against Nazdratenko's objections.[49]

Simultaneously, Yeltsin's presidential representative, Valeriy Butov, and members of the National Control Administration conducted an inquiry into Nazdratenko's notorious behavior and his connections with big business and the mafia. Their findings included more than enough evidence to warrant the governor's removal from office. Instead, Butov was removed and an individual considered sympathetic to Nazdratenko was appointed presidential representative in his place.[50]

The "Thorn" Between the Core and the Periphery. Confident that he had the core's leadership in his pocket, the governor solicited further economic and territorial concessions. He demanded higher freight rates on transit cargoes, which represent the largest category of shipments in Primor'ye; fuel and energy subsidies; investments in Primor'ye enterprises; a ten-year tax holiday for his region; and restricted entry on immigrants to Primor'ye for the next decade. These requests, which were not approved, added up to almost $90 billion through 2010.[51] A native of Severo-Kuril'sk, Nazdratenko hoped to subordinate the Kurile Islands under the control of Primorskiy kray. He aspired to accomplish this with the help of his Kremlin cronies and without the knowledge of the governor of Sakhalin. Acquisition of the islands, which are subsidized by the core, would have meant several billion more rubles in Primor'ye's coffers.[52]

All the while, rumors of Nazdratenko's planned secession from Russia roiled about the country, even embarrassing members of the FEA.[53] By the end of 1995, it appeared that Yeltsin might very well lose the 1996 presidential election. The obviously ailing president increasingly relied on members of the clique surrounding his close friend and adviser, Alexander Korzhakov. Most of Yeltsin's retinue considered Primor'ye strategic to the election's outcome, and they advised the president to proceed with caution in addressing the rumors about Nazdratenko, at least until after the election.

Since the election, Nazdratenko has become more vulnerable. Kirkow correctly has asserted that the Primor'ye governor could not have gone as far as he did, had he not close allies in the president's entourage in Moscow.[54] As a member of Chernomyrdin's party (called Our Home Is Russia), he has had the opportunity to hobnob regularly with some of the most conspicuous, if not the most contemptible, Russian politicians of the day, not the least being Korzhakov. Until 1996, Nazdratenko's other friends in high places included deputy prime ministers Viktor Il'yushin and Oleg Soskovets, a Korzhakov protégé; Yeltsin's chief of staff, Sergey Filatov; and the former security chief, Alexander Lebed'. The governor's close ties with high-ranking individuals in the attorney general's office delayed investigations into his alleged violations of Cherepkov's human rights, not to mention those of the 200,000 Chinese. One of his closest allies was Vladimir Shumeyko, the former chairperson of the Federation Council (1994–1995), who in 1993 was investigated for corruption while serving as one of Chernomyrdin's deputy prime ministers. Not long after the 1996 presidential elections, in which Shumeyko served as one of his campaign managers, Yeltsin fired Korzhakov, Soskovets, Filatov, and Lebed'. Later, Il'yushin was investigated for misuse of funds. Simultaneously, Yeltsin promoted the "incorruptible" Boris Nemtsov and strengthened the position of Nazdratenko's sworn enemy, Anatoliy Chubais.[55]

As proponents of a strong core, both Nemtsov and Chubais have favored a diminishment in the powers of the regions and their anti-Yeltsin governors. Chubais has been especially aggressive in countering the regions' promotion of their own laws over national legislation. He was responsible for expanding the powers of presidential appointees in Russian regions, particularly in monitoring the use of federal funds. Both Nemtsov and Chubais have emphasized the need for the core to tighten its grip over the regions by supporting Yeltsin loyalists in provincial elections. Such efforts have met with limited success, because Russian voters prefer candidates with connections to local enterprises and members of the opposition.[56]

Some Russian analysts believe that the power of the regional governors peaked in autumn 1996, after Chubais's appointment. Before Chubais took office, "the governors felt themselves to be government officials of the highest rank, on par with ministers."[57] As deputy prime minister in charge of the economy, Chubais was given full control over critical financial flows and became a threat to the regional governors: His proposed reforms in local self-government would have forced governors (such as Nazdratenko) to share money with city and district officials (such as Cherepkov), in accordance with federal laws. The governors naturally favored the existing, equivocal situation in which they lobbied the core for funds and favors and then allocated these benefits as they wished, to preferred clients in their own territories. In a manner evoking U.S. pork barrel politics, this is precisely how Nazdratenko operated within his Primor'ye fief. To be fair, however, "he and his" were only the tip of the regional iceberg: The Primor'ye governor's links to big business and the criminal underworld were merely more conspicuous than most other governors', and politically more testable.

Nazdratenko's power over the core began to unravel in March 1996, when the Primor'ye regional duma wrote a letter to Yeltsin and the parliament, threatening to withhold taxes unless the federal government liquidated its $373 million debt to the region. The regional officials argued that without these funds, the kray would suffer power outages, late payment of wages, and inability to satisfy child welfare benefits. The local population, they said, lived in "near–Stone Age conditions" and was vulnerable to mass protests and strikes.[58]

An even more contentious confrontation arose over the constitutionality of the 1991 Soviet-Chinese border agreement. On March 20, 1991, to encourage the creation of the Tumen FEZ, the Yeltsin government agreed to transfer 1,500 hectares (3,700 acres) of disputed territory to China, giving the latter access to the Sea of Japan. Yeltsin's decision was applauded by officials not only in China but also Japan and South Korea, who felt that their countries had much to gain from the potential duty-free manufacturing zone. Nazdratenko and his legislators protested that Yeltsin's decision was illegal under Article 104 of the old RSFSR Constitution, which specified that border changes required the approval of the Congress of People's Deputies. They also pointed out that the treaty violated the June 1990 sovereignty declarations, which demanded that border adjustments be subjected to all-Russian referenda.[59] The governor himself argued that the region was valuable forest and hunting land and contended that if China obtained the property, Russia would lose authority over river transport on the Tumen. Within weeks of the presidential election, Yeltsin suspended the process of demarcation of the disputed zone, which in essence prevented authorities from implementing the treaty. Nazdratenko's interference prompted a harsh rebuke from the Ministry of Foreign Affairs, which castigated the governor for trying to "torpedo" Russo-Chinese relations. Six months later, well after the elections, Yeltsin also warned Nazdratenko to stop "rocking the boat" in Russo-Chinese relations and ordered him to submit any future public statements on the issue to the Russian foreign ministry for clearance before announcing them.[60]

Primor'ye's promised mass protests and strikes erupted over back wages on July 15, twelve days after the presidential runoff election, which Yeltsin won with 52.3 percent of the vote (Map 8.1). The protesters included 10,000 miners who were demanding back wages totaling $22 million; moreover, electric power workers were conducting a hunger strike for the same reason. In early August, the core responded by earmarking $1.2 billion to relieve the pressures on the kray's fuel and energy sectors. A fortnight later, Yeltsin placed the blame for the energy crisis squarely on the shoulders of Nazdratenko, whom he described as "not entirely qualified" to handle such matters. He upbraided the governor and instructed him to fire his deputy responsible for regional fuel and energy, to pay the miners their overdue wages, and to stabilize the situation by mid-September. Nazdratenko agreed to implement emergency measures, but the miners' strike continued well into autumn.[61]

Nazdratenko's woes mounted as his regional duma's electoral term expired in mid-January 1997. New elections originally were to be held on March 30, but they were postponed indefinitely by the incumbent deputies. With Cherepkov in the lead, agitated crowds filled the streets of Vladivostok and demanded the immediate dissolution of the duma, the members of

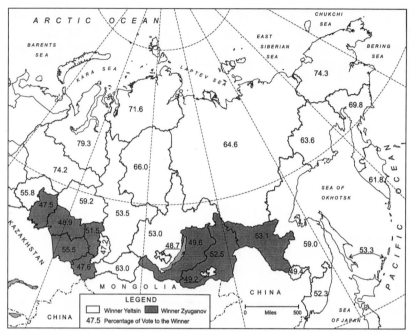

MAP 8.1   *Results of the 1996 Russian Presidential Runoff Election in Greater Siberia*
SOURCE: *"Election Results in Siberia," July 4, 1996. Available on-line at
<http://www.nns.ru/res2/res5-e.html>. Note that Yeltsin's support becomes stronger
from south to north.*

which in support of Nazdratenko had sworn to oust the mayor a second time. Meanwhile, the governor diverted attention from the issue by calling for a regional referendum on the Tumen River question. Evidently, he had not cleared the effort with the foreign ministry, for within 60 days, Yeltsin dispatched Chubais to Vladivostok to demand Nazdratenko's immediate resignation. Simultaneously, in Moscow, Nemtsov, himself a former governor, charged Nazdratenko and his authoritarian duma with irresponsibility in dealing with the kray's energy problems. On May 23, Yeltsin replaced his presidential representative, Nazdratenko ally Vladimir Ignatenko, with Viktor Kondratov, the local chief of the federal security force and possibly the only leading official in Vladivostok with no known connections to organized crime. At his press conference on May 28, Kondratov announced that he, not the governor, henceforth would coordinate all federal activities in Primor'ye, including operations of the navy, army, police, and tax collection offices. Yeltsin has since broadened Kondratov's powers to include oversight of the implementation of presidential decrees; of the fuel and energy sectors; of fish and timber export quotas; and of the allocation and distribution of federal funds.[62]

Nazdratenko immediately accused Chubais of carrying on a blood feud. It was nonetheless a clear case of the chickens coming home to roost: Due to his sloppy handling of the energy crisis, his misuse of funds, and complaints from Russian and international businessmen about his callous disregard for (and probable complicity in) criminal activities in Primor'ye, the governor was stripped of most of his powers. As proof of Nazdratenko's misdeeds, Kondratov noted that approximately $4.3 million, which had been earmarked as back wages for teachers and doctors, had disappeared in just one month—the month of April.[63]

The core-periphery confrontation, in which this was but one striking episode, continues. On the one hand, Yeltsin insists that he has the right to dismiss democratically elected governors. On the other, Nazdratenko gained the support of governors of all persuasions at the meeting of the Federation Council on July 3, 1997, forcing Yeltsin to promise that he would not employ the Primorskiy model of direct rule in any other region. Despite his recent political vulnerability, Nazdratenko has been able to ward off all his detractors. As a member of the Federation Council, he is immune from prosecution; and according to the 1993 Constitution, he cannot be forced to stand down as a popularly elected governor. This was the key to his Pyrrhic victory in summer 1997.[64]

The All-Russian Association of the Numerically
Small Peoples of the North, Siberia, and the Far East

The Association of Peoples of the North (APN) was born in May 1989 as an advisory body to the Gorbachev administration.[65] Originally chaired by Communist writer Vladimir Sangi, the APN has served as an advocate of indigenous rights for native peoples throughout northern Russia. In 1997, the organization's name was changed to the "All-Russian Association of the Numerically Small Peoples of the North, Siberia, and the Far East."[66] Within a year of its establishment, the APN held its first congress in the Kremlin. With Gorbachev in the audience, delegates spoke of job discrimination against indigenous youth, poor ethnic representation on local political councils, the rise of tensions among natives and nonnatives, and the lack of use of native languages in local media. For example, the Mansi, who together with the Khants represented less than 2 percent of the population of their official homeland, had not had a Mansi-language radio broadcast or newspaper for a long time.[67]

The living standards of the native peoples in 1990 were far worse than those of the nonnatives, the delegates asserted. Housing space was less than half that of the *prishliye*. Only 3.0 percent of the dwellings had gas, 0.4 percent had water, and 0.1 percent had central heat. A typical native residence, which was a minimum of thirty years old, had no sewage dis-

PHOTO 8.3   *Yevdokiya Gayer, former member of the Federation Council (ca. 1994).*
SOURCE: *ITAR-TASS, courtesy of Dr. Aleksey Novikov, Moscow State University.*

posal. The Khants and Mansi, for instance, who formerly lived in hundreds of hamlets, now resided in 72 consolidated rural settlements that had been established under Khrushchev. In many villages there were no medical facilities, schools, clubs, bakeries, bathhouses, or shops.[68]

The collapse of the Soviet Union has brought little relief to the native peoples. In spring 1992, the Russian parliament resolved to improve the living conditions of the peoples of the north but failed to follow through. Deputies such as Nanay parliamentarian Yevdokiya Gayer, who represented the numerically small peoples during that time, "demanded that the North be declared an ecological disaster area," but such pronouncements were unlikely to have much effect on the environment or the native peoples of those areas (Photo 8.3).[69] By 1993, an estimated 30 to 50 percent of the Western Siberian taiga had been affected by the development of hydrocarbons. The accident rate at wellheads increased by 20 percent in 1994 alone. Peterson reported that in 1992–1993, a year after the parliament's resolution, no fewer than 20 oil spills occurred in Tyumen' oblast, chiefly in Khantia-Mansia.[70]

During the troublesome transition from the command economy to the free market, the APN itself has experienced growing pains. At its second conference in November 1993, the organization suffered splits and spent much of its time bickering over who would be the association's president. Nevertheless, the APN continues to lobby for indigenous property rights, including guarantees of traditional uses of land and resources. It emphasizes the fact that the numerically small peoples must have control over their homelands and resources if they are to survive as nations. Fondahl notes that the Yeltsin government "has responded [to these demands] *in part*," particularly by increasing native access and control over *renewable* resources.[71] Other laws permit the numerically small nations to select their own way of life in order to preserve their ethnic singularity.

With the debacle of the USSR, the situation has gone from bad to worse. The Yeltsin team has yet to formalize a comprehensive policy for native peoples or regional development of the north.[72] In fact, with advocates of national supremacy like Nemtsov and Chubais in his camp, Yeltsin has been advised to reduce the number of regions and to spend *less* time responding to demands for indigenous property rights—not more.[73] In the Soviet Union, native regions were inevitably subsidized. Today, without state subsidies, the local economies have collapsed, and any efforts by the national government to improve housing, social, and medical amenities have lagged for want of money. The money shortage has forced Yeltsin to prioritize his allocations in terms of regions, production, indigenous peoples, and conservation. Obviously, the natives, especially the tiny Siberian ones, and conservation are assigned lower priorities relative to the requirements of Machiavellian Russian "patriots" such as Mukha and Nazdratenko.

Knowing this, the APN forwarded an open letter headed "Discrimination Against Indigenous People of the Russian North" to Yeltsin, Chernomyrdin, and the chairpersons of both houses of parliament in March 1996. The document was co-signed by spokespersons for the Nentsy, Sakhans, Kets, Buryats, Itel'men, Khants, and Mansi, and the natives of Sakhalin oblast and Krasnoyarsk kray. No longer a member of the Russian parliament, Gayer signed as secretary-general of the International League of Indigenous Peoples and Ethnic Groups.[74] The letter indicted the Russians for causing the extinction of six different native groups "in the past century" and for permitting the endangerment of such nationalities as the Aleut, Ket, Nganasan, Negidal, Orok, Oroch, Tofalar, Enets, and Yukagir.[75]

The authors of the letter reminded the Russian leadership that the Soviet and Russian supreme soviets included eighteen indigenous parliamentarians from 1989 to 1991, who developed a code of laws protecting native rights and interests. Because of the dominance of nonindigenes in the titular homelands, however, only two native deputies were elected in the 1995 parliamentary elections, leaving the peoples of the north virtually without representation. The letter's writers stressed that since that time, authorities in the majority of ethnic homelands had been under great pressure to make decisions that were not in keeping with the interests of numerically small native groups. They complained bitterly that native rights were inadequately defended by the 1993 Constitution, and that the legislation that has been approved has not been appropriately implemented:

"The Government remains indifferent to repeated appeals of the APN."[76] The writers scarified the Yeltsin government by emphasizing the facts that their native lands were being "annexed and barbarously destroyed by rapacious oil, gas, coal, gold, and nonferrous mining interests, *without just compensation*, [and] deprives us of our right to life." They noted that a law of great national significance, the "Basis for the Legal Status of Indigenous Peoples of Russia," had been tabled twice by the president himself. (Several successive drafts of the law, in fact, showed that the native political powers it was designed to codify actually had diminished progressively during the debate.[77]) They concluded by stating that the economic collapse had brought soaring unemployment; increased impoverishment; life-threatening levels of crime and alcoholism; erosion of their traditional outlooks on life; and a decline in the health of their peoples evidenced by death rates one and a half times the Russian averages.[78]

The authors of the letter did not leave the president without a proposed solution to their woes. They demanded: (1) the establishment of procedures to compensate indigenous groups and enterprises for damages resulting from annexation and industrial development of their homelands; (2) licensing procedures to provide for resource use practices, production quotas, and land tenure that would guarantee the perpetuation of traditional native activities; (3) the creation of a native economic development corporation; (4) the establishment of procedures for negotiation between the Russian government and indigenous representatives; (5) the creation of a fully empowered agency to advance native rights within the executive branch;[79] (6) the establishment of a state fund to support native northern peoples; (7) a home rule system for indigenous peoples of the north; (8) guaranteed minimum representation of numerically small peoples in federal, regional, and executive bodies; (9) the creation of a Department of the Arctic, which would have an ambassador to coordinate, "at the international level," issues of northern development; (10) the passage of the pending federal laws on the "Basis for the Legal Status of Indigenous Peoples of Russia" (see above) and the "Status of the Peoples of the North"; (11) the organization of celebrations marking the International Decade of Indigenous Peoples of the World (1995–2005). In response, Russia's minister of nationalities informed an obviously concerned Council of Europe delegation in March 1997 that the Kremlin planned soon to establish an Assembly of the Peoples of Russia, which would represent the interests of all 176 officially recognized Russian ethnic groups.[80]

Because Chubais, Nemtsov, Zhirinovskiy, and other advocates of national supremacy in the Russian government oppose these proposals, the APN has an uphill climb. Moreover, because the glacial pace of the executive's movement on these matters precludes the desired quick solutions, "going international" with their cause may be APN's only alternative. Already, former APN chairperson Sangi has entreated the U.N. General Assembly and the Council of Europe to ensure protection of the environment of the Nivkhi, Oroks, Orochi, and Nanays, whose native lands on Sakhalin Island lie astride the path to and from the international oil and gas developments of Sakhalin I, II, and III.[81] Simultaneously, the APN has forged links with the World Council of Indigenous Peoples, the Inuit Circumpolar Council, and the Saami (Lapp) Council. Such connections have paved the way for cultural exchanges and for the participation of Russian minorities in international conferences. These activities have particularly benefited Russian Eskimos, whose interaction with North American Eskimos (Inuits) has been ongoing since 1989.[82]

THE MICE THAT ROAR

The numerically small peoples of Russia are hardly pushovers. All over Greater Siberia, they struggle to increase their autonomy and control over their native lands. The Khakass, for example, have battled politically with Russian and Cossack factions over seats and offices in the republican duma, in a homeland in which they compose only 11 percent of the population. They also maintain a strained customs relationship with contiguous Krasnoyarsk kray, which they defied when they declared themselves a republic in 1990. Their "sovereign" neighbors in the west, the Altay, whose share of the population is greater at 31 percent, have laid claim to all raw materials within the borders of their homeland.[83] For all the brouhaha raised by others, however, none has been more blatant than that registered by the Khants, the Mansi, the Nentsy, and the Sakhans.

Regional Supremacy or Ethnic Property Rights: Tyumen' Versus the Indigenes

As we have seen, since 1960, the exploitation of Ob' Basin oil and gas resources has thoroughly disrupted the traditional lifestyles of the native Ugrians (Khants and Mansi) and Samoyeds (Nentsy and Sel'kups). Moreover, the use of antiquated hydrocarbon-extractive technologies and equipment, poor supervision and organization, and simple neglect have led to environmental damage far beyond what might have been expected four decades ago.[84] IREX scholar Gail Osherenko, a specialist on indigenous political and property rights in the Circumpolar North, has concluded that "the most feasible approach to environmental protection and revitalization of the traditional economy and lifeways of Siberia's indigenous population *without impeding large-scale extraction of resources* is to accord indigenous groups extensive political and property rights in the areas they have traditionally occupied."[85] As evidenced by their behavior since 1995, native groups of the Ob' Basin are poised to meet the challenge.

Tyumen' oblast is the richest of Russia's administrative regions. Its industrial output, concentrated on oil and gas, is 150 percent more valuable than that of Moscow oblast.[86] Its 1995 population of 3.2 million represented only 2.1 percent of Russia's overall census, but its share of the country's industrial output was 7.5 percent. Tyumen' oblast, however, includes three constituent parts that increasingly are vying for a share of the wealth and property: Tyumen' oblast proper, and the autonomous okrugs of Khantia-Mansia and Yamalia. Khantia-Mansia claimed 1.3 million of Tyumen's residents, comprising 22,000 Khants and 8,300 Mansi, who accounted for 1.4 percent of the okrug census. Yamalia boasted 480,000 of Tyumen's inhabitants, 21,000 of whom were Nentsy—about 4.4 percent of the okrug population.

In Russia's current revenue-sharing formula, 40 percent of the money derived from the marketing of Ob' Basin oil and gas is allocated to the core and to Tyumen' oblast (20 percent to each); 30 percent to the okrug; and 30 percent to the rayon (district) of origin. If the constituent parts were divided, the richest Russian province would be Khantia-Mansia; Yamalia would rank fifteenth; and Tyumen' would fall to fiftieth place. While Yamalia contains approximately 90 percent of Russia's (and one-third of the globe's) natural gas reserves and Khantia-Mansia bears 53 percent of Russia's oil, Tyumen' oblast by comparison has very few natural resources (Photo 8.4). Well aware of their wealth, the nonindigenous majorities and the native minorities of Khantia-Mansia and Yamalia have translated their economic power into political power, which they have wielded at the national level. Their quest has become a true test of Russian constitutionalism.

The 1993 Russian Constitution divided jurisdiction over property rights between federal (meaning national or core) and regional structures. There are now three categories of jurisdiction: an exclusively federal category; an overlapping, joint federal-regional category; and an exclusively regional category. As set forth in Article 72.1, matters of ownership including the use and disposal of land, minerals, water, and other resources are the province of joint federal-regional jurisdiction. However, Article 9.2 is vague about who actually owns the resources. The structure of minerals industries thus becomes the focus of a "trilateral struggle" between the Russian executive branch, the Russian legislative branch, and the regional governments.[87]

In the case of Western Siberia, the crux of the issue is the okrugs' alleged administrative subordination to Tyumen' oblast. Under the original post-Soviet oblast charter, Yamalia and Khantia-Mansia are integral and equal parts of the oblast. Between 1991 and 1993, Tyumen' and okrug officials attempted to create a modified framework of relations, but all efforts failed. Oblast authorities forwarded a bill to the parliament in Moscow

PHOTO 8.4   *East Surgut oil field, Khantia-Mansia (ca. 1994).* SOURCE: *Dmitriy Korobeynikov, Novosti Press Agency (Kemerovo branch).*

that proposed to place energy supply, pipelines, and crime control under the exclusive jurisdiction of the oblast, and resource use under the joint federal-regional category. Not helping the relationship is the 1993 Russian Constitution, which is contradictory and has become a cause for embarrassment to the Russian Constitutional Court. In accordance with Articles 5 and 65 of the document, each constituent part is equal; but in accordance with Article 66.4, autonomous okrugs are subordinate to the administration of the oblast or kray in which they are located. After deliberating for more than a year, on July 14, 1997, the Court ruled in favor of *both* constitutional provisions: "On the one hand, the okrugs are parts of Tyumen' oblast; on the other hand, they have equal rights with the oblast in relations with the core, with other constituent parts of the Russian Federation, and with representatives of foreign countries." As the okrugs became aware of their new political power, Tyumen' authorities increasingly lost both political and budgetary control over them.[88]

Between 1995 and 1996, Russian regional and republican dumas formulated and approved new provincial charters to conform with the national framework. As required by law, by the end of 1996, each region was compelled to hold new elections for governor and chair of the provincial duma, so as to fill the seats of the Federation Council. The Yamalian legislature approved a charter that contained virtually no mention of the authority of Tyumen' oblast within the okrug except for mutually shared responsibilities for social welfare programs. Meanwhile, Tyumen' oblast found it difficult to formulate its charter, because of the uncertain fate of its relations with its constituent parts. On March 23, 1995, representatives of the three regions convened in Tyumen' in an effort to forge an agreement on jurisdictional authority. Oblast officials tried to force the okrug representatives to accept Tyumen' as their superior—or at the very least, to consent to the use of their names as *sub"yekty* (constituent parts) of the oblast in the Tyumen' charter. Both Khantia-Mansia and Yamalia refused to accede to Tyumen's demands.

As voting day approached, leaders of both Yamalia and Khantia-Mansia advocated a boycott of the Tyumen' oblast elections. Although a presidential representative claimed to have acquired an agreement from the legislatures of both okrugs to comply with Yeltsin's decree ordering the okrugs to participate in the election, a subsequent legislative vote in Khantia-Mansia reflected overwhelming support for ignoring the decree. Both okrugs then proclaimed that the oblast election could not take place until after the signing of a power-sharing treaty with Tyumen'. Witnesses feared that if the okrugs did not take part in the gubernatorial election, the oblast would be split three ways and the election would be meaningless.[89] In November 1996, after the elections of its own governor and legislative head, the duma of Khantia-Mansia agreed to participate in Tyumen's elections, simultaneously declaring that the vote would be valid only if 25 percent or more of the okrug's electorate took part. Yamalia continued to resist, insisting that it was not subordinate to Tyumen'.[90]

The Tyumen' oblast gubernatorial election was held on January 12, 1997. As it promised, Yamalia boycotted the affair. Only 13 percent of the Khantia-Mansia electorate turned out, invalidating the votes. The elections, in fact, did nothing to reduce the secessionist tendencies in the maverick regions. Okrug governors continued to press for direct links with Moscow, bypassing the administrative heads in Tyumen'.[91]

As the conflict deepened, it acquired nationwide notoriety, fueling subordination controversies within Arkhangel'sk oblast and Krasnoyarsk kray, which also contain autonomous okrugs. Noril'sk rayon, for example, has aspired to be subordinate to Taymyr autonomous okrug in lieu of Krasnoyarsk kray. The "Tyumen' syndrome" stimulated the involvement of large industrial organizations and federal agencies, which have had the daunting task of taking sides. Gazprom, for example, took the side of the titular minorities, which to a degree explains the current weakness of the Tyumen' administration.

Sakha in the Sky with Diamonds

Resource-rich Sakha (Yakutia) has one of the lowest standards of living in Russia, ranking just above the poorest backwaters of the North Caucasus.

Upon their declaration of sovereignty in 1990, the Sakhans, with vivid memories of the riots of 1979, wanted to immediately shed their Russian name of "Yakut"; but true to their historical propensity to compromise, they adopted the hyphenated appellation "Yakut-Sakha" instead. Within two years, they had deleted the hyphen and called their land the "Sakha Republic (Yakutia)."[92]

Sakhans are descendants of northeast Turkic tribes who migrated to their present homeland during the fifteenth century and are linguistically related to the Altays, Dolgans, Khakass, Shors, Tofalars, and Tyvans. Neither Muslim nor Russian Orthodox in faith, they are culturally linked with the Evens, Evenks, and Yukagirs—shamanist tribal peoples. Although Sakhans have been subjected to some form of Russian rule since 1630, Russian culture has obtained but a superficial foothold.[93] Native occupants of a territory that represents 2 percent of the earth's landmass, Sakhans number fewer than 400,000. More than 96 percent are residents of Sakha (Yakutia), with the remaining 15,000 or so dwelling in Khabarovsk kray, Evenkia, and other parts of Russia. In 1995, Sakhans represented more than 35 percent of the population of their homeland, a proportion that was rising because of the outflow of short-term nonnative workers. Approximately 50 percent of the republic's population was ethnically Russian.[94]

From the perspective of the core, the Sakha Republic is "back of beyond"; but in Greater Siberia, the region forms a bridge between Siberia proper and the RFE. The Turkic Sakhans are uniquely positioned to communicate not only with the Turks of Siberia but also with Turks worldwide. A small number of Sakhans have espoused pan-Turkic goals and have sent delegates to Turkic congresses in Ankara, Baku, and Kazan'. Sakhans also interrelate with the numerically small minorities of the north, some of whom have suffered not only the scars of Russification but also Yakuticization. Several new institutions dedicated to healing these wounds have materialized in the Sakha capital of Yakutsk. The most conspicuous of these are the Association of Northern Minorities of the Sakha Republic and the Institute of Problems of Northern Minority Peoples. The Sakha government's northern interests now extend to peoples beyond the borders of Russia by means of a program entitled "The Cooperation of the Sakha Republic (Yakutia) with Northern States." President Mikhail Nikolayev, who despite his very Russian name is purely Sakhan by birth, is the vice president of the internationally based Northern Forum (an advocacy group for the rights of northern peoples around the world), which maintains a branch office in Yakutsk. In this way, Sakha (Yakutia) has expanded its relations with the peoples of Alaska, Canada, and Scandinavia. Reinforcing their image as an ethnic bridge, Sakhans also have active ties with the Japanese, Koreans, Chinese, and Mongolians, with whom they have distant kinship.[95] The South Koreans, Japanese, and Chinese have developed economic and cultural activities in the Sakha capital.[96]

Mikhail Nikolayev: Sakha's Stephen A. Douglas. Mikhail Yefimovich Nikolayev (Photo 8.5) was born of Sakhan parents in the village of Otemskiy, southwest of Yakutsk, in 1937. He studied veterinary medicine in Omsk through 1961, then returned to Sakha (Yakutia) and became the head of the Yakutsk Komsomol, which placed him on the fast track to future political stardom. In 1963, he became a member of the CPSU and climbed the ladder to Soviet success as a protégé of Yakut party secretaries Gavril Chiryayev and Yuriy Prokop'yev. At the time of the collapse of the Soviet Union, Nikolayev was chairperson of Yakutia's supreme soviet (1989–1991). During the March 1990 elections to the Russian parliament, which he won decisively, he campaigned in his native district of Ordzhonikidze. In December 1993, he ran for a seat on the Federation Council and won again, with two-thirds of the vote. He has served on that body ever since.[97]

Nikolayev's association with Yeltsin began and ended in rivalry. In the 1991 presidential election, he ran against Yeltsin, Nikolay Ryzhkov, Tuleyev, Zhirinovskiy, and others. His platform comprised: (1) state sovereignty for the Yakut-Sakha Republic *within* Russia; (2) transition to a market economy with due consideration of the special characteristics of the north, which included *inter alia* the creation of a national banking system and the simultaneous development of the private and state economic sectors; (3) protection of the social welfare of the population; and (4) encouragement of international agreements.[98] Nikolayev was soundly beaten, but he had made his point on the issue of economic autonomy for Yakut-Sakha. For these and other stands, he was elected president of Yakut-Sakha on December 20, 1991. A week later, while being sworn in, he pleased the native residents of his republic by pledging to serve the "Sakha (Yakut) Republic." Since that time, the Sakhan president has performed double duty as prime minister of his homeland.

President Nikolayev has proved himself one of Russia's ablest politicians in many ways. By supporting

PHOTO 8.5 *Mikhail Nikolayev, President of Sakha (Yakutia) (ca. 1994).* SOURCE: *ITAR-TASS, courtesy of Dr. Aleksey Novikov, Moscow State University.*

Yeltsin for the Russian presidency in 1991, at the time of the August (1991) coup, and in the executive branch's clash with parliament in October 1993, Nikolayev has stayed on the winning side despite opposition from his frequently conservative regional legislatures. During winter 1992, Nikolayev rallied support for Sakhan sovereignty. He contended that Sakha's relations with Russia had to be based on firm legal foundations. It was during this period that he hammered out economic agreements on the disposition of Sakhan diamonds and other resource-sharing policies. Throughout the negotiations, Nikolayev's goals were always geared toward economic and *not* political independence. Until spring 1993, the Sakhan president exercised caution when speaking of reform. Despite his conservative record in parliament,[99] however, he supported Yeltsin's wishes and voted against the ouster of Russian Prime Minister Gaydar in December 1992. Thus, on substantive issues, Nikolayev has been one of the Russian parliament's stronger supporters of President Yeltsin. However, in day-to-day politics, he has been a regionalist and Sakhan patriot. After Yeltsin's victory in October 1993, Nikolayev dissolved his republic's parliament and called for new elections.

The Sakhan president's loyalty to Yeltsin, however, may be more transparent than it at first appears. Under the USSR, Sakha was a classic resource frontier, and Sakhans dreaded that the pattern would persist under the administration of the Russian Federation. Nikolayev and his regional parliaments were determined to accrue as much control as they could over their resources. The core's concessions on these matters might be due less to its grateful generosity to a loyal Nikolayev than to its desire to co-opt Sakha by gaining the republic's promises not to seek independence.[100] Nonetheless, Nikolayev's apparent loyalty to the Russian president would have made it difficult for Yeltsin to refuse his ally's demands without alienating Sakhans.

Diamond Sovereignty.   Nikolayev believed that if his constituency held direct control over only 30 percent of its resources (especially diamonds, gold, oil, gas, and coal), Sakha could become wealthy enough to attract businessmen from all over the developed world.[101] Sakha's most impressive bargaining chip is its diamonds, which represent 99.8 percent of Russia's current production (approximately 24 million carats).[102] Under Soviet authority, all revenues from the sale of such resources went directly into the core's coffers. Rarely if ever did any of the profits return to the region of origin, except indirectly by way of Moscow.

Since 1957, four diamond mining operations have arisen on Sakhan soil. The first of these was a diamond concentrator based on South African–like kimberlite pipes at Mirnyy, south of the Vilyuy River. A decade later, two other diamond centers took root, on sites of similar pipes at Aykhal and Udachnyy, almost due north of Mirnyy and just south of the Arctic Circle. Still farther north of Mirnyy, on the tiny Ebelyakh River (a right-bank tributary of the Anabar), diamond placers were mined through the 1980s. Together, Aykhal, Udachnyy, and Mirnyy produce more than 95 percent of the republic's annual output. Ebelyakh provides an additional million carats per year. By the mid-1990s, the original Mirnyy mines were near depletion, but the proximal Yubileynyy (Jubilee) pipe awaited exploitation. For want of appropriate equipment and sufficient funding, the Jubilee operation had been delayed for four years. Because of environmental concerns, Jubilee was to be a shaft mine instead of the more economical opencast type.

With the demise of the Soviet Union, the question of economic sovereignty over domestic diamond production shifted from a rivalry between Russia and the USSR to one of Russia versus Sakha. In early 1992, Nikolayev advocated Sakha's secession from Russia and vowed to conduct his intercourse with the core on the basis of international treaties.[103] The outcome of the controversy, emerging in late 1992, was a joint-stock relationship (*Almazy Rossii-Sakha*, or Alrosa) that gave Russia 80-percent control over the domestic gem diamond industry and Sakha a 20-percent share. Sakha was permitted to retain 100-percent control over the domestic industrial diamond industry.

The agreement permitted Sakha to "single-channel market" up to half of its 20-percent gem-quality quota to customers other than DeBeers, which maintains a near-monopoly on world diamond markets. Sakhans also formed a joint venture with DeBeers in diamond selection and cutting under the name Polar Star. At inception, representatives of Polar Star announced that they had plans to coordinate fourteen new diamond-cutting operations in Sakha, the first of which went onstream in the Vilyuy River town of Suntar' in November 1992. To the initial dismay of authorities in the core, Polar Star also intermediated between Sakha, independent of Russia, and other cutting firms in Japan, Israel, Belgium, and South Korea.[104]

Sadly, the arrangement has not proved beneficial to the ordinary residents of Sakha. Instead, the old guard Communists in neocapitalist garb have kept most of the profits. This group undoubtedly includes Nikolayev himself. Because of his "special relationship" with Yeltsin, the Sakhan president has been able to obtain advantages for Sakha that other Siberian regions do not possess. For example, the constitution of Sakha stipulates that Sakhan domestic law takes precedence over Russian law. The document also gives the republic the right to secede, should there ever be a catastrophic crisis in the core; but Moscow authorities do not take this provision seriously. Constitutionally, Sakha retains the right to form its own army, but it has not chosen to adopt its own currency, bank network, or other attributes characteristic of independence. In return for the core's peaceful acceptance of these potentially contentious notions, Sakha agreed to participate fully in the governance of the Russian Federation. The republic obtained the right to avoid much of Russia's privatization program, with local retailing remaining in state hands. In another "special arrangement," Yeltsin permitted Nikolayev to keep all federal taxes that he raised until June 1995, when the two sides negotiated a new tax code that has been even more favorable to Sakha.

Tax retention proves to be a two-edged sword: Sakha must pay for all federal and local programs from its own budget. As Barner-Barry and Hody have pointed out, the "money does not ensure economic prosperity, but it puts Sakha in a position to begin rebuilding its infrastructure and to clean up the worst of its environmental problems."[105]

Many of the negotiations that resulted in agreements favorable to Sakha were conducted in secrecy. In the biggest secret maneuver of all, the republic obtained ownership rights over all the diamonds on its territory and the right to sell them abroad, as long as Russia could maintain a 32-percent share of the stock in Alrosa. It was a sweet deal: Sakha had permission to buy its 20-percent share of the output at cost, or approximately 40 percent of the international price. In 1995, Alrosa accumulated gross returns of $721 million, including $250 million in profits. The following year, the company reported revenues of $1.4 billion, $600 million of which derived from exports through DeBeers. A closed joint-stock company, led by the republic's vice president, Vyacheslav Shtyrov, the enterprise provides 70 to 80 percent of Sakha's budgetary revenues.[106]

The Sakhan president's supporters tout the tax treaties as his greatest accomplishment. In Sakha, the vast majority of his compatriots see him as the guarantor of political stability, the person most likely to solve the republic's socioeconomic problems, and a bulwark against potential interethnic quarrels. Most Sakhans are willing to extend his term to 2001.

Nikolayev's administration has not been without its critics inside Sakha, however. His economic ideas tend to be authoritarian. He supports state regulation of the economy, contending that only the state can stimulate business and entrepreneurial activities. The old guard Communists (newly restyled as entrepreneurs) in his parliament, who wrote the republic's constitution, have striven to weaken his authority—but to no avail. In October 1996, Nikolayev's proponents urged him to disband his legislature and to convoke a constitutional assembly to adopt a new constitution that strengthens his already heavy hand.[107] In April 1997, he signed a decree that compels all foreigners who come to Sakha to first obtain permits from local officials and the republic's interior ministry. Simultaneously, the interior ministry announced that it might soon begin a sweep of Sakha to deport all "illegal aliens." Predictably, Nikolayev's parliamentary opponents claimed the decree violated the constitution of the republic.[108]

In summer 1997, it appeared that Nikolayev's honeymoon with the national government was near its end and that external opposition also was growing. When Sakha's bilateral treaty with the core expired in March 1997, the regional duma unilaterally extended it, without permission from the Yeltsin government. Probably jealous of Nikolayev's growing power and popularity, the governor of Krasnoyarsk kray, Valeriy Zubov, summoned the national government to terminate its "secret arrangement" with the republics, particularly with Sakha. In May 1997, when Zubov invited Chubais to Krasnoyarsk to discuss the favoritism issue, the deputy prime minister was only too willing to accept. After the talks, Chubais traveled to Sakha, where he chastised the local leadership for asking for federal subsidies at the same time as they retained would-be federal taxes. He admonished the owners of companies to sell stock as a means of raising capital.

Chubais contended that Sakha could afford to contribute more to the national budget. He argued that as of spring 1997, Sakha had not transferred a single diamond to the core and that Moscow had obtained a mere $3 million of the money garnered from the arrangement with DeBeers, despite its one-third proprietorship in Alrosa. In retaliation, the Russian government refused to approve Alrosa's deal with DeBeers in 1997. By late spring, the company and Sakha were strapped for funds. The young deputy prime minister stressed that Sakha would no longer be permitted to avoid its obligations to the federal budget.[109] Meanwhile, the Yeltsin government sought to find investors in the Lomonosov diamond deposits in Arkhangel'sk oblast—reputedly the world's largest untapped reserves of the precious stones. The goal was "to create a powerful mining center to rival that of Sakha."[110]

In early July 1997, Nikolayev finally surrendered, saying that Sakha would pay taxes just like any other region. In response, Yeltsin signed the decree that allowed Alrosa to conclude a new agreement to export diamonds with DeBeers. The ukase also reduced Sakha's ability to benefit from the diamond sales. Since the decree, Sakha has been allowed to buy only as many diamonds as Russia permits, and only at the prices set by the core. Almost immediately, Sakhans erupted in anger. In September, workers from the Yakutsk water works shut off water supplies to government buildings. They said that they had not been paid in ten months and they intended to keep the water off until all back wages were collected.[111] Nikolayev's honeymoon was indeed over.

Kuzbas: Tuleyev Is Nobody's "Tool"

In autumn 1991, the city of Kemerovo played host to an international trade show. The event was perfectly timed: Summer was ending, and the brief autumn was nigh; the leaves were changing, and the sky was bright

PHOTO 8.6 *Lenin as antihero at Kemerovo Meeting Hall, 1991.* SOURCE: *Dmitriy Korobeynikov, Novosti Press Agency (Kemerovo Bureau).*

with sunlight. Cool breezes from the Tom' blew away much of the air pollution generated by the huge industrial district west of town, at least until the late afternoon. It was Kemerovo's "window of opportunity." Hundreds of foreigners would witness the city at its very best.

A premonitory glow perfused the town. Naive Kuzbas communists-turned-capitalists dreamed of doing big business with the visitors. All manner of technology, both Russian and foreign, was on display in the cumbrous exhibition hall that overlooked the Tom' under the watchful gaze of the now-unfashionable Lenin (Photo 8.6). The biggest attraction was a miniature Dutch mobile bakery that continuously cranked out free baguettes: Whatever else they went without, Siberians must have their *khleb* (bread), which was getting scarcer and more expensive every day.

Curiously, although their presence was needed at the exhibition, host after host would disappear for several hours, but never all at once. The trade show had coincided with the season of harvest on private plots, and the precious produce had to be collected before mid-September lest it rot. Throughout the city, Kemerovans were filled with the urgency that only a people who have known past malnourishment can feel. In contrast to the Occident, Kuzbas society still worried about the availability of the most basic necessities.

All the "Red Directors" (communists-turned-capitalists) were on hand to commune with their former enemies. Aman Tuleyev still seemed unsure that he appreciated the new times. He appeared to be seething at Gorbachev for the latter's having initiated such changes. At the opening ceremony in the downtown opera house, he gave a preprandial address to a capacity audience. A gifted orator, he shook his fist and ranted that the foreign businessmen needed to appreciate Kemerovo oblast's bounty. As a Kazakh, he had inherited coal-black hair and black, bushy eyebrows from his forebears; he was as menacing as a young John L. Lewis, and twice as animated (Photo 8.7). One could tell that he was accustomed to deference. Like the blessing at a dinner table surrounded by nonbelievers, his fiery speech was over in a few minutes. The abrupt termination of his presentation was tantamount to the declaration, "and now, let's eat!"

Siberians, whether Kazakh, Russian, or something else, not only know how to eat, they know even better how to drink. Within an hour after the opening of the buffet line, Tuleyev was roaring drunk. So drunk was he, in fact, that he had to be carried out to his chauffeur-driven Volga by no fewer than four of his lackeys. He continued to rave sibilantly and nonsensically as he vanished into the dusk.[112]

Aman Tuleyev was born in the Turkmen port of Krasnovodsk in 1944. A leading member of the CPRF, Tuleyev has been in Russian politics since 1989, when he ran for the Soviet Congress of People's Deputies. He naturally supported the strikers but distanced himself from their call for Gorbachev's resignation. He did this because he planned to run for the Russian presidency against Yeltsin, Gorbachev's archrival. During the 1990 campaign, he blatantly registered his opinion of Yeltsin by declaring that "a vote for Yeltsin" would be "a vote for a superdictator." Tuleyev came in fourth, surprising many of his detractors. In Kemerovo, he garnered more votes (44.7 percent) than any other candidate.

During the August 1991 coup, he interrupted his vacation, flew

PHOTO 8.7 *Aman Tuleyev, the "Kazakh from Kemerovo" (ca. 1994).* SOURCE: *ITAR-TASS, courtesy of Dr. Aleksey Novikov, Moscow State University.*

directly to Moscow, and held discussions with the coup supporters to ensure that they would not interfere in the affairs of Kemerovo oblast. Tuleyev urged the perpetrators to use state food reserves to gain the support of the people. While the outcome of the putsch was still undecided, the Kemerovo governor met with his oblast presidium and informed the members of his discussions with the coup's leaders. He told them that under no circumstances could he support Yeltsin, and that the coup's leaders had his backing, stressing his willingness to aid them should they need his help. Shortly afterward, an ad hoc committee was established as a contingency to assist the coup. Tuleyev declared martial law in the city of Kemerovo, imposed curfews, and ordered the army and the militia to patrol the streets. To counter Tuleyev's actions, Yeltsin dispatched Mikhail Kislyuk to Kemerovo as his presidential representative. Until summer 1997, Tuleyev had to play second fiddle to Kislyuk in his base oblast; thus, Tuleyev and Kislyuk have never been friends.

The Kazakh was livid over Yeltsin's handling of the parliamentary crisis in October 1993, and he called not only for Siberian independence but also for a nationwide strike against the Russian president (see Chapter 7). Both positions were expected because of Tuleyev's stands on regionalism. In his opinion, the existing system of managing the central budget "drains the provinces of everything" and pumps it into "the coffers of the state treasury." This constrains local budgets and excludes regions from the reform process. To alleviate the crisis, Tuleyev argues against the elimination of extant social structures based on collective principles and advocates the development of new societal forms parallel to and competing with the old ones. In this way, he contends, "you realize a program of stabilization simultaneous with the implementation of a regulated transition to the market economy." He supports wage increases tied to inflation, emphasizes lowering costs, and wants to renovate the industrial base. He has been a strong voice for the rights of vestigial socialist institutions.[113]

The predominantly Russian citizens of the Kuzbas never aspired to sovereignty (see Chapter 7). All they want is a higher standard of living, greater control over their domestic resources, and greater autonomy in decisionmaking. Even on these points their expectations have become more modest over time. Christensen has noted that since 1991, the Kuzbas strike committees have become involved in "rearguard actions" protecting workers' jobs and social benefits, or have "bickered internally" about the appropriate long-term strategies of the labor movement.[114] Under the new market economy, they hoped that the cheapness and competitiveness of their coal (simultaneously the lowest cost at the mine head and the highest Russian domestic grade) would carry them. They did not foresee the dramatic rise of rail tariffs in October 1993, which forced them to their knees. Yeltsin's promises of yesteryear proved as empty as Gorbachev's. Tempers flared. By 1995, Kuzbas miners and elites alike could hardly abide the once-popular economic reforms of the Yeltsin government. The vaunted Kemerovo FEZ foundered on infertile soil. The region's new capitalists could neither ship their coal overseas nor distribute it economically to domestic markets. The former home of the Soviet "working-class elite," by 1997, Kemerovo was swamped with human and economic depression. The steel mills of Novokuznetsk no longer operated, and the coal mining towns were bankrupt. Since 1993, 37 unprofitable mines had closed. Ironically, as unemployment rose, the state of the environment improved. On March 27, faced with further pit closures, the once inspired miners of Prokop'yevsk ignored another call to strike. Fearing unemployment, they simply could not afford to halt work. They could not afford to stop work even though they had not been paid in six months. Meanwhile, filling the streets of the town, wives, children, and pensioners carried placards that read "give the miners their money," "our children are starving," and "save our town."

Governor Kislyuk declared a state of economic emergency in the oblast as early as September 1996. He took the action because local enterprises could not pay their debts. With a nationwide onus of $9 billion in wage arrears, the core could not find sufficient money to pay back wages, pensions, and other social benefits in the region. Within the oblast, 90 percent of the industrial enterprises relied on barter exchanges. Whatever monetary transactions occurred took place outside the province. This left local governments destitute. The situation became so desperate that Kislyuk seemed to side with Nemtsov and Chubais by recommending that his oblast be split into three parts and merged with neighboring Altay kray and Novosibirsk and Tomsk oblasts.

By May, still without wages, Kuzbas workers stoically accepted their fates. Long before, they had taken second and third jobs to tide them over when the core could not pay them. The Kuzbas mafia was flourishing amid general exhaustion and apathy. In the words of a *Los Angeles Times* reporter, "The most drastic change wrought by [the Yeltsin government] is that the poor feel defenseless." Even when a Dahmerish cannibal stalked children in Novokuznetsk, city residents were hardly fazed.[115]

The heat of summer brought tensions to a boil. Yeltsin fired the unpopular Kislyuk and replaced him with Tuleyev, who was to govern the oblast until the new gubernatorial elections took place in October (Tuleyev would win with 95 percent of the vote). Having had prior experience (before 1991) as governor, Tuleyev immediately took the side of the protesters and began to pay out at least some of the wage arrears and child allowances. Meanwhile, he still sneered at Yeltsin's market reforms. A supporter of a strongly bound economic union, or commonwealth, Tuleyev nostalgically favors a return to Soviet-style paternalism.[116]

CONCLUSION

We live in a so-called new world order that more often than not resembles a world of disorder. During the 1990s, groups long fused together by the Cold War were torn asunder. Even in the United States, centrifugal forces have increased in the last score of years. In summer 1993, historian Daniel Boorstin warned, "the menace to America today is in the emphasis on what separates us rather than on what brings us together—the separations of race, of religious dogma, of religious practice, of origins, of language."[117] In the United States, this proclivity is cause for concern, but in the rest of the world, its implications are truly profound. In the United States, the venerable glue of constitutionalism and a common language still counteract centrifugal tendencies. In Eurasia and elsewhere, however, where cultural differences are entrenched and "constitutions" are either nonexistent or weak, the menace is very real. For a while, in the early 1990s, a good slogan appeared to be: If you don't have a country, rush out and make one.

And so it was in Greater Siberia. Toward the end of Gorbachev's administration, the historic precedents of nineteenth-century regionalism reemerged as if they had never dissipated. Although their movements were fleeting and ineffective, Greater Siberian separatists had regrouped under the banners of economic autonomy and ethnic sovereignty. Congresses were held. The message that transpired from all of this was that the region as a whole is hardly unified, but parts of it are: Sakha is one such part, Yamalia another, and Khantia-Mansia still another; and there are others that tend to be less conspicuous. Regional economic confederations, such as the SA and FEA, do not and will not fuse together "nations," but can and do serve useful purposes as interest groups and lobbies in the core.

In 1997, it became apparent that the Yeltsin government was more worried about Greater Siberian "economic separatism" than about its political separatism. To lower inflation rates in 1996, core authorities had to withhold financial support of the regions, including wages for state employees, pensions, and other social payments. In Greater Siberia, the first to respond to the austerity program were Sakhalin and Irkutsk oblasts, both of which discontinued their contributions to the federal budget.

The population of Sakhalin oblast had shriveled from 720,000 in 1992 to 632,000 in January 1997, an implosion of 12 percent. The overwhelming majority of emigrants were highly skilled urban workers who abandoned the province because of the regional government's inability to create conditions that would permit residents to utilize the island's resources—especially because of the delays in the development of oil and gas fields on the continental shelf. During the same period, average life expectancy on the island fell from 68 to 55 years. Other "push factors" comprised a precipitous rise in the crime rate and in drug use. The Sakhalin government's incapacity to cope with its sagging economy was largely monetary. The problems were the same in Irkutsk, where the popular Governor Yuriy Nozhikov complained that federal debts to the province totaled more than $350 million, while Irkutsk transferred almost $700 million to the federal budget during 1996. A month after he presented these statistics, Nozhikov, who had been governor since 1991 and had been supported by 70 percent of the provincial electorate, resigned, saying that the policies of the core had severely damaged the interests of donor regions such as Irkutsk.[118]

Today, Nozhikov, Tuleyev, Nikolayev, and Nazdratenko—not to mention dozens of other governors—are like Siberian salmon swimming upstream. In Soviet times, Siberian workers were granted the northern increment and other incentives for sacrificing their comforts in the core to work in the periphery (see Chapter 6). The prices on their raw materials and consumer commodities were held extremely low, and relative to the ordinary worker back home, nonnatives in Greater Siberia became "rich." Overnight, Yeltsin's reforms erased the high wages and low prices. The real wage of an average Siberian fell by 20 percent below the Russian average in 1992 and has continued to lag ever since, especially in the face of wage arrears (Appendix B).[119]

As we have seen, Sakhalin and Irkutsk are joined by Kemerovo and Primor'ye in their frustrating competition for cooperation from the core. Obviously, these four regions are not alone. Each day, the core must cope with the plea bargains of 89 regions and republics with 89 separate inventories of local problems. Paul Goble contends that the core in 1997 is considerably weaker than it was in 1987, for three reasons: (1) It has lost key levers of control (the CPSU, the KGB, and the Soviet Army), without being able to replace them with democratic institutions in the regions; (2) its authoritarian traditions force regions to be suspicious of its motives; and (3) the core itself is divided, allowing regional governors to play one side against the other. There are also three reasons why regions are stronger than ever before: (1) Governors are elected and are legitimated at the local level; (2) regional leaders face few constraints locally in their control of the media, repression of the opposition, and management of the local purse strings; and (3) they often have close ties with regional business leaders and military commanders (Nazdratenko, for example).[120] When viewed from this perspective, one can easily understand why Nemtsov and Chubais want to simplify the number of administrative units with which Moscow now contends and to constrain the power of regional governors.

Ten purely territorial administrative districts made up Greater Siberia in 1917. Today, the region is composed of twenty-nine ethnic-territorial administrative units (see Appendix A), each with a different environment and very different needs. Compared to those in other Russian regions, Siberian populations are numerically small, and some are *very* small (see Appendix

B). Humanitarians, such as the members of the APN, argue that the numerically small peoples of Greater Siberia should be preserved, no matter what the costs. Pragmatists counter that the costs are too great. In the view of the latter, the opinions of 30,000 Khants and Mansi and 21,000 Yamalo-Nentsy are of no consequence in the face of the need to extract the hydrocarbons of the Ob' Basin, on which tens of millions of people depend for their energy supply. More important, the sale of the energy to other countries still attracts the bulk of the foreign exchange income that Russia requires to carry itself into the twenty-first century.

Were Alexander Hamilton and Thomas Jefferson alive today, they would be simultaneously fascinated and horrified by the struggle between national supremacy and ethnoregional rights in modern Russia. The struggle is a classic example of federalism in the making. As we have seen, it is a process of give and take, of adamancy and compromise, and of constitutionalism and tyranny. Many questions remain. Will the Russian core finally and ruthlessly repudiate ethnic and regional sovereignty in favor of neutral administrative units such as the governorships of the tsarist era? Will the Greater Siberian periphery forge stronger ties among its Little Siberians? Will the Russian economy obtain sufficient stability and concomitant security to balance conservation with production and to protect minority rights in Greater Siberia? Will the ethnic minorities throughout Greater Siberia use the model set by the Khants, Mansi, and Nentsy and practice civil disobedience to acquire what they need to continue their traditional lifestyles and occupance patterns? Will the ethnoregions surrender under the pressure from core lieutenants like Chubais and Nemtsov, as did the Sakhan leadership in 1997? And if they do, is it simply an example of a Leninist pseudoalliance, after which they will rise again at a more appropriate time?

At this juncture, although there is good reason to suggest that parts of Siberia and the RFE might someday become an independent republic (or republics), it is equally clear that as long as Siberians generate their livelihood primarily by trading in raw materials, they will remain a resource frontier dependent on Russia and other world regions for food, finished products, and consumer goods. Siberians are headstrong and hardy people, but their economies are far from self-sufficient. They need the Russian and international markets for their crude resources. Likewise, they depend on Russia and foreigners for sophisticated machinery and know-how, as their region cannot yet supply its own. Sophisticated Western companies such as Amoco, Shell, Exxon, Pennzoil, Marathon, Mustang, Elf-Aquitaine, John Brown, Anglo-Suisse, and many others stand ready to provide Siberians with the same environmentally friendly technology that they are already using in subarctic and arctic locations elsewhere in the world. To date, xenophobic members of the Russian parliament have successfully delayed these provisions because of their lingering fears of Greater Siberia's political separation and their usual paranoia about national security. Remember, it was this same chauvinism that drove Siberia's greatest political protagonist, Murav'yev-Amurskiy, from office in 1861 (see Chapter 3). Without high technology and secondary industries, Siberia and its regions will have neither economic nor political independence.

NOTES

1. Tracey A. Ryan, ed., *Russian Government Today* (Washington, D.C.: Carroll Publishing, 1993), pp. iv–viii.

2. Graham Smith, "Ethnic Relations in the New States," in *The Post-Soviet Republics: A Systematic Geography*, ed. Denis J. B. Shaw (London: Longman Scientific and Technical, 1995), pp. 38–39. For the complete text of the Russian Constitution, see *Konstitutsiya Rossiyskoy Federatsii: Proyekt* (Moscow: Yuridicheskaya literatura, 1993).

3. Peter J. S. Duncan, "The Politics of Siberia in Russia," *Sibirica: The Journal of Siberian Studies*, Vol. 1, No. 2 (1994/1995), p. 17; and James H. Bater, *Russia and the Post-Soviet Scene* (London: Arnold, 1996), p. 118.

4. Smith, "Ethnic Relations in the New States," pp. 38–39; and Jeffrey Taylor, "This Side of Ultima Thule," *The Atlantic Monthly*, April 1997, pp. 37–41.

5. Smith, "Ethnic Relations in the New States," pp. 39–40.

6. The quotation is from Duncan, "The Politics of Siberia," p. 18.

7. *Ibid.*

8. Philip R. Pryde, *Environmental Management in the Soviet Union* (Cambridge: Cambridge University Press, 1991), p. 228; and Paul E. Lydolph, *Geography of the USSR* (2d ed.; New York: John Wiley and Sons, 1970), pp. 277–278.

9. Philip P. Micklin, "Recent Developments in Large-Scale Water Transfers in the USSR," *Soviet Geography: Review and Translation*, Vol. 25, No. 4 (April 1984), p. 262; G. V. Voropayev et al., "The Problem of Redistribution of Water Resources in the Midlands of the USSR," *Soviet Geography: Review and Translation*, Vol. 24, No. 10 (December 1983), p. 714; and Gordon B. Smith, *Soviet Politics: Continuity and Contradiction* (1st ed.; New York: St. Martin's, 1988), p. 127.

10. Smith, *Soviet Politics*, p. 129. Shortly before the collapse of the USSR, Greater Siberia's military-industrial complex comprised 10 percent of Russia's defense industrial enterprises and 18 percent of its labor force (see Victor L. Mote, *An Industrial Atlas of the Soviet Successor States* [Houston, Tex.: Industrial Information Resources, 1994], pp. X-2–X-6); Brenda Horrigan, "How Many People Worked in the Soviet Defense Industry?" *Radio Free Europe/Radio Liberty Research Report*, Vol. 1, No. 33 (August 21, 1992), pp. 33–39; and E. Amosenok and V. Bazhanov, "Oboronyy kompleks regiona," *EKO*, No. 9 (1993), p. 17.

11. Smith, *Soviet Politics*, pp. 135–136.

12. F. M. Borodkin, ed., *Goroda Sibiri i Dal'nego Vostoka: Kratkiy ekonomiko-geograficheskiy spravochnik* (Moscow: Progress, 1990), p. 523.

13. *Sibirskaya gazeta*, October 15–21, 1990, p. 12; and *Omskaya pravda*, March 29, 1995. About the same time, the Interregional Association for Siberian Understand-

ing was founded in Novosibirsk, with a chairperson, executive director, and analytical center for coordinating the shift to a market economy. This group involved representatives from the provinces of Altay, Krasnoyarsk, and Novosibirsk, and focused mainly on analyzing regional industrial surpluses and deficits (*Gudok,* December 13, 1990).

14. Vladimir A. Zhdanov, "Contemporary Siberian Regionalism," in *Rediscovering Russia in Asia,* eds. Stephen Kotkin and David Wolff (Armonk, N.Y.: M. E. Sharpe, 1995), p. 123.

15. A. Glubotskiy, A. Mukhin, and N. Tyukov, *Organy vlasti sub"yektov Rossiyskoy Federatsii* (Moscow: Panorama, 1995), p. 30.

16. Duncan, "The Politics of Siberia," p. 21, citing James Hughes, "Regionalism in Russia: The Rise and Fall of Siberian Agreement," *Europe-Asia Studies,* Vol. 46, No. 7 (1994), pp. 1133–1141.

17. *Rossiyskaya gazeta,* March 4, 1994.

18. Duncan, "The Politics of Siberia," p. 21.

19. *Ibid.*

20. *Vedomosti,* October 8–14, 1993; and Zhdanov, "Contemporary Siberian Regionalism," p. 126.

21. At the time, Polezhayev was a member of Chernomyrdin's "Our Home Is Russia" Party (see G. V. Belonuchkin, *Federal'noye Sobraniye: Sovet Federatsii, Gosudarstvennaya Duma [Spravochnik]* [Moscow: Panorama, 1996], p. 93; and Duncan, "The Politics of Siberia," p. 22).

22. *Rossiyskaya gazeta,* July 27, 1993.

23. Duncan, "The Politics of Siberia," p. 22.

24. *Segodnya,* November 20, 1993.

25. *Segodnya,* January 28, March 5, and June 28, 1994; *Kommersant,* June 21, 1994; and *Vek,* January 21–27, 1994.

26. Zhdanov, "Contemporary Siberian Regionalism," p. 129.

27. *Segodnya,* April 6 and June 28, 1994; and *Vek,* January 21–27, 1994. In the famous U.S. case of *McCulloch v. Maryland* (1819), the State of Maryland tried to tax an agency of the national government, the Bank of the United States. The Supreme Court ruled that Maryland could not tax such an agency because theoretically any state could raise the local tax so high as to force the agency off its territory.

28. *Segodnya,* December 27, 1994.

29. *Moskovskiye novosti,* December 22–29, 1996.

30. *Molodost' Sibiri,* December 19, 1996.

31. *Ibid.*

32. M. Lyashevskaya, "Regional'nyye assotsiatsii oblastey Rossii: Opyt regional'noy integratsii," *Kentavr,* No. 3 (1995), pp. 59–68.

33. "Duma Adopts Law on Federal-Regional Subordination," *Chronology of Events: NUPI,* April 28, 1997, available on line at <http://www.nupi.no/cgi-win/Russland/krono.exe/589> (27 May 1997).

34. *Sibirskaya gazeta,* September 3–9, 1990; and *Gudok,* September 29, 1990.

35. *Moskovskiye novosti,* December 22–29, 1996; Glubotskiy, Mukhin, and Tyukov, *Organy vlasti sub"yektov,* p. 30; and Lyashevskaya, "Regional'nyye assotsiatsii," pp. 59–68.

36. Stephan, "The Russian Far East," p. 294.

37. Vladimir I. Ivanov, "The Russian Far East: The Political Economy of the Defense Industry Conversion," in *Socio-Economic Dimensions of the Changes in the Slavic Eurasian World*, eds. Shugo Minagawa and Osamu Ieda (Sapporo, Japan: Hokkaido University, Slavic Research Center, 1996), p. 180; and Elisa Miller and Alexander Karp, eds., *Pocket Handbook of the Russian Far East: A Reference Guide* (Seattle, Wash.: Russian Far East Update, 1994), p. 123. Since its founding, the FEA has actively courted countries of the APR to join RFE regions in creating a flourishing base of commerce (see *Segodnya*, April 25, 1997).

38. Ivanov, "The Russian Far East," pp. 176, 180, and 185.

39. *Ibid.*, p. 176.

40. *Segodnya*, March 5, 1994.

41. Peter Kirkow, "Russia's Gateway to Pacific Asia," *Sibirica: The Journal of Siberian Studies*, Vol. 1, No. 2 (1994/1995), p. 54.

42. *Ibid.*

43. *Ibid.*, p. 55; and Glubotskiy, Mukhin, and Tyukov, *Organy vlasti sub"yektov*, pp. 168–169.

44. Kirkow, "Russia's Gateway," p. 55. The 213 individuals who founded PAKT—the Primorskiy Joint-Stock Corporation of Manufacturers (*Primorskaya aktsionernaya korporatsiya proizvoditeley*), a sort of local business roundtable—came from the region's 36 leading enterprises, comprising, among others, six defense plants and four fishing and fish-canning industries. Members of PAKT were indicted for the embezzlement of as much as $16 million in 1993, or 3.3 percent of that year's total regional budget (see also Glubotskiy, Mukhin, and Tyukov, *Organy vlasti sub"yektov*, p. 169). To locate Nazdratenko's former enterprise at Vostok, see Mote, *An Industrial Atlas*, p. V-13.

45. Stephan, *The Russian Far East*, p. 294.

46. Kirkow, "Russia's Gateway," p. 55.

47. *Ibid.*

48. Glubotskiy, Mukhin, and Tyukov, *Organy vlasti sub"yektov*, p. 170.

49. Kirkow, "Russia's Gateway," p. 56. For the update, see *Izvestiya*, July 23–26, 1996; and "Political Battle Heats Up in Primor'ye," *Chronology of Events: NUPI*, April 28, 1997, available on line at <http://www.nupi.no/cgi-win/Russland/krono.exe/494> (27 February 1997).

50. Glubotskiy, Mukhin, and Tyukov, *Organy vlasti sub"yektov*, p. 169; and Kirkow, "Russia's Gateway," p. 56. The new representative was Vladimir Ignatenko.

51. *Ibid.*, p. 57.

52. Glubotskiy, Mukhin, and Tyukov, *Organy vlasti sub"yektov*, p. 169.

53. *Rossiyskiye vesti*, April 14, 1995; and *Tulskiye izvestiya*, September 3, 1994.

54. Glubotskiy, Mukhin, and Tyukov, *Organy vlasti sub"yektov*, p. 169.

55. *Kommersant Daily*, September 17, 1996. Between July 1996 and November 1997, Chubais was Yeltsin's chief of staff and first deputy prime minister in charge of the economy. He fell victim to scandal and has since witnessed a reduction of his power.

56. "Chubays Wants to Assert Control over Russia's Regions," *Chronology of Events: NUPI*, September 30, 1996, available on line at <http://www.nupi.no/

cgi-win/Russland/krono.exe/294> (19 September 1997); "Presidential Decree Broadens Powers of Regional Representatives," *RFE/RL Newsline*, No. 73, Part 1, available on-line at <http://citm1.met.fsu.edu/~glenn/russia/msg01296.html> (16 July 1997); and Geir Flikke, "Chubays Wants to Control Regions," *Chronology of Events: NUPI*, September 31, 1996, available on-line at <http://www.nupi.no/cgi-win/Russland/krono.exe/242> (19 September 1997).

57. *Segodnya*, July 9, 1997.

58. Penny Morvant, "Primorsk Kray Threatens to Withhold Taxes," *Chronology of Events: NUPI*, March 15, 1996, available on-line at <http://www.nupi.no/cgi-win/Russland/krono.exe/96> (30 May 1997).

59. Scott Parrish, "Primorsk Kray Challenges Russo-Chinese Border Agreement," *Chronology of Events: NUPI*, March 20, 1996, available on-line at <http://www.nupi.no/cgi-win/Russland/krono.exe/88> (30 May 1997). The treaty was reaffirmed in 1995 (see Lewis A. Tambs, "Demography, Geopolitics, and the Decline of the West," *Policy Counsel*, No. 1 [Spring 1997], p. 68).

60. Scott Parrish, "Foreign Ministry Slams Primorsk Governor," *Chronology of Events: NUPI*, April 19, 1996, available on-line at <http://www.nupi.no/cgi-win/Russland/krono.exe/76> (30 May 1997); and "Nazdratenko Gets Warning from Yeltsin," *Chronology of Events: NUPI*, January 8, 1997, <http://www.nupi.no/cgi-win/Russland/krono.exe/376> (30 May 1997).

61. Penny Morvant, "Hunger Strike Ends as Moscow Seeks to Resolve Primorsk Energy Crisis," *Chronology of Events: NUPI*, August 5, 1996, <http://www.nupi.no/cgi-win/Russland/krono.exe/90> (30 May 1997); Penny Morvant, "Miners' Strike Ends in Primor'ye," *Chronology of Events: NUPI*, August 6, 1996, <http://www.nupi.no/cgi-win/Russland/krono.exe/93> (30 May 1997); Anna Paretskaya, "Yeltsin Punishes Primorskiy Kray Officials for Energy Crisis," *Chronology of Events: NUPI*, August 15, 1996, <http://www.nupi.no/cgi-win/Russland/krono.exe/105> (30 May 1997); and Penny Morvant, "Primorskiy Kray Governor Calls for Cancellation of Referendum," *Chronology of Events: NUPI*, September 17, 1996, <http://www.nupi.no/cgi-win/Russland/krono.exe/157> (30 May 1997).

62. "Governor Nazdratenko Under Attack," *Chronology of Events: NUPI*, May 29, 1997, <http://www.nupi.no/cgi-win/Russland/krono.exe/659> (17 June 1997); *Kommersant Daily*, May 29, 1997; and "Yeltsin Empowers His Representative in Primor'ye," *Chronology of Events: NUPI*, June 6, 1997, <http://www.nupi.no/cgi-win/Russland/krono.exe/682> (17 June 1997).

63. "Governor of Primor'ye Effectively Stripped of Powers," *Chronology of Events: NUPI*, June 9, 1997, <http://www.nupi.no/cgi-win/Russland/krono.exe/683> (17 June 1997). The governor is not friendless. On the same day, he received a telegram from Alexander Lebed' advising him to stay the course.

64. "Kremlin Quandary over Primorskiy Kray," *Chronology of Events: NUPI*, June 30, 1997, <http://www.nupi.no/cgi-win/Russland/krono.exe/726> (19 September 1997); and "Kremlin Asserts Right to Sack Governors," *Chronology of Events: NUPI*, June 30, 1997, <http://www.nupi.no/cgi-win/Russland/krono.exe/725> (19 September 1997).

65. James Forsyth, *A History of the Peoples of Siberia* (Cambridge: Cambridge University Press, 1992), p. 415.

66. "Discrimination Against Indigenous People of the North in the Russian Federation," March 4, 1996, available on-line at <http://www.lib.uconn.edu/ArcticCircle/SEEJ/russia_indig.html> (September 21, 1997), p. 1.

67. Duncan, "The Politics of Siberia," p. 20.

68. Alexander I. Pika and Boris Prokhorov, "Soviet Union: The Big Problems of Small Ethnic Groups," *Russia: Khanty-Mansi Autonomous Area,* available on-line at <http://www.lib.uconn.edu/ArcticCircle/SEEJ/Yamal/pika1.html> (21 September 1997), p. 2.

69. Duncan, "The Politics of Siberia," p. 20; and Gail Osherenko, "Indigenous Political and Property Rights and Economic/Environmental Reform in Northwest Siberia," *Post-Soviet Geography,* Vol. 36, No. 4 (April 1995), pp. 225–237. Gayer is now secretary-general of the International League of Indigenous Peoples and Ethnic Groups ("Discrimination," March 4, 1996, p. 4).

70. Demosthenes James Peterson, "Russia's Environment and Natural Resources in Light of Economic Regionalization," *Post-Soviet Geography,* Vol. 36, No. 5 (May 1995), p. 303.

71. Gail Fondahl, "Assimilation and Its Discontents," in *New States, New Nations,* eds. Ian Bremmer and Ray Taras (2d ed.; Cambridge: Cambridge University Press, 1997), p. 202; and Osherenko, "Indigenous Political and Property Rights," p. 236.

72. Fondahl, "Assimilation and Its Discontents," p. 203.

73. "Too Many Federal Subjects? Siberian Conference: Too Many Federation Members," *Chronology of Events: NUPI,* April 17, 1997, available on-line at <http://www.nupi.no/cgi-win/Russland/krono.exe/725> (19 September 1997). Members of this conference, which took place in Novosibirsk, concluded that Russia's 89 republics and regions are too numerous and suggested resurrecting Sibkray, among other larger entities, to diminish the number of federation members.

74. "Discrimination," March 4, 1996, pp. 1–4.

75. *Ibid.,* p. 1. The "extinct" groups were the Ainu (the last of whom moved to Hokkaido in 1955), Vod, Kamasin, Omok, and Yug. The Kereks were also mentioned, but according to Fondahl, they might still number as many as 100 persons, dwelling on the piedmont of the Koryak Mountains parallel to the coast of the Bering Sea (Fondahl, "Assimilation and Discontents," p. 192). The Kamasins preserved their Samoyedic language in the Eastern Sayan Mountains into the Soviet period. They represented the last tribe of Samoyeds in the Samoyedic hearth, the rest of whom migrated to northern Siberia more than a millennium ago. The Omoks lived on the Kolyma Lowland in the vicinity of Cherskiy (Forsyth, *A History of the Peoples of Siberia,* pp. 10, 18, 123, 125, 134, and 355).

76. "Discrimination," March 4, 1996, p. 2.

77. Fondahl, "Assimilation and Discontents," pp. 202–203.

78. "Discrimination," March 4, 1996, p. 2.

79. Although there is no such agency within the executive branch, a Committee on Matters of the North and Numerically Small Peoples exists in the Federation Council (Glubotskiy, Mukhin, and Tyukov, *Organy vlasti sub"yektov,* p. 17). The Duma has two committees that would seem to overlap: the Committee on Matters of the Nationalities and the Committee on Problems of the North (Belonuchkin, *Federal'noye Sobraniye,* pp. 141 and 148).

80. "Russia to Set Up Body to Facilitate Dialogue with Minorities," *Chronology of Events: NUPI*, March 10, 1997, <http://www.nupi.no/cgi-win/Russland/krono.exe/509> (22 September 1997).

81. "Sakhalin Oil Projects Run into Opposition," *Chronology of Events: NUPI*, March 6, 1997, <http://www.nupi.no/cgi-win/Russland/krono.exe/563> (22 September 1997). Sakhalin I–III will develop five oil and gas fields, containing 400 Mmt of crude oil and 830 Bcm of gas, in the Sea of Okhotsk northeast of Sakhalin Island (Tanya Shuster, "Sakhalin Leads the Way," *Bisnis Bulletin*, September 1997, p. 1; and Matthew J. Sagers, "Prospects for Oil and Gas Development of Russia's Sakhalin Oblast," *Post-Soviet Geography*, Vol. 36, No. 5 [May 1995], pp. 274–290).

82. Fondahl, "Assimilation and Discontents," p. 204.

83. *Ibid.*, pp. 207–208.

84. John Massey Stewart, "The Khanty: Oil, Gas, and the Environment," *Sibirica: The Journal of Siberian Studies*, Vol. 1, No. 2 (1994/1995), pp. 25–34; and Osherenko, "Indigenous Political and Property Rights," p. 225.

85. Osherenko, "Indigenous Political and Property Rights," p. 226.

86. *Izvestiya*, October 8, 1996.

87. Daniel R. Kempton and Richard M. Levine, "Soviet and Russian Relations with Foreign Corporations: The Case of Gold and Diamonds," *Slavic Review*, Vol. 54, No. 1 (Spring 1995), pp. 102–103.

88. *Segodnya*, July 15, 1997; *Konstitutsiya Rossiyskoy Federatsii: Proyekt*; and "Split Deepens in Tyumen,'" *Chronology of Events: NUPI*, April 24, 1997, available on-line at <http://www.nupi.no/cgi-win/Russland/krono.exe/669> (22 September 1997).

89. "Preparations for Regional Elections Continue," *Chronology of Events: NUPI*, August 7, 1996, available on-line at <http://www.nupi.no/cgi-win/Russland/krono.exe/94> (30 May 1997); "Khanty-Mansi Withdraws from Tyumen' Oblast," *Chronology of Events: NUPI*, September 27, 1996, on-line at <http://www.nupi.no/cgi-win/Russland/krono.exe/171> (29 May 1997); Robert Orttung, "Kazakov Resolves Tyumen' Crisis," *Chronology of Events: NUPI*, October 9, 1996, <http://www.nupi.no/cgi-win/Russland/krono.exe/202> (29 May 1997); "Yeltsin Moves Tyumen' Elections Back to December," *Chronology of Events: NUPI*, October 16, 1996, <http://www.nupi.no/cgi-win/Russland/krono.exe/382> (29 May 1997).

90. Ritsuko Sasaki, "Oil Factor in Tyumen' Elections," *Chronology of Events: NUPI*, November 13, 1996, <http://www.nupi.no/cgi-win/Russland/krono.exe/284> (29 May 1997).

91. "Tyumen' Re-elects Roketskiy," *Chronology of Events: NUPI*, January 15, 1997, <http://www.nupi.no/cgi-win/Russland/krono.exe/408> (31 May 1997).

92. Partly in exchange for his signature on the March 1992 (Russian) Federation Treaty, Sakha President Nikolayev signed in the name of the Sakha Republic (Yakutia) (Marjorie Mandelstam Balzer, "The Sakha Republic," in *Rediscovering Russia in Asia*, eds. Stephen Kotkin and David Wolff [Armonk, N.Y.: M. E. Sharpe, 1995], p. 142).

93. Marjorie Mandelstam Balzer, "Turmoil in Russia's Mini-Empire," *Perspective*, Vol. 2, No. 3 (January 1992), pp. 2–3. Dr. Balzer kindly sent me a photocopy of this piece.

94. Out-migration from Sakha was 17,600 in 1991, a figure that was second only to the emigration from Magadan oblast. Sakha's outflow exceeded the republic's

rate of natural increase by 5,600 persons. The migration stream burgeoned after the debacle of the USSR, thus raising the share of Sakhans in their republic (Miller and Karp, *Pocket Handbook*, p. 91; and Balzer, "The Sakha Republic," p. 142). Between 1989 and 1992, the populations of Western and Eastern Siberia imploded by 150,000 (Peterson, "Russia's Environment," p. 304).

95. There are vestigial Sakhan and Evenk groups scattered along the Chinese bank of the Heilongjiang (Amur) River. I spotted Evenk in their native dress in the Hailaerh (Hailar) Railway Station in 1987. As Balzer stresses, they are "Sinocized but hungry for further contacts [with their own kind in Sakha]" (Balzer, "The Sakha Republic," p. 147). For information on the Manchurian Evenk, see Juha Janhunen, "Ethnic Implications of the Sino-Russian Border," in *Socio-Economic Dimensions of the Changes in the Slavic Eurasian World*, eds. Shugo Minagawa and Osamu Ieda (Sapporo, Japan: Hokkaido University, Slavic Research Center, 1996), pp. 202–204.

96. Balzer, "The Sakha Republic," pp. 146–147. While I was in Seoul, in autumn 1990—shortly after Sakha's declaration of sovereignty (September 27)—"plenipotentiaries" of the Yakut-Sakha Republic took part in discussions with representatives of Hyundai about developing the Elgen coal deposit and the private construction of the troubled AYAM Railway.

97. Belonuchkin, *Federal'noye Sobraniye*, p. 91.

98. Glubotskiy, Mukhin, and Tyukov, *Organy vlasti sub"yektov*, p. 153.

99. Ryan, *Russian Government Today*, Spring 1993, p. 52. From 1991 to 1993, Nikolayev ranked -41 on a scale of -100 to 100 (from antireform to proreform).

100. Carol Barner-Barry and Cynthia A. Hody, *The Transformation of the Former Soviet Union* (New York: St. Martin's, 1995), p. 297.

101. Balzer, "Turmoil in Russia's Mini-Empire," p. 3.

102. The rest of the diamond output comes from Kus'ye-Aleksandrovskiy, the site of a tiny mine on the western slope of the central Urals, in Perm' oblast. For more on the Sakhan diamond controversy, see Bond, Levine, and Austin, "Russian Diamond Industry," pp. 635–644; and Kempton and Levine, "Soviet and Russian Relations," pp. 100–102.

103. *Kommersant-Daily*, December 15, 1996.

104. Bond, Levine, and Austin, "Russian Diamond Industry," pp. 637–639.

105. Barner-Barry and Hody, *The Transformation*, p. 298. The absolute "worst" of Sakha's environmental problems is radioactive plutonium pollution, the remains of windblown fallout from a 58-megaton, above-surface explosion of a hydrogen bomb over Novaya Zemlya in 1961. The perpetrators waited until the winds blew from the west in order to avoid contaminating the core, thereby concealing their secrets. Instead, the fallout precipitated on Sakha, "smothering the land with an invisible layer of plutonium 239 and 240, the most poisonous substances known to man and comparable to the fallout from Chernobyl." No one was told. Today, almost 40 years after the explosion, thousands of Sakhans suffer from disorders of the blood, hair, connective tissues, digestion, and immune system. See Svetlana Yegorova, "Yakutia: Siberia's Chernobyl," *Sibirica: The Journal of Siberian Studies*, Vol. 1, No. 2 (1994/1995), pp. 35–37.

106. *Sovetskaya Rossiya*, October 19, 1996.

107. *Ibid*.

108. *Segodnya*, April 26, 1997.

109. *Izvestiya*, May 16, 1997; *Segodnya*, May 15, 1997; and *Kommersant-Daily*, May 15, 1997.

110. "Russia to Offer Diamond Rights to Foreign Companies," *Today's Headlines International: PR Newswire*, Story 71096 (May 23, 1997).

111. "Yakutsk Workers Shut Off Water to Local Government," *RFE/RL Newsline*, No. 115, Part 1, available on-line at <http://citm1.met.fsu.edu/~glenn/russia/msg01409.html> (11 September 1997), p. 3.

112. I was an eyewitness to this display. Later, as I emerged from the opera house, I noticed a staggering Tuleyev, "walking it off" alone in the city square. His chauffeur obediently awaited his recovery (Kemerovo, early September 1991).

113. *Sibirskaya gazeta*, No. 38, September 1991.

114. Paul T. Christensen, "Property Free-for-All: Regionalism, 'Democratization,' and the Politics of Economic Control in the Kuzbas, 1989–1993," in *Rediscovering Russia in Asia*, eds. Stephen Kotkin and David Wolff (Armonk, N.Y.: M. E. Sharpe, 1995), p. 220.

115. *Los Angeles Times*, May 26, 1997; "Siberian Miners Ignore Strike Call, Fearing Job Losses," *Industry Track from Business Wire*, Document 7086896 (March 27, 1997), pp. 1–2; "Kemerovo Oblast to Be Dismembered?" *Chronology of Events: NUPI*, February 12, 1997, on-line at <http://www.nupi.no/cgi-win/Russland/krono.exe/467> (27 May 1997); and "Kemerovo Governor Declares State of Economic Emergency," *Chronology of Events: NUPI*, September 10, 1996, <http://www.nupi.no/cgi-win/Russland/krono.exe/155> (30 May 1997).

116. "Yeltsin Sacks Siberian Governor," *Chronology of Events: NUPI*, July 3, 1997, <http://www.nupi.no/cgi-win/Russland/krono.exe/733> (9 July 1997); and "Day of Protest in Kemerovo," *RFE/RL Newsline*, No. 72, Part 1, on-line at <http://citm1.met.fsu.edu/~glenn/russia/msg01292.html> (16 July 1997), p. 3.

117. *Parade Magazine*, July 25, 1993, p. 4.

118. "Sakhalin Population Shrinks," *Chronology of Events: NUPI*, April 30, 1997, on-line at <http://www.nupi.no/cgi-win/Russland/krono.exe/773> (22 September 1997); "Regional Leaders Seek Economic Independence," *Chronology of Events: NUPI*, March 13, 1997, <http://www.nupi.no/cgi-win/Russland/krono.exe/530> (31 May 1997); *Segodnya*, March 6, 1997; and *Kommersant-Daily*, April 21, 1997.

119. James Hughes, "Yeltsin's Siberian Opposition," *RFE/RL Research Report*, Vol. 2, No. 50 (1993), p. 30. In 1995, the average Siberian real wage lag was 31 percent among the 15 losing regions, with Primor'ye, Chita, and the JAR all below -50 percent. When Tyumen' and Sakha, with 107 percent and 13 percent, respectively, above the Russian average, are added in, the deficit average real wage becomes -20 percent. Chukotka, Kamchatka, and Koryakia were still receiving government subsidies but endured enormous wage arrears. Kamchatka, for example, suffered a 30-percent unemployment rate (see "Administrative Units," on-line at <http://www.nupi.no/cgi-win/Russland/a_enhet.exe/> (30 May 1997); and *New York Times*, June 15, 1997).

120. Paul Goble, "Russia: Analysis from Washington—Federalism by Default," July 14, 1997, on-line at <http://www.rferl.org/nca/features/1997/07/F.RU.970714131730.html> (27 August 1997), pp. 1–2.

· Appendix A ·

TABLE A.1   Greater Siberian Governorships in 1917 and Ethnoregions in 1997

Regions in 1917	Regions in 1997	Area in 1997 1,000 km²	Population in 1993 millions	Share Titular Group
Western Siberia		2,427.2	15.2	n/a
Tobol'sk guberniya	Tyumen' oblast	1,435.2	3.1	n/a
	Khantia-Mansia	(523.1)	(1.3)	1.4
	Yamalia	(750.3)	(0.5)	4.4
	Omsk oblast	139.7	2.2	n/a
Tomsk guberniya	Tomsk oblast	361.9	1.0	n/a
	Novosibirsk oblast	178.2	2.8	n/a
	Kemerovo oblast	95.5	3.1	n/a
	Altay kray	169.1	2.7	n/a
	Altay republic	92.6	0.2	31.0
Eastern Siberia		4,122.8	9.2	n/a
Yeniseysk guberniya	Krasnoyarsk kray	2,339.7	3.0	n/a
	Evenkia	(767.6)	(0.02)	14.0
	Taymyria	(862.1)	(0.05)	10.7
	Khakassia	61.9	0.6	11.1
	Tyva	170.5	0.3	64.3
Irkutsk guberniya	Irkutsk oblast	767.9	2.8	n/a
	Ust'-Orda Buryatia	(22.4)	(0.1)	36.3
Transbaykalia oblast	Buryatia	351.3	0.6	24.0
	Chita oblast	431.5	1.4	n/a
	Aga-Buryatia	(19.0)	(0.08)	54.9
Russian Far East		6,215.9	7.9	n/a
Yakutsk oblast	Sakha (Yakutia)	3,103.2	1.1	35.0
Amur oblast	Amur oblast	363.7	1.0	n/a
	Jewish aut. oblast	36.0	0.2	4.2
Maritime oblast	Primorskiy kray	165.9	2.3	n/a
	Khabarovsk kray	788.6	1.6	n/a
Kamchatka oblast	Kamchatka oblast	472.3	0.4	n/a
	Koryakia	(301.5)	(0.03)	16.5
	Chukotka	737.7	0.1	7.3
	Magadan oblast	461.4	0.3	n/a
Sakhalin island	Sakhalin oblast	87.1	0.7	n/a

SOURCES: Donald W. Treadgold, *The Great Siberian Migration* (Princeton, N.J.: Princeton University Press, 1957), pp. 263–265; Goskomstat Rossii, *Rossiyskaya federatsiya v 1992 godu* (Moscow: Respublikanskiy informatsionno-izdatel'skiy tsentr, 1993), pp. 8–10, 91–93; and James H. Bater, *Russia and the Post-Soviet Scene* (London: Arnold, 1996), p. 118.

Appendix B

TABLE B.1 Socioeconomic Characteristics of Ethnoregions in Greater Siberia in 1997

Ethnoregion	Ethnic Groups (and Population)	Language	Religion	Real Wage in 1995[a]	Wage Arrears in 1995[b]
Western Siberia					
Altay republic	Altay (60,000)	NE Turkic	Orth/Lamaist	0.75	10,500
Altay kray	Altay (4,000)	NE Turkic	Orth/Lamaist	0.75	10,500
Kemerovo oblast	Tatars (63,116)	NW Turkic	Muslim	0.54	n/a
	Shors (12,585)	NE Turkic	Orthodox	0.54	n/a
Khantia-Mansia	Tatars (97,689)	NW Turkic	Muslim	1.87	323,600
	Khants (11,892)	Ugrian	Orth/Shamanist	1.87	323,600
	Mansi (6,562)	Ugrian	Orth/Shamanist	1.87	323,600
	Nentsy (1,144)	Samoyedic	Shamanist	1.87	323,600
Novosibirsk oblast	Tatars (29,428)	NW Turkic	Muslim	0.72	15,400
Omsk oblast	Tatars (49,784)	NW Turkic	Muslim	0.83	n/a
Tomsk oblast	Tatars (20,812)	NW Turkic	Muslim	0.91	n/a
	Sel'kups (1,347)	Samoyedic	Shamanist	0.91	n/a
	Khants (804)	Ugrian	Orth/Shamanist	0.91	n/a
Tyumen oblast	Tatars (103,303)	NW Turkic	Muslim	2.07	205,000
	Nentsy (1,702)	Samoyedic	Shamanist	2.07	205,000
	Khants (1,232)	Ugrian	Orth/Shamanist	2.07	205,000
	Mansi (756)	Ugrian	Orth/Shamanist	2.07	205,000
	Sel'kups (102)	Samoyedic	Shamanist	2.07	205,000
Yamalia	Tatars (26,431)	NW Turkic	Muslim	1.25	457,800
	Yamalo-Nenets (20,917)	Samoyedic	Shamanist	1.25	457,800
	Khants (7,247)	Ugrian	Orth/Shamanist	1.25	457,800
	Sel'kups (1,530)	Samoyedic	Shamanist	1.25	457,800

Eastern Siberia

Aga-Buryatia	Buryats (42,362)	Mongolic	Lamaist	0.45	82,900
Buryatia	Buryats (249,525)	Mongolic	Lamaist	0.62	3,100
	Tatars (10,496)	NW Turkic	Muslim	0.62	3,100
	Evenks (1,679)	Tungussic	Shamanist	0.62	3,100
Chita oblast	Buryats (66,625)	Mongolic	Lamaist	0.45	82,900
	Tatars (12,335)	NW Turkic	Muslim	0.45	82,900
	Evenks (1,271)	Tungussic	Shamanist	0.45	82,900
Evenkia	Evenks (3,480)	Tungussic	Shamanist	n/a	n/a
	Sakha (937)	NE Turkic	Orth/Shamanist	n/a	n/a
Irkutsk oblast	Tatars (39,609)	NW Turkic	Muslim	0.72	60,700
	Jews (4,796)	Semitic	Judaic	0.72	60,700
	Evenks (1,369)	Tungussic	Shamanist	0.72	60,700
	Tofalars (630)	NE Turkic	Orth/Shamanist	0.72	60,700
Khakassia	Khakass (62,859)	NE Turkic	Orthodox	0.90	n/a
Krasnoyarsk kray	Tatars (54,052)	NW Turkic	Muslim	1.16	n/a
	Khakass (6,466)	NE Turkic	Orthodox	1.16	n/a
	Kets (994)	Kettic	Shamanist	1.16	n/a
	Evenks (902)	Tungussic	Shamanist	1.16	n/a
	Dolgans (521)	NE Turkic	Orthodox	1.16	n/a
	Nganasans (279)	Samoyedic	Shamanist	1.16	n/a
Taymyria	Dolgans (4,939)	NE Turkic	Orthodox	n/a	n/a
	Entsy (103)	Samoyedic	Orthodox	n/a	n/a
	Nganasans (849)	Samoyedic	Shamanist	n/a	n/a
Tyva	Tyvans (198,448)	NE Turkic	Lamaist/Sham	0.53	n/a
	Khakass (2,258)	NE Turkic	Orthodox	0.53	n/a
Ust'-Orda Buryatia	Buryats (49,298)	Mongolic	Orth/Lamaist	0.72	28,700
	Tatars (4,391)	NW Turkic	Muslim	0.72	28,700

(continues)

(continued)

Ethnoregion	Ethnic Groups (and Population)	Language	Religion	Real Wage in 1995[a]	Wage Arrears in 1995[b]
Russian Far East					
Amur oblast	Evenks (1,617)	Tungussic	Shamanist	0.92	77,400
Chukotka	Chukchi (11,914)	Paleo-Asiatic	Shamanist	0.80	412,500
	Tatars (2,272)	NW Turkic	Muslim	0.80	412,500
	Eskimos (1,452)	Eskimo-Aleut	Shamanist	0.80	412,500
	Evens (1,336)	Tungussic	Orthodox	0.80	412,500
	Chuvans (944)	Paleo-Asiatic	Orthodox	0.80	412,500
Jewish autonomous oblast	Jews (8,887)	Semitic	Judaic	0.56	56,900
Kamchatka oblast	Evens (1,489)	Tungussic	Orthodox	1.39	156,100
	Koryaks (618)	Paleo-Asiatic	Orth/Shamanist	1.39	156,100
	Aleuts (390)	Eskimo-Aleut	Orthodox	1.39	156,100
	Itel'men (262)	Paleo-Asiatic	Orthodox	1.39	156,100
Khabarovsk kray	Tatars (17,591)	NW Turkic	Muslim	0.68	114,500
	Jews (14,014)	Semitic	Judaism	0.68	114,500
	Nanays (10,582)	Manchu	Orth/Shamanist	0.68	114,500
	Evenks (3,691)	Tungussic	Shamanist	0.68	114,500
	Ul'chi (2,733)	Manchu	Orthodox	0.68	114,500
	Nivkhi (2,386)	Paleo-Asiatic	Shamanist	0.68	114,500
	Evens (1,919)	Tungussic	Orthodox	0.68	114,500
	Udegeys (697)	Manchu	Shamanist	0.68	114,500
	Negidals (502)	Manchu	Shamanist	0.68	114,500
	Orochi (499)	Manchu	Shamanist	0.68	114,500

				a	b
Koryakia	Koryaks (6,572)	Paleo-Asiatic	Orth/Shamanist	0.68	249,800
	Itel'men (1,179)	Paleo-Asiatic	Orthodox	0.68	249,800
	Evens (713)	Tungussic	Orthodox	0.68	249,800
Magadan oblast	Tatars (8,024)	NW Turkic	Muslim	1.45	412,500
	Evens (3,769)	Tungussic	Orthodox	1.45	412,500
	Koryaks (1,013)	Paleo-Asiatic	Orth/Shamanist	1.45	412,500
	Chukchi (649)	Paleo-Asiatic	Shamanist	1.45	412,500
	Itel'men (509)	Paleo-Asiatic	Orthodox	1.45	412,500
	Eskimos (79)	Eskimo-Aleut	Shamanist	1.45	412,500
	Chuvans (41)	Paleo-Asiatic	Orthodox	1.45	412,500
Primorskiy kray	Tatars (20,211)	NW Turkic	Muslim	0.33	33,200
	Koreans (8,454)	Altaic	Buddhist	0.33	33,200
	Udegeys (766)	Manchu	Shamanist	0.33	33,200
Sakha (Yakutia)	Sakha (365,236)	NE Turkic	Orth/Shamanist	1.13	296,600
	Tatars (17,448)	NW Turkic	Muslim	1.13	296,600
	Evenks (14,428)	Tungussic	Shamanist	1.13	296,600
	Evens (8,668)	Tungussic	Orthodox	1.13	296,600
	Yukagirs (697)	Altaic?	Orthodox	1.13	296,600
Sakhalin oblast	Koreans (35,191)	Altaic	Buddhist	0.59	141,400
	Tatars (10,496)	NW Turkic	Muslim	0.59	141,400
	Nivkhi (2,008)	Paleo-Asiatic	Shamanist	0.59	141,400
	Orochi (212)	Manchu	Shamanist	0.59	141,400
	Evenks (188)	Tungussic	Shamanist	0.59	141,400
	Nanays (173)	Manchu	Orth/Shamanist	0.59	141,400
	Oroks (129)	Manchu	Orthodox	0.59	141,400

a Share of Russian average (Russia=1.00)
b Amount per capita over/under the Russian average in 1995 rubles (Russia=37,100)
SOURCES: "Ethnic Groups," <http://www.nupi.no/cgi-win/Russland/etnisk_b.exe/> (30 May 1997), numerous ethnic groups and OMRI. RRR, <http://www.omri.cz/Elections/Russia/Regions/About/.html> (20 June 1997), numerous regions.

▪ Selected Bibliography ▪

RUSSIAN NEWSPAPERS

Amurskaya pravda
Blagovest (Kuzbas writers' newspaper)
Delovaya Sibir' (Private business newspaper in Novosibirsk)
Den'
Doveriye (Novosibirsk oblast trade union newspaper)
Ekonomicheskaya gazeta (Replaced by *Vestnik statistiki*)
Gudok (Newspaper of the ministry of transportation; privatized in 1992)
Izvestiya
Kommersant
Kuzbass
Levyy bereg (Kuzbas newspaper)
Literaturnaya gazeta
Molodost' Sibiri
Moment istiny (Independent Novosibirsk weekly)
Moskovskiye novosti
Nasha gazeta (Daily of the Laborers of the Kuzbas)
Na smenu! (Daily of Sverdlovsk *obkom*)
Nauka v Sibiri
Nedelya
Nezavisimaya gazeta
Omskaya pravda
Pravda
Reporter (Kuzbas weekly newspaper)
Rossiyskaya gazeta
Rossiyskiye vesti
Segodnya
Sibirskaya gazeta
Sibirskiy biznes
Sovetskaya gazeta
Sovetskaya Sibir' (Novosibirsk daily)
Tulskiye izvestiya
Vash posrednik (Novosibirsk oblast newspaper)
Vecherniy Novosibirsk
Vecherniy Sverdlovsk

Vedomosti
Vestnik statistiki
Vostok Rossii (Vladivostok weekly)
Vremya (Kuzbas trade union newspaper)
Yavo (Daily of Kemerovo *oblispolkom*)

SOURCES IN RUSSIAN

"Administrativnoye deleniye." *Sibirskaya Sovetskaya entsiklopediya.* Vol. 1 (1929), pp. 20–22.

Aganbegyan, A. G. *Zapadnaya Sibir' na rubezhe vekov.* Sverdlovsk: Sredne-Ural'skoye knizhnoye izd., 1984.

Aganbegyan, A. G., and A. I. Kin, eds. *BAM: Pervoye desyatiletiye.* Novosibirsk: Nauka, 1984.

Aganbegyan, A. G., and D. D. Moskvin. *Chto, gde, pochemu?* Moscow: Prosveshcheniye, 1987.

Aganbegyan, A. G., and V. P. Mozhin, eds. *BAM: Stroitel'stvo i khozyaystvennoye osvoyeniye.* Moscow: Ekonomika, 1984.

Agranat, G. A., and V. Loginov. "Ob osvoyenii severnykh territorii." *Kommunist.* No. 2 (1976), pp. 39–48.

Akademiya nauk SSSR. Khabarovskiy filial. *Sotsial'naya ekologiya i zdorov'ye cheloveka.* Khabarovsk: Znaniye, 1988.

Akademiya nauk SSSR. Komissiya po problemam Severa. *Letopis' Severa.* Moscow: Geografgiz, 1957.

Akademiya nauk SSSR. Sibirskoye otdeleniye. *Problemy BAM.* Novosibirsk: Gos. publichnaya nauchno-tekhnicheskaya biblioteka, 1975–1983, annually.

Akademiya nauk SSSR. Sibirskoye otdeleniye. *Sibirskiy geograficheskiy sbornik.* No. 2. Moscow: Izd. Akademii nauk SSSR (ANSSSR), 1963.

Aleksandrov, S. I., G. N. Rechko, and Yu. A. Fridman. *Kuzbass: Strategiya sotsial'no-ekonomicheskoy rekonstruktsii.* Novosibirsk: Nauka, Sibirskoye otdeleniye, 1991.

Alekseyev, A. I. *I tayga pokoryayetsya nam.* Moscow: Prosveshcheniye, 1980.

———, ed. *Problemy osvoyeniya severa Buryatskoy ASSR.* Novosibirsk: Nauka, Sibirskoye otdeleniye, 1978.

Amosenok, E., and V. Bazhanov. "Oboronyy kompleks regiona." *EKO.* No. 9 (1993).

Andreyevich, V. K. *Istoriya Sibiri.* St. Petersburg: Tip. V. V. Komarova, 1889.

Argudyayeva, Yu. V. *Trud i byt molodezhi BAMa: Nastoyashcheye i budushcheye.* Moscow: Mysl', 1988.

Arsen'yev, V. K. *Dersu Uzala skvoz' Taygu.* Moscow: Pravda, 1989.

———. *Po Ussuriyskomu krayu.* Khabarovsk: Khabarovskoye knizhnoye izd., 1988.

Artemov, N. Ye., and V. I. Lebedev. *Istoriya SSSR s drevneyshikh vremen do XVIII v.* Moscow: Gos. uchebno-pedagogicheskoye izd., 1959.

Assotsiyatsiya Sibirskikh gorodov. *Goroda Sibiri: Spravochnik.* Moscow: Progress, 1990.

Ayzmana, N., Ye. Bugayenko, and V. Klipelya. *Yevreyskaya avtonomnaya oblast'.* Khabarovsk: Khabarovskoye knizhnoye izd., 1984.

Azarkh, E. D. *BAM: Stroyka veka.* Vol. IV. 4 vols. Moscow: Sovremennik, 1978.

Azarkh, E. D., et al. *Blagosostoyaniye gorodskogo naseleniya Sibiri.* Novosibirsk: Nauka, Sibirskoye otdeleniye, 1990.

Bakhrushin, S. V. *Ocherk po istorii kolonizatsii Sibiri v XVI i XVII vv.* Vol. III of *Nauchnyye trudy.* Moscow: Izd. Akademii nauk SSSR, 1955.

BAM posle fanfara. Soviet television documentary. 1988.

Bashkuyev, B. V., and L. G. Pasternak. *Geografiya Buryatskoy ASSR.* Ulan-Ude: Buryatskoye knizhnoye izd., 1983.

Bazhentsov, Yu. N., and A. I. Chistobayev. *Ot problemy k tseli.* Moscow: Mysl', 1987.

Belonuchkin, G. V. *Federal'noye Sobraniye: Sovet Federatsii, Gosudarstvennaya Duma (Spravochnik).* Moscow: Panorama, 1996.

Bilimovich, A. D. *Kooperatsiya v Rossii do, vo vremya i posle bol'shevikov.* Frankfurt/Main: Possev-Verlag, V. Gorachek KG, 1955.

Bochanova, G. A. *Obrabatyvayushchaya promyshlennost' Zapadnoy Sibiri.* Novosibirsk: Nauka, Sibirskoye otdeleniye, 1978.

Bogdanova, Milana. *Samizdat i politicheskiye organizatsii Sibiri i Dal'nego Vostoka.* Moscow: Panorama, 1991.

Bolkhovitinov, N. "Kak prodali Alyasku." *Mezhdunarodnaya zhizn'.* No. 7 (1988), pp. 120–131.

Bol'shaya Sovetskaya entsiklopediya. 30 vols. Moscow: Sovetskaya entsiklopediya, 1970–1981.

Borodkin, F. M., et al. *Goroda Sibiri i Dal'nego Vostoka: Kratkiy ekonomiko-geograficheskiy spravochnik.* Moscow: Progress, 1990.

Boronikhin, A. "K biografii Yermaka." *Voprosy istorii.* No. 10 (October 1946), pp. 98–100.

Botvinnikov, V. I., ed. *Problemy razvitiya gazovoy promyshlennosti Sibiri.* Novosibirsk: Nauka, Sibirskoye otdeleniye, 1983.

Brezhnev, L. I. *Zhizn' po zavodskomu gudku: Chuvstvo rodiny.* Moscow: Politizdat, 1981.

Chichkanov, V. "Problemy i perspektivy razvitiya proizvoditel'nykh sil Dal'nego Vostoka." *Kommunist.* No. 16 (November 1985), pp. 93–103.

Chudnyy, V. P. *BAM: Stranitsy velikoy stroyki.* Kiyev: Izd. politicheskoy literatury Ukrainy, 1985.

Dal'niy Vostok: Fotoal'bom. Moscow: Planeta, 1989.

Danilov, A. D., et al. *Ekonomicheskaya geografiya SSSR.* Moscow: Vysshaya shkola, 1983.

Derevyanko, A. P., ed. *BAM: Problemy, perspektivy.* Moscow: Molodaya gvardiya, 1976.

Drobizhev, V. Z., I. D. Koval'chenko, and A. V. Murav'yev, eds. *Istoricheskaya geografiya SSSR.* Moscow: Vysshaya shkola, 1973.

D'yakonov, F. V., and O. A. Kibal'chich, eds. *Baykalo-Amurskaya Magistral'.* Vol. 105 of *Voprosy geografii,* ed. S. A. Kovalev. Moscow: Mysl', 1977.

Federal'noye sobraniye Rossiyskoy Federatsii (see Informatsionno-ekspertnaya gruppa "Panorama").

Fekhner, M. V. *Torgovlya russkogo gosudarstva so stranami vostoka v XVI veke.* Moscow: Izd. gos. istoricheskogo muzeya, 1952.

Fridman, Yu. A., and S. I. Aleksandrov, eds. *Khimizatsiya i intensifikatsiya narodnogo khozyaystva Sibiri.* Novosibirsk: Nauka, Sibirskoye otdeleniye, 1979.

Galaziy, G. I., ed. *Klimaticheskiye osobennosti zony BAM.* Novosibirsk: Nauka, Sibirskoye otdeleniye, 1979.

Gavrilov, A. T., and I. I. Lavrov. *Zabastovka.* Moscow: Profizdat, 1989.

Glavnoye upravleniye geodezii i kartografii pri Sovete Ministrov SSSR. *Atlas obrazovaniya i razvitiya Soyuza SSR.* Moscow: Akademii nauk SSSR, Institut istorii SSSR, 1972.

Glinka, G. V., et al., eds. *Atlas' Aziatskoy Rossii.* 3 vols. St. Petersburg: A. F. Marks', 1914.

Glubotskiy, A., A. Mukhin, and N. Tyukov. *Organy vlasti sub"yektov Rossiyskoy Federatsii.* Moscow: Panorama, 1995.

Golovachev, P. M., ed. *Sibirskiye voprosy: Periodicheskiy sbornik.* St. Petersburg: Izd. Al'tshulera, 1905.

Golovanov, V. D., et al. *Zapovedniki Dal'nego Vostoka.* Moscow: Mysl', 1985.

Goryushkin, L. M. *Sibirskoye krest'yanstvo na rubezhe dvukh vekov.* Novosibirsk: Nauka, Sibirskoye otdeleniye, 1967.

———. *Istochniki po istorii krest'yanstva i sel'skogo khozyaystva Sibiri vo vtoroy polovine XIX–nachale XX vv.* Novosibirsk: Novosibirsk State University, 1988.

Goskomstat Rossii. *Narodnoye khozyaystvo Rossiyskoy Federatsii: 1992.* Moscow: Respublikanskiy informatsionno-izdatel'skiy tsentr, 1992.

Goskomstat SSSR. *Demograficheskiy yezhegodnik SSSR.* Moscow: Finansy i statistika, 1990.

Granberg, A. N., ed. *Ekonomika Sibiri v razreze shirotnykh zon.* Novosibirsk: Nauka, Sibirskoye otdeleniye, 1985.

Granberg, A. N., and A. Rubensteyn. "Uchastiye Sibiri vo vneshneekonomicheskoy deyatel'nosti: Problemy i perspektivy." *Vneshnyaya torgovlya.* No. 8 (1989), pp. 25–29.

Grekov, B. D., and A. Yu. Yakubovskiy. *Zolotaya Orda i yeye padeniye.* Moscow-Leningrad: ANSSSR, 1950.

Gushchin, N. Ya., ed. *Krest'yanstvo i sel'skoye khozyaystvo Sibiri.* Novosibirsk: Nauka, Sibirskoye otdeleniye, 1991.

Informatsionno-ekspertnaya gruppa "Panorama." *Federal'noye sobraniye Rossiyskoy Federatsii: Spravochnyye materialy.* Moscow: Panorama, January 24, 1994.

Iofa, L. Ye. *Goroda Urala.* Moscow: Gos. izd. geograficheskoy literatury, 1951.

Ivanov, V., and P. Minakir. "Opyt roli vneshneekonomicheskikh svyazey v razvitii tikhookeanskikh rayonov SSSR." *Mirovaya ekonomika i mezhdunarodnyye otnosheniya (MEMO).* No. 5 (1988), pp. 59–70.

Ivashentsov, A., and A. Rozentsvit. *Severnoye Zabaykal'ye: Zapadnaya chast' BAMa.* Moscow: Sovetskaya Rossiya, 1977.

Kabo, R. M. *Goroda Zapadnoy Sibiri.* Moscow: Gos. izd. geograficheskoy literatury, 1949.

Kallantar', A. A. "Molochnoye khozyaystvo." In *Aziatskaya Rossiya.* Vol. 2 of *Atlas' Aziatskoy Rossii,* ed. G. V. Glinka. 3 vols. St. Petersburg: A. F. Marks', 1914.

Katayeva, Nina. *I byla zhizn'.* Moscow: Molodaya gvardiya, 1990.

Khromov, Yu. B., and V. A. Klyushin. *Organizatsiya zon otdykha i turizma na poberezh'ye Baykala.* Moscow: Stroyizdat, 1976.

Khrushchev, A. T. *Geografiya promyshlennosti SSSR.* Moscow: Vysshaya shkola, 1990.

Kistanov, V. V., A. B. Margolin, and L. V. Starodubov, eds. *Zapadno-Sibirskiy ekonomicheskiy rayon.* Moscow: Nauka, 1967.

Kolesov, L. I. *Mezhotraslevyye problemy razvitiya transportnoy sistemy Sibiri i Dal'nego Vostoka.* Novosibirsk: Nauka, Sibirskoye otdeleniye, 1982.

Komissarov, V. N. "Stalinskiye lagerya Zapadnoy Sibiri." *EKO.* No. 1 (1990), pp. 58–59, inside back cover.

———. "Stalinskiye lagerya Urala." *EKO.* No. 2 (1990), pp. 58–59, inside back cover.

Konovalenko, V. D. *Vladimir Dmitriyevich Buchichevich-Sibirskiy.* Kemerovo: Redaktsionno-izd. otdel., 1990.

Konstitutsiya Rossiyskoy Federatsii: Proyekt. Moscow: Yuridicheskaya literatura, 1993.

Kopytov, A. I., ed. *Toboy my slavny, Shoriya.* Kemerovo: Panorama, 1989.

Kosmachev, K. P., and Yu. P. Mikhaylov, eds. *Geografiya osvoyeniya resursov Sibiri.* Novosibirsk: Nauka, Sibirskoye otdeleniye, 1979.

Kostennikova, V. M., ed. *Ekonomiko-geograficheskiye rayony SSSR.* Moscow: Prosveshcheniye, 1965.

Kostyukovskiy, Viktor. *Kuzbass: Zharkoye leto 89-go.* Moscow: Sovremennik, 1990.

Kovalev, A. "Svobodnyye ekonomicheskiye zony: Opyt zarubezhnykh stran i perspektivy ikh sozdaniya v SSSR." *Vneshnyaya torgovlya.* No. 11 (1989), pp. 16–19.

Kovtun, V. F., ed. *Khabarovskiy krayevoy krayevedcheskiy muzey*. Khabarovsk: Upravleniye kul'tury Khabarovskogo kraispolkoma, 1985.

KPSS. *Materialy XXVII s"yezda Kommunisticheskoy partii Sovetskogo Soyuza*. Moscow: Politizdat, 1986.

Krivosheyeva, Ye. *Bol'shoy Bill v Kuzbasse*. Kemerovo: Kemerovskoye izd., 1990.

Krotov, V. A., et al. *Vostochnaya Sibir'*. Moscow: Gos. izd. geograficheskoy literatury, 1963.

Krotov, V. V. *K vostoku ot Urala*. Moscow: Mashinostroyeniye, 1979.

Kryuchkov, V. V. *Chutkaya subarktika*. Moscow: Nauka, 1976.

————. *Krayniy Sever: Problemy ratsional'nogo ispol'zovaniya prirodnykh resursov*. Moscow: Mysl', 1973.

————. *Sever: Problemy i chelovek*. Moscow: Nauka, 1979.

Kudryavtsev, F. A., ed. *Sibir' v epokhu kapitalizma*. Vol. 3 of *Istoriya Sibir'*, ed. A. P. Okladnikov. 5 vols. Leningrad: Nauka, 1968.

Kuznetsov, V. L., ed. *Yakutiya zolotaya: Fotoal'bom*. Yakutsk: Yakutskoye knizhnoye izd., 1984.

Lebedev, D. M., and V. A. Yesakov. *Russkiye geograficheskiye otkrytiya i issledovaniya*. Moscow: Mysl', 1971.

Lenin, V. I. *Razvitiye kapitalizma v Rossii*. Vol. 3 of *Sochineniya*. 40 vols. Moscow: Institut Marksa-Engel'sa-Lenina, 1941.

Leont'yeva, G. A. *Zemleprokhodets Yerofey Pavlovich Khabarov*. Moscow: Prosveshcheniye, 1991.

Levchenko, S. V., and D. L. Mozeson. *Za rudami v Sibir'*. Moscow: Nauka, 1978.

Levin, M. G., and L. P. Potapov, eds. *Istoriko-etnograficheskiy atlas Sibiri*. Moscow-Leningrad: Izd. Akademii nauk SSSR, 1961.

Lifanchikov, A. N., et al. *Pishchevaya promyshlennost' Sibiri i Dal'nego Vostoka*. Moscow: Legkaya i pishchevaya promyshlennost', 1983.

Livshits, R. S. *Ocherki po razmeshcheniyu promyshlennosti SSSR*. Moscow-Leningrad: Gos. izd. politicheskoy literatury, 1954.

Lyashevskaya, M. "Regional'nyye assotsiatsii oblastey Rossii: Opyt regional'noy integratsii." *Kentavr*. No. 3 (1995), pp. 59–68.

Margolin, A. B., ed. *Rossiyskaya Federatsiya: Dal'niy Vostok*. In the series *Sovetskiy Soyuz*, ed. S. V. Kolesnik. 22 vols. Moscow: Mysl', 1971.

Martynovo, A. I. *Pisanitsa na Tomi*. Kemerovo: Kemerovskoye knizhnoye izd., 1988.

Matveyev, N. P. *Kratkiy istoricheskoy ocherk g. Vladivostok*. Vladivostok: Ussuri, 1990.

Meysak, N., ed. *Zemlya Novosibirskaya*. Moscow: Sovetskaya Rossiya, 1983.

Mikhaylenko, V. Ya., and P. I. Ovsyannikova, eds. *Atlas zheleznykh dorog SSSR*. Moscow: Glavnoye upravleniye geodezii i kartografii, 1986.

Mikhaylov, N. I. *Priroda Sibiri*. Moscow: Mysl', 1976.

Miller, G. F. *Istoriya Sibiri*. Moscow-Leningrad: ANSSSR, 1937.

Minakir, P., and V. Syrkin. "Strategiya kompleksnogo sotsial'no-ekonomicheskogo razvitiya Dal'nego Vostoka." *Ekonomicheskiye nauki*. No. 12 (December 1987), pp. 3–12.

Ministerstvo kul'tury RSFSR. *Kul'tura malochislennykh narodov Kraynego Severa SSSR: Materialy i bibliografii*. Moscow: 1991 (offset).

Ministerstvo vysshego i srednego spetsial'nogo obrazovaniya RSFSR. *Iz istorii partiynykh organizatsiy Vostochnoy Sibiri*. Irkutsk: Irkutsk State University, 1962.

Morozov, A. T. *Zemlya trudovogo podviga*. Yakutsk: Yakutskoye knizhnoye izd., 1982.

Morozova, T. G., and D. M. Zakharina. *Novaya geografiya Sibiri*. Moscow: Prosveshcheniye, 1972.

Moshkov, A. V. "Etapy khozyaystvennogo kompleksoobrazovaniya v yuzhnoy zone Dal'nego Vostoka." *Geografiya i prirodnyye resursy.* No. 1 (1988), pp. 112–120.
Mosunov, V. P., Yu. S. Nikul'nikov, and A. A. Sysoyev. *Territorial'nyye struktury rayonov novogo osvoyeniya.* Novosibirsk: Nauka, 1990.
Mozhin, V. P., ed. *Ekonomicheskoye razvitiye Sibiri i Dal'nego Vostoka.* Moscow: Mysl', 1980.
Narodnoye khozyaystvo RSFSR. Moscow: Finansy i statistika, 1970–1989. Various issues.
Narodnyye deputaty SSSR: Kto yest' kto. Moscow: Vneshtorgizdat, 1990.
Narodnoye khozyaystvo SSSR. Moscow: Finansy i statistika, 1970–1990. Various issues.
Nikol'skaya, V. V. *Dal'niy Vostok.* Moscow: Gos. izd. geograficheskoy literatury, 1962.
Nikul'nikov, Yu. S., ed. *Ekologo-geograficheskoye kartografirovaniye i rayonirovaniye Sibiri.* Novosibirsk: Nauka, Sibirskoye otdeleniye, 1990.
Ogorodnikov, V. I. *Ocherk istorii Sibiri do nachala XIX stol.* Irkutsk: Tip. shtaba voyennogo okruga, 1920.
Okladnikov, A. P., ed. *Drevnyaya Sibir'.* Vol. 1 in *Istoriya Sibir'*, ed. A. P. Okladnikov. 5 vols. Leningrad: Nauka, 1968.
Orudzhev, S. A. *Gazovaya promyshlennost' po puti progressa.* Moscow: Nedra, 1976.
Otpetyy, V., ed. *Altay, budushchaya Kaliforniya Rossii i tsarstvovavshiye na Altaye.* Leipzig: Tipografiya Bera i Germanna, 1882.
Partiynnyy arkhiv Novosibirskogo oblastnogo komiteta KPSS. *Partizanskoye dvizheniye v Zapadnoy Sibiri (1918–1920 gg.).* Novosibirsk: Novosibirskoye knizhnoye izd., 1959.
Pavlovskaya, R. F. *Putevoditel' po otdelu istorii muzeya "Kuzbass za gody Sovetskoy vlasti."* Kemerovo: Redaktsionno-izdatel'skiy otdel, 1990.
Pechenyuk, I. L., ed. *BAM: Doroga sozidaniya.* Moscow: Sovetskaya Rossiya, 1983.
Pinneker, Ye. V., and B. I. Pisarskiy. *Podzemnyye vody zony Baykalo-Amurskoy magistrali.* Novosibirsk: Nauka, Sibirskoye otdeleniye, 1977.
Pistuna, N. D., ed. *Ekonomicheskaya geografiya SSSR.* Kiyev: Golovnoye izd. ob"yedineniye "Vishcha shkola," 1984.
Pobozhiy, A. *Skvoz' severnuyu glush'.* Moscow: Sovremennik, 1978.
Pokshishevskiy, V. V., ed. *Rossiyskaya Federatsiya: Vostochnaya Sibir'.* In the series *Sovetskiy Soyuz*, ed. S. V. Kolesnik. 22 vols. Moscow: Mysl', 1969.
Pomus, M. I., ed. *Rossiyskaya Federatsiya: Zapadnaya Sibir'.* Of the series *Sovetskiy Soyuz.* Edited by S. V. Kolesnik. 22 vols. Moscow: Mysl', 1971.
Popov, V. E., ed. *Toplivo-energeticheskiy kompleks Sibiri.* Novosibirsk: Nauka, Sibirskoye otdeleniye, 1978.
Preobrazhenskiy, V. S., ed. *Voprosy geografii Zabaykal'skogo Severa.* Moscow: Nauka, 1964.
Pushkar', Arnol'd. *Zdes' nachinayetsya Rossiya.* Moscow: Sovetskaya Rossiya, 1977.
Rafik, Sh. -A. Aliyev. "Vneshnyaya politika Sovetskogo Soyuza v Vostochnoy Azii: Kriticheskoy analiz." *Acta Slavica Iaponica.* Vol. 8 (1990), pp. 67–83.
Rasputin, Valentin. *Sibir', Sibir'.* Moscow: Molodaya gvardiya, 1991.
Razgon, I. M., ed. *Sibir' v period stroitel'stva sotsializma.* Vol. 4 in *Istoriya Sibiri,* ed. A. P. Okladnikov. 5 vols. Leningrad: Nauka, 1968.
Razvitiye yedinoy transportnoy seti SSSR. Moscow: Transport, 1963.
Rossolimo, L. L. *Baykal.* Irkutsk: Vostochno-Sibirskoye knizhnoye izd., 1971.
Ryabov, N. *Khabarovsk.* Khabarovsk: Khabarovskoye knizhnoye izd., 1987.
Rybakovskiy, L. M., ed. *Neryungrinskoye prityazheniye.* Yakutsk: Yakutskoye knizhnoye izd., 1983.
Sapozhnikov, V. V., and N. A. Gavrilov. "Zemli Kabineta Yego Velichestva." In *Aziatskaya Rossiya.* Vol. 2 of *Atlas' Aziatskoy Rossii,* ed. G. V. Glinka et al. St. Petersburg: A. F. Marks', 1914.

216 ■ SELECTED BIBLIOGRAPHY

Semenov-Tyan'-Shanskiy, V. P., ed. *Rossiya: Polnoye geograficheskoye opisaniye nashego otechestva.* St. Petersburg: A. F. Devriyena, 1907.

Serebrennikov, I. I. *Sibirivedeniye.* Kharbin": Svet", 1920.

Seredonin, S. M. "Zavoyevaniye Aziatskoy Rossii." In *Aziatskaya Rossiya.* Vol. 2 of *Atlas' Aziatskoy Rossii,* ed. G. V. Glinka et al. St. Petersburg: A. F. Marks', 1914.

Sergeyev, V. I. "K voprosu o pokhode v Sibir' druzhiny Yermaka." *Voprosy istorii.* No. 1 (January 1959), pp. 118–129.

Shafirkin, B. I., ed. *Ekonomicheskiy spravochnik zheleznodorozhnika.* Moscow: Transport, 1978.

Shcherbakov, Yu. G., and V. I. Sotnikov, eds. *Mineralogiya i geokhimiya rudnykh mestorozhdeniy Sibiri.* Novosibirsk: Nauka, Sibirskoye otdeleniye, 1977.

Shinkarev, L. *Sibir': Otkuda ona poshla i kuda ona idet.* Moscow: Sovetskaya Rossiya, 1978.

Shmelev, N. "Avansy i dolgi." *Novyy mir.* No. 6 (1987), pp. 142–158.

Shunkov, V. I., ed. *Sibir' v sostave feodal'noy Rossii.* Vol. 2 of *Istoriya Sibiri,* ed. A. P. Okladnikov. 5 vols. Leningrad: Nauka, 1968.

"Sibirskaya zheleznaya doroga." *Entsiklopedicheskiy slovar',* Vol. 58 (1900).

Singur, N. "Dal'niy Vostok: Kompleksnoye razvitiye proizvoditel'nykh sil." *Planovoye khozyaystvo.* No. 3 (1988), pp. 94–98.

Sklyarov, L. F. *Pereseleniye i zemleustroystva v Sibiri v gody Stolypinskoy agrarnoy reformy.* Leningrad: Izd. Leningradskogo universiteta, 1962.

Skorokhodov, Yu. T. "Sovetskiy Dal'niy Vostok: Problemy i perspektivy." *Problemy Dal'nego Vostoka.* No. 2 (February 1988), pp. 6–19.

Skrynnikov, R. G. "Podgotovka i nachalo Sibirskoy ekspeditsii Yermaka." *Voprosy istorii.* No. 8 (August 1979), pp. 44–56.

Slovtsov, P. A. "Istoricheskoye obozreniye Sibiri." *Sibirskiye ogni.* No. 2 (1991), pp. 101–119.

Sobolev, Yu. A. *Zona BAMa: Puti ekonomicheskogo razvitiya.* Moscow: Mysl', 1979.

Sokolov, Maksim. "Zhizn' zamechatel'nogo Rossiyanina." *Stolitsa.* No. 5/115 (1993), pp. 8–11.

SSSR. Ministerstvo putey soobshcheniya. *Statisticheskiy otchet o rabote zheleznodorozhnogo transporta.* Issue No. 474. Moscow: Soyuzblankoizdat, 1991.

SSSR. Sovet Ministrov. *Chislennost' naseleniya SSSR.* Vol. 1 of *Itogi vsesoyuznoy perepisi naseleniya 1970 goda.* 7 vols. Moscow: Statistika, 1972.

Svatikov, S. G. *Rossiya i Sibir'.* Praga: Izd. obshchestva sibiryakov v ChSR, 1931.

Tochenov, V. V., et al., eds. *Atlas SSSR.* Moscow: Glavnoye upravleniye geodezii i kartografii pri Sovete Ministrov SSSR, 1983.

Tolstikhin, O. N. *V krayu naledey.* Leningrad: Gidrometeoizdat, 1978.

Tsvyutkov, M. A. "Zhivotnovodstvo." In *Aziatskaya Rossiya.* Vol. 2 of *Atlas' Aziatskoy Rossii,* eds. G. V. Glinka et al. St. Petersburg: A. F. Marks', 1914.

Tsymek, A. A. *Listvennyye porody Dal'nego Vostoka: Puti ikh ispol'zovaniya i vosproizvodstva.* Khabarovsk: Khabarovskoye knizhnoye izd., 1956.

Tugolukov, V. A. *Kto Vy, Yukagiry?* Moscow: Nauka, 1979.

Turgan-Baranovskiy, M. I. *Sotsial'nyye osnovy kooperatsii.* Petrograd: Knigoizd. Slovo, 1922.

Tyukavkin, V. G. "Potrebitel'skiye kooperativy v sel'skom khozyaystve Sibiri v nachale XX v." In *Ekonomicheskoye i obshchestvenno-politicheskoye razvitiye Sibiri v 1861–1917 gg.* Vol. 2 of *Sibir' perioda kapitalizma.* Novosibirsk: Nauka, Sibirskoye otdeleniye, 1965.

Urvantsev, N. N. *Otkrytiye Noril'ska.* Moscow: Nauka, 1981.

Vartanov, V. N., et al. *Konflikt na KVZhD*. Khabarovsk: Khabarovskoye knizhnoye izd., 1989.

"Vladivostokskiye initsiativy: Dva goda spustya." *Mezhdunarodnaya zhizn'*. No. 7 (July 1988), pp. 141–155.

"Vladivostokskaya programma: Impul's novogo myshleniya." *Problemy Dal'nego Vostoka*. No. 4 (April 1988), pp. 3–8.

Vlasov, I. V. "Poseleniya Zabaykal'ya." Pp. 21–32 in *Byt i iskusstvo russkogo naseleniya Vostochnoy Sibiri*, ed. I. V. Makovetskiy and G. S. Maslova. Novosibirsk: Nauka, Sibirskoye otdeleniye, 1975.

Vol'f, M. B. *Geograficheskoye razmeshcheniye russkoy promyshlennosti*. Moscow-Leningrad: Gos. izd. geograficheskoy literatury, 1927.

Vol'naya Sibir'. 7 vols. 1926–1929.

Vorob'yev, V. V., and A. V. Belov. *Geograficheskiye problemy zony BAM*. Novosibirsk: Nauka, Sibirskoye otdeleniye, 1979.

Vypov, A. I., ed. *Novokuznetsk*. Moscow: Sovetskaya Rossiya, 1983.

Vyzhutovich, Valeriy. "Rol' i ispolnitel'." *Stolitsa*. No. 47/105 (1992), pp. 8–10.

Yadrintsev, N. M. *Sibir' kak koloniya*. St. Petersburg: I. M. Sibiryakov, 1892.

Yakovleva, Ye., ed. *My zhivem na Kiye*. Kemerovo: Panorama, 1990.

Yakushev, I. A. *Sibir' v tsifrakh*. Praga: Izd. obshchestva sibiryakov v ChSR, 1931.

Yatsenko, V. A. *Port na Morskom beregu*. Moscow: Mysl', 1985.

Yegorova, L. N., et al., eds. *Atlas istorii SSSR*. Part 1 (of 3). Moscow: Min. geologii i okhrany nedr SSSR, 1960.

Yurkov, A. *BAM: Magistral'*. Moscow: Planeta, 1976.

Zlobin, A. "Na Sibirskoy magistrali." *Novyy mir*. January 1959, pp. 120–130.

SOURCES IN ENGLISH

Aganbegyan, Abel. *Inside Perestroika: The Future of the Soviet Economy*. New York: Harper and Row, 1989.

Allison, Anthony P. "Siberian Regionalism in Revolution and Civil War, 1917– 1920." *Sibirica*. Vol. 1, No. 1 (Summer 1990), pp. 78–97.

Armstrong, Terence, ed. *Yermak's Campaign in Siberia*. London: Hakluyt Society, 1975.

Artamonov, M. I. "Frozen Tombs of the Scythians." *Scientific American*. May 1965, pp. 101–109.

Aslund, Anders. "Gorbachev's Economic Advisors." *Soviet Economy*. Vol. 3, No. 3 (1987), pp. 246–269.

Bakich, Olga. "A Russian City in China: Harbin Before 1917." *Canadian Slavonic Papers*. Vol. 28, No. 2 (June 1986), pp. 129–148.

Balzer, Marjorie Mandelstam. "Introduction." *Anthropology and Archeology of Eurasia*. Vol. 31, No. 1 (Summer 1992), pp. 3–6.

———. "The Sakha Republic (Yakutia)." In *Rediscovering Russia in Asia*. Eds. Stephen Kotkin and David Wolff. Armonk, N.Y.: M. E. Sharpe, 1995, pp. 139–159.

———. "Turmoil in Russia's Mini-Empire." *Perspective*. Vol. 2, No. 3 (January 1992), pp. 2–3 and 7.

Baradat, Leon P. *Soviet Political Society*. 3d edition. Englewood Cliffs, N.J.: Prentice-Hall, 1992.

Barner-Barry, Carol, and Cynthia A. Hody. *The Politics of Change: The Transformation of the Former Soviet Union*. New York: St. Martin's, 1995.

Barr, Brenton M., and Kathleen E. Braden. *The Disappearing Russian Forest*. Totowa, N.J.: Rowman and Littlefield, 1988.

Barraclough, Geoffrey, ed. *The Times Atlas of World History*. 6th ed. Maplewood Cliffs, N.J.: Hammond, 1984.

Barrat, Glynn. *Voices in Exile: The Decembrists' Memoirs*. Montreal and London: McGill-Queen's University Press, 1974.

Bassin, Mark. "Expansion and Colonialism on the Eastern Frontier: Views of Siberia and the Far East in Pre-Petrine Russia." *Journal of Historical Geography*. Vol. 14, No. 1 (1988), pp. 3–21.

————. "Inventing Siberia: Visions of the Russian East in the Early Nineteenth Century." *American Historical Review*. Vol. 96, No. 3 (June 1991), pp. 763–794.

————. "Russia Between Europe and Asia: The Ideological Construction of Geographical Space." *Slavic Review*. Vol. 50, No. 3 (Spring 1993), pp. 1–17.

————. "The Russian Geographical Society, the 'Amur Epoch,' and the Great Siberian Expedition, 1855–1863." *Annals of the Association of American Geographers*. Vol. 73, No. 2 (March 1983), pp. 240–256.

————. "Russian Views of Siberia: Meeting Report." Xerox. Washington, D.C.: Woodrow Wilson Center, Kennan Institute for Advanced Russian Studies, December 12, 1988.

Bater, James H. *Russia and the Post-Soviet Scene: A Geographical Perspective*. London: Arnold, 1996.

Biryukov, Victor. "The Baykal-Amur Mainline." *Soviet Geography: Review and Translation*. Vol. 16, No. 4 (April 1975), pp. 225–230.

Bond, Andrew R. "Noril'sk: Profile of a Soviet Arctic Development Project." Unpublished Ph.D. dissertation. University of Wisconsin–Milwaukee, 1983.

————. "Spatial Dimensions of Gorbachev's Economic Strategy." *Soviet Geography*. Vol. 28, No. 7 (September 1987), pp. 490–523.

Bond, Andrew R., Richard M. Levine, and Gordon T. Austin. "Russian Diamond Industry in State of Flux." *Post-Soviet Geography*. Vol. 33, No. 10 (December 1992), pp. 635–644.

Bower, B. "Siberian Site Cedes Stone-Age Surprise." *Science News*. Vol. 145, No. 6 (February 5, 1994), p. 84.

Bradshaw, Michael. "Foreign Trade and Inter-republican Relations." Pp. 132–150 in *The Post-Soviet Republics: A Systematic Geography*, ed. Denis J. B. Shaw. London: Longman Scientific and Technical, 1995.

————. *Siberia at a Time of Change*. Special Report No. 2171. London: Economist Intelligence Unit (EIU), 1992.

————. "Siberia Poses a Challenge to Russian Federalism." *Radio Free Europe/Radio Liberty [RFE/RL] Research Report*. Vol. 34, No. 8 (1992).

Bridge, Richard. "The Northern Economy in the 1970s and 1980s." *Sibirica*. Vol. 2 (1986), pp. 16–27.

Brigham, Lawson W., Captain, USCG, ed. *The Soviet Maritime Arctic*. Annapolis, Md.: Naval Institute Press, 1991.

Broekmeyer, Marius J. "Some Questions Concerning the Construction of the BAM." Pp. 315–320 in *Siberia I: Siberian Questions*. Ed. Boris Chichlo. Paris: Institut d'études slaves, 1985.

Carr, E. H. *A History of Soviet Russia*. Vol. 1: *The Bolshevik Revolution, 1917–1923*. New York: W. W. Norton, 1985.

Chard, Chester S. "Archaeology in the Soviet Union." *Science*. Vol. 163 (February 21, 1969), pp. 774–779.

Chernykh, Ye. N. *Ancient Metallurgy in the USSR*. Cambridge: Cambridge University Press, 1992.

Christensen, Paul T. "Property Free-for-All: Regionalism, 'Democratization,' and the Politics of Economic Control in the Kuzbas, 1989–1993." Pp. 207–223 in *Rediscovering Russia in Asia*. Eds. Stephen Kotkin and David Wolff. Armonk, N.Y.: M. E. Sharpe, 1995.

———. "Regionalization and Politics in the Kuzbas." Pp. 207–223 in *Rediscovering Russia in Asia*. Eds. Stephen Kotkin and David Wolff. Armonk, N.Y.: M. E. Sharpe, 1995.

Chung, Han-ku. *Interest Representation in Soviet Policymaking: A Case Study of a West Siberian Energy Coalition*. Boulder: Westview, 1987.

———. "Politics of Siberian Development Policy: Comparison of Two Siberian Lobbies." *American and Soviet Studies Annual*. 1986, pp. 41–69.

Collins, David N. "Plans for Railway Development in Siberia, 1857–1890, and Tsarist Colonialism." *Sibirica*. Vol. 1, No. 2 (Winter 1990–1991), pp. 128–150.

Connoly, Violet. *Beyond the Urals*. London: Oxford University Press, 1967.

———. "The Second Trans-Siberian Railway." *Asian Affairs*. No. 2 (February 1975), pp. 23–29.

Conquest, Robert. *The Great Terror*. London: Macmillan, 1968.

———. *The Great Terror: A Reassessment*. New York: Oxford University Press, 1990.

———. *Kolyma*. London: Macmillan, 1978.

Constable, George. *The Neanderthals*. New York: Time-Life Books, 1974.

Coox, Alvin D. *Nomohon: Japan Against Russia, 1939*. 2 vols. Stanford: Stanford University Press, 1985.

DeSouza, Peter. *Territorial Production Complexes in the Soviet Union—with Special Focus on Siberia*. Gothenburg, Sweden: University of Gothenburg Press, 1989.

Dewdney, John C. *A Geography of the Soviet Union*. 2d ed. Oxford: Pergamon, 1971.

Dibb, Paul. *Siberia and the Pacific*. New York: Praeger, 1972.

Dienes, Leslie. "Comment on the New Development Program for the Far East Economic Region." *Soviet Geography*. Vol. 39, No. 4 (April 1988), pp. 420–422.

———. "Economic and Strategic Position of the Soviet Far East." *Soviet Economy*. Vol. 1, No. 1 (1985), pp. 146–176.

———. "Economic Geographic Relations in the Post-Soviet Republics." *Post-Soviet Geography*. Vol. 34, No. 8 (October 1993), pp. 497–529.

———. "Investment Priorities in Soviet Regions." *Annals of the Association of American Geographers*. Vol. 62, No. 3 (September 1972), pp. 437–454.

———. "Prospects for Russian Oil in the 1990s: Reserves and Costs." *Post-Soviet Geography*. Vol. 34, No. 2 (February 1993), pp. 79–110.

———. *Soviet Asia: Economic Development and National Policy Choices*. Boulder: Westview, 1987.

Dienes, Leslie, and Theodore Shabad. *The Soviet Energy System*. Washington, D.C.: Victor H. Winston and Sons, 1979.

Dmytryshyn, Basil. "Russian Expansion to the Pacific, 1580–1700: A Historiographical Review." *Sibirica*. Vol. 1, No. 1 (Summer 1990), pp. 4–37.

Duncan, Peter J. S. "The Politics of Siberia in Russia." *Sibirica: The Journal of Siberian Studies*. Vol. 1, No. 2 (1994/1995), pp. 13–23.

Edwards, Mike. "Siberia in from the Cold." *National Geographic*. Vol. 177, No. 3 (March 1990), pp. 2–49.

Feshbach, Murray, and Alfred Friendly, Jr. *Ecocide in the USSR*. New York: Basic Books, 1992.

Fisher, Raymond H. *The Russian Fur Trade*. Berkeley: University of California Press, 1943.

Florinsky, Michael T. *Russia: A History and Interpretation in Two Volumes*. Vol. 2. New York: Macmillan, 1964.

Fondahl, Gail. "Siberia: Assimilation and Discontents." Pp. 190–232 in *New States, New Politics: Building the Post-Soviet Nations*. Eds. Ian Bremmer and Ray Taras. Cambridge: Cambridge University Press, 1997.

———. "Siberia: Native Peoples and Newcomers in Collision." Pp. 477–510 in *Nations and Politics in the Soviet Successor States*. Eds. Ian Bremmer and Ray Taras. Cambridge: Cambridge University Press, 1993.

Forsyth, James. *A History of the Peoples of Siberia*. Cambridge: Cambridge University Press, 1992.

French, R. A. "The Development of Siberia: Peoples and Human Resources." Xerox. London: University of London, School of Slavonic and East European Studies, Great Britain–USSR Association, April 1986.

Friedgut, Theodore, and Lewis Siegelbaum. "The Soviet Miners' Strike, July 1989." *The Carl Beck Papers*. No. 804 (March 1990), pp. 1–43.

Friedmann, John. *Regional Development Policy: A Case of Venezuela*. Cambridge, Mass.: MIT Press, 1966.

Garrett, Wilbur E., ed. "The Peopling of the Earth." And related articles in *National Geographic*. Vol. 174, No. 4 (October 1988), pp. 434–509.

George, Dev. "Search for Nuclear Wastes May Hold Up Sakhalin Program." *Offshore International*. November 1993.

Gibson, James R. *Feeding the Russian Fur Trade*. Madison: University of Wisconsin Press, 1969.

———. *Imperial Russia in Frontier America*. New York: Oxford University Press, 1976.

———. "Interregional Migration in the USSR, 1981–1985 and 1971–1975." *The Canadian Geographer*. Vol. 35, No. 2 (1991), pp. 143–156.

———. "Interregional Migration in the USSR, 1986–1990: A Final Update." *The Canadian Geographer*. Vol. 38, No. 1 (1994), pp. 54–56.

———. "The Rush to Meet the Sun: An Essay on Russian Eastward Expansion." *Siberica*. Vol. 1, No. 1 (Summer 1990), pp. 68–77.

———. "The Sale of Russian America to the United States." *Acta Slavica Iaponica*. Vol. 1 (1983), pp. 15–37.

Gill, Graeme. *The Origins of the Stalinist Political System*. Cambridge: Cambridge University Press, 1990.

Gore, Rick. "The Dawn of Humans." *National Geographic*. Vol. 191, No. 5 (May 1997), pp. 80–95.

Goryushkin, L. M. "Late-Nineteenth- and Early-Twentieth-Century Siberian Regionalists' Views on the Economic Independence of Siberia." *Siberica*. Vol. 1, No. 2 (Winter 1990/1991), pp. 152–168.

Grant, Bruce. "Indigenism on Sakhalin Island." Pp. 160–171 in *Rediscovering Russia in Asia*. Eds. Stephen Kotkin and David Wolff. Armonk, N.Y.: M. E. Sharpe, 1995.

Graves, William S. *America's Siberian Adventure, 1918–1920*. New York: Peter Smith, 1941.

Hardman, Ric. *Fifteen Flags*. Boston: Little, Brown, 1968.

Hardt, John. "The Military-Economic Implications of Soviet Regional Policy." Pp. 235–250 in *Regional Development in the USSR*. Newtonville, Mass.: Oriental Research Partners, 1979.

Hausladen, Gary. "Russian Siberia: An Integrative Approach." *Soviet Geography*. Vol. 30, No. 3 (March 1989), pp. 223–246.

———. "Siberian Urbanization Since Stalin." Xerox. Washington, D.C.: National Council for Soviet and East European Research, August 1990.

Helf, Gavin. *A Biographic Directory of Soviet Regional Party Leaders.* 2 parts. 2d and 3d editions. Munich: Radio Liberty Research, 1987 and 1988.

Holzner, Lutz, and Jeane M. Knapp, eds. *Soviet Geography Studies in Our Time.* Milwaukee: University of Wisconsin, 1987.

Horrigan, Brenda. "How Many People Worked in the Soviet Defense Economy?" *RFE/RL Research Report.* Vol. 1, No. 33 (August 21, 1992), pp. 33–39.

Hough, Jerry, and Merle Fainsod. *How the Soviet Union Is Governed.* Cambridge, Mass.: Harvard University Press, 1979.

Hoyt, Joseph Bixby. *Man and the Earth.* 3d ed. Englewood Cliffs, N.J.: Prentice-Hall, 1973.

Hughes, James R. *Stalin, Siberia and the New Economic Policy.* Cambridge: Cambridge University Press, 1991.

———. "Yeltsin's Siberian Opposition." *RFE/RL Research Report.* Vol. 2, No. 50 (1993).

International Institute for Development (IID). *World Competition Almanac.* Lausanne, Switzerland: IID, 1997.

Ivanov, Vladimir I. "The Russian Far East: The Political Economy of the Defense Industry Conversion." Pp. 174–195 in *Socio-Economic Dimensions of the Changes in the Slavic-Eurasian World.* Eds. Shugo Minagawa and Osamu Ieda. Sapporo, Japan: Hokkaido University, Slavic Research Center, 1996.

Jackson, W. A. Douglas. *The Russo-Chinese Borderlands.* 2d ed. Princeton, N.J.: D. Van Nostrand, 1968.

Janhunen, Juha. "Ethnic Implications of the Sino-Russian Border." Pp. 199–220 in *Socio-Economic Dimensions of the Changes in the Slavic-Eurasian World.* Ed. Shugo Minagawa. Sapporo, Japan: Hokkaido University, Slavic Research Center, 1996.

Japanese Ministry of Foreign Affairs. *Japan's Northern Territories.* Black-and-white version. Tokyo: Government Publishing House, 1987.

Jensen, Robert G., Theodore Shabad, and Arthur W. Wright, eds. *Soviet Natural Resources in the World Economy.* Chicago: University of Chicago Press, 1983.

Jordan, Terry G., and Lester Rowntree. *The Human Mosaic.* San Francisco: Canfield Press, 1976.

Josephson, Paul R. "New Atlantis Revisited." Pp. 89–107 in *Rediscovering Russia in Asia.* Eds. Stephen Kotkin and David Wolff. Armonk, N.Y.: M. E. Sharpe, 1995.

Kabuzan, V. M. "The Settlement of Siberia and the Far East from the Late 18th to the Early 20th Century (1795–1917)." *Soviet Geography.* Vol. 32, No. 9 (November 1991), pp. 616–632.

Karlinsky, Simon. "Memoirs of Harbin." *Slavic Review.* Vol. 48, No. 2 (Summer 1989), pp. 284–290.

Keegan, John. *Fields of Battle.* New York: A. A. Knopf, 1995.

Keenan, Edward Lewis. "Muscovy and Kazan': Some Introductory Remarks on the Patterns of Steppe Diplomacy." *Slavic Review.* Vol. 26, No. 4 (December 1967), pp. 545–560.

Kempton, Daniel R., and Richard M. Levine. "Soviet and Russian Relations with Foreign Corporations: The Case of Gold and Diamonds." *Slavic Review.* Vol. 54, No. 1 (Spring 1995), pp. 80–110.

Kennan, George. *Siberia and the Exile System.* 2d ed., abridged. Chicago: University of Chicago Press, 1958.

Kennan, George F. *Soviet-American Relations, 1917–1920.* Vol. 1: *Russia Leaves the War.* New York: W. W. Norton, 1956.

———. *Soviet-American Relations, 1917–1920.* Vol. 2: *The Decision to Intervene.* New York: W. W. Norton, 1958.

Kennan Institute for Advanced Russian Studies. "Speeches of Egor Kuz'mich Ligachev at the Kennan Institute." *Occasional Paper.* No. 247 (Fall 1991).

Kim, Hakjoon. "The Emergence of Siberia and the Russian Far East as a 'New Frontier' for Koreans." Pp. 302–311 in *Rediscovering Russia in Asia.* Eds. Stephen Kotkin and David Wolff. Armonk, N.Y.: M. E. Sharpe, 1995.

Kingsbury, Robert C., and Robert N. Taaffe. *An Atlas of Soviet Affairs.* New York: Praeger, 1965.

Kirkow, Peter. "Russia's Gateway to Pacific Asia." *Sibirica: The Journal of Siberian Studies.* Vol. 1, No. 2 (1994/1995), pp. 51–59.

Klein, Richard G. *The Human Career.* Chicago: University of Chicago Press, 1989.

———. "Mousterian Cultures in European Russia." *Science.* Vol. 165 (July 18, 1969), pp. 257–265.

Kolarz, Walter. *The Peoples of the Soviet Far East.* New York: Praeger, 1954.

Kotkin, Stephen, and David Wolff, eds. *Rediscovering Russia in Asia.* Armonk, N.Y.: M. E. Sharpe, 1995.

Kropotkin, Peter. *Memoirs of a Revolutionist.* Vol. 1. 2 vols. New York: Houghton, Mifflin, 1899.

Levin, M. G., and L. P. Potapov, eds. *The Peoples of Siberia.* Chicago: University of Chicago Press, 1964.

Lexis Nexis. *Dialogue SovData DiaLine—SovLegisLine.*

Linden, Eugene. "The Tortured Land." *Time.* September 4, 1995, pp. 42–53.

Lorimer, Frank. *The Population of the Soviet Union: History and Prospects.* Geneva: League of Nations, 1946.

Luckett, Richard. *The White Generals.* London: Longman Group, 1971.

Lyashchenko, Peter I. *History of the National Economy of Russia to the 1917 Revolution.* New York: Macmillan, 1949.

Lydolph, Paul. *Climates of the Soviet Union.* Vol. 12 of *World Survey of Climatology.* Ed. H. E. Landsberg. 13 vols. New York: Elsevier Scientific Publishing, 1977.

———. *Geography of the USSR: Regional Analysis.* 3d ed. New York: John Wiley and Sons, 1977.

———. *Geography of the USSR: Topical Analysis.* 3d ed. Elkhart Lake, Wis.: Misty Valley, 1977.

———. *Geography of the USSR: Topical Analysis.* 5th ed. Elkhart Lake, Wis.: Misty Valley, 1990.

Mandel, William. "Soviet Miners Speak." *The Station Relay.* Vol. 5, Nos. 1–5 (1988–1991).

Marks, Steven G. "Conquering the Great East: Kulomzin, Peasant Resettlement, and the Creation of Modern Siberia." Pp. 23–39 in *Rediscovering Russia in Asia.* Eds. Stephen Kotkin and David Wolff. Armonk, N.Y.: M. E. Sharpe, 1995.

———. *Road to Power: The Trans-Siberian Railroad and the Colonization of Asian Russia, 1850–1917.* Ithaca, N.Y.: Cornell University Press, 1991.

Maslyukov, Yu. "The Far East: A New Stage." *Soviet Union.* No. 7 (July 1989), p. 4.

Mazour, Anatole G. *The First Russian Revolution, 1825.* Stanford: Stanford University Press, 1977.

Medvedev, Roy. *Let History Judge: The Origins and Consequences of Stalinism.* New York: Columbia University Press, 1989.

Menges, Karl H. *An Outline of the Early History and Migrations of the Slavs.* New York: Columbia University Press, 1953.

Micklin, Philip P. "Recent Developments in Large-Scale Water Transfers in the USSR." *Soviet Geography: Review and Translation.* Vol. 25, No. 4 (April 1984).

Miller, Elisa, ed. *Russian Far East Update.* Vols. 1–5 (1991–1995), various issues.

Miller, Elisa, and Alexander Karp, eds. *Pocket Handbook of the Russian Far East: A Reference Guide.* Seattle, Wash.: Russian Far East Update, 1994.

Minakir, Pavel A., and Gregory L. Freeze, eds. *The Russian Far East: An Economic Handbook.* Armonk, N.Y.: M. E. Sharpe, 1994.

Moses, Joel C. *Regional Party Leadership and Policy-Making in the USSR.* New York: Praeger, 1974.

————. "Regionalism in Soviet Politics." *Soviet Studies.* Vol. 37, No. 2 (1985), pp. 184–211.

Mote, Victor L. "AYAM: Soviet Concept or Reality." *Professional Geographer.* Vol. 39, No. 1 (February 1987), pp. 13–23.

————. "The Baikal-Amur Mainline and Its Implications for the Pacific Basin." Pp. 133–187 in *Soviet Natural Resources in the World Economy.* Eds. Robert G. Jensen, Theodore Shabad, and Arthur W. Wright. Chicago: University of Chicago Press, 1983.

————. "BAM, Boom, Bust: Analysis of a Railway's Past, Present, and Future." *Soviet Geography.* Vol. 31, No. 5 (May 1990), pp. 321–331.

————. "The Cheliabinsk Grain Tariff and the Rise of the Siberian Butter Industry." *Slavic Review.* Vol. 35, No. 2 (Summer 1976), pp. 304–317.

————. "Containerization and the Trans-Siberian Land Bridge." *Geographical Review.* Vol. 74, No. 3 (July 1984), pp. 304–313.

————. "Environmental Constraints to the Economic Development of Siberia." Pp. 15–71 in *Soviet Natural Resources in the World Economy.* Eds. Robert G. Jensen, Theodore Shabad, and Arthur W. Wright. Chicago: University of Chicago Press, 1983.

————. *An Industrial Atlas of the Soviet Successor States.* Houston, Tex.: Industrial Information Resources, 1994.

————. "New Soviet Economic Strategy in Asia and the Pacific." *Acta Slavica Iaponica.* Vol. 8 (1990), pp. 85–108.

————. "Pacific Siberian Growth Centers: A New Soviet Commitment." *Soviet Union.* Vol. 4, No. 2 (1977), pp. 256–270.

————. "Siberia." In *Compton's Encyclopedia.* Vol. 21 (1990), pp. 280–283.

————. "The South Yakutian Territorial-Production Complex." Pp. 163–184 in *Soviet Far East.* Ed. Allan Rodgers. London: Routledge, 1990.

————. "A Visit to the Baikal-Amur Mainline and the New Amur-Yakutsk Mainline Rail Project." *Soviet Geography.* Vol. 26, No. 9 (November 1995), pp. 691–717.

Mowat, Farley. *The Siberians.* New York: Bantam Books, 1970.

Newby, Eric. *The Big Red Train Ride.* New York: St. Martin's, 1978.

Nogee, Joseph L., and R. Judson Mitchell. *Russian Politics: The Struggle for a New Order.* Boston: Allyn and Bacon, 1997.

North, Robert N. "The Soviet Far East: New Centre of Attention." *Pacific Affairs.* Vol. 51, No. 2 (Summer 1978), pp. 195–215.

————. *Transport in Western Siberia.* Vancouver, B.C.: University of British Columbia Press, 1979.

Norton, Henry Kittredge. *The Far Eastern Republic of Siberia.* Westport, Conn.: Hyperion Reprint, 1981.

NUPI (Norsk Utenrikspolitisk Institutt). *Centre for Russian Studies—Database.* On-line at <http://www.nupi.no/cgi-win/Russland/.exe[morethan].

OMRI (Open Media Research Institute). *Russian Regions Page.* On-line at <http://www.omri.cz/Elections/Russia/Regions/About.html>.

Osadchy, Mykhaylo. *Cataract.* New York: Harcourt Brace Jovanovich, 1976.

Osherenko, Gail. "Indigenous Political and Property Rights and Economic/Environmental Reform in Northwest Siberia." *Post-Soviet Geography.* Vol. 36, No. 4 (April 1995), pp. 225–237.

"Panel on Siberia: Economic and Territorial Issues." *Soviet Geography.* Vol. 32, No. 6 (June 1991), pp. 363–432.

"Panorama" Information-Expert Group. *Who Is Who in the Russian Government. Supplement 1.* Moscow: Panorama, 1993.

Parkanskiy, Alexander B. "Current Issues of Foreign Direct Investment in Russia." *Acta Slavica Iaponica.* Vol. XI (1993), pp. 18–33.

Pereira, N.G.O. "The Partisan Movement in Western Siberia, 1918–1920." Paper presented at the British Universities Siberian Studies Seminar, "Siberia in the Twentieth Century: Social and Economic Developments," Glasgow, Scotland, September 4, 1989.

———. "Regional Consciousness in Siberia Before and After October 1917." *Canadian Slavonic Papers.* Vol. 30, No. 1 (March 1988), pp. 113–133.

Peterson, Demosthenes James. "Russia's Environment and Natural Resources in Light of Economic Regionalization." *Post-Soviet Geography.* Vol. 36, No. 5 (May 1995), pp. 291–309.

———. *Troubled Lands: The Legacy of Soviet Environmental Destruction.* Boulder: Westview, 1993.

Petrov, Victor P. *Geography of the Soviet Union: Electric Power.* Washington, D.C.: Victor Kamkin, 1959.

Pika, Alexander, and Boris Prokhorov. "Soviet Union: The Big Problems of Small Ethnic Groups." *Russia: Khanty-Mansi Autonomous Area.* Available on-line at <http://www.lib.uconn.edu/ArcticCircle/SEEJ/Yamal/pika1.html>.

Polosmak, Nataliya. "A Mummy Unearthed from the Pastures of Heaven." *National Geographic.* Vol. 186, No. 4 (October 1994), pp. 80–103.

Pond, Elizabeth. *From the Yaroslavsky Station: Russia Perceived.* Revised ed. New York: Universe Books, 1984.

Prideaux, Tom. *Cro-Magnon Man.* New York: Time-Life Books, 1975.

Pryde, Philip R. *Environmental Management in the Soviet Union.* Cambridge: Cambridge University Press, 1991.

———, ed. *Environmental Resources and Constraints in the Former Soviet Republics.* Boulder: Westview, 1995.

Quinn-Judge, Sophie. "Partners Preferred." *Far Eastern Review.* February 2, 1989, p. 54.

———. "Pragmatists and Pioneers Near the End of the Line." *Far Eastern Economic Review.* August 4, 1988, pp. 20–30.

Rahr, Alexander. *A Biographic Directory of 100 Leading Soviet Officials.* 3d and 4th eds. Munich: Radio Liberty Research, 1986 and 1989.

Resnick, Abraham. *Siberia and the Soviet Far East: Endless Frontiers.* Moscow: Novosti Press Agency, 1983.

RFE/RL Newsline. Available on-line at <http://citm1.met.fsu.edu/~glenn/russia/msg>.

Riasanovsky, Nicholas V. *History of Russia.* 2d ed. New York: Oxford University Press, 1969.

Rigby, T. H., and Bohdan Harasymiw, eds. *Leadership Selection and Patron-Client Relations in the USSR and Yugoslavia.* London: George Allen and Unwin, 1983.

Rodgers, Allan, ed. *The Soviet Far East: Geographical Perspectives on Development.* London: Routledge, 1990.

Ryan, Tracey A., ed. *Russian Government Today.* Washington, D.C.: Carroll. Spring 1993–Fall 1994 (published twice per year).

Sagers, Matthew J. "The Energy Industries of the Former USSR: A Mid-Year Survey." *Post-Soviet Geography.* Vol. 34, No. 6 (June 1993), pp. 341–418.

———. "News Notes." *Soviet Geography* and *Post-Soviet Geography.* Vols. 28–. 1987–. Numerous citations.

———. "Prospects for Oil and Gas Development of Russia's Sakhalin Oblast." *Post-Soviet Geography.* Vol. 36, No. 5 (May 1995), pp. 274–290.

Sakwa, Richard. *Gorbachev and His Reforms.* New York: Prentice-Hall, 1991.

Sallnow, John. *Reform in the Soviet Union: "Glasnost'" and the Future.* London: Pinter, 1989.

Santalov, A. A., and Louis Segal. *Soviet Union Yearbook, 1929.* London: George Allen and Unwin, 1929.

Segal, G. "CIA's Dire Forecast for USSR Oil Looks Accurate as Output Slumps." *Petroleum Review.* January 1979, pp. 17–18.

Shabad, Theodore. *Basic Industrial Resources of the USSR.* New York: Columbia University Press, 1969.

———. "Geographic Aspects of the New Soviet Five-Year Plan, 1986–1990." *Soviet Geography.* Vol. 27, No. 1 (January 1986), pp. 1–16.

———. *Geography of the USSR: A Regional Survey.* New York: Columbia University Press, 1951.

———. "News Notes." *Soviet Geography: Review and Translation* and *Soviet Geography.* Vols. 1–28, 1960–1987. Numerous citations.

Shabad, Theodore, and Victor L. Mote. *Gateway to Siberian Resources: The BAM.* New York: John Wiley and Sons, 1977.

Shaw, Denis J. B., ed. *Post-Soviet Republics: A Systematic Geography.* London: Longman Scientific and Technical, 1995.

———. "Siberia: Geographical Background." Pp. 9–34 in *Siberia: Problems and Prospects for Regional Development.* Ed. Alan Wood. London: Croom Helm, 1987.

Shaw, Denis J. B., and Michael J. Bradshaw. "Free Economic Zones." *Post-Soviet Geography.* Vol. 33, No. 6 (June 1992), pp. 409–414.

Sheehy, Ann. "Fact Sheet on Declarations of Sovereignty." *Report on the USSR.* Radio Liberty Research Report No. 464/90 (October 31, 1990), pp. 23–25.

Sherrat, Andrew, ed. *The Cambridge Encyclopedia of Archaeology.* New York: Crown, 1980.

Shuster, Tanya. "Sakhalin Leads the Way." *Bisnis Bulletin.* September 1997, pp. 1 and 5.

Smith, Allen B. "Soviet Dependence on Siberian Resource Development." Pp. 481–500 in *Soviet Union in a New Perspective.* Washington, D.C.: U.S. Government Printing Office (for U.S. Congress, Joint Economic Committee), 1976.

Smith, Gordon B. *Soviet Politics.* New York: St. Martin's, 1988.

Smith, Graham. "Ethnic Relations in the New States." Pp. 34–45 in *The Post-Soviet Republics: A Systematic Geography.* Ed. Denis J. B. Shaw. London: Longman Scientific and Technical, 1995.

———. "Gorbachev's Greatest Challenge." *Political Geography Quarterly.* Vol. 8, No. 1 (1988), pp. 7–20.

———, ed. *The Nationalities Question in the Soviet Union.* London: Longman, 1992.

Solomon, Michael. *Magadan.* Princeton, N.J.: Vertex, 1971.

Solzhenitsyn, Alexander. *Gulag Archipelago.* Vol. 1. 2 vols. New York: Harper and Row, 1974.

Stephan, John J. "'Cleansing' the Soviet Far East, 1937–1938." *Acta Slavica Iaponica.* Vol. 10 (1992), pp. 43–64.

———. "Far Eastern Conspiracies? Russian Separatism on the Pacific." *Australian Slavonic and East European Studies.* Vol. 4, Nos. 1/2 (1990), pp. 135–152.

———. *The Kuril Islands.* Oxford: Clarendon, 1974.

———. *The Russian Far East: A History.* Stanford: Stanford University Press, 1994.

———. *Sakhalin: A History.* Oxford: Clarendon, 1971.

Stewart, John Massey. "The Khanty: Oil, Gas, and the Environment." *Sibirica: The Journal of Siberian Studies.* Vol. 1, No. 2 (1994/1995), pp. 25–34.

Suh, Dae-Sook. *Koreans in the Soviet Union.* Honolulu: Center for Korean Studies/Center for SUPAR, 1987.

Surovell, Jeffrey. "Ligachev and Soviet Politics." *Soviet Studies.* Vol. 43, No. 2 (1991), pp. 355–374.

Suslov, S. P. *Physical Geography of Asiatic Russia.* San Francisco: W. H. Freeman, 1961.

Swearingen, Rodger, ed. *Siberia and the Soviet Far East.* Stanford: Hoover Institution Press, 1987.

Taylor, Jeffrey. "This Side of Ultima Thule." *The Atlantic Monthly.* April 1997, pp. 24–28, 36–41.

Taylor, Peter J. *Political Geography: World-Economy, Nation-State, and Locality.* London: Longman, 1985.

Teruyuki, Hara. "Japan Moves North." Pp. 55–67 in *Rediscovering Russia in Asia.* Eds. Stephen Kotkin and David Wolff. Armonk, N.Y.: M. E. Sharpe, 1995.

Toffler, Alvin. *The Third Wave.* New York: Bantam Books, 1981.

Toffler, Alvin, and Heidi Toffler. *Creating a New Civilization: The Politics of the Third Wave.* Atlanta, Ga.: Turner Publishing, 1994.

Treadgold, Donald W. *The Great Siberian Migration.* Princeton, N.J.: Princeton University Press, 1957.

Tupper, Harmon. *To the Great Ocean.* Boston: Little, Brown, 1965.

Turner, Samuel. *Siberia: Travel and Exploration.* New York: Charles Scribner's Sons, 1905.

United States. Central Intelligence Agency (CIA). *The International Energy Situation: Outlook to 1985.* Washington, D.C.: Government Printing Office, 1977.

―――. *USSR Agricultural Atlas.* Washington, D.C.: CIA, 1974.

―――. *USSR Energy Atlas.* Washington, D.C.: CIA, 1985.

United States. Defense Intelligence Agency (DIA). *Gorbachev's Modernization Program: A Status Report.* Washington, D.C.: DIA, 1987.

Urban, Michael. *The Rebirth of Politics in Russia.* Cambridge: Cambridge University Press, 1997.

Ushakov, Nikolay. "The Origins of the Yakuts." *Yakutia: Frozen Gem of the USSR,* 1978. Available on-line at <http://www.maximov.com/Russia/Sakha/ yakutia_past. html#origins> (28 September 1997).

Vitebsky, Piers. "Perestroika and Cultural Change Among the Reindeer Herders of Siberia: A Field Report." Paper presented at the conference on "Siberia in the Twentieth Century: Social and Economic Developments." Glasgow, Scotland, September 1989.

―――. "Yakut." Pp. 304–319 in *The Nationalities Question in the Soviet Union.* Ed. Graham Smith. London: Longman, 1992.

Voropayev, G. V., et al. "The Problem of Redistribution of Water Resources in the Midlands of the USSR." *Soviet Geography: Review and Translation.* Vol. 24, No. 10 (December 1983).

Wallerstein, Immanuel. *The Modern World System.* New York: Academic Press, 1974.

―――. *The Modern World System II.* New York: Academic Press, 1980.

Weekes, Richard V., ed. *Muslim Peoples: A World Ethnographic Survey.* 2 vols. Westport, Conn.: Greenwood, 1984.

Werth, Alexander. *Russia at War, 1941–1945.* London: Barrie and Rockcliff, 1964.

Wheatcroft, Stephen G. "Glasnost' and Rehabilitations." Pp. 199–218 in *Facing Up to the Past.* Ed. Ito Takayuki. Sapporo, Japan: Hokkaido University, Slavic Research Center, 1989.

Whiting, Allen S. *Siberian Development and East Asia: Threat or Promise?* Stanford: Stanford University Press, 1981.

Wolff, David. "Russia Finds Its Limits." Pp. 40–54 in *Rediscovering Russia in Asia*. Eds. Stephen Kotkin and David Wolff. Armonk, N.Y.: M. E. Sharpe, 1995.

Wood, Alan. "Settlement and Unsettlement: Massive Criminal Exile to Siberia in Tsarist Russia." Paper presented at the conference on "The Development of Siberian Territories: Historical and Economic Aspects." Kemerovo, USSR. September 1991.

———. "Sex and Violence in Siberia: Aspects of the Tsarist Exile System." Pp. 23–42 in *Siberia: Two Historical Perspectives*. London: Eyre and Spottiswoode, 1984.

———. "Siberian Exile in the Eighteenth Century." *Siberica*. Vol. 1, No. 1 (Summer 1990), pp. 38–63.

———. "Siberian Regionalism Resurgent." *Sibirica: The Journal of Siberian Studies*. Vol. 1, No. 1 (1993/1994), pp. 71–86.

———, ed. *Siberia: Problems and Prospects for Regional Development*. London: Croom Helm, 1987.

Wood, Alan, and R. A. French, eds. *The Development of Siberia: People and Resources*. London: Macmillan, 1989.

Yegorova, Svetlana. "Yakutia: Siberia's Chernobyl." *Sibirica: The Journal of Siberian Studies*. Vol. 1, No. 2 (1994/1995), pp. 35–37.

Yeltsin, Boris. *Against the Grain*. New York: Summit Books, 1990.

Zemtsov, Ilya. *Chernenko: The Last Bolshevik*. New Brunswick, N.J.: Transaction Publishers, 1989.

Zhdanov, Vladimir A. "Contemporary Siberian Regionalism." Pp. 120–132 in *Rediscovering Russia in Asia*. Eds. Stephen Kotkin and David Wolff. Armonk, N.Y.: M. E. Sharpe, 1995.

▪ Index ▪

Abakan, 106
Abaza, A.A., 49
Academy of Sciences, Siberian branch, 17, 108, 109, 116
Achinsk, 114
Administration
  central, 184
  of frontier, 40, 44
  joint (of Sakhalin), 47
  local, 89
  oblast, 180–181
  public, 62
Administrative structure, 3(map), 62, 64, 66, 76, 90, 156–157, 193–194
Afanas'yevans, 34, 53
Aga-Buryatia (Aginskiy Buryat Autonomous District), 23, 25, 73, 159
Aganbegyan, A.G., 109, 117, 119, 123, 125, 150, 158
Agriculture, 34, 69, 87, 109–110, 118, 164
Ainu, 27, 29, 32, 39, 199
Air pressure, 9, 28
Akademgorodok, 107–110, 116–117, 123
Alaska, 10, 46, 182
Alenin, V.T. See Yermak
Aleuts, 27, 29, 39, 176
Alexander I, tsar, 70
Alexander II, tsar, 48–49, 55
Alexander III, tsar, 49, 63, 66, 71
Allied powers, 82–84
Alphabet, 99–100
Altay, 13, 15–16, 34, 58–59, 68, 109–110, 146
Altay kray, 16, 19, 86, 93, 145, 151, 159, 164, 191, 196
Altay Mountains, 13, 15–16, 32–33, 35, 53
Altay Republic (former Gorno-Altay Autonomous Oblast), 16, 19, 138, 142, 151, 160
Altays, 16, 19, 36, 73, 123, 138, 178, 182
Altay-Sayan region, 36–37, 44
Amur Basin, 26–29, 35, 37, 43–44, 46, 73, 76

Amuria, 26, 28, 44–47, 49–50, 55, 58, 68–69, 85, 123
Amur oblast, 29, 84, 165
Amur River, 8, 23, 26–28, 35, 43–44, 46–47, 50, 91, 97, 119, 142, 201
Amursk, 166
Amur-Yakutsk Main Line project (AYAM), 120(map), 125, 128, 201
Anabar River, 21, 185
Anadyr' River, 26, 43
Andronovians, 34, 35(photo), 36
Andropov, Yu.V., 116, 122–123
Angara River, 19, 21–22, 24, 32, 54, 110
Angarsk, 121
APN. See Association of Peoples of the North
APR. See Asia-Pacific Region
Arctic, 28, 37, 73, 177
Arctic Circle, 17, 185
Arctic Ocean, 8–9, 51
Aristov, A.B., 114, 126
ASC. See Association of Siberian Cities
Asia-Pacific Region (APR), 89, 102, 108, 116, 145, 166–167, 197
Asiatic Russia, 7, 94, 107, 111
Assimilation, 31, 40, 68
Association of Peoples of the North (APN), 174–178, 194
Association of Siberian Cities (ASC), 157–159
Attila, 36–37, 43
August coup attempt (1991), 143, 147, 184, 189–190
Authoritarianism, 89, 99, 144, 156, 169, 173, 186, 193
Authorities
  central, 133, 137, 162, 164, 167–168, 185, 192
  local, 88, 176, 179
  regional, 2, 7, 49, 87, 167, 180
  Russian, 5, 58, 71
  Soviet, 7, 86, 87, 100, 105, 124
  tsarist, 59, 63, 70
Autocracy, 2, 4, 49–50, 61, 70

228

Autonomy
    cultural, 156
    economic, 89, 145–147, 169, 183, 192
    political, 26, 74, 82, 178, 190
Avalyani, Teymuraz, 133
Avars, 31, 36–37
Average, comparisons of Siberia to national,
    6–7, 45, 51, 69, 91, 93, 96, 107, 109, 118,
    129, 134–135, 177, 193, 202
Avvakum, Archpriest, 61, 68
AYAM. See Amur-Yakutsk Main Line
Aykhal diamond mine, 185

Bakunin, Mikhail, 64, 76
BAM. See Baykal-Amur Main Line
Baraba Steppe, 15, 39, 71, 73
Barnaul, 51, 91, 110
Batu, 37–38, 43
Baykal-Amur Main Line (BAM), 23–24, 55, 97,
    107, 109–110, 116, 119, 120(map),
    121–123, 125, 127–128, 132, 139–140,
    158–159
Baykal, Lake 8, 11, 19, 21–24, 33–34, 37, 43, 47,
    55, 65, 71, 84, 89, 109, 119
Belorussians, 51, 68
Belovo, 136
Berezovo, 112
Berezovskiy, 136
Bering Sea, 9, 199
Bering Strait, 9, 32, 40, 43
Bering, Vitus, 44
Birobidzhan, 142, 152
Biryusa River, 23
Biya River, 15
Biysk, 51
Black earths. See Soils, chernozems
Blagoveshchensk, 47, 51, 69, 96, 145–146
Blyukher, V.K., 95
Bogomyakov, G.P., 117–119
Bolsheviks, 60, 80–87, 99–100, 102, 137–138
Borders
    Russo-Chinese, 8, 26, 44, 47, 51, 76, 121, 172
    Russo-Korean, 26, 28
    Russo-Mongolian, 8, 47, 51, 95
Bratsk, 22, 110–111
Brezhnev, L.I., 7, 111, 114–119, 122–124,
    126–128, 131–133, 144, 146
    period under, 7, 116, 149
Bronze Age, 34–36
Budget
    federal, 51, 147, 156, 163–164, 187, 190,
    192–193
    local, 80, 137, 156, 163, 169, 186, 190, 197
Bureya River, 26, 165

Buryatia, 21, 23, 25, 34, 71, 84, 99, 160, 164–165
Buryats, 23, 25, 37, 39–40, 43, 67–73, 99–100,
    141, 176
Butashevich-Petrashevskiy, M.V., 64
Butov, Valeriy, 170
Byrranga Mountains, 15, 19, 21

Canada, 8, 10, 80, 182
Catherine II the Great, empress, 63, 70
Cattle, 26, 71, 124
Caucasoids, 5, 33
Center, the (central power, "the core"), 2, 4, 7,
    40, 46, 50, 66, 72, 74, 76, 86, 101, 109, 116,
    124, 133, 136–137, 143–146, 157, 159–160,
    165, 167, 171–172, 179–180, 184, 187,
    191–194
Centers, industrial, 21, 90–91, 117
Central Asia, 4, 34, 36, 38, 40, 70, 91, 96, 158
Central Committee (of Communist Party), 86,
    89, 96, 115, 119
Central Siberian Upland, 13, 19, 37, 68, 121
Centuries
    5th, 11, 36
    9th, 39
    10th, 70
    13th, 16
    15th, 40, 54, 182
    16th, 11, 38
    17th, 39, 43–45, 57–58, 70
    18th, 5, 32, 43, 45, 69
    19th, 18, 32, 43, 57–60, 62, 69, 71, 101, 146,
    176
    20th, 33, 49, 51, 57, 65, 75, 99, 139, 146
    21st, 10, 194
CER. See Chinese Eastern Railway
Chany, Lake, 16
Chelyabinsk, 6, 59, 82, 83, 110
Chelyabinsk oblast, 2, 154
Chelyabinsk Tariff Break, 59–60
Cherepkov, Viktor, 169, 172
Chernenko, K.U., 114–115, 119, 123
Chernomyrdin, V.S., 160, 161(photo), 162,
    169–171, 176, 196
Chernyshevskiy, N.G., 65
Cherskiy Range, 26, 199
China, 9, 37, 44, 46–47, 50, 67, 145–146, 153,
    172, 201
Chinese, 5, 34–38, 44, 47, 49, 66, 87, 89, 95, 121,
    163, 167, 169–170, 182
Chinese Eastern Railway (CER, KVZhD), 50,
    56, 81, 84, 102, 167
Chiryayev, G.I., 121–122, 128, 183
Chita, 47, 49–50, 69, 80, 82, 85, 102, 106
Chita oblast, 25, 84, 145, 159, 164–165, 202

Chubais, Anatoliy, 171, 173–174, 176–177, 187, 191, 193–194, 197
Chukchi, 26, 29, 32, 35, 39–40, 43, 65, 72–73, 99, 123, 141
Chukchi Peninsula, 9, 26, 28, 44, 97, 107
Chukchi Sea, 9
Chukotka (Chukchi Autonomous District), 2, 28, 141, 152, 165, 202
Chulym River, 15
Chuvans, 35, 39
Chuvashs, 51, 68
Cities, 4, 6–7, 29, 62, 66, 69, 86, 124, 158–159
Civilization, 5, 10, 34, 72, 96
Civil War (1918–1922), 60, 79, 81–85, 89, 99
Clans, 71, 123, 137
Climate, 8, 14(map), 16, 18, 24–25, 27–28, 31–32, 69
Coal miners, 4, 93, 132–135, 137, 142–143, 145, 147, 149, 166, 191
Coasts, 9, 26, 28, 199. See also Pacific Coast
Collectivization, 60, 88–89, 99, 101, 124
Colonization, 44, 50
Colony, Siberia as a, 4, 57, 60, 64–65, 74, 90, 136
Commander Islands, 27
Commodities, 43, 45, 59–60
    coal, 16, 21, 27, 90, 92, 96, 110, 118, 132, 134, 137, 143, 146, 151, 153, 166, 190–191
    diamonds, 144, 184–185, 187
    electricity, 12, 110, 164, 166–167, 169
    furs, 5, 39–40, 43–44, 57–58, 73, 99
    grain, 17, 58–60, 70, 87–88, 110
    iron ore, 90, 110, 126
    machinery, 6, 69, 106, 194
    natural gas, 112, 119, 127
    oil, 91, 112, 122, 127
    oil and gas, 6, 58, 60, 119, 121, 125, 152, 179
    salt, 16, 39, 70
    sulfur, 27
    timber, 24, 110, 173
    wheat, 16–17, 34, 60, 109, 126
Commune, peasant, 48, 67, 69
Communism, 64, 85, 108, 149, 156
Communist Party congresses
    17th (1934), 96
    18th (1939), 96
    20th (1956), 106, 109
    21st (1959), 116
    24th (1971), 121–122
    25th (1976), 118–119
    27th (1986), 128, 158
Communist Party of Russian Federation (CPRF), 154, 162, 164–165, 189
Communist Party of Soviet Union (CPSU), 86–87, 89, 96–97, 99, 108–109, 114–115, 118, 132–133, 138, 147, 158, 183, 193

Communist Party's December 1977 plenum, 119
Communists, 86, 96, 107, 133, 138, 143, 149, 162, 185–186
Companies
    Almazy Rossii-Sakha (Alrosa), 185–187
    DeBeers, 185–187
    foreign, 6–7, 116, 127, 144, 153, 194
    Russian-America Company, 46
Competitiveness, 11, 190
Congresses of People's Deputies, 133, 141, 172, 189
Conquest of Siberia, 39–41, 42(map), 43–48, 62–63
Constitution
    Soviet (1977), 114, 133, 143–144, 148–149, 155, 172
    Yeltsin's (1993), 155–157, 163, 165, 174, 176, 179–180, 195
Constitutional Democrats, party of (Kadets), 80–81
Consumer goods, 11, 193–194
Conversion (of the defense industry), 160, 166–167
Core-periphery relations, 4–5, 7–8, 11, 60, 74, 89, 105, 107, 121, 131, 143–144, 147, 149, 156–157, 160–161, 166, 171, 174, 185
Corruption, 64–65, 71, 169, 171
Cossacks, 39–41, 42(map), 43–44, 62, 66, 69, 72–73, 75, 82, 142, 178
Costs
    labor, 7, 59
    transportation, 7, 59, 166–167
Council of Ministers, 7, 158
Council for the Study of Productive Forces (SOPS), 117–118, 123
Countryside, 34, 71, 80, 86, 88, 140
CPRF. See Communist Party of Russian Federation
CPSU. See Communist Party of Soviet Union
Crimean War (1853–1855), 46–47
Criminals, 43, 60–61, 74, 94, 107, 171
Cro-Magnons, 32
Culture, 32, 34–35, 37, 39, 53, 62, 66, 68, 123, 143, 182
Customs duties, 145, 163, 167, 169
Czech Legion, 82–84

Dams and reservoirs, 97, 108, 110–111, 124, 158
Dauria, 26, 145–146. See also Chita oblast
Davydov Plan. See Dams and reservoirs
Decades of the 20th century
    1900s, 67, 69–72, 102
    1910s, 60, 66, 75
    1920s, 64, 71, 87, 89, 95, 99–101, 111, 121, 124

1930s, 26, 89–92, 99–101, 104–106, 111, 124, 138
1940s, 93–94, 97. *See also* World War II
1950s, 73, 77, 100, 106, 109–111
1960s, 25, 60, 109–112, 114, 116, 121, 124, 128, 158
1970s, 23, 91, 97, 116, 118, 128, 144, 165
1980s, 23, 107–108, 117, 122, 124, 129, 157, 185
1990s, 7, 143, 162, 185, 192
Decembrists, 61–64, 74
Decentralization, 55, 133, 137
Demidov family, 58–59, 75
Democracy, 60, 62, 65, 74, 80, 142, 156
Deportation, 68–69, 94–95, 97, 100, 186
Derber, Peter, 81–83, 102
Development
    cultural, 99, 160
    economic, 45, 66, 107, 110, 125, 145, 147, 167
    industrial, 21, 50, 91, 177
    of natural resources, 6–7, 91, 97, 121, 138, 165, 201
    of oil and gas fields, 7, 15, 102, 107, 111–112, 113(map), 116–118, 128, 175, 178, 192, 200
    regional, 2, 50, 105, 111, 176
Development programs and projects, 7, 109, 117–119, 122, 138–139, 158, 165
Dezhnev, Semen, 41
Dialects, 21, 39, 68
Dolgans, 21, 25, 72–73, 182
Dolgikh, Vladimir, 115–116, 119, 122, 127
Dudinka, 21, 91
Duma (lower chamber of parliament)
    provincial, 156, 162, 171–173, 178, 180–181, 187
    Russian (after 1993), 165, 199
    Russian (before 1917), 66, 79–80
    Siberian, 80–83, 102
Dzhugdzhur Range, 26

Eastern Siberia, 19–25, 30, 67
East Siberian Sea, 9
Ebelyakh River, 185
Economic base, 7, 87
Economy
    global, 2, 4–5, 10
    market, 7, 148, 160, 175, 183, 190, 196
    national, 132, 149–150, 194
    planned ("command"), 127, 175
    regional, 4, 10, 62, 80, 145, 156–157, 163, 186
    of Siberian regions, 5, 8, 66, 85, 147, 149, 161, 163, 165, 169, 193–194
    traditional, 71, 176, 178
Ecosystems, 10, 18, 165
EKO. *See* Institute of Economics and Organization of Industrial Production

Elections, 86–87, 137, 162, 171–172, 176, 180–181, 183–184, 191
    presidential (1996), 165, 170–172, 173(map)
Electric power stations, 27, 90, 107, 110–111, 124, 165
Entsy, 19, 37, 70, 100, 176
Environment, 15, 33, 108–109, 112, 125, 129, 139, 175, 178, 191, 193
Eskimo-Aleuts. *See* Aleuts
Eskimos, 26, 32–33, 37, 65, 73, 123, 178
Ethnic groups, 19, 20(map), 23, 25, 29, 32, 39, 68–69, 137, 139, 141, 152, 156, 176–177
Ethnicity, 10, 36, 64, 67, 74, 151, 157
Ethnic regions, 3(map), 157, 160, 176, 194
European Russia, 49–50, 59, 63–67, 74, 85–87, 91–93, 107, 109, 118, 131, 144
Europoids, 33–35
Evacuation of industry during World War II, 92–93
Evenkia (Evenk Autonomous District), 9, 21, 25, 156, 160, 182
Evenks, 21, 23, 25, 29, 33, 39–40, 43, 69, 72–73, 99–100, 114, 123, 140, 152, 182, 201
Evens, 26, 29, 33, 39, 43, 69, 72, 100, 123, 182
Exile, 45–46, 48, 59–61, 65, 69–70, 74–75, 90, 94, 124
Exploration of Siberia, 26, 40, 43, 46, 54
Export quotas, 162, 169, 173
Exports, Siberian, 6, 51, 60, 87, 122, 125, 160, 186, 187
Extinction, 33, 39, 44, 69, 176, 199

Famine. *See* Starvation
Far East, 6, 25–29, 32, 45, 47–48, 65–66, 84, 89, 91, 95–96, 99, 101–102, 104, 108, 110, 121, 142, 144–146, 149, 153, 165–167
Far East and Baykal Association for Economic Cooperation (FEA), 159, 165–167, 192, 197
Far Eastern Republic (FER), 66, 83–85, 89, 168
Farmers, 25, 34–35, 38, 85–86
Farming, 4, 23, 26, 36, 71, 86
Farms, 69, 88, 110, 140, 151
FEA. *See* Far East and Baykal Association for Economic Cooperation
Federalism, 80, 142–149, 156, 194
Federation Council (upper chamber of parliament), 156, 171, 174, 180, 183, 199
Federation Treaty (1992), 144, 155, 165, 200
Fedorov, Valentin, 145, 154
Fedorovo oilfield, 112, 113(map)
FER. *See* Far Eastern Republic
FEZ. *See* Free Economic Zones
Financial aid, 111, 136
First Siberian Regional Congress, 81

Fishing, 15, 27, 33, 37, 68, 72–73, 123
Five-Year plans (FYP), 90–91, 111
Foreigners, 46, 49, 64, 71, 90, 169, 186, 188
Foreign intervention (1918–1921), 83–85, 89
Foreign investment, 144–146, 149, 157
Forestry, 109
Forests, 4, 11, 33, 38, 43, 64, 111, 134, 172
  broadleaf, 18
  coniferous, 8, 18, 24–25, 28. See also Taiga
  mixed, 18, 28
Fossil fuels, 5, 8, 21, 27, 148
Free Economic Zones (FEZ), 145–147, 153, 172, 191
Freight rates, 7, 12, 59, 170
Frontier, 5–7, 10, 39–40, 42(map), 45–46, 48, 51, 54, 60, 91, 109, 184, 194
Fur trade, 40, 43, 58, 99
Fur tribute, 38, 40, 69–70, 99
FYP. See Five-Year plans

Gaydar, Ye.T., 147, 184
Gayer, Yevdokiya, 175(photo), 175–176, 199
Genghis Khan, 37
Glaciation, 15, 23, 31–32
Glasnost', 132, 139–141, 149, 157, 166. See also Reforms, Gorbachev's
Gold, 26–27, 34, 58, 74–75, 91, 94, 100, 144
Gold miners, 48, 94
Gorbachev, M.S., 89, 116–117, 125, 127, 131–133, 137, 139, 141, 143, 149–151, 158, 160, 174, 189
  period under, 60, 114, 141, 147, 192
Gornaya Shoriya, 16, 151
Gosplan. See State Planning Agency
Government
  Bolshevik, 82, 84
  central, 12, 67, 80, 117, 141, 163–164, 169–171, 176, 187
  foreign, 84, 172
  Gorbachev, 143, 145, 174
  provisional, 81–83
  regional, 4, 80–84, 88, 146, 159, 179, 182, 191–192
  Russian, 146, 162, 177, 187
  Soviet, 7, 118, 146
  Stalin, 89
  tsarist, 49, 55, 59, 65, 68
  Yeltsin, 7, 156, 163, 169, 172, 176–177, 187, 191–192
Grasslands. See Steppes
Great Terror. See Repression, Stalinist
Growth
  economic, 7, 93, 164
  population, 7, 12, 19, 28, 45–46, 51, 61, 70, 100, 110, 201

Gubkin, I.M., 104, 111
Gulag, 93–97, 98(map), 103–104, 131, 152. See also Labor camps
Gulf of Ob', 17, 113(map), 158
Gulf of Pos'yet, 142
Gydan Peninsula, 16, 72, 113(map)

Harbin, 81, 84, 102
Hard currency, 6, 60, 87, 125, 167, 194
Harvest, 17, 109–110
Herzen, Alexander, 63–64
Hinterland, 4, 49, 89, 159
Hokkaido, 27, 32, 199
Homeland (ethnic), 16, 23, 37, 39, 99–100, 123, 128, 137–138, 140–142, 144, 174, 176–178, 182
Homestead, 48, 69
Horvath, D.L., 81–83, 102
Huns, 1, 31, 35–37
Hunting, 32–33, 37, 68, 72–73, 100, 140, 172

Igarka, 97
Immigrants, 45–46, 48, 51, 55, 64, 66–68, 70, 85, 99, 170
Imports, Siberian, 6, 11, 87, 160, 166–167
Independence
  economic, 2, 65, 89, 133, 154, 184, 195
  political, 102, 137, 142–143, 146, 149, 163, 166, 186, 190, 195
Independent Siberia, idea of, 55, 63, 83, 149, 161, 163
Indigenous peoples, 20(map), 40, 44–45, 64, 69, 71–73, 99, 123, 125, 129, 137, 140, 149, 176–178. See also Native Siberian peoples
Indigirka River, 37, 43
Industrial enterprises, 12, 52, 58–59, 91–93, 131–132, 136, 164, 166, 170–171, 191
Industrialization, 60, 87, 89–93, 100, 124, 139, 149
Industrial output, 52, 91–93, 109, 116, 147, 160, 165–166, 179
Industrial Revolution, 5, 49, 62
Industry, 87, 92, 118, 146, 166
  aluminum, 93, 107, 110–111
  butter, 51, 59, 75
  coal mining, 15, 21, 23, 27, 30, 133, 143, 169, 191
  coke-chemical, 90
  defense-related, 91, 93, 108, 148, 166
  diamond, 184–185
  food processing, 51–52, 70, 87
  gold mining, 59
  heavy, 134, 149
  logging, 91, 110
  machine-building, 6, 87, 91, 93

manufacturing, 91, 144, 147, 166
metallurgic, 52, 58, 90–93, 110, 135(photo), 191
metalworking, 6, 91, 93
mining, 4, 19, 106, 109, 131, 148
oil, 30, 117, 180(photo)
oil refining, 91, 111
petrochemical, 7, 117
pulp and paper, 107, 110–111
wood processing, 52, 91, 93, 110–111
Infrastructure, 118, 158–159, 186
Inhabitants. *See* Population
Insects, 9, 112
Institute of Economics and Organization of Industrial Production (EKO), 117, 119
Intelligentsia, Siberian, 65, 71, 169
Interest groups, 132, 157–178, 192
Investment, 7–8, 49, 59, 90–91, 93, 111, 118–119, 125, 132, 159, 170
Irkutsk, 19, 22, 25, 46–47, 49, 62, 64, 69, 71, 82, 84, 102, 110, 121, 123, 160–161
Irkutsk oblast, 4, 25, 103, 140, 159, 164, 192–193
Iron Age, 36–37
Irtysh River, 8, 13, 15, 34, 38–39, 41, 111, 158
Iset' River, 15
Ishim River, 15, 38
Ishim Steppe, 15
Isker (Sibir'), 11, 38, 41
Itel'men, 27, 29, 35, 39, 43, 69, 73, 123, 176
Ivan IV the Terrible, tsar, 38–40
Ivankov, Vladimir, 163

Japan, 27, 32, 34, 44, 50–51, 67, 82, 91–92, 94, 102, 116, 122, 144, 146, 172, 185
Japanese, 27, 49, 66, 85, 89, 102, 182
Japanese troops, 22, 84–85, 95, 102
JAR. *See* Jewish Autonomous Region
Jewish Autonomous Region (JAR), 28, 99, 142, 145–146, 152, 165, 202
Jews, 68–70, 94, 99, 102, 114
Joint ventures (JV), 144–145, 149, 153, 165, 185
JV. *See* Joint ventures

Kadets. *See* Constitutional Democrats
Kalmykov, I.P., 102
Kama River, 39, 41, 54
Kamchatka oblast, 28–29, 141, 165, 202
Kamchatka Peninsula, 9, 26–28, 44
Kansk-Achinsk Coal Basin, 21, 118
Kara Sea, 9, 17
Karasuks, 34–36
Karymy, 68
Katun' River, 15
Kazakhs, 36, 67–68, 70, 73
Kazakhstan, 8–9, 13, 15–16, 18, 110, 158

Kazan', 70, 182
Kemerovo, 17, 53, 133, 135–136, 143, 150–151, 154, 159, 187–188, 190, 202
Kemerovo oblast, 4, 19, 90, 132, 137, 145–148, 153–154, 159, 189–191, 193
Kerenskiy, A.F., 80, 82
Ket' River, 15, 100
Kets, 21, 39, 69, 72–73, 176
Khabarov, Yerofey Pavlovich, 26, 44
Khabarovsk, 26, 28–29, 47, 50, 91, 96, 99, 110, 123, 145, 165
Khabarovsk kray, 29, 84, 95–96, 142, 145, 165–166, 182
Khakass, 23, 25, 43, 69, 72, 100, 114, 123, 137, 178, 182
Khakassia, 23, 25, 99, 137, 142, 151, 159–160, 164
Khanka, Lake, 26, 68
Khantia-Mansia (Khanty-Mansi Autonomous District), 2, 19, 125, 139, 142, 152, 160, 164, 175, 179, 181, 192
Khants, 15, 19, 34, 37, 40–41, 53, 72–73, 100, 123, 140(photo), 140–141, 158, 174–176, 178–179, 194
Khanty-Mansiysk, 15
Khatanga River, 19, 21
Kheta River, 21
Khingan Mountains, 37
Khozraschet (cost accounting), 7, 132, 159
Khrushchev, N.S., 89, 106, 108–111, 114, 146
period under, 107–108, 114, 124, 175
Kipchaks, 37–38
Kiselevsk, 133, 150
Kislyuk, Mikhail, 153–154, 190–191
Kolchak, Alexander, 82–85, 102, 142
Kolyma, 26, 59, 94–97, 100, 106
Kolyma Lowland, 199
Kolyma River, 37, 43
Kolyvan, 58, 68
Komi, 68, 123, 128
Komsomol'sk-na-Amure, 91, 100, 107, 166
Konda River, 15, 111
Korea, 9, 27, 146, 172, 185
Koreans, 27, 29, 66, 85, 95, 142, 182
Koryakia (Koryak Autonomous District), 29, 141, 165, 202
Koryak Mountains, 199
Koryaks, 27, 29, 33, 35, 37, 39, 72–73, 123, 141
Kosygin, A.N., 114, 118–119, 121, 153
Kotuy River, 19, 21
Krasnoshchekov, A.M., 84, 103, 149, 168
Krasnoyarsk, 6, 19, 25, 80, 86, 93, 110, 115, 150, 160, 187
Krasnoyarsk kray, 25, 103, 114–115, 159, 164, 176, 178, 181, 187, 196

Kremlin, 118, 170, 174, 177
Kuchum Khan, 39, 41
Kulaks, 86–90, 100–101, 137. *See also* Peasants
Kulomzin, Anatoliy, 49–50, 55, 66–68, 71
Kulunda Steppe, 15, 17, 32, 35
Kurgan oblast, 2, 154
Kurile Islands, 9, 26–28, 47, 56, 145–146, 170
Kuzbas, 4, 15–17, 21, 34, 36, 87, 90, 92, 110, 117, 126, 132–136, 143, 145–147, 151, 154, 166, 187–188, 190–191
Kuzbas coal miners' strikes (1989, 1991), 132–137, 134(photo), 143, 147, 149–150
Kuznetsk Alatau, 13, 15–16, 134
Kuznetsk Basin. *See* Kuzbas
Kuznetsov, Vladimir, 167
KVZhD. *See* Chinese Eastern Railway
Kyakhta, 101
Kyrgyz, 36–37, 43
Kyzyl, 23, 24, 124

Labor camps, 21, 77, 94, 97, 98(map), 106. *See also* Gulag
Labor force, 45, 68, 87, 92–93, 96–97, 106–107, 112, 117–118, 195
Language
    native, 21, 29, 37, 39, 53, 70–71, 123, 156, 174, 199
    Russian, 72, 100, 123
    Turkic, 36
Laptev Sea, 9
Lavrent'yev, M.A., 108–109, 116
LDPR. *See* Liberal Democrats
Lena Basin, 24, 26, 30, 32, 37, 59, 126
Lena River, 8, 19, 26, 43, 54, 110, 122
Lenin, V.I., 81, 83–85, 102, 188(photo)
Leninsk-Kuznetskiy, 136
Liberal Democrats, party of (LDPR), 162
Ligachev, Ye.K., 105, 106(photo), 115–117, 119, 122, 127
Little BAM, 91, 93, 120(map), 121–122, 125, 128
Lobbies, 117, 119, 122, 125, 159, 163, 164, 171, 175, 192
Lomakin, V.P., 121, 128

Magadan, 145
Magadan oblast, 2, 6, 29, 94, 141, 146, 165, 200
Majority, ethnic, 23, 137–138, 141, 157
Mammoths, 32–33
Manchu Dynasty, 46–47
Manchuria, 37, 49–50, 84, 96, 102, 119, 201
Manchus, 27, 39, 43, 46–47, 49, 67
Mansi, 15, 19, 34, 37, 40–41, 43, 53, 72, 123, 140–141, 158, 174–176, 178–179, 194
Medical care, 55, 62, 136
Medvezh'ye gas field, 112, 113(map)

Megion oilfield, 111, 113(map)
Merchants, 38–40, 69–70, 89
Mesolithic era, 32–33
Metals, 5, 58, 91
    cobalt, 21, 23
    copper, 16, 21, 58, 121
    ferrous, 21
    lead, 16, 23, 26, 58
    manganese, 16
    mercury, 16, 26
    molybdenum, 23, 26, 91
    nickel, 21, 93
    nonferrous, 21, 109
    platinum, 21
    precious, 21, 57, 74
    tin, 26, 34, 91
    titanium, 23
    tungsten, 23, 26, 91, 167
    zinc, 16, 23, 26
Mezhdurechensk, 133–134, 136, 147
Middle Volga region, 37, 70, 83
Migration, 18, 37, 44–46, 48, 50–51, 55, 61, 67, 71, 74, 86, 107, 123, 192, 200–201
Military-industrial complex, 158, 166, 195
Military service, exemption of, 48, 55, 89
Mineral deposits, 16, 21–24, 26, 40, 47, 59, 91, 109, 111–112, 119, 151, 187, 201
Miners, 6, 172. *See also* Coal miners
Mines
    coal, 21, 133–137, 143, 191
    diamond, 110, 124, 185
    gold, 45, 58–59, 68, 94
    silver, 45, 58
Minorities, ethnic, 23, 29, 31, 52, 61, 70, 74, 81, 100–101, 123, 132, 138–139, 142–143, 178–179, 181–182, 194
Minusinsk Basin, 23, 33–35
Mirnyy diamond mines, 110, 184–185
Mongolia, 9, 23–24, 33, 37, 71, 146
Mongoloids, 5, 33–35
Mongols, 36, 38–39, 73, 82, 182
Mongol-Tatar invasion, 4, 37–38, 70
Mongol-Tatars, 31, 38
Moscow, 4, 5, 8, 28, 58, 88–89, 95, 97, 99, 101, 103, 108–109, 112, 114–116, 122–123, 127, 132, 136, 138, 145, 161–163, 167, 170, 173, 181, 184, 190, 193
Mt. Klyuchevskaya, 27
Mukha, Vitaliy, 148–149, 161(photo), 161–162, 165, 167–168, 176
Murav'yev-Amurskiy, N.N., 46–49, 55, 58–59, 66, 71, 142, 195
Muscovites, 38, 40, 57
Muscovy, 38, 40, 53, 58
Muslims, 67–68, 70, 182

Nadym River, 15
Nakhodka, 96, 122, 145–146
Nanays, 26–27, 35, 69, 73, 99, 100, 142(photo), 178
Nationalities, titular, 2, 23, 138, 151, 156
National supremacy, idea of, 157, 176–177, 194
Native Siberian peoples, 1–2, 13, 20(map), 23, 26, 29, 32, 34, 38–40, 44–45, 54, 67–69, 72–73, 99–100, 139, 156–158, 174–177, 183, 194. See also Indigenous peoples
Natural gas fields, 112, 113(map), 114
Nazdratenko, Yevgeniy, 149, 167–174, 168(photo), 176, 193, 197
Neanderthals, 31–32
Nefteyugansk, 111
Negidals, 26, 72, 176
Nemtsov, Boris, 157, 171, 173, 176–177, 191, 193–194
Nentsy, 15, 19, 33, 37, 40, 43, 53, 70, 72, 99, 123, 140, 142, 176, 178–179, 194
Neolithic era, 23, 33–34
NEP. See New Economic Policy
Nerchinsk, 58–59
Neryungri, 7
Nesselrode, Count Karl Vasilyevich, 47, 60, 62
Nevel'skoy, Admiral, 46
Nevel'skoy Strait, 96, 97
Newcomers, 19, 28, 38, 40, 43–45, 72, 74, 137, 174, 176, 193
New Economic Policy (NEP), 60, 85–90, 100–101, 132
Nganasans, 19, 37, 69, 100, 114, 176
Nicholas I, tsar, 46–47, 69
Nicholas II, tsar, 50
Nikolayev, M.Ye., 182–187, 183(photo), 193, 200–201
Nikolayevsk Incident (1920), 85, 102
Nikolayevsk-na-Amure, 46, 85, 96
Nivkhi, 26–27, 29, 35, 39, 73, 140, 152, 178
Nizhnevartovsk, 121
Nomadism, 15, 33, 36, 71–72, 99, 124
Noril'sk, 21, 91, 93, 97, 100, 110, 135, 181
Northern wage increment, 107–108, 117, 193
North Siberian Lowland, 21–22
North Siberian Railway (NSR), 121
Novaya Zemlya, 15, 201
Novokuznetsk, 90, 135(photo), 135–136, 191
Novonikolayevsk. See Novosibirsk
Novosibirsk, 6–7, 12, 19, 51, 92(photo), 93, 100, 108, 115, 117, 123, 145, 148, 159–162, 196, 199
Novosibirsk oblast, 19, 148, 159, 162, 164–165, 191, 196
Nozhikov, Yuriy, 161, 193
NSR. See North Siberian Railway

Ob' Basin, 17–18, 34–35, 60, 97, 104, 107, 111–112, 113(map), 122, 178–179, 194
Ob'-Irtysh Basin, 16, 38, 43, 158
Oblastnichestvo. See regionalism
Ob' River, 8, 13, 15, 37, 40, 110–112, 123
October 1993 parliamentary crisis , 155, 161–162, 168, 184, 190
Oil fields, 15, 17, 112, 113(map), 117–118, 122, 132, 180(photo)
Oil and gas fields, 113(map), 139, 142, 178
Oirots. See Altays
Olenek River, 19
Omsk, 6, 17, 19, 28, 51, 65, 69, 82–83, 92–93, 111, 160, 183
Omsk oblast, 19, 159, 162, 164
Orochi, 26–27, 176, 178
Oroks, 27, 72, 140, 176, 178
Osinniki, 136
Ostyaks. See Khants
Oymyakon, 8–9

Pacific Basin. See Asia-Pacific Region
Pacific Coast, 26, 29, 39, 43, 46, 55, 119, 121–122
Pacific Fleet, 62, 108
Pacific Ocean, 8–9, 27–28, 51, 63, 83
Paleo-Asiatic peoples, 26–27, 35, 39, 67
Paleolithic era, 31–33
Party, the. See Communist Party of the Soviet Union
Pavlutskiy, 44
Peasant Majority Party, 85
Peasants, 48, 51, 55, 61, 67, 74, 81, 85–89, 100. See also Kulaks
Perestroyka, 117, 125, 132, 144, 149–150, 159–161. See also Reforms, Gorbachev's
Periphery, 2, 5, 8, 10, 50, 58, 64, 66, 74, 86, 101, 109, 111, 117, 146–147, 165, 193–194
Perm', 39, 83
Permafrost, 9, 17–18, 24–25, 55, 97, 110, 121
Perm' oblast, 201
Peter I the Great, tsar, 22, 44–45, 58
Peter the Great Bay, 28
Petropavlovsk-Kamchatskiy, 46–47
Petrovsk-Zabaykal'skiy, 47, 52
Pipelines, 111–112, 113(map), 118, 121–122
Polezhayev, L.K., 162, 196
Policy
    colonial, 64, 86
    development, 4, 59
    economic, 8, 60, 90, 193
    migration, 7, 48, 50, 55, 63, 68
    nationalities, 99–100, 137–142, 177
    protectionist, 59, 163, 166
    religious, 70–71
Politburo, 89, 114–116, 118–119, 124–125, 144

Pollution, 21, 123, 133–135, 135(photo), 139, 150–151, 153, 188, 201
Popular fronts, 141, 149, 152, 157
Population
  density, 6, 43
  ethnic composition of, 19, 25, 29, 43, 45, 51, 66–67, 85, 99, 124, 182
  growth, 7, 12, 19, 28, 45–46, 51, 61, 70, 100, 110, 201
  rural, 19, 25
  of Siberia, 1, 6, 8, 45–46, 51, 62, 125
  of Siberian peoples, 1, 39, 69–70, 151, 174, 178–179, 182
  of a Siberian region, 18, 28, 45–46, 68, 85–87, 99, 160, 165, 179, 192–193
  urban, 6, 18, 25, 29, 52, 110, 123, 159
Port Arthur, 22, 50
Post-Soviet period, 2, 7, 26, 179
Postyshevo, 110, 121
Pos'yet, Konstantin, 49
Potanin, G.N., 64–66, 79–81, 85, 101, 137, 149
POW. See Prisoners, of war
Poyarkov, Vasiliy, 26, 43–44, 54
Pravdinsk oilfield, 111, 113(map)
Precipitation, 8–9, 17, 24, 28
Primorskiy kray, 4, 28–29, 84, 95, 116, 121, 145, 147, 149, 165–174, 193, 202
Primor'ye, 8, 28, 45, 47–50, 68, 85
Prisoners, 50–51, 82, 94–97, 100
  political, 26, 61, 74, 94
  of war (POW), 61, 82, 94, 96, 100
Procurement of grain, 86–88, 124. See also Requisitioning
Production, 6, 125, 160, 176, 194
  of butter, 59
  of coal, 90, 134, 136, 143
  of consumer goods, 166
  of diamonds, 26, 184–186, 201
  of electricity, 90
  of gold, 26, 59, 91–92
  of grain, 110
  of machinery, 6, 87
  of nickel, 93
  of petroleum, 112, 117–119
  of steel, 90, 92
  of timber, 24
Prokop'yevsk, 135–136, 150–151, 191
Provincial People's Assembly (1917), 80
Prudenskiy, G.A., 116–117
Pur River, 15
Pushkin, Alexander, 61–62
Putoran Plateau, 15, 21, 24

Radishchev, Alexander, 61
Rasputin, Valentin, 57

Raw materials, 4–5, 8–10, 21, 27, 34, 107, 110, 146, 165, 178, 193–194
Red Army, 83, 85, 95–96, 102
Reforms, 157, 184
  economic, 117, 127, 171
  Gorbachev's, 132–133, 137–138, 141, 149, 159. See also Perestroyka; Glasnost'
  Yeltsin's, 161, 163, 166, 191, 193
Regime
  communist, 88, 103, 107, 138, 161
  tsarist, 46, 66
Regionalism, 63–66, 74, 76, 79–83, 85, 95–96, 100, 115, 142–149, 160, 162, 165, 168, 190, 192
Reindeer herding, 15, 36–37, 72–73, 100, 123–124, 139, 140(photo)
Religions
  Buddhism, 69, 71, 100
  Christianity, 70–71
  Islam, 69–70
  Lamaism, 71
  Orthodoxy, 62, 67–68, 70–71, 182
  Shamanism, 32, 67, 69–71, 99–100, 182
Religious sects, 61, 66–69
  Baptists, 68
  Dukhobors and Molokans, 61, 67, 69
  Mennonites, 68
  Old Believers, 61, 67–68, 77
  Skoptsy, 67, 69
Repression, Stalinist, 96, 115, 124. See also Gulag
Requisitioning of grain, 81, 86, 114. See also Procurement
Reserves
  coal, 8, 21, 23, 26, 47, 121, 138, 184, 201
  diamond, 184, 186–187
  gold, 16, 23, 26, 184
  hydroelectric, 21
  natural gas, 8, 15, 26, 112, 114, 165, 179, 184
  ore, 16, 21, 23, 26, 121, 138
  petroleum, 8, 15, 22, 26–27, 104, 111–112, 117, 179, 184
  timber, 110
  water, 22
Resource base, 5, 8, 62, 89
Revolutionary movement, 64, 70, 76, 79–81
Revolution of 1905, 68
Revolution of 1917, 51, 60, 73–74, 79, 81–82
  period before, 29, 137
River reversal schemes, 158
Rubtsovsk, 32, 93
Rule by decree, 147–148, 155
Russian advance to Siberia, 26, 31, 39–41, 42(map), 43–44, 46, 51, 53, 123
Russian Far East. See Far East

Russian parliament, 146–148, 156, 167, 175–176, 183–184, 194
Russians, 2, 19, 29, 39, 45, 47, 50–51, 54, 58, 62, 64, 67–70, 72, 76, 79, 84–85, 99–100, 123–124, 138–139, 142, 149, 157, 176
Russian troops, 39, 47, 95, 100
Russification, 27, 57, 66–72, 74, 114, 123, 182
Russo-Japanese War (1904–1905), 22, 50, 56, 79

SA. See Siberian Agreement
St. Petersburg, 5, 48, 58, 64, 66, 80–81
Sakha; Sakhans. See Yakutia; Yakuts
Sakhalars, 37
Sakhalin Island, 26–28, 32, 46–47, 50, 56, 85, 91, 96–97, 102, 123, 140, 145–146, 165, 178, 200
Sakhalin oblast, 4, 6, 29, 84, 116, 127, 145, 152, 154, 165, 170, 176, 192–193
Salair (settlement), 58
Salair Ridge, 13, 15–16, 58, 134
Salekhard, 17
Samotlor oilfield, 112, 113(map), 121
Samoyeds, 24, 37–39, 68–69, 73, 178, 199
Sangi, Vladimir, 141, 152, 174, 178
Sarmatians, 35, 36
Satraps, 44, 64, 72, 116
Sayan Mountains, 19, 23, 45, 199
Sayanogorsk, 110
Scythians, 35, 52–53
SD. See Social Democrats
Sea of Japan, 8, 167, 172
Sea of Ob'. See Dams and reservoirs
Sea of Okhotsk, 26–27, 40, 46, 54, 73, 200
Seasons of the year, 8–9, 15–18, 22, 24–25, 28, 73, 108, 112, 134
Secession, 8, 64, 144, 161, 170, 181, 185
Sedentary, 16, 26, 34, 38, 71–72
Self-government, 62, 64, 80, 133, 137, 171
Sel'kups, 15, 19, 37, 69, 73, 100, 123, 178
Semenov, Grigoriy, 82–83, 102, 142
Separatism, 46, 55, 62, 64–67, 74, 76, 160, 162, 166, 192
Serfdom, 45, 48, 59, 65, 75
Settlement of Siberia, 18, 23, 32, 40, 42(map), 44–46, 48, 50–51, 63, 67–68, 140
Settlements, 6–7, 32, 43, 47, 140, 175
Settlers, 39, 51, 67, 72–74, 76, 86, 96, 108
Shaim oilfield, 111, 113(map)
Shashkov, S.S., 65
Shchadov, M.I., 133–134, 136, 150
Shchapov, A.P., 64
Shcherbina, B.Ye., 117, 119
Shor Mountains. See Gornaya Shoriya
Shors, 19, 138, 138(photo), 151, 182
Siberian Agreement (SA), 148, 159–165, 192

Siberian Khanate, 38–39, 41
Siberian kray (Sibkray), 87–90, 96, 100–101, 103, 199
Siberian republic, idea of, 162–163
Siberian Ridges. See Sibirskie Uvaly
Siberian Tatars, 16, 19, 38–40, 62, 70, 72
Siberian University, 65
Sibir'. See Isker
Sibirskiye Uvaly, 15
Sibkray. See Siberian kray
Sikhote-Alin' Mountains, 26, 28, 68
Silver, 16, 58, 74
Slavophilism, 49, 63
Slavs, 67–68, 74
Slovtsov, P.A., 63–64, 76
Social Democrats, party of (SD), 81
Socialism, 108, 132
Social Revolutionaries, party of (SR), 80–83
Soils, 9, 14(map), 18, 23, 25, 28, 109
chernozems, 18, 25, 51
Solzhenitsyn, Alexander, 94
SOPS. See Council for the Study of Productive Forces
Sos'va River, 15
South Siberian Railway, 97, 110, 126, 134
Sovereignty, 99, 137, 141, 143, 149, 156, 168, 182–185, 190, 192, 194, 201
Sovetskaya Gavan', 97, 121
Soviet Europe. See European Russia
Soviet Far East. See Far East
Soviet period, 5–7, 11, 116, 156, 176, 184, 193
Soviets (local councils), 86–87, 95, 148, 160
Soviet Union, collapse of, 2, 26, 132, 143–146, 161, 166, 175–176, 183, 185, 195, 201
Speranskiy, Mikhail, 58
SR. See Social Revolutionaires
Stalin, J.V., 26, 66, 87–90, 95–97, 99, 101, 104, 106, 114, 146
period after, 105–109, 146
period under, 77, 90–98, 105, 108
Stalinsk. See Novokuznetsk
Stanovoy Range, 24, 26, 44
Starvation, 43, 86, 94
State Planning Agency (Gosplan), 117, 158, 164
Steppes, 15–18, 23–25, 34, 37–38, 45
Stolypin, P.A., 59
Stone Age, 33–34
Strike committee (of Kuzbas coal miners), 136–137, 141, 143, 147, 148(photo), 190. See also Kuzbas coal miners' strikes
Stroganov family, 39, 41
Subsidies, 7, 131, 149, 166–167, 169–170, 176, 187, 202

Supreme Soviet
of Russian Federation, 137, 145, 152, 161, 176
of Soviet Union, 117, 176
Surgut, 17, 111–112
Sverdlovsk. *See* Yekaterinburg
Sverdlovsk oblast, 2, 154
Syrtsov, S.I., 87–89

Tagarians, 35
Taiga (coniferous forest), 8, 18, 24–25, 28, 32, 43, 77, 121, 140, 175
Talnakh, 21
Tannu-Ola Range, 23
Tariffs, 39, 163, 169, 190. *See also* Customs duties
Tashtyks, 35–36, 53
Tatars, 38–41, 51, 67–68, 70, 73, 123
Tatar Strait, 47, 121
Taxation, 39, 48, 55, 66, 87, 159, 163, 169
Tax collection, 66, 68–69, 146, 156–157, 171, 173, 186, 187
Taymyria [Taymyr (Dolgano-Nenets) Autonomous District], 25, 160, 181
Taymyr Peninsula, 19, 21, 24–25, 72
Tayshet, 97, 110, 121, 126
Taz River, 15
Technology, 36, 139, 144, 178, 194
Teletskoye, Lake, 53
Temperatures, 8, 17–18, 24, 27, 112, 134, 158
Tobol River, 15, 34, 38–39
Tobol'sk, 11, 38, 68–71, 86, 111
Tofalars, 23, 37, 72, 176, 182
Tom' River, 15–16, 53, 134–135, 150, 188
Tomsk, 51, 65, 69, 71, 80–83, 100–101, 122, 160, 162
Tomsk oblast, 19, 115, 117–118, 125, 159, 191
TPR. *See* Trans-Polar Railway
Trade, 38, 40, 47
foreign, 6, 8, 51, 58, 60, 122, 144, 153, 157, 160, 167–168, 194
interregional, 6, 60
Transbaykalia, 24, 35, 37, 50, 68, 71
Trans-Polar Railway project (TPR), 97, 98(map), 104
Transportation, 9, 48, 73, 104, 111, 121–122
Trans-Siberian Railroad, 6, 8, 10, 16–19, 21–22, 24, 48–51, 59, 61, 63, 66, 73, 82–84, 91, 92(photo), 96, 110, 119, 121, 148, 162
Treaty of Aigun' (1858), 47, 121
Treaty of Brest-Litovsk (1918), 81–82
Treaty of Nerchinsk (1689), 44–46, 58
Treaty of Peking (1860), 45, 47, 121
Treaty of Portsmouth (1905), 50

Treaty of Shimoda (1855), 47
Tribes, 1, 23, 31, 40, 44, 71, 124, 182, 199
Trofimuk, A.A., 116–117, 119
Trotsky, Leon, 84, 88
Tuleyev, Aman, 147, 148(photo), 149, 154, 183, 187, 189(photo), 189–191, 193, 202
Tumen River, 142, 145–146, 153, 167, 172–173
Tundra, 15, 18, 24–25, 28, 32–33, 37
Tungus, 27, 33, 35, 39, 43, 67–68, 72–73
Tungus Coal Basin, 21
Tunguska rivers, 19, 21–22, 26, 43
Turana Mountains, 26
Tura River, 15, 38–39, 41
Turkestan, 35, 38, 52, 92
Turkestan-Siberian Railroad (Turksib), 91, 103
Turkic peoples, 16, 23, 26, 36–39, 43, 72–73, 124, 182
Turksib. *See* Turkestan-Siberian Railroad
Tuva (*also* Touvinian Republic, Tyva), 2, 19, 23, 25, 56, 123–124, 142, 160
Tuvans, 23–25, 72, 124, 142, 182
Tym River, 15, 100
Tynda, 7, 91, 120(map), 122
Tyumen', 38, 41, 71, 111, 150, 160, 181
Tyumen' oblast, 2, 4, 19, 113(map), 117–118, 125, 148, 159, 175, 179–181, 202
Tyva; Tyvans. *See* Tuva; Tuvans

Udachnyy diamond mine, 185
Uda River, 23
Udegeys, 26, 35, 73
Udokan, 121
Ufa, 83
Ugrians, 15, 32, 37–40, 67, 69–70, 72–73, 152, 178
UKK. *See* Urals-Kuznetsk Combine
Ukraine, 35, 48, 52, 66, 82, 90, 93
Ukrainians, 19, 29, 51, 68, 85, 124
Ulan-Ude, 84, 159
Ul'chi, 26
Unemployment, 166, 177, 191, 202
United States of America, 2, 8, 13, 47, 51, 61–62, 82, 84, 90, 144, 151, 157, 192, 196
Ural Mountains, 8–9, 15, 17, 39, 41, 58, 63, 68, 123, 154, 201
Urals, 2, 6, 37, 58, 75, 83, 92, 111–112
Urals-Kuznetsk Combine (UKK), 90–92
Urengoy gas field, 112, 113(map)
Ussuri River, 26, 28, 46, 48, 142
Ust'-Balyk oilfield, 111–112, 113(map)
Ust'-Ilimsk, 110–111
Ust'-Kut, 110, 121
Ust'-Orda (Ust'-Ordynskiy Buryat Autonomous District), 25, 160

Uygurs, 37
Uy River, 15

Vakh River, 15
Vanino, 96
Vasyugan swamps. *See* Vasyugan'ye
Vasyugan'ye, 8, 15–16, 37
Vegetation, 14(map) 18, 24–25, 33
Verkhoyansk, 8–9, 26
Vilyuy River, 19, 54, 110, 184–185
Virgin Lands, 109–110, 126, 128
Vitim River, 24, 54
Vladivostok, 28–29, 32, 47–48, 50, 66, 80, 82, 84–85, 89, 94, 96, 142, 145–146, 150, 153, 167, 169, 172–173
Voguls. *See* Mansi
Volga River, 34, 38, 40–41, 82–83
Volga-Urals region, 34, 117, 127
Voronov, G.I., 114, 118, 126–127
Vostochnyy, port of, 122
Vyatka (Kirov), 63

Wages, 7, 11, 107, 118, 166, 171–172, 174, 187, 191–193. *See also* Northern wage increment
Western Siberia, 13–19, 38, 51, 55, 59, 67, 72, 86, 90, 93, 103, 112, 114, 117, 119, 127, 139, 158, 179
West Siberian Lowland, 8, 13, 15, 21, 37
West Surgut oilfield, 111, 113(map), 180(photo)
White Army, 83, 85
White Russians, 82–83, 102
Wigwam, 33, 73
Wilderness, 6, 10, 111, 140
Wind chill, 17, 24
Witte, Sergey, 49–50, 55, 66–67
Workers, 6, 50, 96, 107, 122, 124, 132–133, 136, 138, 140, 157, 172, 182, 187, 190–193
World War I, 51, 60, 81
World War II, 27, 92–95, 100, 106, 110, 121
    period after, 96, 106
    period before, 91, 96

Yablonovyy Range, 23–24, 45, 58
Yadrintsev, N.M., 64–65, 76, 79, 137, 149
Yakut horse, 73
Yakutia, 2, 8, 11, 19, 21, 24–26, 28–30, 34–35, 69–71, 73, 99–100, 121, 123–124, 141, 144, 151–152, 156–157, 165, 181–187, 192, 200, 202
Yakut Lowland, 26
Yakuts, 13, 21, 26, 29, 37, 39, 68, 70, 72–73, 99–100, 122, 124, 141, 157, 176, 178, 182, 184–187, 201
Yakutsk, 32, 91, 122, 124–125, 128, 182–183, 187
Yamalia (Yamalo-Nenets Autonomous District), 2, 19, 123, 125, 139, 160, 164, 179–181, 192
Yamal Peninsula, 16, 72, 113(map)
Yamburg gas field, 112, 113(map)
Yekaterinburg, 6, 154
Yeltsin, B.N., 115, 126, 137, 141, 143–144, 146–149, 148(photo), 153–154, 157, 160–162, 169–174, 173(map), 176, 183–185, 187, 189–191
Yenisey River, 7–8, 13, 15, 17, 19, 21, 33, 43, 59, 91, 97, 110
Yermak, 40–41, 62–63, 72
Yugra, 39–40
Yukagirs, 29, 32, 35, 37, 39–40, 69, 72, 176, 182
Yurt, 70, 73

Zapolyarnoye gas field, 112, 113(map)
Zaslavskaya, Tatyana, 109, 117
Zemstvo, 64
Zeya-Bureya Plain, 26, 28, 68
Zeya River, 110
Zheleznogorsk, 126
Zhirinovskiy, V.V., 154, 157, 162, 177, 183
Zhukov, G.K., 95
Zmeinogorsk, 58
Zubov, Valeriy, 187
Zyuganov, G.A., 154, 173 (map)